FREEING YOUR CHILD FROM ANXIETY

ALSO BY TAMAR E. CHANSKY, PH.D.

Freeing Yourself from Anxiety

Freeing Your Child from Negative Thinking

Freeing Your Child from Obsessive-Compulsive Disorder

REVISED AND UPDATED EDITION

FREEING YOUR CHILD FROM ANXIETY

PRACTICAL STRATEGIES TO OVERCOME FEARS, WORRIES, AND PHOBIAS AND BE PREPARED FOR LIFE—FROM TODDLERS TO TEENS

TAMAR E. CHANSKY, PH.D.

ILLUSTRATIONS BY PHILLIP STERN

Published in the United States by Harmony Books, an imprint of the Crown Publishing Group, a division of Random House LLC, a Penguin Random House Company, New York.
www.crownpublishing.com

Harmony Books is a registered trademark, and the Circle colophon is a trademark of Random House LLC.

Originally published in paperback in the United States by Broadway Books, an imprint of the Crown Publishing Group, a division of Random House LLC, New York, in 2004.

Library of Congress Cataloging-in-Publication Data
Chansky, Tamar E. (Tamar Ellsas), 1962– author.
Freeing your child from anxiety : practical strategies to overcome fears, worries, and phobias and be prepared for life—from toddlers to teens / Tamar Chansky, Ph.D.— Revised and updated edition.
1. Anxiety in children. I. Title.
RJ506.A58C48 2014
618.92'8522—dc23 2013050665

ISBN 978-0-8041-3980-9
eBook ISBN 978-0-8041-3981-6

Printed in the United States of America

Book design by Lauren Dong
Illustrations by Phillip Stern
Cover design by Gabriel Levine
Cover photograph: istock © pixdeluxe
Author photograph: Phillip Stern

10 9 8 7 6 5 4 3 2 1

Revised Edition

For Phillip, Meredith, and Raia

CONTENTS

FREEING YOUR CHILD FROM ANXIETY

AUTHOR'S NOTE TO SECOND EDITION

When I first sit down with a new family in my office, I tell them that my goal is to teach them everything I know—in a first meeting! While not exactly realistic, the point is that I want the families I see to quickly become experts (and believe that they really can become so), to learn all the tricks, strategies, solutions, ins and outs of how worry works, so they can ensure that their child overcomes the hurdles that anxiety can place in a child's life. And they do! The fact is, I have learned so much from my patients in the ten years since this book was first published—from the youngest worry warriors who learn to stomp their feet and shake their bossy fingers at worry brain when it's scaring them and say no!, to the teenagers who bravely share their worry thoughts, risking great shame and embarrassment, only to find that their worries are normal and typical, and that there are some very clear things they can do to stop these thoughts from running the show in their minds—that my goal in writing this second edition is to teach you everything I've learned in the past ten years, all in one sitting! You can become an expert, or what I call a "worrywise parent" to your "worrywise kid." You'll know exactly what to do when worry comes barging into your child's life, and beyond that, how to make sure that your child knows exactly what to say and do to ensure that worry stays far out of the way of your child's much better and more important plans. It's easier than you think! So get ready and away we go!

INTRODUCTION

How to Be a Worrywise Parent and Raise a Worrywise Kid

I want life to be easier for Jake. He's an exact replica of me. I was the kid who always had a stomachache, always worried about doing something wrong, kept thinking I was going to get in trouble—and of course I never, ever did. I was the model child. He's always on edge, looking around at what other kids are doing, making sure he's not doing anything different. He's only five years old. Why can't he relax like the other kids? It kills me.

My husband says that our daughter will outgrow her separation anxiety when she's older and not to worry. I worry. Every time the front door closes, she calls out: "Mom!" And starts crying because she thinks I'm gone. She can't go to the bathroom on her own, certainly can't sleep by herself. I know lots of kids still feel afraid at nine, but it seems like things are getting worse with time, not better.

Sarah has never been a worrier; she was always my confident, straight-A student who would go for anything, but suddenly she has become paralyzed with fear about everything. She is hesitant to try anything new, she's doubting her abilities, she second-guesses everything. It's heartbreaking—we don't know what happened to our girl, and we don't know how to get her back.

The day I found out that Dan had been eating his lunch in a bathroom stall rather than face the kids in the cafeteria, I died a thousand deaths. I knew he was shy, but I didn't realize how unbearable life had become for him. This can't be the story of his life. We've got to help him, but I don't know where to begin.

Marty has never been a worrier; he's a really put-together kid. I was stunned when he turned around and walked right off the bus he was supposed to take for his school overnight trip, and in front of all the kids said, "I can't do it." I knew he had some trouble falling asleep, but this was so humiliating for him. How do I help him get over this?

TEACHING YOUR CHILD TO BE PREPARED FOR WORRY TO PREVENT A WORRIED WAY OF LIFE

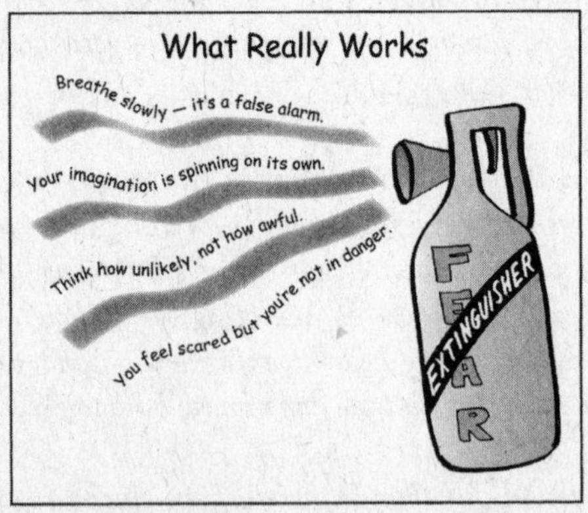

> *The test of a first-rate intelligence is the ability to hold two opposed ideas in mind at the same time, and still retain the ability to function.*
>
> —F. SCOTT FITZGERALD

We all want our children to succeed in life. We would do anything to protect them from bumps in the road, but if we listen honestly to that little voice in the back of our minds, we know we can't. But we can do something better: Teach our children how to protect themselves. How to be prepared, not scared, when they hit those obstacles. What do they need to be prepared for? Situations, struggles, failures, and unknowns, yes, but even more than that, they need to be prepared for worry. Why? Because worry is a great primitive, unreliable exaggerator, and it's a built-in first-responder for all of us. It casts tall shadows on otherwise ordinary or uneventful situations of life—saying hello to a teacher, taking a test, or touching a doorknob—and makes our children think that something bad will happen if they were to take that risk. But worry has it wrong. When children don't take reasonable risks, that's when bad things happen: they miss out on important experiences and opportunities in life. This book is about teaching our kids to be smarter than their worry by fact-checking it: to first look at worry's unreliable, distorted version of the story and next, what they really believe to be true, and compare those two stories side by side for accuracy—and not only to retain the ability to function, as Fitzgerald suggests, but far beyond that, by choosing the facts over the fears, to cultivate the opportunity to thrive. To make good choices for a good life, to have fun, connect, grow, learn—to be kids! That's exactly what this book is about. You now hold in your hands dozens of practical take-home strategies to do just that.

Worry is an inevitable part of growth and change. Worry rushes in every time we experience some uncertainty and fills the gap between the exposure to something new and the mastery of that experience. That is why we need to teach our children to be as prepared as they can be, to get worries out of the way, rather than let the unreliable stories worry is telling them detour them. Why is this necessary? Because if we conducted an exit interview about all those stressful moments our children lose sleep over, we would see that for every book report, test, bedtime, audition, parent outing—over and over again—worry is wrong. It tells our kids the wrong things about what will happen. Worry narrows the mind to focus all the attention on the most far-flung, unlikely scenarios, meanwhile distracting our children from focusing on what they actually need to do in order to feel prepared and confident for the situations they face. We don't want our children to waste their time, but given how attention-grabbing worry thoughts are, kids don't know how and when (or that it is safe) to switch gears unless we teach them. That's the essence of being what I call worrywise children. These are children who can't be outsmarted by worry because they've been taught how to spot and not fall for the tricks the brain can play. Worry won't change—but our kids absolutely can.

When wrestling with every what-if that comes down the pike—*What if you faint, what if you hurt your mother, what if you get hurt? What if today is your last day on Earth?*—the natural reaction for kids is to be scared and say, "Make the thoughts stop!" But a worrywise kid knows that you don't have to *stop* your worry thoughts; you just have to decide whether to listen. That the thoughts' mere presence doesn't grant their authority. By changing their relationship with worry, children can learn to be the boss and to downgrade worry's authority by tapping into other departments of the brain and generating other options. Your child shifts his perspective: worry goes from something to trust to something to test. A worrywise kid looks past the worry to the other side of the story and decides which advice is better, more true, and more helpful. When you let the worry speak for itself, rather than just trying to convince your child everything is fine, worry won't have the last word. After doing the "side-by-side comparison" of fears vs. facts, your child will see worry's shortcomings and distortions and choose the side of the truth; in so doing he is choosing to step out into life, even if cautiously, rather than retreating to the sidelines.

ANXIETY AND OUR CHANGING WORLD

Since the original release of *Freeing Your Child from Anxiety*, much has changed in the world. Not a month goes by where parents are not put in the position to have to explain something difficult either in the world at large—terrorism, school shootings, natural disasters, a fiscal crisis, or in their own world: the neighbor or schoolteacher with cancer—and still tuck their child into bed and send them to school the next day. In many ways, the anxious frame has now become the new normal. Anxiety continues to be the primary mental health problem facing children and teens today; the incidence according to some estimates is as high as 20 percent. More children are more anxious. Parents are more anxious. According to one study by psychologist Jean Twenge, even typical schoolchildren today without any diagnoses have baseline stress levels higher than psychiatric patients in the 1950s.[1]

Parents are more concerned than ever, too—not just about their children, but in general (think economic pressures, unemployment concerns, college admissions competitiveness, and more). Parental uncertainty about the future often translates into more pressure on kids. The impulse is to turn outward: enrolling preschoolers in Kumon classes; pressuring high school students to take multiple AP classes; entering young athletes in travel sports teams so that their achievements will look good on a resume or earn them a sports scholarship; hiring coaches for college admissions, application essay writing, and SAT prep. But these extra advantages often lose their benefit when they translate into more pressure, especially when the place that children truly need reinforcement is by strengthening their inner resources and emotional resilience.

Anxiety doesn't go away on its own. And anxiety-producing situations are not going to disappear. It is my firm belief that our future depends on recognizing the essential need for anxiety prevention for our youth. The urgency of addressing the needs of anxious kids is undeniable.

It's clear that if ever there was a time when parents needed simple, trusted direction on how to teach children to overcome the tricks and trials that worry plays on the mind and be free to pursue their path unencumbered by the obstacles of anxiety, it is now.

In order to teach your child how to be in charge and talk back to his fears and worries, you, as a parent, need to help your child separate himself from the worry, and distinguish between what worry is saying and what your child truly believes deep down. How do you do this? Instead of saying, "What are you worrying about?" you can ask, "What's worry bugging you about, or what's worry telling you to think here?" If your child says, "I'm scared!" or "I'm freaked out," rather than telling him "Don't be scared," you can say, "It sounds like the yikes button got pushed. Let's do a system reset. Is this really a yikes button moment?" or ask, "So part of you is scared. What does another part of you think?" Instead of putting them in a position to defend to you why they are worried, notice how this nuance of phrasing separates worry from your child and lets worry speak for itself—and come up short. You want to shine a light on that, so your child can see worry's limitations and, though it gets there first in his mind, not give worry the last word; that belongs to your child. By separating worry from your child, you are also encouraging your child to use his "thinking brain" to stop and think realistically about what he truly expects will occur.

CHILDREN ALREADY HAVE THE SKILLS TO OVERCOME WORRY (YOU JUST NEED TO TELL THEM IT'S OKAY TO USE THEM)

We know kids worry. Today we want to know how parents can teach their kids to get competent at managing their worry. The good news: your child already has the skills they need to overcome worry and anxiety and they use them every day—sometimes for good, sometimes not so much. But regardless—your child has these skills! They may not know that they are allowed to use them, and even that they are *supposed* to use them in certain situations. Our job as parents is to teach them that they are allowed to (and need to) use these skills with their worries and fears.

- Children know how to *ignore things that come up*: like when you are telling them to turn off the TV or a video game. Or if they're in school and think, "I'm hungry" or "I want to go out to recess"—they understand that they don't have to jump just because a thought is there. That's what they are going to learn to do when worry keeps bugging them with unnecessary warnings.
- They know how to be *bossy*: like when their sibling is in their room without permission. They are going to use that voice and that stance to refuse to be bossed around by their worry.
- They know how to *expect trouble*: like if a neighbor always cheats in hide-and-seek, they know to predict the pattern and call them on it. They are going to use those prediction skills to learn worry's habits and tricks. That way they won't be surprised when worry pops up; they'll know to expect it and be prepared to say, "Oh, you again."
- They know how to *be flexible* and *solve problems*: like when their batteries run out on their Wii, they borrow them from their remote-control car. Or when they are losing at a video game or get thwarted, they try a different route. They are going to learn not to stick with their first reaction—worrying—and instead get in the habit of switching gears to consider other, more realistic interpretations of the real risk in a situation.
- They know how to *use facts appropriately*, *argue with authority*, and *prove people wrong:* like when they know better than you how electronic devices work or what the carpool schedule is. They are going to learn to trust their own authority, put worry to the test, and fact-check the claims that worry makes. They are going to show that they can prove worry wrong and feel proud of their triumphs.
- They know how to *get used to things that are hard at first*. Just like when they learned to ride a bike, tie their shoes, or play the trumpet, they learned that practice is the way. They'll rely on practice and hard work to put themselves in uncomfortable situations with worry—and learn that they can not only get used to new situations but also be glad that they made the effort!
- They know how to *do what's best for them* even under pressure:

like on the playground if people are insisting that they play soccer, but they want to play on the swings or play basketball, they'll do what they want. This is what they'll learn to decide when it comes to worry. Instead of thinking it's safer to stay home, they'll *decide* that it's not fair to miss out on things that are safe just because worry is telling them that they're not safe.

Kids don't have to stop the thoughts. They simply need to change their relationship to their thoughts. The more your child can learn to trust themselves, and not their anxiety, the more they will be able to put the worry thoughts aside.

WORRY: NATURAL BUT NOT NECESSARY

One in five children will develop an anxiety disorder, and many more will be on the fringes of that statistic. But beyond those statistics, we know that no child is immune to the challenges and pressures of life. Anxiety is a natural by-product of those stresses, and a natural first reaction to feeling overwhelmed or encountering uncertainty. But it's not necessary. Although there are many better and more accurate ways of seeing a situation, anxiety prevents children from looking for other ways of thinking. Running marathons in their minds, round and round the worry track, they suffer on the inside. For the vast majority of kids, it's not the situations themselves that are the problem, but what their minds are telling them about their lives. Their minds are playing tricks on them—making them run through the equivalent of dress rehearsals and fire drills for disaster, embarrassment, and dangers on a daily basis—things that will never happen, and that other children, whose minds aren't spotting trouble out of every corner, will never have to consider.

As parents, we have to be on the lookout for anxious children. In the vast majority of cases, anxious children appear to be fine to their peers, teachers, and sometimes even their parents. Better than fine, actually—they are perceived as competent and model students, and rightly so; their efforts not to stand out or be found out come at a great cost. As much as they are doing their best to manage the constant worry and the pressure that it generates, continuing with the status quo is not a sustainable solution. Worry takes its toll physically, emotionally, socially, even academically, though often invisibly. A child who is anxious and hiding anxiety is like the swan seemingly gliding across the surface of a pond but paddling like crazy underneath—the work is exhausting and relentless. Stuck with a worry sound track playing in their minds, these children don't know there is a choice, that there are specific steps they can take to change the score. They need our help.

Just because worry is "normal," in the sense that it is universal and everyone experiences it from time to time, does not mean that it should be ignored or brushed aside. Runny noses are normal too—but we certainly don't tell kids' noses to just "stop running"! We teach kids a system to take care of a runny nose: how to use tissues or their sleeve (options are always good!), and also how to prevent one: bundling up in the cold and washing their hands (occasionally anyway) to reduce the spread of germs. Kids wouldn't know how to do these things on their own—witness the ever-drippy toddler. But once they've got it, they've got it, and goodness, don't hand them a tissue, because as soon as they're able to reach, they want to get the tissues themselves. Kids want to know how to take care of themselves. So it is with worry. And fortunately the worry lessons are simple. Here are the first three to get you started.

LESSON: It's Not the Situation; It's Just the Story Worry Brain Is Telling You

Lesson one for being anxiety-savvy is knowing that the problem isn't the test, or the dark, or the playdate, or college. Those things are ultimately very manageable parts of life. The problem is what your child's mind is *telling them* about those things. Anxious children are tangled up in a widening web of "what-if" and worry. We can't get rid of the dark or the test or the playdate; it's our job instead to encourage the child to focus on what the worry brain is saying. It's not a good companion. It won't help your child find *the way* to handle the situation competently; the worry brain would be *in the way* of your child's clear thinking. Learning this is the beginning of being a worrywise kid. It's about realizing there is a choice; that worry's take on the situation is the first (and the worst), but it's not the accurate one.

So how do we help kids extricate themselves from their worry so they can decide what to think and do? Rather than rushing to reassure them or argue with them rationally, we must devalue the worry message in the first place and help kids see they have a choice. If your child came to you distressed about a telemarketer's insistence that they buy new siding, you would likely respond by saying, "That's just a telemarketer; his job is to make everything sound urgent. What does he know about what you need?" Substitute the phrase "worry brain" for "telemarketer" and you've begun to understand how to enlist your child's critical thinking. For young children, it helps to give the worry a name—the buzzing of the worry bug, the overprotection of protector brain. For older children, referring to it as the worry tape or the exaggerator opens up the possibility of hearing the worry with an analytical ear. The mountain has now been reduced to a molehill, and kids are more willing to approach their worry situation and overcome it one step at a time. Encourage your child to "stamp" the thought as unnecessary, to use a thought sorter to separate the fears from the facts. Help him relabel the voice of worry and both of you can roll your eyes when you hear it exaggerating the risks as usual. Your child will appreciate that you're not upset with him, you're fed up with worry!

LESSON: Do the Side-by-Side Comparison: Choose the Real Deal

Children are natural choosers. They write more if they get to choose what color ink. The desire to make their own choices is so strong and innate that one study of four-month-olds found that they would get upset if they couldn't pull the strings themselves to hear music, even though they heard the same amount of music when someone else pulled the strings for them. So lesson two: Let kids pull the strings. Don't tell kids what to think; instead ask them questions about what they *want* to think. This gives kids choices, so that they can choose better interpretations than what their worry brain is telling them. Help your child see worry as a choosing moment. He can't help that the worry thoughts are there or that they got there first, but he doesn't have to settle for worry's version of the story. He can't control that the thoughts are there, but he can choose whether they get all of his attention; he can instead search his mind for better options. Parents can help their child learn to stop, not to reinforce worry's take on the situation by adding more and more what-if's, but rather to look and think *past* the worry. To what? To the truth that every time is completely different (and better!) than what worry threatened it would be.

How does this translate to the home front? When your child asks questions (often questions to which they know the answers), like "What if this happens?," "Is this safe?," "What's going to happen if I . . . ," rather than just saying "It's fine" or "Don't worry," take the opportunity to separate your child from the worry and create choices. Say things like this: "Is that what worry is telling you?" or "What do you really think?" Or, "You're having worry thoughts right now. I wonder what you think will actually happen when you do go to the dance. How do you think it will turn out? And why do you think that is the case?" This is how you create the side-by-side comparison of fears vs. facts. Then like good consumers they can choose which version of the story sounds more likely or more true. Ask them how different parts of the brain might interpret that situation: the thinking brain, the protector brain, the scientist brain. Ask them what else they might feel besides scared. Excited? Curious? By not seeing it as a matter of either/or, scared or not, but rather thinking in parts or drop-down menus, kids are able to tap into a range of thoughts and feelings that actually coexist within them. Thinking to look for the pull-down menu of hypotheses and interpretations in their mind? That's the hallmark of a worrywise kid.

LESSON: Exposure and Desensitization: Using Planned Discomfort to Prove That Worry Is Wrong

What's the third secret of being a worrywise kid? The secret advantage that unlocks your child from the grips of worry and doubt? Experience, or what cognitive behavior therapists call "exposure."

Kids achieve this by going ahead and interacting with the thing they've been afraid of: going to a pet shop and looking at dogs, raising a hand in class, ordering in a restaurant, texting a friend about going to the mall. Anything that worry said they can't do, they shouldn't do, it's too hard, bad things will happen—put worry to the test and watch it fail and your child win. It's one thing to shrink your worries down by correcting the story that worry tells you, but seeing is believing. When kids avoid something that frightens them, or when parents help them to avoid those things, kids get the message that it is too scary, or dangerous, or that other kids can handle this but they can't. Avoidance makes fear stronger, but experience weakens fear and builds your child's confidence. They've proven to themselves that they can handle it and even master the challenges they face.

We say approach *on purpose* because anxious children have been avoiding *on purpose*—interacting with what they fear only under duress or by accident. Their plan for dealing with feared situations up to this point is to hope that a snowstorm closes school or that they get sick so they won't have to give their book report. Planning the right-size exposure for your child's anxiety level (not too hard, but not too easy) will give your child the confidence that they don't have to be afraid. For example, when a child who is terrified of throwing up sees that they are able to watch a video of someone getting sick, and eventually even laugh (because of the weird texture of the . . . vomit . . . not because someone got sick), that's a confident child. Or when a child with OCD for the first time touches a doorknob and then eats a snack without washing his hands, the world opens up. The most exciting thing is that they hold the key. Where do you come in as a worrywise parent? By encouraging them to try, or simply being willing for them to try these things, you give them the signal loud and clear: This must be okay. My mom wouldn't want me to do it if it weren't.

To make this work, parents need to notice or create exposure opportunities. And they are everywhere in a child's day. For a child who has social anxiety, a parent may always order for them in a restaurant. A worrywise parent would start to share that job, by first having the child order the drink (or whatever is an easier first step) and ordering the rest of the meal him- or herself. Gradually the parent would shift the responsibility ratio over time until the child can do it all himself—and feel proud! Your job is to create or simply not overlook the natural opportunities available to help this competence grow.

I summarize these lessons as follows: "shrink" the worry down to size by creating thinking choices, and then "approach" the situation one small step at a time to see that your child can tackle that challenge safely and proudly. These are cognitive and behavioral elements used in cognitive behavior therapy, the most effective treatment for anxiety disorders. The best news about anxiety disorders is that treatment works—these disorders are the most treatable psychiatric condition, and cognitive behavior therapy is our most powerful tool. Hundreds of studies have shown that kids are able to overcome their symptoms and maintain their progress long after treatment has ended. What's more, the lessons they learn are internalized for life. As anxiety experts Drs. John Walkup and Golda Ginsburg of Johns Hopkins write: "It is dramatic to observe a child 'anxious since birth' or even 'in the womb' respond to treatment with what appears to be substantial changes in 'temperament and personality.'"[2] Importantly, often treatment doesn't have to take place in a therapist's office. You can learn to do what a cognitive behavior therapist would do, and do it in your living room, your car, your child's classroom, the backyard. That's my ultimate purpose in writing this book.

I'd like you to meet some parents who understand that the goal is not to take away their children's pain or stop their children's thoughts (though, like any parent, there's nothing they'd rather do), but to teach their children to hold the worry thought *and* the other opposing thought and choose the most accurate "caption" to the situation they're in. These parents understand that their child can and needs to do this themselves—with their coaching.

Here are some of the brave (and occasionally edgy or unorthodox) things that worrywise parents do, because they know that they're safe, and they need to confidently show this to their children:

A mother of a child with a bug phobia reached into her purse and brought out a sealed plastic bag with a bunch of ants. We proceeded to have a picnic in my office, bugs and all. And in the end, that child could see that she didn't have to run, that her life and plans no longer had to come to a screeching halt just because there were bugs present.

Another mom who was trying to explain to her child that worry is fake, like junk mail—an idea she had read in the first edition of this book—did a demonstration on her own with the solicitations she'd received. She put a bunch of junk mail on the table and then put in a bill or two, and said, "See the difference? These letters aren't important. What do we do with junk mail? Rip it up and throw it away."

And finally there was a mother whose daughter, suffering with OCD, was terrified that she might somehow, unwillingly or by accident, decide to follow Satan or allow demons to possess her. The family had a strong Christian faith, and the mother knew this wasn't her daughter talking—it was OCD. To prove to her daughter that a thought doesn't mean anything more than the value we give it and can't change who we are, she did a very brave thing. She said (much to her daughter's initial shock): "I'm going to show you that you are safe no matter what thoughts go through your mind. I am going to say these words: 'I am going to choose to follow Satan.'" The mother was devout and had no intention of changing that! She was showing her daughter that these intrusive thoughts that characterize OCD don't have any power, that they are different from our actions and intentions and beliefs, and that we don't need to be afraid of our thoughts or of ourselves. That even though unpleasant thoughts may pop up, they are meaningless, and ultimately *we* are in charge; we decide what we believe and what we do. Worry is just playing the "what-if" trick on us. Seeing her mother, whom she trusted more than anyone, demonstrate this lesson was deeply relieving to the daughter and gave her the confidence to jump in and start "bossing back" her OCD.

Their tactics may be unorthodox and edgy at times, but these are parents who get it: their job is to teach their children (and *show* them) that we need to be prepared for worries and fears, that we don't have to be scared, that worry doesn't have instant authority in our lives, that its exaggerations are wrong. Then they know that, when their child is afraid of something, they need to start planning—not to avoid the situation, but to understand the situation differently and reduce the risk down to size, so that the child will not be afraid to approach it. They also know that if they can't be brave and show their children that risks—of touching doorknobs, tackling their fear of heights, being assertive with a salesperson—are reasonable, then they can't expect their children to take risks. This work is a two-person job. Model reasonable risk-taking.

I'm not afraid that I will do x, or that x will happen; that's only what my worry brain is telling me.

At first when you're working on worry, you will be the one coaching your child to think differently about their thoughts. But your ultimate goal is to teach your child the skills to take charge of worry themselves. In so doing, you are giving them the autonomy to do what you would do *for* them. You are teaching them how to at the same time have these uncomfortable thoughts and learn a new way to approach their thinking. One that feels much better (and truer!). As much as there's a natural avoidance, kids also have a natural curiosity and a desire to master new skills. You are giving your child skills that will last a lifetime.

How do we do this? The most important lesson is not to take worry at face value. Worry is not the calm, still voice of reason that we could really use on our side when we're in a pinch. On the contrary, worry is a relentless exaggerator, a distorter of the facts, and for anxious kids it is the default first reaction. To them, the worry sounds convincing, but in truth it operates independently of reality—there's no interface. Managing worry means challenging the credibility of those automatic thoughts and cultivating a strong second reaction—speed-dialing that voice of reason, connecting to some truth circuits, and in so doing, bringing that magnified risk down to a manageable size. Second, give kids permission to play with their own thinking and you open up the possibility that kids can actually doubt and "boss back" the worry, with authority, rather than being held hostage by it.

We have more reasons than we can count to take on the job of teaching our children how to manage their anxiety. To start, we need to understand the lessons ourselves. In this book you will find the nuts and bolts of how worry works, and solutions for how to reduce it step-by-step. When you learn the principles of how anxiety builds and resolves, you will feel prepared rather than overwhelmed by your child's fears and worries and will be empowered to introduce simple strategies into daily life. This practice with the small stuff helps kids be prepared to competently handle the big stressors when they come along.

Taking this job seriously doesn't mean that you need only keep a serious tone. As you will see in these pages, worrywise parents use whatever creative means they need to reach their audience. Take your child's distress seriously, but play with the worry; this will reassure your child, more than anything, that worry's messages aren't worth heeding.

This book is organized into four parts. In Part I we explore the causes of anxiety, how to diagnose it, and what treatments are available for kids. In Part II we take a closer look at the mechanisms of anxiety. We'll discuss user-friendly ways to talk to your child about anxiety, and give you and your child a "master plan" to implement in anxiety situations.

Part III takes a closer look at specific anxiety issues, including worry, phobias, social anxiety, separation anxiety, obsessive-compulsive disorder, and tics and habits. Applying the techniques introduced in Parts I and II, these chapters illustrate how to adapt the strategies to address the particular concern your child is having. In Part IV we take a brief look at issues that can impact anxiety levels and learn how to manage hot spots for anxious kids—including going to school, dealing with siblings, and going to sleep. Talking to children about real-life tragedies and turning down the heat on our pressure cooker children are also addressed in Part IV.

Whether you are a newcomer to the subject of anxiety in children or are a veteran of the struggles it creates, my hope is that through the examples of other families facing the same situations you'll be inspired to see that worry management is not only a skill, but an essential gift that you can work on with your child.

In these pages you will meet many children and families who know well what life with anxiety is like because they live it too. These generous families have agreed to share their stories—their struggles and ultimately their triumphs—so that others may learn and perhaps find the path a bit easier because they know that they are not alone. These are parents who may have started out knowing nothing about anxiety, or have known the dark side of it from their own childhoods. They have succeeded because they learned how anxiety works so that they could explain it to their children. They learned not to be afraid of their children's fears, and instead to be strategic—to teach their child to "think twice" when worry is talking, or to ask "the million-dollar question": If their child could win a million dollars by saying whether worry is right or wrong—could they do it? They've learned to back up when their child is afraid, but not to back off. They know that helping their child to approach fearful situations is exactly how they will prove to themselves that they don't have to be afraid. Just as children need to be brave and see beyond the anxious moment to the success and relief on the other side, to understand that this discomfort is temporary, parents need to do the same. Get ready. You are going to get braver and wiser through this process too.

Remember the goal: It's not to talk your children out of their fears; it's to teach them how to *talk themselves through* their fears, to put worry to the test and see how it falls short. Parents can do better than removing hurdles for their children; they can let their children be the heroes by teaching them how to jump over the hurdles themselves.

DO IT TODAY: EVERYONE CAN LEARN TO WORRY LESS.

One great thing about the worry lessons you'll teach your child is that they will find more and more opportunities to apply them—even with you! Don't be surprised (and do be gracious) when your child gets so good at spotting "worry brain" that they bring this home to you. One youngster recently told me that when his dad was driving them to a ball game his dad was saying: "We're going to be late. We're going to miss the whole first inning! And look at the gas gauge; it's only a quarter of a tank!" He told his dad: "That's your worry brain. I think it's making things worse. We can't get there any faster if you worry, but it's making this ride really stressful. And didn't you tell *me* that you only have to worry about the gas tank when the light comes on? Can we try to have fun now?"

As long as it is done in a respectful spirit, this is a great opportunity to thank your child. Really. We all do better with less worry!

Part I

ANXIETY DISORDER BASICS

What You Need to Know to Set Your Child Free

Parents are excellent leaders when they know where they are going. But many parents feel so overwhelmed by their child's anxious distress that they get confused about where they are headed. Are they trying to make their child feel *better*, or are they trying to help their child be *stronger*? Torn between these two options, parents often feel at an impasse. In this section I'll tell you what you need to know to tackle both goals at once. By learning the fundamentals of how anxiety works, how to identify it, and how to successfully intervene, you will become competent in teaching your child to overcome their fears and worries—and nothing feels better than that!

In Chapter 1 we look at the potential causes of anxiety in children. I'll explain the "no-fault" nature of anxiety disorders. It's important that parents accept their child for who he or she is—which is the key to making the first steps toward change. In Chapter 2 I'll introduce the different types of anxiety disorders so that you can find the anxiety-disorder type that best fits the theme of your child's worry. Chapter 3 covers the "when" and "how" of treatment for childhood anxiety.

Chapter 1

"I CAN'T; I'M TOO SCARED"

Understanding Children's Fears and Worries

From the children:

When I was little my mom worked the "graveyard shift" at the hospital. Every night I was so worried that meant she was going to die and I'd never see her again.

I hate having to worry all the time. I can't do anything without thinking—Are my parents okay? Is my family okay? It is always in the back of my mind. I wish I could just turn off my mind, but then I feel like a bad person for feeling this way, because I love my family and I don't want anything bad to happen to them.

My parents get mad at me for staying up late working. They keep telling me to stop worrying. That stresses me out more. They have no clue the pressure I'm under. It wasn't like this for them. Everything I do counts for college. There's nothing to cut out, this is just my life.

From the parents:

Until he knows for sure, he can't, he won't. How do I convince him life is okay?

I feel like the worst parent. I want to help my son, but I lose it and I know that's not helping anything. I start out patient, but nothing I say makes him feel better. Then I get frustrated and it's a mess.

My son is so worried all the time; he's constantly in this bubble of stress. The other kids are oblivious all around him. They are just being kids. I wish so much that he could be more like them.

If you want to make things better, you first need to know what's wrong. In this chapter we're going to explore exactly what an anxious child's inner experience is like and the different ways that anxiety can manifest. We'll explore the fine line between when anxiety is "normal" and when it's not, and we'll take a look at what causes anxiety. All of this will help you empathize with your child's experience so that you can better help him overcome his worries and fears.

THE PROBLEM OF LIVING ON HIGH ALERT

"Don't run into the street! Stop climbing on that. Careful, that will break!" Words like these are staples in most parents' rule books, but most parents of anxious children find they never have to utter them. The mind of a worrying child is already fielding hundreds of internal "be careful" or "watch out" or simple "don't!" messages every day. Rather than insisting that their child do their homework as in most families, you may be wresting papers from your kid, convincing him he has done enough and it's time for bed. In fact, you may even find yourself kept in check by your worrying child—"Did you lock the door? Is the gas tank full? Did you send in the permission slip?"

Though it can often be confusing or frustrating to parents that their child must feel every wrinkle in the day and race ahead to prepare for every eventuality, we must understand that anxious kids are just following the instructions that their worry brain is giving: Proceed with caution; handle with care; warning: danger ahead.

Whether they are worrying too much about typical concerns such as grades or friends, or being frightened by unlikely disasters like getting a fatal disease or becoming homeless, anxious children are highly cautious because their mind is giving them unreliable, biased information and overcorrecting for the possibility of danger. *But they don't know that.* They are oriented—by their wiring, or their experiences—to see danger when it's not there. Though it sometimes seems that anxious children go looking for trouble—whether it is overhearing a conversation in the hallway about lice, or financial stress, or heart attack, their hearts sink and their worry soars—they don't want to be this way. They are equipped with a system that is programmed to be highly sensitive to any hint of uncertainty, to risk, to danger. But it's a system that is not very good at interpreting that risk or uncertainty. So kids notice everything but don't get any help putting those observations into perspective.

Sometimes anxious kids recognize that they are different from their peers, but oftentimes they assume that this is just who they are, rather than seeing this as a problem that can change. But to be an anxious child—at any age—is to juggle; it is to live a double life. As one articulate youngster said: "My heart is telling me things that make my stomach feel bad." On one hand, there is a constant barrage of catastrophes, worries, and disasters flashing through their minds. Their default setting is high alert. Meanwhile, on the other hand, their parents and teachers tell them not to worry, and sometimes these adults even get frustrated with them for feeling the way they do. This adds to their worry, because now they feel they're doing something wrong!

Conducting their lives as if they're in the middle of a fire station, anxious children are constantly on edge, waiting for the next alarm to sound, the next disaster to strike, and amazingly with all of that going on in their minds, to the outside world anxious children often fly right under the radar of the best-trained eyes. It is much to their credit that they can keep all the balls in the air and do so well—but it is not without a cost.

Parents juggle too. On one hand, they feel embarrassed when it's their child who is hiding in the corner at the birthday party, in tears at the school play, or unable to go on the school camping trip. In these moments they just want to make the problem stop. On the other hand, they feel scared: If my child is struggling with all these hypothetical fears in the midst of a pretty great life, how will they ever survive when they have a *real* problem? Caught between these two views and feeling helpless, they may try to diminish the fear, ignore it, or even get frustrated at their child for being anxious. But what they need to do is understand what is going on. That's the beginning of finding a new solution.

MAKE IT STOP! THE PROBLEM WITH ANXIETY: THE EMERGENCY THAT ISN'T

All children need to know that they are safe and that their parents will protect them. Anxious children are no exception, but helping them feel safe is a complicated and often frustrating endeavor. This is the poignancy of an anxious child.

He or she comes to you, drops their fear, unhappiness, or uncertainty in front of you, and waits for you to fix it. Struggling with invisible enemies, they want you to save them as you would protect them from any concrete danger. You see your child unraveling and that the degree of distress your child is feeling is out of proportion to the situation, but what he's experiencing *feels* like an emergency, and he wants *you* to take away the emergency or he wants to *escape*.

Put those two together and your child might get angry or frustrated at you for not being able to save him and make him feel better. He might think that you are being mean because you can't make it better, or even that you're choosing not to make him feel better because you won't do the simple things he asks (like letting him stay home from school or assuring him for the twentieth time that morning that he won't throw up). And you probably feel frustrated yourself that the usual magic touches of parenthood—a hug, a kiss, and some reassuring words—aren't doing a thing. While you could do all the things that your anxious child asks, you know that meeting these surface needs will not free him in the long term, but will only engender dependence on you for reassurance forever!

Anxious children feel trapped, and they want *you* to get them out. The more that you understand that what is trapping your child is the faulty information their brain is telling them, the more you will be able to separate the worry from your child and help them begin to correct the distortions and mistakes—by *themselves*.

FEAR: A NORMAL AND NECESSARY PART OF LIFE

What is the setup for anxiety? Fear. On one hand, fear is an adaptive human reflex and an essential safeguard for survival, for children and adults alike. Fears and worries can help children put on the brakes in unfamiliar situations. Rather than hurling yourself into a swimming pool when you don't know how to swim, for example, a good dose of fearful "what if?" can keep a healthy degree of caution in the picture. Because our natural inclination is toward growth and development, we would not survive as a species if it were not for our ability to hold back and appraise and avoid danger. It is a protective mechanism and a normal part of development.

Fear can be considered the emotional response that occurs in the space between confronting a new situation and actually mastering it. Anxious children are wired to notice these gaps more than others. Rather than responding with delight and curiosity—a desire to master something new—they become derailed by an overwhelming feeling of distress and concern. The "what's new" is eclipsed by "what's wrong."

Temporary fears are a normal and healthy part of development. In the same way that adults may be fearful of a new piece of technology until we have figured out how it works—and may even entertain unrealistic scenarios of blowing up the computer by pushing the wrong button—kids' fears are fueled by an active imagination, trying to piece together an explanation for how the world works in the high-stakes context of their safety. A little information goes a long way. A four-year-old at the aquarium is afraid of seeing the sharks because she's old enough to understand that sharks are dangerous, but she's not old enough to understand that she can watch safely from outside the tank. An eight-year-old is beginning to understand about germs and disease, but he can't yet grasp how unlikely it would be to get sick just from engaging in normal activities.

THE TYPICAL DEVELOPMENTAL SEQUENCE OF FEARS IN CHILDREN

There is a normal unfolding of fears for all children, not just anxious ones, over time. A healthy safeguard, these fears mirror their development as their world broadens and they encounter new experiences that they have not yet mastered. As children interact with the new experiences they gain confidence and competence and move on to the next stage.

Infancy: Babies' fears are immediate and concrete. In response to a growing ability to differentiate familiar faces from unfamiliar faces, stranger anxiety (clinging and crying when a stranger approaches) develops around seven to nine months and typically resolves by the end of the first year. Infants fear separation, loud noises, and sudden movements.

Early childhood: As a healthy attachment to parents grows, separation anxiety (crying, sadness, fear of desertion upon separation) emerges around one year of age and improves over the next three years, resolving in most children by the end of kindergarten. As children's worlds expand, they may fear new and unfamiliar situations, as well as real and imagined dangers such as big dogs, spiders, or monsters.

Elementary school: With access to new information and a growing ability to grasp the gravity of events, children begin to fear real-world dangers—fire, burglars, kidnappers, storms, illness, drugs. With experience, they normally learn that these risks present remote, rather than imminent, danger. They continue to struggle with what is real and what is not—so fears of ghosts, witches, and zombies are common.

Middle school: The growing importance of social status leads to social comparisons and worries about social acceptance. Concerns about test grades, crime, social isolation, athletic performance, and social-group identification are normal.

High school: Teenagers continue to be focused on social acceptance, but with a greater concern for finding a group that reflects their chosen identities. They tend to worry about the narrow focus of their social relationships as well as about the larger world, moral issues, and their future failure or success.

The chart that follows provides an example of the top ten fears for typical boys and girls (in this study, ages nine to thirteen), without any anxiety or other diagnosis, and how they differ by gender.

Boys' Fears	**Girls' Fears**
1. Spiders	1. Spiders
2. Predators	2. Being kidnapped
3. Being hit by a car	3. Parents dying
4. Snakes	4. The dark
5. Burglar	5. Frightening movies
6. Frightening movies	6. Thunderstorms
7. The dark	7. Being teased
8. Being teased	8. Bats
9. Frightening dreams	9. Bats/ghosts/spooky things
10. Medical operations	10. Sleeping in the dark/ making mistakes

Source: Muris, P., Merckelbach, H., & Collaris, R. (1997). Common childhood fears and their origins. *Behavior Research and Therapy,* 35(10), 929-937.

ANXIETY: UNNECESSARY AND DISRUPTIVE

In contrast to fear, which is a natural, adaptive, immediate reaction to a stimulus, anxiety is the tense emotional state that occurs when you can't predict the outcome of a situation or guarantee that the outcome will be the desired one. It's the mind doing guesswork, and by always guessing catastrophe, it doesn't guess well. It is not adaptive but *disruptive*—at the very moment when it would be helpful to lean in and get more information about an unknown or new situation, anxiety takes our attention ninety miles an hour into the future, into disasters that will probably never happen. Meanwhile, the real problem is still waiting for us to solve it—but we've been so dragged around by worry that we can't think straight or see our options.

Even in the best circumstances children experience some fear and worry. Anxiety becomes a disorder when a child automatically exaggerates risks and underestimates his ability to cope with a given situation to the extent that this interferes with his functioning (more about this in Chapter 2). Anxiety is debilitating internally to children, causing chronic fatigue and putting children at other physical risks like hypertension, heart disease, and gastrointestinal and respiratory disorders. It is also implicated in the development of depression and substance abuse, and it is associated with decreased immune function in general. Just as dangerous, anxiety hinders and restricts children's movement in the world around them, affecting how they function in school, how they interact with peers, and their role in their family. The familiar stereotype of the worrywart belies the serious physical and emotional risks and consequences of untreated anxiety.

WHO IS THE ANXIOUS CHILD?

Anxiety has many faces. Some children appear visibly stressed, while others keep their anxiety under cover and worry silently. Still others are angry-anxious kids, reacting to their limitations with frustration. Approximately one in five children will develop an anxiety disorder of some kind. We know that the rates of anxiety disorders tend to increase slightly with age, but most studies of anxiety disorders draw from a sample of children over seven, so the prevalence of anxiety disorders in very young children is unclear. Girls tend to be diagnosed with anxiety disorders more often than boys. Interestingly, though, more boys are brought to treatment as the outward signs of anxious behavior, like crying, shying away, and overt distress, tend to be less socially acceptable in boys than in girls.

The consensus across numerous studies is that the majority of anxious children have more than one anxiety disorder at the same time, which is referred to as "comorbid." If left untreated, anxiety symptoms become more disabling over time, and the course of anxiety disorders is considered to be chronic with fluctuations across the lifespan.

Though children with anxiety disorders are as impaired as children with more overtly disruptive disorders (e.g., children with attention-deficit/hyperactivity disorder who are impulsive, interrupt the teacher, talk in class, can't sit still), they often stay below the radar of adults and go undiagnosed because their symptoms are internalized and don't interfere in the classroom. Their worry conversation goes on only inside their own head. But the invisibility of the symptoms makes them no less detrimental to the child. In addition to the serious medical and psychological risks I already mentioned, anxious children may have fewer friends because of social fears, or because their free time is consumed by worry or rituals. They may spend inordinate amounts of time preparing for an event, trying to fall asleep at night, getting their homework just right, or seeking reassurance about their safety. They may not go out for a sport to avoid the risk of being humiliated. They may not go to friends' houses or not consider college, because of panic or separation concerns. At home, family life may lose its sense of spontaneity and fun, as participating in ordinary events may be too anxiety-provoking.

There isn't one type of anxious child. Anxiety disorders differ by diagnosis, and by their presentation. Here are some common ways that an anxious child might present. Take a look and see which best matches your anxious child's situation.

Verbal-anxious: These children talk openly—and at times endlessly—about their fears and worries. They want to tell you everything they are thinking. Sometimes they feel better when they explain their fears, but often their fears build on themselves and they can get more worked up as they talk. Setting compassionate limits on "talking" or "telling" time will teach them that it's okay and important to switch gears from worrying to working things out.

Undercover anxious: These children seem to have it all together in public—they give seamless, Oscar-worthy performances of being gracious, positive, even gregarious. But inside their stomachs are churning and their minds are going a hundred miles an hour with what-if's. They tend to fall apart at home given all the stress that they subject themselves to during the day. By helping them create more sustainable expectations for themselves and leave some room for mistakes, you'll allow your child to feel less anxious, so they'll have less to hide. Helping these children see the "seams" in life—the doubts and mistakes that we all have—can help them ease up on themselves and take the pressure off the perfect valve.

The somaticizer: These are children who can't tell you what they are worried about, and truly they may not have thoughts or images about what they are anticipating. Their worry is expressed through the body—they may throw up before school or have stomachaches or headaches frequently. You can help them use relaxation strategies and coping cognitions to calm the body down.

The angry-anxious child: Walking on eggshells, prickly to the touch, the angry anxious child is as much in need of your help as he is insistent that he isn't. He doesn't want to be in the situation he's in—the vulnerability he feels is unacceptable to him. When you try to help, he may feel at first as if you are shining a light on his worst attribute. Your job as a parent of an angry-anxious child is to help him understand that even very successful people have anxiety. You'll learn to reassure him that anxiety is not his fault, and that there are straightforward ways to take charge of it so it doesn't interfere with his life or define him.

The avoider: "I'm not anxious. I just don't want to go to parties." This is what you might hear from the child who solves his worry problems by simply avoiding situations that are difficult for him. "Socializing isn't important to me. I don't care about eating lunch on my own." "I don't have to go out on weekends." "I don't need to talk to the teacher about extra credit." These are kids for whom approaching situations is so mortifying that they would rather work their life around avoiding anxiety-provoking situations. These children may also procrastinate (which only creates more anxiety), or stay home "sick" on days when there are challenging situations to face such as oral presentations or show and tell. Your job is to help the child approach such situations in small steps, do "research" first to find out what is likely to happen if they do participate, and show them how unfair it is that they are missing out on exciting things because of anxiety.

WHAT MADE MY CHILD ANXIOUS?

Whether their child has been anxious since birth or is having an acute episode, all parents spend time wondering what caused their child's anxiety. Many entertain the dark question of whether they somehow brought the anxiety on their child—either by their own behavior or by genetic transmission. While there are some genetic links for anxiety disorders, the relationship is complex. The best answer is that children's anxiety, like any aspect of a child's functioning, is the result of the knitting together of multiple influences: genetics, natural temperament, and life stressors. No one factor accounts for everything. "Bad parenting" can't cause these problems, and good parenting alone can't fix them.

In this book you will learn many new ideas about handling your child's anxiety that may be different from how you were approaching your child's anxiety before. You could spend time lamenting what you did "wrong," but don't! It's good to find new solutions—this is exactly what you would hope to find! Your child's difficulties may inspire you to turn over a new leaf in your parenting style, but please understand that these changes will only help the process. They're not the reason there was trouble in the first place. It is important to maintain a no-fault approach to the problem. We would never blame our children for their asthma or diabetes—or blame ourselves for passing it on—and we should take the same stance when it comes to their anxiety.

Nature? Nurture? Our understanding of the causes of anxiety in children comes from an appreciation of the interaction of multiple factors. These include (1) genetics and brain physiology, (2) temperament, (3) environmental factors, including stressful events and parenting style.

Genetics: Born to Be Anxious?

> *Genes are not destiny. They are a risk factor, but they are not a determining factor.*
>
> —DR. JORDAN SMOLLER, MASS GENERAL HOSPITAL

It is commonly said that evolution selects for anxious genes, and it's not hard to see why. It is better to have too many false positives (ever on the lookout for the possible tiger lurking around the bend) than to have one fatal oversight (being surprised by the tiger). But when you scale that down to the individual child's narrow shoulders, that explanation doesn't make anxiety a positive trait for the owner of those anxious genes.

Genetics determine one's overall susceptibility to an anxiety disorder, but they are not the direct cause. Genes affect how different cells in the body's alarm system operate—the sensitivities and reaction times—and some children are born more sensitive and reactive, with lower "distress tolerance." There are likely multiple genes that contribute to a child's anxiety disorder, not one identifiable "anxiety gene."

Genetics researchers have found some support for the genetic transmission of anxiety: Children of anxious parents are as much as seven times more likely to develop an anxiety disorder as children whose parents don't have a problem with anxiety, but this is due to a combination of genetics and modeling, as we'll see in a minute. Genetics explains about 30 to 40 percent of all transmission—so although genetics are important, the majority of children with anxious parents do not develop an anxiety disorder. The bottom line? Genetics alone aren't responsible for anxiety disorders. Other factors intervene to tip the scales.

Temperament and Behavioral Inhibition

"Temperament," according to Ralph Waldo Emerson, "is the iron wire upon which the beads [of life] are strung." Many anxious children appear to be very sensitive to change and risk from birth. As a result, they have an extremely cautious style and a curbed approach to exploration. This predisposition is a blueprint for predicting children's needs and experiences in any given situation. Harvard University's Dr. Jerome Kagan identified this trait, which he calls behavioral inhibition, in children as young as twenty-one months old. While other infants respond to the most minor changes in their environment—a new mobile or cup—with excitement or delight, infants with behavioral inhibition respond with distress. Dr. Kagan hypothesized that these children had a lower threshold for responsivity in the emotion-regulating limbic system and as a result were susceptible to greater sympathetic nervous system (fight-or-flight reactions) when exposed to novel situations. Dr. Kagan found that these inhibited children had a higher than average likelihood of developing an anxiety disorder later in life. According to meta-analytic studies, approximately half of the 15 percent of children exhibiting behavioral inhibition as infants will develop social anxiety disorder.[3] As we have seen in our genetics discussion above, the recipe for temperament combines many different genes and factors, so while behavioral inhibition can be a heritable trait, many children will not have this temperament style even if their parents do.

Behavioral inhibition is the single most robust variable associated with the development of social anxiety disorder. As with any risk factor, it can be modulated by environment, parenting, adaptive emotion-modulating skills, and encouragement.

Environmental Factors: Stressful Events and Parenting Factors

Not all children who develop an anxiety disorder have a traumatic event in their history. In fact, most do not. However, many children and adolescents today are exposed to traumatic experiences; more than two-thirds of children report experiencing a traumatic event by age sixteen. These may include witnessing a violent crime, being exposed to sexual abuse, or receiving emergency care as a result of a car accident, fall, fire, dog bite, and so forth. Many studies suggest that the majority of children who undergo trauma do recover without incident. But a child who has experienced a traumatic event is *twice as likely* to develop some type of difficulty—whether anxiety, depression, or a behavioral disorder. Children faced with stressful or traumatic situations may go through periods of greater sensitivity, clinging, and regression. This is not only normal; it is adaptive—it enables them to get the nurturing they need to recover emotionally and physically. Some kids, though, will cross the line into a disorder. In Chapter 17, we look at treatments for children who are experiencing post-traumatic stress disorder. In Chapter 20, we discuss how to handle stressful and tragic events in ways that are most constructive for your child.

FAMILY ENHANCEMENT OF ANXIOUS THINKING

At a recent visit to my daughter's dentist, as I sat respectfully at a distance, the doctor was complaining about "helicopter parents" who hover over the child, making sure they are okay, constantly asking, "Now, does that hurt?" While his concern was how these "pilots" get in the way of the equipment, the real concern is how this hovering impacts kids' experiences in potentially stressful situations like in the dentist's chair. Though we know that parent interaction/instruction alone cannot cause anxiety reactions, studies suggest that the style of family interaction can enhance an anxious child's perceptions about a situation and influence his actions. While parents may be trying to protect kids from potential dangers, to an already anxious child this behavior reinforces the idea that these situations are scary. Rather than turning down the volume on that worry sound track, the child is now hearing it in stereo. All parents want their children to feel safe and secure in the world, but the best way to do this is to focus on *how* to be safe and savvy (things the child can do to help himself), rather than focusing on how dangerous the world is (something that is distorted, out of the child's control, and will engender more fear). We will explore the behaviors associated with optimal parenting style in Chapter 10, but for the moment, when you are talking to your child about a situation do a quick check-in with yourself: Is what I am telling them going to help them feel *prepared* or *scared*? The more you keep tabs on your own anxiety, the better off your child will be.

A classic paper by Ginsburg and Margaret Schlossberg of Johns Hopkins University School of Medicine summarized over twenty studies of parenting factors associated with anxiety in children.[4] A synopsis of these findings is given below, listing the factors that either reinforce or reduce anxious behavior in children. It is crucial to understand that these studies could show only the correlations between anxious behavior in children and certain parenting behaviors; the studies were not designed to indicate which came first. As you're reading the following lists, keep in mind a recent interaction with your child. Review the list and see what is going well and what you might need to work on.

PARENTING BEHAVIORS ASSOCIATED WITH ANXIETY IN CHILDREN

- Parental overcontrol: intrusive parenting, exerting control in conversation, limiting of autonomy and independence in conversation
- Overprotection: excessive caution and protective behaviors without cause
- Modeling of anxious interpretation: agreeing with child's distortion of the risk in a situation, reinforcing the idea that normal things in the world are too scary to approach

- Tolerance or encouragement of avoidance behavior: suggesting or agreeing with not trying something difficult
- Rejection or criticism: disapproving, judgmental, dismissive, or critical behavior
- Conflict: (not as strong a factor) two out of five studies found fighting, arguing, and disharmony in a family to be associated with high levels of anxiety

POSITIVE PARENTING BEHAVIORS THAT BUFFER STRESS

- Rewarding coping behavior: focusing on means, not ends, rewarding children for taking on challenges, recognizing partial successes
- Extinguishing excessive anxious behavior: reducing anxious behavior by not responding to it excessively, with either concern or anger
- Managing one's own anxiety: limiting displays of distress, not introducing parents' worries into the mix
- Developing family communication and problem-solving skills: open-house policy for positive communication and problem-solving opportunities
- Authoritative/democratic parenting style: Parents directing children's behavior while valuing independence is associated with lower levels of anxiety (versus authoritarian style—parents demand obedience, limit autonomy; or permissive style—parents avoid any attempts to control behavior)

DO IT TODAY: CONNECT WITH YOUR CHILD, NOT WITH HER ANXIETY

When our children are afraid, our first reaction is that we want it to stop—as soon as possible! We want them to stop feeling scared and see that everything is fine. We get pretty uncomfortable ourselves. It's important to know that the fastest way to get there is to take what may seem like a slower route. Rather than trying to stop the anxiety, or convince or reassure your child he's fine—understanding and empathizing with your child's experience will help your child move on from it. Remember that his "first reaction" of fear is as no-fault as his brown eyes or right-handedness. And it's just how he feels right now. Stay connected; lean in to where your child is emotionally by saying things like the following: "I understand this feels really scary right now to you," or "This is feeling really hard. I want to help." The simple fact that you are not criticizing, doubting, or correcting how your child feels is exactly what will help him feel more secure and confident and ready to move on and follow your lead to the next idea. Your connection and understanding will be a stepping-stone for him to begin to do something different with his fear, rather than having to hide it or convince you that it's real.

Chapter 2

MAKING THE DIAGNOSIS FOR ANXIETY

Is It Just a Phase?

When I meet with parents for an initial intake evaluation about their child, I am happiest when I conclude that their child doesn't meet the criteria for an anxiety disorder. This may sound obvious. Of course it would be preferable for a child not to have a severe condition! But this isn't the only reason. I am happy that they've come in for help now, rather than waiting till their child's symptoms start to interfere so much with his functioning that it would not take an hour's interview with an expert to see how bad the problem is—it would be obvious immediately. The fact is, there is so much parents can do, instantly and easily, so that they will never have to reach that point.

When parents come in to meet with a professional, it's because they are confused and they've run out of their own ideas for how to alleviate their child's suffering. Whether or not there ends up being a diagnosis, this is an opportunity for parents to learn how to change the conversation with their child at home so that they have a better chance of avoiding those diagnostic criteria. Similarly, as you read through the descriptions of the different anxiety diagnoses in this chapter, keep in mind that any child who is feeling anxious—whether he meets criteria for a diagnosis or not—deserves to feel better. And he can, with some new direction from you. Rather than stand idly by waiting to see whether this is just a phase, whether things heat up or resolve, you can teach your child what to do to take charge of worry *now*. In this chapter you'll learn which subtype of anxiety best fits your child's behavior; then you can refer to the chapters in Section III that will provide the most relevant road map for you. We first review general red flags for problem anxiety, and next describe features of specific anxiety disorders. Sometimes anxiety isn't the only issue your child is contending with, so the chapter closes with brief descriptions of other common diagnoses that may co-occur with anxiety.

Is this your child?

Six-year-old Matthew is taking swimming lessons for the first time. He has lots of questions: Is the teacher going to be mean or nice? Will he have to be in the water the whole class? Will the teacher let him out of the water if he's cold? Does he have to tread water? He doesn't want to tread water, because that's what you have to do so you don't drown, and he doesn't like to think about drowning. But he's excited about learning how to be a stronger swimmer and hopes that he will be allowed to try the diving board. He asks his mom if she can stay for the class.

At the end of class Matthew is excited that he's going to go on the diving board in a few weeks, he says his teacher is okay, and he thought that learning how to tread water was funny—they called it the "doggy-paddle"! He did get cold and wants his mom to ask the teacher if he can get out of the water next time if he's too cold. Matt still wants Mom to be there for the next class, but he's excited to go.

Or is this your child?

Six-year-old Jason has always had a hard time with new situations. He doesn't want to try swimming lessons and has been crying and refusing to go ever since his mom mentioned it weeks before. He can't talk about why he's scared; he just doesn't want to go. On the day of the class he hides behind the chair in the living room, refuses to get dressed, and cries the whole time his mom is leading him out to the car. When he arrives he hangs on to his mom as she helps him up to class. Jason is unable to participate like the other children; he keeps looking to his mom when the teacher asks him to try something. The same scenario continues for two more weeks until Jason's mom and dad decide it would be best to drop the class.

Matthew might be considered temperamentally a "slower to warm up" child. He is cautious and needs more details than other kids. His imagination leads to some worries—but he seems to be able to take them in stride, given a little time.

Jason, on the other hand, is stuck. Not only does he get extremely distraught when he's anticipating an event, as do his parents; he also comes away with a sense of failure and a confirmation that the best way to deal with something hard is to avoid it.

Take another example: Cara goes through a litany of nighttime questions, like many young children. "Where are you going to be? Why can't I sleep in your bed? I'm scared!" When Cara's parents kindly but firmly cut her off and leave ("I think you know the answers already! Love you, goodnight!"), she is able to take those answers in stride. She doesn't spiral into more worry; instead the routine—the outcome of which she already knows—settles her. She is able to trust her parents' reassurance and close down the thinking for the night.

By contrast, Maggie, if you can wrangle her into bed, starts with the same nightly routine of twenty questions: "Where are you going to be? Will you be upstairs? When are you going to bed? Are you sure the doors are locked and there are no bad guys? Why can't you stay? I can't sleep without you! What if I can't sleep all night?" Unlike Cara, Maggie gets more worked up the more questions she asks, rather than settling down. With each of her parents' answers she gets more upset and tearful. In fact, she's not really listening; she is too upset. Turning out the light is like turning on the switch for the imagination: She imagines she sees something move or hears a noise; her heart is racing; her stomach feels sick. Unable to stand it anymore, she runs into her parents' room. Looking like a trapped animal, she begs them to let her stay in their bed. Knowing that Maggie will never be able to sleep in that state, and that school will be a disaster the next day, they relent.

As we see from these two examples, it isn't the content of the fear, or the "what" of your child's worries, that distinguishes problem anxiety from transitory anxiety. Cara and Maggie were afraid of the same things. The difference is the way the children process their worry. If your child seems to be unable to use your calming presence to move forward, or worry just seems to get stuck in your child's mind and won't let go, this is a situation in need of an action plan. This chapter will help you decide whether what is needed is therapy or a take-action plan at home. Either way: Don't wait. No matter how big or small your child's fears, she will benefit from knowing how to handle them.

WHEN YOU SHOULD WORRY: RED FLAGS FOR ANXIETY IN YOUR CHILD

As you read in Chapter 1, there are normal fears of childhood. It can be confusing for parents to tell when their child's anxiety is diverging from the expected track. Even though your child's fears may be "normal" in content—dogs, shots, the dark—this doesn't mean that the process your child, and by extension your family, is going through is normal, tolerable, or desirable. Rather than thinking normal or not normal, ask yourself the following questions:

1. Is your child's worry out of proportion to the risk or demands of the situation?
2. Are you unable to reassure your child with logical explanations?
3. Are there physical symptoms of anxiety: headaches, stomachaches, sleep disturbances?
4. Are you changing plans or spending inordinate amounts of time preparing, convincing, or reassuring your child in order to participate in ordinary activities?
5. Has the anxiety persisted for a long period of time (six months or more)?
6. Does the anxiety lead to avoidance?

7. Does the anxiety interfere with social, family, or academic functioning?

Signs of Transitory Anxiety	Signs of Problematic Anxiety
Fears and concerns are reasonable and expectable.	Fears and concerns are unreasonable and out of proportion to the event.
The child is responsive to suggestions for change.	The child becomes overwhelmed and inconsolable and may regress or melt down in response to suggestions for change.
The child has many questions, to which there are answers, and the child accepts those answers.	Reassurance is never enough; no answer is good enough. Concerns are taken deeply to heart and create distress in the present and worry about the future.
The child takes pride in doing work neatly and correctly.	The child is perfectionistic; nothing is good enough; nothing is ever right. School work or simple tasks of daily living may take an inordinate amount of time because of the child's insistence on precision.
The child is learning to take responsibility for mistakes and oversights, although he may need consoling.	The child is constantly concerned that others are mad at him, or that he is going to make a mistake or be at fault for making something bad happen.
Symptoms diminish in intensity over time, and take less time to deal with.	Symptoms increase in intensity over time and the worry takes on a life of its own.
The child understands why he needs to face the situation.	The child is more focused on how to avoid the situation than on how or why to face it.
The symptoms catalyze/facilitate positive change.	The symptoms interfere with growth and productivity.
Themes are in synch with the child's developmental stage.	Themes are out of synch with the developmental stage of the child.

MAKING THE DIAGNOSIS: CRITERIA FOR THE PRIMARY ANXIETY DISORDER DIAGNOSES

The summaries that follow provide a snapshot of the specific diagnostic criteria for each type of anxiety disorder. I'll explore each one in greater depth in Part III.

Generalized Anxiety Disorder

Children with generalized anxiety disorder (GAD) have excessive, uncontrollable worry about a number of different situations: friends, health, academic or sports performance (even when their performance is not being evaluated by others). They are extremely suggestible, and the mere mention of an adverse event such as an illness or accident or someone being laid off sets off a chain reaction of worry and reassurance seeking. Their worry is out of proportion to the likelihood or impact of the event, and it is difficult to console or redirect a child with GAD. Children with GAD are on edge making sure that they (and the others around them, too) are doing "the right thing," that no one is getting in trouble, breaking a rule, or misbehaving. They fear the worst consequences for small actions. They are unable to relax or enjoy situations because they are constantly thinking about what could go wrong or what they need to do next. They often look stressed and have difficulties with headaches, stomachaches, and falling asleep at night. In order to meet criteria for the diagnosis, symptoms of excessive worry plus one of the following must be present for at least six months: restlessness or feeling keyed up or on edge, being easily fatigued, difficulty concentrating or mind going blank, irritability, muscle tension, sleep disturbance (difficulty falling asleep, staying asleep, or restless sleep). (See Chapter 11.)

Specific Phobias

Phobias are sometimes considered the "narrow-minded" brand of anxiety. Children with a specific phobia have a marked fear of a specific object or situation—think bees, dogs, or throwing up—

that is out of proportion to the actual risk presented. They react to the possibility of contact with that object or situation with immediate fear, anxiety, crying, tantrums, freezing, clinging, or otherwise becoming dysregulated emotionally and even out of control. They are so consumed with avoiding the phobic situation that they may unknowingly put themselves into high-risk situations—for example, running into the street to avoid a dog, running away from a party to avoid a bee, running out of class if another student looks ill. Whereas other anxiety disorders tend to lead to anxiety in multiple situations, children with specific phobias are generally okay if they are able to avoid the feared object or situation, although they may not trust that they won't encounter the phobic situation and may ask questions repeatedly—"Will someone get sick today at school?" "What if there's a dog in the parking lot?" To meet criteria for the diagnosis, the fear must be persistent (lasting six months) and interfere with significant areas of functioning or create significant distress. Sometimes phobias develop after a traumatic event (being knocked over by a dog, having an especially painful shot, seeing a clown for the first time), but they can also be triggered by observing someone else experiencing a traumatic event (having an allergic reaction, vomiting, drowning). (See Chapter 12.)

Social Anxiety

Imagine if every moment of life was a performance during which the world is watching and there is no "backstage" and you begin to approach the feeling of exposure that the socially anxious child experiences. "Social anxiety" refers to a persistent fear of social or performance situations. Not shy by choice, the socially anxious child feels under constant scrutiny by others in any social encounter. Children may suffer far in advance of a social interaction, anticipating their embarrassment. Some children may have this fear only with regard to speaking or performing in public; for others, just being in the presence of others—in class, standing in line in the cafeteria, or even simply stepping out their door into public—causes anxiety. To meet the diagnostic criteria, symptoms must be present for at least six months and interfere with participation in social, academic, or family activities. For children, these symptoms must occur when they are with peers, not just in interactions with adults. (See Chapter 13.)

Selective Mutism

Children with selective mutism (SM) are consistently unable to speak in a specific situation (such as at school), whereas they are completely able to speak in other situations (most typically at home with family). Different from a shy or reluctant child, who may need time to acclimate to a new situation, a child with SM does not benefit from more time or invitations to participate. Their inability to speak in school interferes with their participation and teachers' assessment of their skills. To meet the diagnostic criteria, a child's failure to speak must last at least one month (not the first month of school) and cannot be due to another factor, such as a communication disorder or not knowing the language. (See Chapter 13.)

Separation Anxiety Disorder

Children with separation anxiety disorder (SAD) have extreme difficulty separating from their parents in most situations—whether going to school, staying with a babysitter while parents are out, at bedtime, when the parent (or child) needs to use the bathroom, or even simply not sitting right next to them on the couch at home. Children with SAD often express fears about harm befalling their parents or other attachment figures (illness, disaster), or harm happening to themselves, which would result in a separation from their attachment figures (kidnapping, accidents, illness). Kids with separation anxiety disorder cling or shadow parents' every move, needing to know their whereabouts at all times. They are typically unable to sleep alone and often have difficulty attending school, playing at friends' houses, or going on field trips. SAD may be triggered by losses or deaths of relatives or pets, divorce, transitions, change of schools, relocation, or other traumatic events that involve separation. Physical symptoms, such as nausea, vomiting, headaches, or stomachaches, may be present when the child anticipates separation from parents. To meet the diagnostic criteria, symptoms that are developmentally inappropriate must be present for at least four weeks. (See Chapter 14.)

Panic Disorder and Agoraphobia

Children with panic disorder suffer from recurrent panic attacks—sudden surges of anxiety and dread that are accompanied by physical symptoms (heart palpitations, sweating, shaking, shortness of breath, choking, chest pain, nausea or abdominal distress, dizziness, light-headedness, chills or sensations of heat, numbness or tingling sensations). Panic attacks appear out of the blue and peak within minutes. Children interpret this very frightening surge in physical symptoms as life-threatening or life-changing and feel they need to escape the situation in order to stop the symptoms. Following an attack, the child avoids the situation or setting in which the initial attack occurred, believing that this is a way of avoiding future panic attacks. Over time, they may begin to limit their activities in anticipation that they may have an attack. This is called agoraphobia: the inability to leave the house, be in a car, use public transportation, be in stores, stand in a line, or be in an enclosed place, due to a fear of developing panic-like symptoms and being unable to get help. To meet the diagnosis for panic disorder, sufferers must have had at least one panic attack, followed by one month or more of worry about having another, or resulting in significant interference in their functioning. (See Chapter 14.)

Obsessive-Compulsive Disorder

In contrast to the child with GAD, who has unrealistic fears about everyday concerns, the more than one million children with obsessive-compulsive disorder (OCD) have fears that are senseless—even to them. They suffer from intrusive thoughts, images, and impulses that are bizarre and often diametrically opposed to who the child is (a loving child pictures stabbing a parent; a religious child fears that she hates God; an innocent child believes he was sexually inappropriate). Children engage in rituals or compulsive behaviors, such as excessive washing, checking, redoing, counting, or tapping, to relieve the anxiety triggered by the intrusive or "bad" thought. A child can have either obsessions or compulsions or both; in order to meet the criteria for the diagnosis, symptoms must cause distress; rituals must take more than one hour a day, or significantly interfere with a child's home life, school life, or social functioning. (See Chapter 15.)

Post-Traumatic Stress Disorder

Children with post-traumatic stress disorder (PTSD) have been exposed to a traumatic event that was perceived as life-threatening or resulted in death, and which caused them to experience intense fear, horror, or helplessness. They may suffer frightening and disabling residual symptoms such as flashbacks, nightmares, physiological reactivity, inability to sleep or concentrate, or emotional reactivity in situations that are similar to or remind them of some aspect of the traumatic event, and they may try very hard to avoid thoughts, feelings, conversations, and places that remind them of the trauma. Other emotional reactions include detachment, a sense of a foreshortened future, and a diminished interest in activities. To meet the diagnostic criteria, symptoms must be present for more than one month and cause significant distress or impairment in important areas of functioning. (See Chapter 17.)

Other Diagnoses to Consider

The following diagnoses may either be confused for an anxiety disorder because of overlapping symptoms, or may co-occur with anxiety, what is referred to as a comorbid condition. If your child exhibits the symptoms of these other disorders, you may wish to seek professional intervention to address your concerns. Resources are also available on my website: www.tamarchansky.com.

Tourette's Syndrome

Tourette's syndrome is a neurological condition that involves involuntary motor and vocal activity. Motor tics can include eye blinking, face grimacing, pinching, kissing, or throwing things. Vocal tics include throat clearing, squeaking, clicking, or words that are spoken unintentionally. It can be difficult to distinguish OCD symptoms from tics. For example, a child may tap objects symmetrically; if the child has OCD, there is typically a feeling that they will have bad luck or will feel not "just right" if they don't tap; whereas a child with tics may simply say that their body just "taps" or gets a "warning" that they need to tap, but beyond that there isn't a reason (they may even be unaware that it is happening until someone brings it to their attention). Tics in isolation are not Tourette's syndrome—it is when motor and vocal tics are both present that the diagnosis is made. The treatment of tics and Tourette's syndrome is described in Chapter 16.

Trichotillomania (Hair-Pulling Disorder)

Compulsive hair pulling, or "trich," is considered an obsessive-compulsive–related disorder. Like OCD, trich begins with a cycle of strong urges, and even a tingling or "itch-like" sensation that is relieved by engaging in hair pulling. Unlike OCD, however, there is a temporary feeling of pleasure and/or relief associated with pulling the "right" hair. Immediately following that brief relief there is intense shame and embarrassment over one's actions, and the visible repercussions of the disorder. Despite this, the strength of the urges to pull are so great that they are extremely difficult to resist: Imagine having a mosquito bite that you don't itch. To meet the diagnostic criteria, hair pulling must result in hair loss, and there must be repeated attempts to stop the hair pulling. See Chapter 16 for more on treating trich.

Depressive Disorders

While all children have good days and bad days, a depressed child has little hope that anything could get better. Most days are laden with a heaviness that won't lift or fade, or a struggle against an anger that won't break. Importantly, these feelings don't come and go in response to good or bad events. Children with OCD or other anxiety disorders may experience depression if their symptoms are not improving or they are not getting treatment. Though we may think of depression as signaled by sadness and crying, children often express depression through irritability and low tolerance of frustration. Additional symptoms are changes in appetite, overeating or loss of interest in food, changes in sleep habits, and talking about suicide. Children may lose interest in friends, sports, or schoolwork, or lose themselves for hours at a time in television or computer games. If this constellation of symptoms is present for at least two weeks, reflects a marked change in your child's usual behavior, and is interfering with your child's functioning, it is time to pursue professional help.

Attention-Deficit/Hyperactivity Disorder

While all children can have their "hyper" moments when they are overtired, overstimulated, or have eaten too much sugar, children with attention-deficit/hyperactivity disorder (ADHD) show these symptoms across situations, unrelated to specific triggers. The child is not intentionally manifesting bad behavior or a will to disobey; his brain likes to "get up and wander" regardless of the setting. ADHD is a neurodevelopmental disorder characterized by inattention and/or hyperactivity-impulsivity that interferes with functioning, and it generally occurs *before* the age of twelve. Common behaviors include hurrying through work, missing details, having difficulty paying attention to instructions, not following through on instructions, avoiding tasks that require sustained mental effort, losing things, and forgetfulness in daily activities.

While many symptoms of anxiety and ADHD overlap on the surface—fidgeting, restlessness, distractibility—the underlying reasons for the symptoms are quite different. ADHD is caused by the child's inability to harness attention and focus on the demands of a situation. Kids with ADHD have wonderful, busy minds that can engage deeply in novel, exciting, or interesting information. This is why they can seem so distracted in school or at dinner, but focus for hours on something they like—the brain has found the *right* stimulation. In contrast, anxious kids' minds are busy anticipating risk, overestimating danger, fearing the worst. While anxious kids may be fidgety, restless, and inattentive, they aren't distracted by what is going on around them, but rather by their imagination and thoughts. Importantly, the treatment of choice for ADHD is medication along with behavioral interventions to maximize attention and focusing at home and school. But medications for ADHD, psychostimulants, can often increase nervousness in children with anxiety disorders. For children who have both anxiety and ADHD, ask your child's doctor for the best course of treatment.

DIFFERENTIATING ANXIETY AND ADHD SYMPTOMS

Symptom	Anxiety Cause	ADHD Cause
Inattention, easily distracted, doesn't seem to listen, doesn't follow through on instructions	Distracted by worries, intrusive thoughts, rituals, and fears; may be afraid of hearing the question wrong; may race through assignment or not follow instructions because thoughts are interfering with focus	Distracted by kids and noises; may notice that teacher is saying something, but doesn't process the instructions; may rush to get unwanted task done quickly and go on to something more fun
Unable to concentrate on work	Afraid that work will be too hard or will have to be done perfectly so avoids getting started; can't tolerate the feeling of not being sure something is right	Difficulty sitting still due to boredom or excess energy; need to get up and move, or simply do something that feels more interesting
Impulsivity; blurts out answers, interrupts, can't wait one's turn	Fear that he will forget the answer; needs reassurance that he is right; unable to leave a mistake as is; uncertain if heard teacher exactly right and can't tolerate feeling of uncertainty	Not enough processing available between having an idea and putting it into action—no mental brakes or filter; unaware of interrupting

Hyperactivity; fidgety, gets up from seat; talking excessively	Fidgety from adrenaline, stress, anticipation, tension, or worry: can't sit still, wants to go home, get the day over with. Nervous energy: may be doing rituals, or feel the need to leave the room due to panic; may be experiencing trauma flashbacks (PTSD)	Excess energy, physically needs to move or keep hands busy; moving around or fidgeting may actually be child's strategy for not being bored

Bipolar Disorder

The cardinal symptoms of bipolar disorder include abrupt or rapid mood swings; irritable mood states; increased activity; rapid, loud, pressured speech that is difficult to interrupt; decreased need for sleep; protracted, explosive temper tantrums or rages, usually triggered by limit setting (being told no); and periods of depression. As with ADHD, many symptoms overlap with anxiety disorders, including excessive separation anxiety or worry and difficulties sleeping. Careful assessment is needed to differentiate the two.

Sensory Integration Dysfunction

Some children don't seem to be able to "go with the flow," feeling every bump in the road, whether it's the tag on their clothing, a strong food smell, or the seam on their sock. It's as if every piece of sensory input is registered as an obstacle to overcome. These children are described as having sensory defensiveness; though adults may perceive them as "picky" and "oversensitive," the hypersensitivity is not a factor of their personality; it is a reflection of the efficiency, coordination, and maturity of their central nervous system.

This may manifest in frustration, anxiety, or tantrum behavior. Children may be unable to focus on the task at hand because their brain resources are largely occupied processing the minutia of sensory experience—the elastic is bothering my waist, my underwear isn't right, my hair isn't tight enough, this food is too soft. Motor coordination is typically affected, and children may appear clumsy, fidgety, or unable to sit still—excessive movement is the body's way of trying to get the sensory feedback it needs.

Autism Spectrum Disorders

This category of neurodevelopmental disorders—including the disorders previously known as Asperger's syndrome and pervasive developmental disorder—has been receiving much attention in recent years. There are two cardinal symptoms of autism spectrum disorders (ASDs): (1) significant impairments in several areas of development, including negotiating social interactions and understanding the nuances of social situations and social communication; and (2) a narrow range of interests, repetitive behaviors or activities. Children with autistic spectrum disorders (ASDs) may or may not have an intellectual or language impairment. The continuum of functioning in ASDs is very broad; some children are severely impaired and require a special academic or residential setting, while many children (and adults) with ASDs are in our midst, their symptoms not obvious at all. Children with ASDs may have excessive social anxiety because they have difficulty with the ambiguous nature of social interactions. Without a script to predict what will happen in a situation, they may feel quite nervous and not know how to manage their anxiety. While some anxiety-management strategies may be helpful, it is best to focus on generating "new rules" or a formula for how to handle a given situation. Children with ASDs may engage in repetitive behaviors, such as tapping, head banging, or repacking and redoing, but it feels right to them. In children with ASDs there is not the subjective experience of the senselessness and unacceptability of the action that one would see in OCD, nor is there necessarily the feared consequence of not performing the behavior. Still, many of the behavioral strategies used to treat OCD may be used with a child with ASDs if adapted to his or her developmental level. The prevalence of ASDs is 1 percent.

In this chapter we have previewed the different subtypes of anxiety disorders, the treatment of which we will describe in more detail in Part III. If you recognize your child in these descriptions, you may be feeling relieved to see that what your child is contending with is a known quantity, not a mystery: It has a name, and more important—a solution! If, on the other hand, you are feeling overwhelmed because you recognized your child's struggles in many of the descriptions here, take heart. Remember that many children may exhibit *some* aspects of different anxiety disorders, but it is the degree of distress and interference that distinguishes a passing anxiety from a disorder. Ask yourself these questions: Is this fear or struggle interfering with your child's (or the family's) day-to-day life? Is your child very upset about the problem: crying, fighting, losing sleep, wracked with fear? If this is the case, then treatment may be indicated. Remember that either way, the prognosis for children with anxiety disorders is very good, we have excellent treatments to change the course of their life, and many strategies are easily implemented at home. We now explore the "who," "what," and "when" of treatment when professional help is needed.

Chapter 3

WHEN AND WHERE TO TURN FOR HELP

Treatments for Childhood Anxiety

I feel like for the first time someone actually understands what it's like to be me—what it sounds like in my head. It's such a relief. It makes me believe that there's hope that I can get better.

I'm afraid if I go for help that my child will be labeled, but I don't want my issues to get in the way of her getting help.

WHEN TO GO FOR HELP

Problems need solutions. And when we look for them, we usually find them. This is what we teach our children. If they are having trouble with math, we don't let it sit until they are completely lost. We step in, we learn more about the problem, we help, and we may even enlist a tutor when we've exhausted our solutions. We take charge because we know that the longer our children limp along, the worse the problem will become. If anxiety is interfering with your child's happiness and quality of life or making it difficult for your child to navigate their day-to-day activities—getting dressed, going to school, having friendships, doing homework, sleeping—it's a problem. Many anxious kids think that their worry problems cannot be solved. They think, "This is just the way I am"—even though they are miserable. Nothing could be further from the truth. Your action plan is to help them see, every time worry comes up, that it is optional, that they have choices, that making life different is completely within their reach every day.

When a child has a "what-if?" orientation to life, anything and everything is fair game for worry, and the more they worry, the more they seem to find to worry about. The concept of neuroplasticity teaches us that the brain is flexible and gets better at whatever it practices. If it is practicing worry, the brain gets the message to keep prioritizing those types of thoughts. But, just as powerfully, when a child learns not to be tricked by the worry brain, a myriad of possibilities open up. Instead of catastrophizing and avoiding, kids learn to relabel that unreliable worry voice, stamp the thought as inaccurate or unnecessary or even preposterous, "underreact" to the hype, and act on their fact-driven smarts. As we will see in this chapter, the prognosis for children with anxiety is very good. Highly effective, life-changing treatments are available to put children back in the driver's seat of their lives, prepared to navigate around the obstacles that worry drops in their path, seeing the mountains as molehills that they are fully capable of climbing. But don't think that if your child needs treatment that means you have to take a backseat. Working with the strategies in this book, you as the parent are in a unique position to be an essential at-home coach: spotting opportunities to help your child practice "thinking twice" if they are freaking out about a test, or having your child be (a little) uncomfortable "on purpose" by approaching a dog or ordering in a restaurant (and being proud of their success). Your collaboration and encouragement will make the process move along that much faster.

Despite the excellent outcomes awaiting anxious children, parents first considering seeking treatment for their child often worry themselves: Will my child feel different or singled out for having a problem? Will others find out? Parents have to think past their own worry, too, to the fact that their child needs help, and they are the ones who can make that happen. Whatever risks you fear must be weighed against the negative effects of ongoing stress or anxiety for the child and the family, and the limitations and missed opportunities that will result from it. Going for treatment is not about labeling a problem; it's about getting powerful solutions and a game plan, so that parents can be proactive instead of reactive. Treatment, when needed, is the opportunity for your child to learn the essential skills to have the life he deserves, the same opportunities and experiences as other children have. While you may have your fears and doubts, remember that being a worrywise parent means allowing your fear and the facts to coexist, and making the choice to be brave. This is exactly what you are asking your child to do. This is your chance to be your best self and a good role model.

If your child is suffering and you don't have a plan to move through it, it's time to go for help. About half of adults with anxiety disorders report that their symptoms began in childhood. They will say (and if you are one of them, you know) how much they wish that their parents had gotten them help when they were young. You may recall from Chapter 2 that many diagnoses of these disorders are made when acute symptoms persist for a month. Use that as a rule of thumb. Even if your child doesn't meet all criteria for a diagnosis, err on the side of seeking consultation. Early intervention is the best strategy for keeping problems small and keeping your child growing.

MAKING TREATMENT STIGMA-FREE AND MATTER-OF-FACT

If your child is feeling uneasy about going to therapy, your challenge as a parent is to clear the path for your child, telling her that coaching of this sort is as matter-of-fact as getting braces if your teeth need straightening, or allergy shots if you are allergic. There is no stigma attached to those conditions, and mental health should be no different. A skilled therapist will help your child feel comfortable, and empower your child to understand that these issues are normal, universal, and entirely manageable when she learns the skills to overcome them. With cognitive-behavior therapy, not only do most children leave treatment feeling more confident about themselves, but they feel more compassionate toward other people who are suffering. I have had many a child tell me how they helped their friends who were scared at a sleepover, or who were nervous before a sports tournament, or even how they talked their parents down from their own anxiety spiral. These are not the signs of children who feel embarrassed or defined by a label; these are worrywise kids who are taking a matter-of-fact approach to thinking past worry's tricks.

TREATMENT OPTIONS: COGNITIVE BEHAVIOR THERAPY AND MEDICATIONS

We are fortunate that we live in a time when very effective treatments are available for children who suffer from stress and anxiety. These treatments, which are in general short-term—lasting often just a few months—can be life-changing, shifting the path from limitation, avoidance, fear, and isolation to one of participation, possibilities, connection, and progress. The efficacy of cognitive behavior therapy (CBT) for anxiety disorders has been documented for decades; the majority of children (as high as 66 percent) no longer met the criteria for a diagnosis after treatment was completed.[5] More recently, large-scale, multi-site studies have confirmed that both cognitive behavior therapy and medication are effective in treating anxiety, with the combination of treatments producing the greatest treatment effect.[6] Does this mean that every anxious child should be doing both? Not necessarily. In my clinical experience treating thousands of patients with anxiety disorders, I have found that most children's symptoms begin to improve within a few sessions. For those cases, the addition of medication—which typically takes a minimum of a month to take effect—is not necessary. Furthermore, medications may provide faster relief for some problems such as severe panic or sleep disturbance, and this relief can be essential, but if they do not learn the skills so that they do not fall for the tricks that anxiety can play, children tend to relapse once medication is discontinued. In addition, while therapy is not a magic bullet, certain CBT "seeing is believing" exposures/experiences can rapidly accelerate a child's confidence in the recovery process—for example, a child with panic spins round and round with her therapist and sees she doesn't faint or panic! Or a boy with a dog phobia shows mom a picture of him petting a dog. These positive experiences—though they take grit and courage to start—

work quickly and have great staying power for kids as they cross these heretofore impossible things off their worry list.

WHOM DO I CALL FIRST?

For a parent considering treatment, your first step would be to talk to your child's pediatrician to get a referral to a therapist who practices cognitive behavior therapy. Once your child starts with a therapist, the therapist can help you determine if medication is also indicated. If so, the therapist or your pediatrician can recommend a psychiatrist who can prescribe medications.

Understanding How Cognitive Behavior Therapy Works

Unlike other types of less directive psychotherapy or talk therapies, which may look for underlying causes for why a child is anxious, the cognitive behavioral model of anxiety understands fears and avoidances as a result of no-fault, default anxious thought patterns—distorted assessments that the brain is making. The focus of treatment is to teach children to be experts in understanding how to retrain the brain to correct anxious thought patterns to get worry out of the way. Here's what it looks like in action.

What Happens During Cognitive Behavior Therapy?

Psychoeducation: The therapist normalizes the child's experiences by teaching children that anxiety is universal and that anxious feelings come from distorted thoughts and assessments that the brain is making, all in the service of trying to protect you. Psychoeducation also introduces the skills the child will learn to reduce and manage anxiety.

Somatic management skills: The child learns techniques such as breathing and progressive muscle relaxation to counter the unnecessary triggering of the body's fight-or-flight response.

Cognitive restructuring: The child identifies negative or anxiety-producing automatic thoughts and learns to counter those thoughts with realistic, coping thinking based on the evidence available.

Exposure: Replacing the worry about what could happen with real-life experience about what actually does happen; exposure includes practicing new behaviors one step at a time in the target situations: a child with OCD touching "contaminated" items; a child with social anxiety ordering in a restaurant; a child with separation anxiety spending time away from mom and dad.

Relapse prevention: The therapist identifies with the child the signs of a possible relapse and potential stressors and devises a plan the child can use to quickly address any setbacks that may occur in the future. Like having an essential first-aid kit available, relapse-prevention skills will help him be prepared and protected from any anxiety episodes he may encounter in the future.

In Chapters 4–7 we will take an in-depth look at the new lessons of CBT in plain language so that you can be on the same page as your child's therapist, as well as implement these techniques at home.

How Do I Find a Qualified Therapist Who Performs CBT?

Many licensed psychologists have received specialized training in CBT. Some social workers and even psychiatrists are turning to CBT so they can provide their patients effective, time-limited treatments for anxiety. You can ask your pediatrician or school counselor for a recommendation, or consult the web for practitioners who specialize in treatment of anxiety in children.

When you are looking for a therapist, don't be afraid to ask questions. Let the therapist demonstrate her qualifications by describing her techniques and telling you how many children she has treated who have suffered from your child's particular problem. Don't mention techniques first—see what the therapist says. He or she should specifically mention cognitive behavior therapy, systematic desensitization, exposure treatment, and (for OCD) exposure and ritual prevention. Find out the ways parents are included in the treatment. Parent participation in some form is an essential component of treatment success. I have spoken to many parents who have done so much research on their child's issues that they find they are more informed than their child's therapist. If your gut tells you this is the situation, find someone who is going to teach *you*. Also gauge your own reaction to the clinician's personality. Is he warm, caring, patient, and confident in his ability to help you? Chances are, if you feel comfortable with the therapist, your child will. If you are not clicking, it is likely that your child will not either.

Remember that there are numerous specific techniques for challenging anxious thoughts and approaching anxious situations. If a therapist talks about helping a child get her mind off the anxiety, distracting her, or simply using relaxation strategies, this may be a red flag that he or she doesn't understand how anxiety treatment works. Though distraction may be a strategy, it is not the one with teeth. It's also most likely the one your child has been using unsuccessfully up to this point, and the reason you are currently seeking professional services. Listen for new ideas, optimism, and a plan.

QUESTIONS TO ASK A PROSPECTIVE THERAPIST

- What is your approach to working with children with anxiety?
- Do you use cognitive behavior therapy? What strategies would you use in working with my child?
- How many children with this type of problem have you treated, and what is your success rate?
- How do you explain anxiety and cognitive behavior therapy to kids? (Listen for creative, user-friendly ideas.)
- How do you help kids get interested in and cooperate with treatment?
- How soon do you begin to address the issues?
- How do you work with parents?
- Who is in the room with you during sessions? Do parents participate? (You want to make sure that you aren't just left out in the waiting room, not understanding the treatment and having to guess what to do.)
- Is there an opportunity for parents to speak to you privately?
- Do you do exposure work outside the office?

- Do you assign homework? How do you help us work on goals outside of sessions?
- Are there physicians you work with who can prescribe medication if needed?
- Do you have contact with the school?
- What is the best way to contact you in a crisis?
- What insurance do you accept?
- How long is the typical treatment? Are you available for periodic follow-ups?

Can Young Children Participate in Cognitive Behavior Therapy? Cognitive behavior therapy may sound rather grown-up, and most of the literature documenting the effectiveness of CBT in children studied children at least eight years old. But we know anecdotally that children as young as three or four can learn the concepts when they are playfully presented (and often they are the fastest students). They love to shake their bossy finger at the worrybug, make worry mad by doing courage challenges, or draw a silly monster-makeover for the beasts who are frightening them at night. Young children often have a great time in CBT—the structure, the hands-on experiential nature of the work, and the clear goals and rewards are right up their alley, and they feel very proud of their accomplishments. Young children's abundant creativity, active imaginations, and righteous desire to be in charge easily compensate for any cognitive maturity they lack.

Medications

Some parents feel that because an anxiety disorder is physiological in nature, a child necessarily requires medication to treat it. Other parents believe that medications would be harmful to their child and categorically refuse to use them. There is no one-size-fits-all answer for treating anxious kids. While most children will benefit from cognitive behavior therapy, and it is the treatment of choice for anxiety disorders, some children may require medication in order to be ready to participate in therapy. You need to be informed about the issues and your options so that at the end of the day you know that you are doing what's best for your child. In an ideal world we would have more precise information about what works best with the least cost physically, psychologically, and economically for kids who suffer from anxiety—and one day this may be possible. For today, be a good consumer: Learn what you can about different treatments and their appropriateness for your child.

There are certain circumstances in which the use of medications may be indicated from the start. If a child is suffering from depression, has not been sleeping for weeks, or is struggling with some other disruptive or intolerable symptoms, medication will likely be initiated early in the process to resolve the symptoms themselves, and also because the symptoms—irritable mood, low mood, low energy—are preventing the child from being able to participate successfully in the cognitive behavior therapy.

Absent these factors, though, how does one decide whether medication should be included in the therapy? A rule of thumb is to begin with CBT and then consider adding medication if the child is not showing some response within approximately four to six weeks.

When medication is indicated, there is a wide range of options for children. It is outside the scope of this book to provide a comprehensive review of psychiatric medications for anxiety. If your child is on medication, or if it has been recommended as part of his treatment, please consult your pediatrician or psychiatrist for information about efficacy, side effects, dosages, and other pertinent topics.

Is Your Child a Candidate for Medication?

While some parents want to avoid medications due to safety concerns, others may look desperately to medications for a quick fix for their child's painful situation. All medications have to go through FDA approval before they can be prescribed in this country. Often, however, medications that are used for kids have not been specifically approved by the FDA for use in children. This doesn't mean that the drugs are not safe, but certain types of testing have not been conducted on that age group. There are times when the risks or unknowns are outweighed by the potential benefits of the medication. If a child has not been sleeping for weeks and is so overtired that she is not able to respond to behavioral or parental interventions, then goal number one is to get her sleeping again—here medications may make sense in the short term. Once the child has recouped some sleep she will be more receptive to learning how to control her anxiety so she can calm herself into a reasonable night's sleep. Likewise, if a child is significantly depressed and has OCD, medication may be an essential first step to relieve the symptoms of depression so that she may then have the energy and resources to devote to her OCD treatment.

Who Can Prescribe Medications?

For any childhood concern, most parents start at the pediatrician's office. Pediatricians are qualified to prescribe medications for anxiety and may feel comfortable doing so. Because pediatricians have a broad range of conditions on which they need to be up-to-date, often they will recommend that parents consult with a pediatric psychiatrist if medication is being considered. A psychiatrist is a physician with special training in treating these conditions with medication. Most child psychologists do not prescribe medications at this time.

QUESTIONS TO ASK YOUR DOCTOR ABOUT MEDICATIONS

- What are the immediate and long-term side effects of the medication?
- How effective is the medication?
- How soon should I expect to see improvement?
- What is the target dose for this medication? In what increments and how quickly will you increase the dosage?
- What are the warning signs of an adverse reaction?
- How frequently will my child be seen at first to monitor for an adverse reaction?
- Are there any blood tests or other screening required prior to or during administration of the medication?
- Are there any food or drug interactions I should know about?

- What do we do if my child misses a dose?
- How long will my child stay on the medication?
- How will we decide when my child is ready to discontinue medication?
- How often will I need to come in for appointments?

By the time outside help including medication is considered, parents and/or kids are often at their breaking point and feel that things need to change immediately. Still, it is best to think about medication as part of your tool kit, not an instant fix, because most medications take time—days, weeks, or typically months—before their full effect is felt or achieved. Taking the sharp edge off disruptive or distressing symptoms, medications can open up previously unavailable opportunities for parents (i.e., parents can move out of crisis-management mode and into therapeutic mode), and also put children in a better position to use their thinking and strategies for getting used to new situations (a term I refer to as GUTI: Getting Used to It, which is described in Chapter 4) to face the challenges in front of them. As one of my young patients described it, "Medications can open the door, but you still have to walk through." Just as with other physiological conditions, such as asthma or diabetes, medications are a part of the answer, but behavioral management issues, such as watching diet, exercise, or sleep, are equally critical in maintaining good health.

In this chapter we've explored the basics of treatment options for childhood anxiety. While your work as parents will be invaluable in teaching your child how to live a worrywise life, we are fortunate to have powerful treatments in CBT and medications that are there when needed. Each child is different; your pediatrician or child psychologist will be able to advise you on the steps to take in guiding your child's recovery. There are organizations that can provide lists of professionals specializing in childhood anxiety; see the online resource page for links at www.tamarchansky.com.

Part II

BEHIND THE SCENES IN YOUR BRAIN

Teaching Your Child to Outsmart the Tricks the Brain Can Play

---

The goal isn't to make the anxiety disappear, but to change your response to it. The more you underreact to the false alarms, the more, in fact, they do disappear—there's no longer a need for them. You've changed the default settings; worry no longer gets priority attention—it gets the boot!

These next several chapters are your instruction manual. You'll find crystal clear explanations that will help you, as a parent, to understand your child's experiences and the strategies he or she needs to learn. I'll give you sample scripts and exercises for bringing the lessons into your home, whether your child is in preschool, high school, or beyond. In Chapter 4 you will learn how to talk about worry with your child. Rather than just convincing her to stop, which you know hasn't worked, you're going to teach her to correct or dismiss the rude interruptions of worry thoughts by helping her see how unreliable and downright inaccurate worry always is. In Chapters 5, 6, and 7 you will learn strategies for acquiring new thinking patterns, new ways to calm the body, and new ways to change anxious behavior by teaching your child to approach rather than avoid situations that feel uncomfortable. All of the strategies in this section are based on sound cognitive behavioral principles whose effectiveness has been proven in study after study, but these techniques translate easily from the lab to your living room.

We've already seen how important it is to have options, so in keeping with that, there are many different ideas to try. As you are reading, put a sticky note for easy reference on the pages where you think a certain explanation or strategy will work well for your child. If you are reading for more than one child, or for yourself, use different-color sticky notes.

Throughout these chapters we will connect the new lessons and strategies with ideas with which your child is already familiar—for example, teaching them about how to tackle their worry by first looking at how they would help a friend who was worried about something that they themselves aren't afraid of. A child who is afraid of field trips might first learn the thought-shifting principles by considering how they would help a friend who is afraid of skiing—because skiing is your child's favorite sport! That's what I call long-distance learning. Your child is learning strategies at a safer distance from their emotions, because we are talking about someone else's fears, not their own. If the subject matter isn't *their* fear, they aren't in defensive mode, they are in an open-minded learning mode—like in school. They are learning in what I call an "amygdala-friendly" state. The amygdala is the part of the brain that controls the fight-or-flight reaction. When kids are frightened, they are in an amygdala-triggered state and can't think; they can only defend themselves. However, if they can learn a principle from a distance first, the amygdala is neutral—it's not engaged—and the child is free to learn what you are teaching them, as they would something that is interesting to them at school. Then they can apply the strategy to themselves, because they've already seen that it works, and that they are experts at the strategy. So center yourself, take a deep breath, exhale slowly, and remember that although you may wish you had learned these lessons yesterday, feeling the pressure is not going to help anyone today. There is a learning curve, and you are already well on your way. Your patience and persistence are the keys to the success of this work. Here we go.

Chapter 4

HOW TO EXPLAIN WORRY TO YOUR CHILD

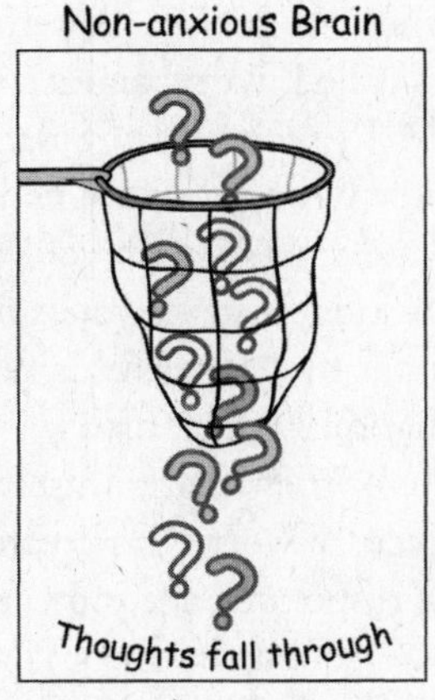

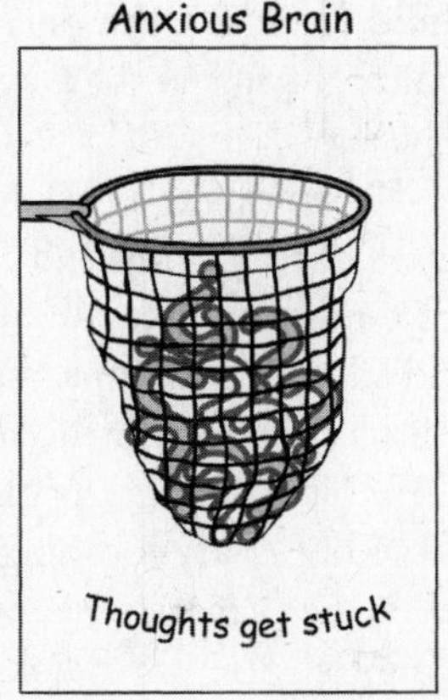

PIN THE PROBLEM ON THE PROBLEM: IT'S NOT YOUR CHILD; IT'S NOT THE SITUATION; IT'S THE TRICKS THAT WORRY IS PLAYING

I can't help it; something in my mind won't let me try it.

—A SIX-YEAR-OLD WITH ANXIETY

I've lived through a thousand tragedies, none of which actually happened.

—MARK TWAIN

"Don't worry, everything's fine, don't be a worrywart." Reassuring, cajoling, convincing, bribing, even picking up and dragging, these are the tactics parents use when their child is scared. The pressure is on: How do I get my child to do something that is clearly safe, but of which she is afraid? As parents we are trying to convince our children to "stop" worrying and just do it; meanwhile, worry is pulling the rope the other way, convincing them that they can't and shouldn't.

How do you win? Or not let worry win? Or get on the same team as your child? Rather than trying to get him to just "stop being afraid," you are the one who can explain that the "*something*" that is getting in the way is called worry, and it's not to be trusted; rather, it should be *tested.* If, with your guidance, your child uses his smarts to prove worry wrong, you are no longer in the business of reassuring and convincing—which you've already witnessed doesn't work for anxious kids. Instead, you can support your child in taking actions that are in line with his new, more accurate understanding of the situation, that is, reality.

Your child is scared not because of the situation itself, but because of the big, scary looming picture worry has created in his mind, the misinformation his first responder, the protector brain, is providing for him. The quick assessment the amygdala is making is to run—and he's outta there! But wait, he's really in a Mark Twain moment—failing the test, being knocked over by the dog, being tongue-tied in front of the class, throwing up at school—they're only happening in his mind. When he says, "I can't!" his body and emotions are synched perfectly with the picture in his head, but not at all connected to reality. But if you just tell him, "It's fine, you're safe," your child is not convinced. He might even be more confused. Why are you getting mad at him for being scared when he's already so upset?

Rather than addressing your child by asking, "Why are you worrying?," pin the problem on the problem: Worry is playing tricks, making things feel dangerous that are really safe. Instead of telling him what to think, ask your child questions to help him discover the truth for himself: "What is worry telling you about this? What do you think is true? Does that sound right to you? Do you think that is really going to happen, or is it just scary to hear that idea?" When parents pose questions this way, it is a great relief for children. They get to see their worry at a distance, and have their opportunity to "tell on worry" rather than feeling responsible or blamed for what worry is telling them.

If we want to help children be unafraid to participate in their lives, first we need to change the picture in their minds to make it more accurate. I call this strategy: "shrink and approach." Don't try to convince your child *not* to worry. He has a picture in his mind, and he's using it as a reference point. Help him to correct (shrink) that picture, and he will be convinced all by himself that he need not be afraid. Then, seeing things more accurately, he'll be willing to approach the challenge. By asking the right questions, getting him thinking differently about worry, he will be able to turn the mountain back into the molehill. This is how we teach a child to outsmart the tricks his mind can play.

The great thing about this strategy is that it's 100 percent doable. We don't need to change school, dogs, or book reports! They are fine as is. Your goal is to get your child to take another look before he assumes that he's in a dangerous or impossible situation. Rather than letting his primitive protector brain decide if a playdate, a test, or riding the school bus is safe, he needs to give the job to the right part of the brain—his smart brain.

Teach him to take the elevator up to the top of his head—to the cortex—and take a second look at the situation from the thinking part of the brain: "Your worry is saying *x*. What do you really believe is going to happen, and why?" Don't be afraid to challenge worry's authority when talking to your child. You want to teach your child to expect worry, but also to remember worry's terrible track record. It's always wrong. Instead of saying, "Don't worry!" say: "Of *course* worry would say something like that," or, "That's exactly what worry would tell you, but if worry took a test in school—would worry be right, or would worry get all the answers wrong?" These kinds of questions help your child to pause and fact-check what worry is saying and shift the picture in his mind from the worry picture to a picture that is more accurate.

ASK, DON'T TELL

Worry isn't the only part of the brain that can size up a situation, and really, it's not the best one for the job. It's just the first to chime in. Your best tool isn't reassurance; it's asking questions. Children can tune out your lectures, but they will believe the truths that they discover when they've put their own effort into finding them.

"What is worry telling you?"
"Is that what you really think? Why?"
"What does another part of you know or think?"
"Do you think that's really true? Why or why not?"
"What do you think is more likely?"

THE BACKSTORY: WHAT YOU AND YOUR CHILD NEED TO KNOW

Worry Is Universal, and Universally Unreliable

For all of us, anxious thinking is distorted, exaggerated, and unreliable; this is essential information that children need to know. To provide something much more powerful and longer lasting than reassurance, parents can learn to reveal to their child the worry tricks, so that the child can see the situation more realistically and dismiss the worries on his own.

Without the concept that *worry is always wrong, it is to be tested, not trusted,* children take their worry thoughts at face value and begin to look for evidence to support the possibility that their worries could be true.

GUTI: Anxious Behavior Is Learned, and It Can Be Unlearned Through Experience

A second fundamental concept is that anxiety can be reduced by breaking the fearful situation into manageable chunks and approaching it, rather than retreating. If you ask children to explain how they got over a past fear, a situation or task that now is no problem for them, they almost always say, "Oh, I just 'got used to it'" (GUTI). In cognitive behavior therapy terms, this translates as "graduated exposure and systematic desensitization," the benchmark of state-of-the-art anxiety intervention. But I prefer to use the kid's term and will refer throughout the book to the idea of GUTI exercises. Anxious kids should neither be kept away from new input nor be inundated; they should be encouraged to keep on trying things, even hard things, on purpose, because they will, as they have with everything else, get used to them and in so doing their world will open up for them.

A child encounters static shocks on a slide at school and refuses to go on the slide again. Without intervention, situations like this, often imperceptible to adults, tend to become the model, or template, for every subsequent similar situation the child faces. Anxious children adopt the "once and done" rule. If something bad (or just new or confusing or uncomfortable) happens once, they're done! Someone needs to give the child the opportunity for a "redo": to approach his feared situation again, learn why he reacted the way he did, see that it all turns out well, have a successful experience, one step at a time, and repeat it as much as he needs to until he masters it.

So for the little boy scared of the slide, we would engage the powers of modeling, observation, and experimentation, and say,

"Let's watch someone else on the slide and see what happens. What are their faces saying? Are they happy? Did they get a shock? Let's send your favorite stuffed animal down the slide, walk up the slide, and come back down." Anxiety will never encourage this kind of learning, but you can. As time goes on, intervention can make the difference between getting on or staying away from the playground of life.

The Anxiety Equation looks like this:

Overestimation of Threat + Underestimation of Ability to Cope = Anxious Response

The Taking Charge Equation looks like this:

Shrink the Fear by Fact-Checking + Approach the Situation in Small Steps = Mastery Response

---

DON'T LET YOUR CHILD'S AMYGDALA RUIN HIS DAY (OR YOURS): ENLISTING THE MIND TO CHANGE THE BRAIN

The amydgala is the brain's round-the-clock security system. If we are crossing the street and suddenly a car appears, the amygdala alerts us instantly and gets us safely back on the curb. The problem is that when we are in an anxious state, it operates on the "just in case" principle. The amygdala doesn't take a close look at the details of a situation to see if it really is dangerous. It errs (really errs) on the side of caution and sets off the flares at the smallest hint of uncertainty or risk. It derails your child's solid thinking and puts him in emergency mode. This is why he can't listen to reason at certain times—the program that instantly gets engaged by the amygdala is not a "study and learn," not a wisdom track; it's the "run for your life!" track. This kind of response is essential if your child were in an actual emergency, but it's quite distressing and distracting when your child is taking a test or competing in a swim meet.

But that's just the first take. By going back and taking a second look, your child can learn to come to a very different conclusion. This "fact-checking" habit is a solid shift in approach that can really stick, if you remind your child to put it into practice. Do this by saying: "Worry is jumping to conclusions. The amygdala is taking over. We need your smart brain to assess the situation. Let's look again!"

As we saw earlier in our discussion of neuroplasticity, advances in the neurosciences are documenting the great capacity of the brain to change or rewire connections, given the right kind of practice. And practice is the key. The mind gets used to whatever it does most of. In other words, whichever brain circuits we engage the most enlist the greatest numbers of neurons or brain cells. The more we engage in worry, the more, the faster, and the more easily the brain will be mapped to make those anxious connections. When we recognize our worries for what they are and begin to dispute and dispel them, we are actually harnessing the transforming power of the mind to reroute the brain's processing map. The more we invest our time and energy in connecting to healthy circuits, the more automatic that response will become. The mind repairs itself.

TEACHING YOUR CHILD ABOUT THE BRAIN: TEACHING THE BRAIN TO BE MORE TRUTHFUL

Children can learn about the brain, even young children. What are we teaching them? That they have wonderful, amazing brains that enable them to do amazing things—like gymnastics, baseball, art, math, hopping on one foot! But even the brain, while trying to protect us, makes mistakes, like making us feel scared that something bad is going to happen when really everything is fine. Children need to be taught that they don't need to stop these thoughts; they just need to expect that the thoughts will show up when we're not sure about something. Our task is to quickly figure out that such thoughts are giving us the wrong information for the job. How do you help your child reach that conclusion? By sharing the job: asking questions rather than making statements. Why? Because if we lecture at our children or even give reassurance, they can be passive and not really hear us—and importantly, not shift out of the fear program that their brain has engaged. However, when you ask a question—"What is your worry saying?," "What do you really believe?," "What would you like your mind to be telling you here?," "What part of the brain do you think is best for this job, your worry brain or your smart brain?"—kids have to think; they get to think! They literally do a neural program shift out of fear mode and into competent mode—you can see it in their face and hear it in their voice. They have gone from reacting to thinking it through. So although throughout this chapter I offer "scripts" for explaining these concepts, these are examples of the language you can use. They should be presented as questions to include your child in the conversation wherever possible. Importantly, take snippets freely from different examples; the scripts needn't be shared in their entirety or verbatim. Your child will appreciate your putting your own signature stamp on these new concepts.

SCRIPT: For Young and Old Children—Welcome to the Different Parts of Your Brain! Let's See Who Is Here!

"Your brain is wonderful. It has many different parts that help you do all the things you like to do like play and learn and eat! One of the parts is making it hard right now for you to do the things you want and need to do, making you scared, not because it's a bad part, it's just a busy part. It says things like 'Oh no! Trouble! You can't! Watch out! It's too hard!' even when things aren't dangerous or too hard. It always says the same thing. We could call that part protector brain because it's trying to protect us, but we could also call it worry brain because the things it says make us more scared! Imagine a frog sitting on a lily pad, and suddenly something long and brown moves in the grass. What do you think worry brain says? It won't say, 'Wait a minute and see what it is'; it says, 'Danger! Hop away from there!' But was the frog really in danger?

"There's another part of the brain that's the 'take a closer look and evaluate it' part. Let's meet that part of the brain now. If we look more closely we see that it wasn't a snake at all; it was just a stick that fell from a branch over the water. This is called a 'false alarm.' If you think about how many times worry made you scared about something (monsters at night, something bad happening to Mom, getting in trouble at school) and we go back and test worry, how many times was it right? How many times was it a 'false alarm'? So now you can be wise to worry's tricks. If it scares you about something, you're going to think again and ask yourself: 'Do I really need to worry, or is this another one of worry's false alarms?'"

SCRIPT: For Older Children and Teens—How to Talk to Your Child About False Alarms and the Brain's Mistakes

"Imagine you are making your breakfast, cooking up some toast, and the smoke detector goes off. Is there really a fire? Is there really a danger? Right, no. You're just making your morning toast. There's really no cause for alarm; that's why we call these 'false alarms.' They are wrong. They go off even when everything is really fine. But how do we feel when we hear an alarm? Right, we can't help that our first reaction when we hear the *beep-beep-beep* of the alarm is to feel scared. Not because we need to, but just because that's what a certain part of our brain does. We feel scared at first when worry is talking to us, but then just like with the smoke detector, we have to take a closer look and see that there isn't an emergency.

"Why are we built this way? We were built in a time when danger crawled on all fours. We needed to be ready for the tiger or bear in the woods so that we could be safe. We are programmed to react before taking the time to think just in case there really is a danger. We wouldn't want to stop and think about it too long; what would happen? It might be too late. This automatic response would be really helpful if there were a danger that couldn't wait—like a tiger or bear. But that's not what's happening in this case. The alarm is going off even though there isn't a tiger or bear. So when our protector brain gets involved it knows how to do only one thing: get us moving away from a situation to safety. Even though our protector brain can't tell the difference between a tiger and, what, a book report, or a baseball game, or riding the school bus—can we tell the difference? Yes! We have to be smart and tell our protector brain, 'Thanks, but no thanks!' Because if there's no real danger, why would we need to move away? We wouldn't. So the protector brain isn't the best part of the brain for handling a lot of things that we encounter in life. It's just the part that gets there first. So we need to take a closer look at the situation to see what really needs to happen here. For that, 'the closer look' brain is a different department. What do you want to call it? Your thinking brain? Your smart brain? Your competent brain? You decide."

SCRIPT: How to Talk to Your Child About Taking Charge of Worry

Taking Charge Script for Young Children

"Worry makes you feel bad inside when you don't need to. If something bad really happens, like if you lose a toy, or your ice-cream cone falls, how do you feel? Right, you feel bad. But worry makes you feel bad when nothing is wrong. It whispers in your ear things that aren't true, like 'It's going to be too hard. You can't do it. It will be too scary. Something bad will happen. You shouldn't try!' What does your worry say to you? These thoughts can be sticky! They stick around in your mind and demand more and more of your attention! When you pay attention to worries, they grow and grow. You can think of this lots of different ways—like when a plant gets a lot of water and sunshine, it grows! Or like if you feed a guest a cupcake or special treats, it wants more and more and keeps coming back. Or like feeding a puppy scraps under the table—what happens? The puppy keeps coming back for more!

"Worry stays a long time, and it keeps coming back if we pay attention to it and treat it well. So we can't help if worry sneaks one cupcake from us, or the dog sneaks one scrap from the table—that's like having your first worry thought. But you don't have to keep going with it. You can stop it right there and say, 'I'm not giving worry any more of my attention!' Just like the puppy may keep whining and begging, worry may keep sending worry thoughts, but if you just say no to worry, just like the puppy, worry will give up! And then, over time, it won't keep coming back. We can teach worry to leave you alone so you won't feel bad inside when you go somewhere new or try something that's a little scary. You'll have your smarts to help you, instead of your worries. You'll see that things are much easier to do when you take charge and don't listen to worry's advice."

Note: For younger children you can use stuffed animals, finger puppets, or just your two hands to play out the different parts of the brain. Share the job. Ask your child to help you find different voices or accents or stuffed animals to represent the different parts of the brain. A very serious voice or a very silly voice may represent worry—a regular voice may represent the voice of reason. There are no right or wrong answers! Get creative and jump in.

EXERCISE: HAVE YOUR CHILD CREATE A DIRECTORY

What are the different "parts" of the brain that your child has? He can draw pictures or have you help. This way your child can put different parts of his brain on "speed dial"—smart guy, fun guy—so he can have them around when he wants them. And he can let worry guy's calls go unanswered! Check out the portrait gallery on the next page for some ideas, but your child may surprise you with the names and personalities he comes up with.

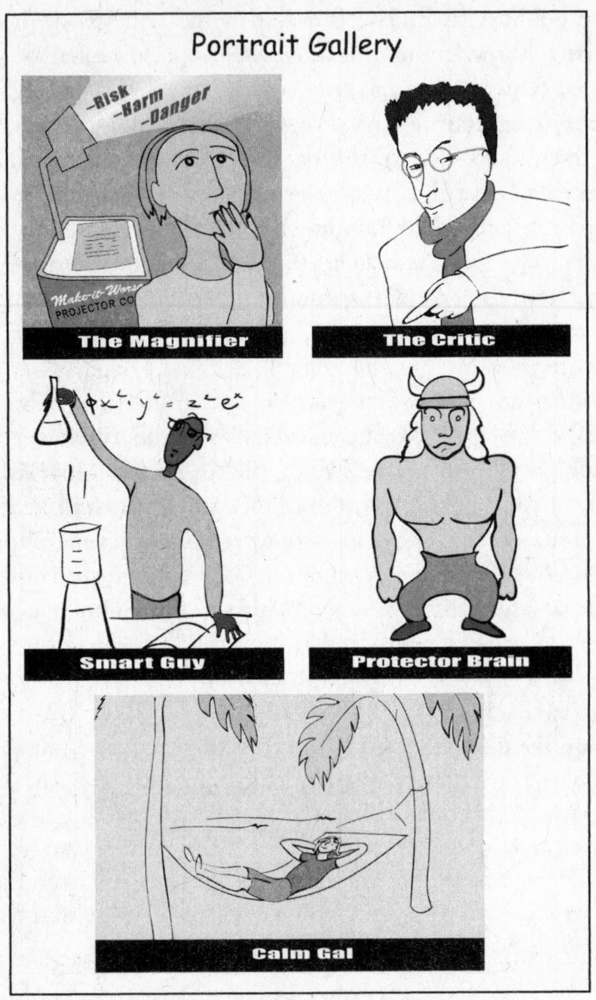

Taking Charge Script for Older Children

"The worry brain has a one-size-fits-all policy. Meaning that no matter what the threat, it has the same response. It was built in a time when the threats we faced were the kind that crawled, prowled, or slithered—like lions, tigers, bears, and snakes—and were really a threat to our lives. The worry brain has only one setting. With any hint of a problem, any crinkle in the grass, it won't take chances and it says: 'Big danger, run!' When the worry brain perceives a danger of any size—whether it's something huge like a tiger (we don't see many tigers anymore!), or something medium-sized like a test that you're nervous about, or something small like not being sure exactly what you want to say when the teacher calls on you in class—the same response is triggered, getting you ready to run or fight for your life. This is super convenient when it is a tiger, and super *inconvenient* when it's a test! How can you think calmly and clearly about math or geography when your worry brain is telling you to run as fast as you can? You can't. But what you *can* do is to teach your brain about what is dangerous and what is not.

"If you think back on the times that you've been worried—what actually happened? Would you say that worry was reliable, or was it really off base? Would it have gotten an A, or would it have really failed the test? Was it also really distracting and upsetting and kind of a waste of time to worry, or did it help? What is the truth about how those situations turned out? What would you like your brain to have told you? How about: 'You've got this. You're not in danger. You're just a little nervous. That's normal. You don't need to drop everything and treat the test like an emergency just because that's how your body responded—by getting all pumped up.'

"You can expect that worry is going to show up—and show up first—when you're not exactly sure how things will turn out. But you can also remind yourself that you don't have to listen to worry because it's a just-in-case first responder. You can make sure your amygdala doesn't ruin your day. Instead, you can think again, and teach your brain when you need to get worked up and run, versus when you just need to give it a little time to settle in and adjust.

"When you feel worry kick in, remember to ask yourself: What part of the brain is best for the job? The amygdala, or the 'ground floor' part of the brain, is best for darting away from animals or jumping back when a car comes. But deciding if you studied enough for a test, or if your family is safe? That's not a good job for the amygdala. Take the elevator up to the top floor and let the thinking part of your brain, your cortex, answer instead. That's the part that can look at details, evaluate outcomes, and make good predictions. So make sure you choose to listen to the part of your brain that is best qualified for the job!

"You are in charge and you can 'reset' your system preferences. You can teach your brain to switch out of worry mode faster and faster as you practice taking control. It will learn the new program from you."

TEACHING YOUR CHILD TO CHOOSE THE SMART TRACK: CREATING NEW PATHWAYS IN THE BRAIN

Your child's first reaction to an anxious situation—yikes!—is a default response. It's as natural as flinching when someone bumps into you. But just because worry gets there first and starts children down a track of fears, worries, and catastrophes, it doesn't mean kids have to stay on that track. In fact, there is much more accurate and helpful information on their smart track, but they have to know how to get there. The key to rewiring the anxious brain is teaching kids to build in a second, more realistic reaction—to "think twice." When your child challenges that automatic worry thinking, a new, healthy circuit is set in motion, and that circuit is made stronger and more available each time the challenge is repeated.

The fundamental premise of cognitive behavior therapy is that our perceptions of events, not the events themselves, dictate our experiences in life. Our internal commentary, what is referred to as "self-talk," can be filled with worry thoughts and distorted appraisals of a situation, or it can be filled with accurate information. When we perceive a threat, the brain sends a message to the body to mobilize against the threat. In response to our perceptions, the body, like a revving engine, amps up to either stay and fight or run. The final component—our behavior—is what we do to "survive" the situation. But what if the situation we were in only felt "high-risk" but really wasn't? If we are all set to run or defend ourselves, how do we convince ourselves the coast is clear? When we change how we look at a situation—by verbalizing and analyzing—seeking more accurate appraisals of the true risk, we will travel down a completely different track, which will lead us to different conclusions, feelings, and actions. Children can best understand this concept of the "two-track mind" by way of the metaphor of the brain train.

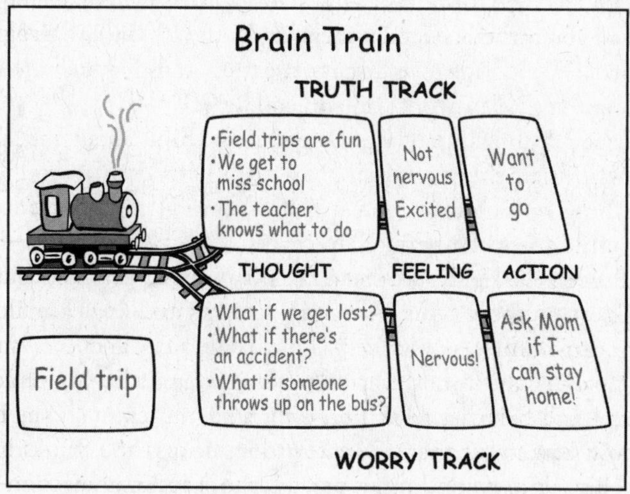

Your Child Can Choose Which Track the Brain Train Will Travel Along

As we see from this illustration of the brain train, one situation can generate very different outcomes: a field trip can bring either dread or delight, all depending on how your child is thinking about the situation. The two-track model of the brain train reflects the two tracks that run through your child's mind. The worry track is the first reaction, the automatic path for an anxious child, but in working with your child on exercises like these, you can point to the fork in the road and begin to develop a second reaction, the other, more constructive direction your child's thinking can take. The lesson of the brain train: The object or situation isn't the problem. You don't have to change the field trip, the dog, the book report, or the school dance, you just have to tune in to the story your mind is telling you about it and make sure it is the accurate one!

Amygdala-Friendly Teaching: Down, Dog, Down!

It may be too difficult for your child to immediately apply this strategy to their own challenges, because they are feeling so stressed about them. To help them sit for the lesson, use the long-distance learning idea we discussed earlier and demonstrate how the brain train can work "on someone else." With this distance from their feelings, they are more able to think about the situation with their smarts, rather than react with their worry. Take something your child is good at that other kids might be afraid of and run it down the brain train tracks. If she loves cats or dogs, you can remind her that other kids are afraid of cats or dogs and imagine how those other kids must see cats and dogs as dangerous, mean animals, while she has the inside story and knows they are safe. See where those very different thoughts lead in terms of feelings and behavior. Ask her—what was different in the end? Did you have to change the cat or dog, or just the thinking? If your child is a skateboarder, ask him to imagine how someone else might view skateboarding and how that attitude would affect their feelings and actions. Our head tells our gut how to feel—and this tells our feet what to do: run or approach. Sometimes the gut talks first, but we might be able to override it if we see that it's off. Anything can be run down the brain train track—riding a bike, skiing, taking the train, doing algebra. How would someone think, feel, and act if they were afraid? How is your thinking different? See how that thought leads down a different track and to a very different conclusion.

SCRIPT: Helping Your Child Understand the Connection Between What We Think, Feel, and Do

For all children: "Let's explore the brain train by looking at how a dog reacts to a situation. Let's say that the situation is a knock on the door. The dog barks every time someone comes to the door. What's in that dog's thought bubble, like in the cartoons? 'Uh-oh, intruder.' His body responds by getting keyed up. The dog barks and jumps up and down. He judges that there is a danger and behaves accordingly by defending himself. But if we could communicate with dogs we would say, 'Hey, Fido, it's just the mailman.' And if Fido could understand, he wouldn't jump. Instead he'd think, 'Oh, right, the mailman again,' and would remain at his post, scratching, enjoying a bone, waiting for a real alarm instead of a false one. What was the difference in those two tracks? What changed? Did the mailman have to change, or was it the way Fido was looking at the situation? Fido's very different interpretations of a simple knock on the door was the thing that changed. Just like Fido, we are the ones who decide the meaning of what happens in our lives."

For older children: "What's something that you like to do that your friends are afraid of—gymnastics, surfing, football? What kind of thoughts might your friend have about surfing? 'What if you fall? You're going to crash! You're going to wipe out!' How do you think your friend would feel if thinking that? Scared! And what would your friend do: approach surfing or run the other way? Interesting. Now, you like surfing, so what are your thoughts about it? 'The waves are great today! I need to focus on keeping my knees bent.' And how would you feel if you were thinking those thoughts? Right! Eager to get in the water. And so what would you do? Get in the water. So in one scenario the water was inviting, and in the other it was terrifying—how come? Did the water change? Were you looking at two different waves? What was it that made all the difference in what happened next? Right, it was which story you and your friend were listening to in your mind: the worry story or the realistic story. Isn't it amazing that we get to choose how to interpret the stories of our lives? We just have to remember that worry is going to jump in and narrate first, but because worry is always wrong, we need to go back and correct the script. That's our job."

Once you establish with your child the idea of the two tracks in the mind, and refer to it regularly with phrases like "What do things look like from the worry track, and how about from the realistic track?" Or, "What's your first thought, and what's your second thought?" Or, "What is protector brain saying, and what does smart brain know instead?" Or, "Do you really think that it's going to turn out badly, or is that just what your worry brain is telling you?" You won't have to convince your child to think differently or more accurately. He'll create a new program in his mind: Think twice. After he looks again, he'll see it isn't the situation that changed; it's the way he was thinking about it. He won't stop at those first thoughts; he'll know that the job is only halfway done, and that he needs to look (and think) again before he makes a decision about how risky the situation is. He will be convinced that he has a choice and some power in the situation, and knowing that will be very reinforcing. This is the fundamental lesson of cognitive behavior therapy—the split in the track—the choice we can make in how we experience life, simply by not taking our automatic worry thoughts at face value as the indisputable authority, but instead questioning them. With this opening many other changes can follow.

When I was explaining the brain train to seven-year-old Isabel, I asked her, "Which thoughts would make you feel better—the worry thoughts or the smart thoughts?" She answered, "Do you mean which ones would I rather think?" Then she asked, "Do I get to choose?" "Yes!" I said, "but you have to remind yourself you have a choice, because your worry brain always acts as if it has the last word, and probably won't give you that information itself." I suggested, "Remember that you have two hands. How about the worry goes in one hand, and the calm thoughts go in the other? That should be easy to remember—when you go into a situation, just remember to take both hands!"

DO IT TODAY

Think in parts! Have your child name and create characters for the two (or more!) parts of the brain. By doing this you're helping her to build the pull-down menu or multiple lifelines that will become the go-to in her mind. Say, "So your worry part says *this*. What do you want to call the other part?" Or, "What do the other parts of your brain think about it?" Children may want to compile an operating instructions manual as below, or younger children may draw pictures of their worry brain (or protector brain, or jumpy brain, or pain in the neck brain) versus their smart brain (or competent brain, or thinking brain, or good brain). Older children could create an ID card, or a mock Facebook profile to capture the true identities and functions of the very different parts of the brain. Even if the exercise sounds campy, it will drive home the point: Worry is unreliable—count on it to always be there, and count on it to always be wrong.

OPERATING INSTRUCTIONS

Smart Brain™	**Worry Brain™**
Speeds	**Speeds**
Challenging (but you can do it)	Scary
Manageable	Scarier
Watch me go	Scariest
Functions	**Functions**
Accurate, realistic thinking	Jumps to conclusions and catastrophizes
Reminds you of your skills and strengths	Underestimates your abilities
Narrows down risks, identifies benefits	Exaggerates risks, sees no benefits
Takes time to slow down and investigate	Races ahead, generating negative thoughts
Stores your knowledge	Prevents you from thinking clearly
Keeps you focused on what you can do	Leaves you feeling helpless
Fine Print: We guarantee that we're available anytime you turn down the volume on your worry brain.	**Fine Print:** We guarantee that the product does not tell the truth.

Chapter 5

HOW TO CHANGE YOUR CHILD'S THINKING AND GET THEM UNSTUCK

You've learned the language to explain worry to your child—now she's thinking in "parts" and isn't surprised (and doesn't look at you like you've got two heads) when you mention "worry brain" as a third person in the conversation. The next step is to teach your child how to put worry to the test and see how its tricks, distortions, exaggerations, and all-around unreliability make it not the best brain to rely upon. Remember: Your job isn't to *tell* your child this information (you've tried!); it's by *asking* the right questions that you help them to come to the right conclusions on their own.

Your child is smarter than his worry. With your help, he can quickly learn to spot the tricks that worry plays and call its bluff. The more familiar you are with the common thinking errors or worry tricks, the more easily you will be able to identify them in your child's thinking right away. Rather than asking, "Why are you worried?"—a question that puts him in a position of defending himself rather than looking for truth—you can be prepared to ask questions that get your child to find the truth for himself: "What is worry bugging you about? What do you really think is true?" Or, "I hear protector brain. Do we really need *him* for this job?" Or, "Do you think your amygdala is acting up again? How do you want to prove worry wrong and do a system reset?" By asking these kinds of questions, you're putting your child in charge and helping her broaden her search for more likely scenarios and decide which version or interpretation of the moment is more accurate. That's what this chapter is about. First we look at the common tricks that worry plays, so that you will have answers when your child asks, "Why would my mind do this?" Then we review strategies for helping your child take charge of the worry brain and engage his thinking brain, which is infinitely smarter and more flexible than the primitive workings of worry. Bottom line: Before your child *freaks* out—help him *test out* his worry.

TEACHING YOUR CHILD TO THINK ABOUT HIS THINKING: DON'T LET WORRY HAVE THE LAST WORD

As we saw in the last chapter, where we learned about taking a ride on the brain train, when we hear scary thoughts, we *feel* scared, and that might make us feel that those thoughts are actually true, but they're not. These are just *first* thoughts. Your child needs to be a detective and question the authority of the thoughts, see if they make sense, and if they don't make sense, replace them with more accurate ones. You can help him see that even though he feels totally scared, that doesn't mean he is actually in danger. The body is just responding to the pictures it's seeing. But the pictures don't necessarily fit what's really happening in the situation. We can change the pictures by changing our thoughts. Then the body will calm down, and we won't feel scared, and we'll know it's okay to approach whatever situation faces us. Ask your child: "What do we end up with after going through worry's list? Did something jump out from the stairs? Did we forget the words to our solo? Did we fail the test? Nope, it's the big 'so what?'! Nothing bad happened."

> *"What's that?! A lion? Turn on the light and you see—it's your laundry."*
>
> *"What's that?! A monster? Turn on the light and you see—it's your curtain."*
>
> *"What if I fail the test?! Think again: I'm nervous about the test, but I don't think I'll fail."*

"What if something bad happens to my mom? Think again: That's just worry; everything is fine. There's no reason that something bad will happen just because I thought it."

LESSONS ABOUT THE TRICKS THAT WORRY CAN PLAY

If only worry glitches showed up in red, or distinguished themselves from other thoughts by first announcing: "Okay, this is a false alarm; it's just the very worst-case scenario, but here goes!" Then kids (and parents) wouldn't have to go through the dress rehearsals of worry and disaster. They'd know that those thoughts were exaggerations, unreliable and irrelevant to whatever is going on. But instead, worries hide out—errors disguising themselves as authorities. Given how serious their anxieties are, kids would never think that worry might be a voice they could ignore. That's where you come in. Here's worry's playbook; now your child will be prepared.

LESSON: The Power of Suggestion: Don't Be Fooled!

"But I feel so scared, it must be true!" To help kids see the power of their thoughts, try the following exercise yourself, then try it with your child. Say the word "poison ivy" or even "lice." Do you feel itchy even though you didn't two seconds ago? Craving a hot-fudge sundae? The kind with swirls of chocolate and whipped cream that melts in your mouth? Did you know you wanted that before I mentioned it?

That's the power of suggestion. Thoughts dictate how we feel and what we do. When we think itchy, we feel itchy; when we think food, we feel hungry; when we think that the creak in the floorboards is a robber instead of the settling of an old house, we feel scared. Use these examples with your child. Unveil worry's secret weapon: The worry brain makes us feel scared just by suggesting a risk or threat. But it doesn't have any proof to back it up. It can change how we feel, but it can't change what is true or what's going to happen.

So when your child says, "I'm scared because I think someone might break in the window," you can say, "Yes, anyone thinking that might feel scared. Worry brain is using that power of suggestion trick on you. You're scared because you had the thought, not because it's true!" Thoughts change how you feel inside, but they can't change what's going to happen. Worry doesn't put you in danger.

LESSON: Fight All-or-None Thinking: Possible Doesn't Mean Likely

At the base of all anxiety is a risk. Will I get laughed at if I raise my hand? Will I get sick if I touch the doorknob? Will I have a panic attack if I go to the movies? The problem with anxious thinking is that the risk is all or none. Your goal is to help your child see how the worry brain is turning a maybe into a definite. Identify other situations where your child is able to take risks without a problem. For example: You let others borrow your belongings even though they *might* break them; you run a race even though you *might* fall or lose; you play on the computer even though it *might* crash. Just because bad things are possible doesn't mean that they are likely and that we need to be braced for them every day. Ask him why he knows it's okay to do those things. Highlight that his brain is working properly in those situations, keeping the risk in proportion to the likelihood. He is automatically thinking "low-risk situation." He'll start to see that in worry situations, his brain is making a mistake, warning him, "If there's any risk, don't try." Help your child use new self-talk: "This is a risk, but it's a small risk. I can handle it. Possible doesn't mean likely. My brain shouldn't be bothering me with the small risks, only the big ones. I'm pushing this one through the net!"

LESSON: When Estimating Risk, Go with the Facts, Not with Your Feelings

If you ask the right questions, you can help your child access her smarts about a situation that feels scary. Work on getting the facts. For example, Anna is afraid that if she goes to school, something terrible will happen to her mom. She thinks every morning that her mom will get in an accident, faint, or get sick. On a feeling level, Anna feels awful. But when you pose the question "If you had to take a test on what you think will really, truly happen today, what would you say?" you see that Anna knows the facts. She would mark the thinking part right, and the feelings part all wrong.

Help your child to separate his feelings from the facts by asking him the following questions: "How much of you feels scared something bad will happen? How much of you really, truly believes it will happen?" You won't have to convince your child that the risk is low; by putting his feelings aside, he discovers the truth for himself. Over time your child will learn that when the facts are in charge, he's in charge. When his scared feelings are in charge, worry is calling the shots.

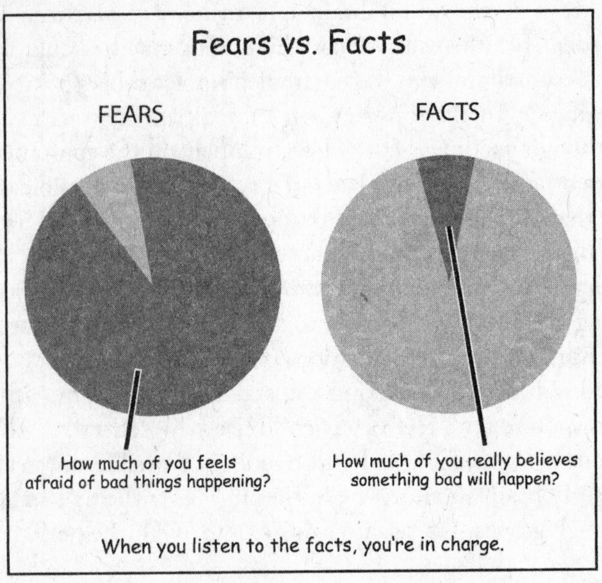
Fears vs. Facts
FEARS
FACTS
How much of you feels afraid of bad things happening?
How much of you really believes something bad will happen?
When you listen to the facts, you're in charge.

LESSON: Once Does Not Mean Always! It Means RARE!

Your child got a stomachache one time at soccer game, and now he's afraid to go. Your child shadows you around the house because one time you had to run out after the dog and you didn't tell him you were leaving—how does he know it won't happen again? Worry is playing the "single trial learning" trick on your child—trying to be the good protector, worry is thinking, "If it happened once, I'm going to keep warning him about it!" But worry's got to let it go! It's last year's news, or even last week's. But it's not what's happening now. Your child needs to be more of a scientist looking at the facts, less of a historian thinking about the past. Ask your child: "If you had your shoe come untied and *almost* tripped—would that mean that you would have to keep checking your shoes always because they *might* come untied?" In fact, what does your child say when you keep reminding him to tie his shoes tight? Doesn't he ignore you? Or get annoyed? Exactly. He does that (respectfully, we hope) because his thought sorter is working and it's telling him that a might, a maybe, something that is rare, doesn't need our constant attention. He needs to tell worry to let it go.

LESSON: Confusing Outcome with Likelihood: Don't Think About How Awful Something Would Be; Think About How Unlikely

If any one of us thought about something sad, difficult, or tragic, we would feel upset. That's our nervous system and humanity working properly. But just because we can imagine how bad something could be, that doesn't mean it's any more likely to happen. That's the trick of confusing a bad outcome with the likelihood of that outcome.

Research on risk perception suggests that people are more inclined to focus on outcomes than probability. So, for example, we may think that flying means a terrorist attack, even though the risk of that happening is very low. We hop in our cars every day although the risk of an auto accident is hundreds of times greater than a terrorist attack on a plane. You can help your child see through this tendency by asking questions: "Just because something could happen, how likely is it that it will?" and "What is more likely to happen?" The first goal is to get better at estimation, but an even more important goal is to choose where to focus your thinking: on imagining how terrible something would be *if* it happened, or on assessing what is most realistically going to happen (nothing!). So when your child comes to you in tears because she is afraid that you'll forget to pick her up at school, rather than reassure her immediately, tell her, "Yes, that is a scary thought. Anyone would feel upset thinking about being left at school. But your brain is playing a mean trick by focusing on how awful that would be, and forgetting the most important fact, which is how absolutely unlikely that is. Do parents forget about their kids? No! That's not how it works, worry brain!"

LESSON: Thought-Likelihood Fusion: Magical Thinking Increases Miserable Thinking

Thought-likelihood fusion occurs when a child feels that something will happen just because he was thinking about it, or that he must want something bad to happen because he just thought of it. It is a very unfortunate and quick way of mentally taking responsibility for something that's not your fault: "I thought about my mom dying. That means it's going to happen, or that I want it to happen. I'm a terrible person." It's also a way of becoming alarmed by coincidental occurrences: "I heard an ambulance. That means that someone in my family is going to die."

Our brain may make the erroneous connection between coincidence and catastrophe, but we can be smarter. One fix is to help your child track the logic and look for signs of thought-likelihood fusion. Sure, when we think something scary (like "What if that ambulance is going to my house?") we have an automatic, normal first reaction of fear. But the intensity of your emotions isn't any gauge of how likely something is; it's simply a result of entertaining the thought. Feeling something or picturing something—even really vividly—can't make it happen; it doesn't change real life. Here are some examples of ways to coach your child not to fall prey to thought-likelihood fusion.

- "That's not how the world works; that's just thought-likelihood fusion."
- "Just because you thought it doesn't make it true."
- "You can think anything; it's just a thought. You decide what to do with it!"
- "Thoughts aren't magic; they only have the power you give them."

- "The only thing those thoughts can do is make you nervous. Say no thanks!"
- "Tell your worry brain: If thinking something makes it true—then how come I'm not on a major-league baseball team right now?"

LESSON: Anxious Thinking Is Future Thinking: Snap Back to the Present and Set Limits on Worry

Quick, what will you be doing five years from now? When we are thrust into the future in our thinking, we naturally feel uneasy. We can't know exactly how things will be, and frankly, we're not supposed to know for sure. Life is full of surprises. Therefore, predicting the future becomes a very anxiety-provoking venture. If you listen to kids' worry talk, it is filled with "what-ifs." Usually these "what-ifs" get strung together, and what started out as a question about a sixth-grade math exam quickly leaps to "What if I can't get into college?" So instead of your child's anxiety reflecting her feelings about how she'll do on the math exam, it gets supersized to her feelings about figuring out the *rest of her life*. Worry is stretching her responsibility and the consequences for her actions far into the future. Snap it back. Otherwise she is borrowing trouble on a problem that she'll probably never encounter, and wasting time coming up with solutions now that will be obsolete by the time she gets there. Like your child deciding now what birthday present he wants three years from now—so much will change between now and then, it doesn't make sense to invest time in that now. Non-anxious thinking is more calm, logical, and present-oriented.

Encourage your child with the following:

- "Don't supersize your worry; just stick to what you need to think about now."
- "Put your worry on a 'what-if diet': Feed it the 'what-else's' instead."
- "If a friend told you that worry story, would you believe it?"

One important fix for "what-if" thinking is to realize that in the present we can solve problems; by projecting ourselves into the future we can only get worked up about what we think will happen, and then we get stuck and can't do anything right now. Help your child realize that worry is making him feel that he has to solve problems right now that, chances are, will never even happen. Let him know he has permission to keep the time frame small. Just because worry is flipping ahead in the book of his life doesn't mean he has to.

LESSON: You Don't Have to Stop the Thoughts; Even Things That Sound Important May Not Be Important to *You*

> *But they're important—I can't (and shouldn't) stop thinking about them!*

One of the tricks that trips children up is that the topics worry is talking to them about—danger, illness, failing—are serious topics. Like most children, anxious kids are accustomed to thinking that if something is important, we should listen. But you need to explain to your child that just because worry *sounds* important doesn't mean that the issues it is raising are important or necessary for *him*. Think of worry like a teacher talking to the class. If she's saying everyone needs to work harder on their English paper but you know you already finished it, you tell yourself, "She's not talking to me." She's giving a generic message. So is worry.

Kids need to be armed with some additional questions to put worry to the test: Is this topic really important to *me*? Is this important for me to think about *right now*? If worry hadn't brought it up, would this have been on my mind anyway?

LESSON: When You're in Worry Mode, More Things Seem More Scary

You probably notice that when you're stressed, little things set you off. Your child is the same. You may notice that your child's fears tend to spiral; it may feel like he's regressing and moving backward instead of forward. First he needed you to tuck him in again; now he's afraid for you to go downstairs while he's in bed; next he can't go upstairs without you at all. Because his stress bucket is getting full, it takes less to put him over the worry edge. Help your child to regain his ground by explaining that his protector brain is on high alert but it doesn't need to be. Ask him how he would have responded to the situations he is worrying about now—last year—before protector brain was bugging him. See how much of those old (good!) patterns he can start modeling again now.

STRATEGIES FOR CHANGING WORRIED THINKING AND PUTTING WORRY TO THE TEST

In the last section we learned worry's tricks, how it gets us to squirm and jump in the face of what turns out to be a catastrophe-no-show every time. In this section it's your turn. Here come the strategies for counteracting these tricks, strategies that you can teach your child so she can quickly spot the glitches and choose to spend time on getting more prepared for life, rather than more scared.

STRATEGY: Make a Thought Sorter to Sort Your Brain Mail

As we saw in the introduction, identifying worry as "junk mail" in the brain is a quick way to know right away that the incoming information is a nuisance (and impersonal) rather than an important message, so we don't spend any time on it. Your child can develop this skill of instant recognition to handle his worry thoughts. Demonstrate this idea by showing a younger child your mail for a couple of days. See if she can distinguish between the real letters and bills, and the junk that comes through the same mail slot but should be shredded and recycled. With an older child you can use the example of your e-mail in-box, which has a program that can "spot" spam and even says things like: "Mail thinks this message is junk." The goal is to have a sorting system: Keep or toss. Your child can create a physical sorter: two envelopes, one marked "worry" and the other "real," or as one young girl decided, "preposterous" versus "true." Or you can just address these ideas through your questions: "Do you think we detect spam here? Is this warning really about what's happening in your life right now, or is it that generic, automatic first reaction that everyone has until we think again and see that it's just a spam worry alert?"

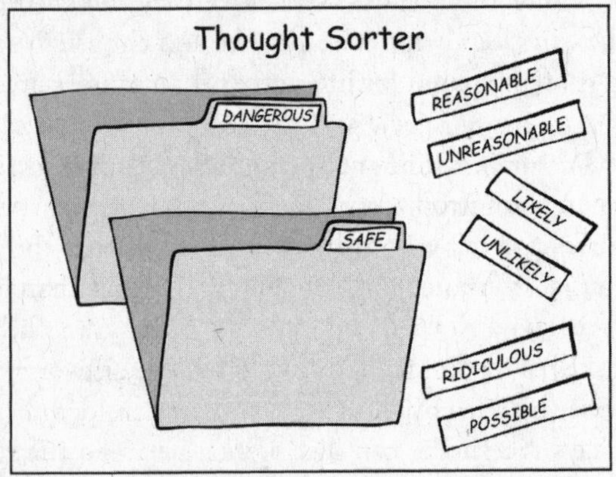

STRATEGY: Do the Side-by-Side Comparison

This set of strategies will get your child to think past the fears to the facts. Find the strategies that speak best to you or your child. In time you won't have to explain the strategies when your child comes to you with a "what-if." You might just say: "Do the side-by-side," or, "Wait, can you answer the million-dollar question?" or "Can we have a fact-checker, please!" In time, your child will catch on to the pattern of worry being wrong and will start to be able to anticipate the outcome—that worry is exaggerating again.

The simplest version of the side-by-side comparison is to have your child list her fears on one side of a piece of paper (or aloud), then on the other side ask her to write down what she *really* thinks will happen and why. Worry says: "If I touch my backpack and my backpack was on the floor, I'm going to get sick!" Or, "I'm going to have no friends at my new school!" Or, "I'm going to fail this test and then I'll be held back!" Rather than disagreeing with these outlandish charges, remember the rule of thumb: Ask, don't tell. Take each statement and turn it into a question: "If you touch your backpack, will you really get sick?" Or, "What do you think will really happen? And why?" Or, "Do you really think you *will* have no friends at school?" Or, "Do you really think you *will* fail the test and be held back—what do you think is more likely . . . and why?" You are helping your child be more wise to the tricks the mind can play, and helping him train his brain to be more honest and accurate with him. Have your child read each side of the story and then ask him to rate his fear level and the accuracy level of each script. Like a good consumer, once your child does the side-by-side comparison, he will see that worry is just making him scared, but that worry has nothing to back up its story. Then, if your child has that same worry again, you can just fold back the page to cover up the worries and reveal . . . the truth!

Worry says bad things are going to happen. Let's put worry to the test. Here's how the test might look:

Worry Says	Turn It into a Question	Answer with Your Smart Brain
"You're going to get lost!"	"Am I really going to get lost?"	"No. I am going with another family. I'll stick with them. And they want to stick with me!"
"You're going to have a bad time!"	"Am I really going to have a bad time?"	"No, I'm going to a movie—and movies are fun! Mom wouldn't let me go to something bad."
"I'll get hurt or bad things are going to happen."	"Do I really think I'll get hurt or bad things are going to happen?"	"No, there's no reason for me to get hurt. Bad things don't just happen. I'm just uncomfortable because it's new and unfamiliar."

If your child answers the questions with more worry answers, say: "That's what worry says. Worry is being sneaky. What does another part of your brain say? What would you say if worry weren't allowed to answer? What would be the answer that gets the A in school?"

Who's Talking? Change the Sound of the Voice

If you hear something scary, you feel scared. That's your nervous system doing its job. But if you *hear something scary* when it is actually harmless, that's worry giving your child a hard time. So another way of doing the side-by-side comparison and cracking worry's hold on your child is to appreciate that the voice sounds scary, and if we can begin to play with that voice, then it loses its power. If I told you that you could be scared by Elvis Presley, you'd be skeptical. But what if Anthony Hopkins or Arnold Schwarzenegger had first uttered the words—"You're nothing but a hound dog!" The messenger matters. By the same token, imagine if Schwarzenegger's famous line "I'll be back" had been delivered by Adam Sandler. Worry speaks with authority it doesn't have. Since we can't just go in there and unhook worry's wires, we can put it through a voice warbler. If your child was thinking, "Monsters are going to come into my room," have him say it like SpongeBob or even let Daffy Duck give it a go and watch the worry temperature drop. You can use stuffed animals or puppets to represent the two sides of the story. What's the nervous part saying? What are other parts saying? Let worry speak first because it's there first—you can give it a silly voice. Then ask your child to "correct" worry, or ask, "What does another part of you think?"

STRATEGY: Ask the Million-Dollar Question: "You Want to Make a Bet About That, Worry?"

One powerful way to help your child not get mired down in thinking these far-out worry thoughts is to change the question: If you could win a million dollars by predicting what's really going to happen—if worry is really right or wrong here—would you be able to guess right? So, for example, if your child is having worry thoughts about failing a test, ask him, "What's the answer to the million-dollar question: Are you going to fail the test?" Your child will probably answer right away: no. You can remark: "Wow! See how quickly you said that? Good for you! Now that you're seeing past the worry, is there anything that you actually need to do to prepare for the test, or are you good to go?" The conclusions to reinforce at the end of these conversations are as follows: (1) "So that was just a worry thought," and (2) "Now that you know you don't have to avoid that situation, is there anything you need to do to be more prepared?"

STRATEGY: Get More Information: Make Up a True/False Test

Worries are notoriously unreliable and incorrect—but they sound convincing. Help your child to do the research. If your child is afraid of being on an airplane because worry says it's going to crash, read up on airplane safety and then make a true/false test about the worry and have family members take it. For instance: Air travel is the safest mode of transportation—even safer than an escalator. True or false? According to research at the Massachusetts Institute of Technology, that one's true! Get the facts! Go truth! (Of course, use your judgment and keep the research age appropriate.)

STRATEGY: Do the Red Pen Edit

Worried children often put out absolute statements, which lead parents to feel that their child has decided that this is what is true and there's no way to change their minds. Fortunately, we don't need to run around changing the situation to change their minds; we just need to help them to begin to think differently. We can hand them the red pen to edit, or keep an "editing basket" with helpful phrases and sentence starters for them to edit their thoughts identifying "worry" as the speaker. Tell them to be the teacher or editor to correct worry's statements. Start by removing the exclamation points and inserting some qualifiers that reinforce the changeableness of the situation. So, for example, when your child says, "I'm going to fail!" or "No one is going to talk to me at lunch!" say to your child, let's rephrase that as "Worry is telling me that . . . (I'm going to fail)," "I'm having a thought that . . . (no one will talk to me at lunch)," "I'm feeling right now like . . ." These edits diminish worry's authority and change the fixedness of your child's thinking to reflect what it really should be: a temporary feeling that will pass. Have your child read/say each version of the story and rate their fear temperature.

I'm too scared! I'm feeling ~~too~~ *scared* right now.

I can't do this! My worry is telling me that *I can't do this.*

I'll mess up! I'm having worry thoughts that *I'll mess up.*

Everything is terrible! My worry is telling me that *everything is terrible* right now.

Nothing will work out! Some parts ~~Nothing~~ *will work out! There's just one part that I'm not sure about.*

STRATEGY: Fast-Forward to the End

What if? What if? What if? If your child is worrying about an event that is coming up in the future—whether that's three hours from now when the babysitter arrives, three days from now when he will have to give his book report, or three months from now when he goes on the school trip—ask your child to break the rules, fast-forward to the end of the show, and let him give away the answer. Ask him to tell you what he thinks will really happen at the end: The next morning at breakfast—what will he be saying? Or, after the test, will he really be looking at a failing grade? Chances are he's seen this movie before and he knows how it ends. Help him see that he can choose not to keep going back to the cliff-hanger moment of the movie, and trust that all will end well.

STRATEGY: Invite the Possibility Panel on Board

When you're trying to counter worry's version of the situation, your perspective as a parent often carries the least weight. Your child will respond, "Of course you're saying I'll be great—you have to, you're my dad!" Often parents feel the limitations of their authority because their child is only thinking about how her parents are biased. No problem. Ask your child to assemble a trusted inner board of directors. Who is her dream team? If your child is struggling with sports, ask her to choose her top three favorite players. Ask her what she thinks those players would say if they were in that situation. For example, a child strikes out in a game and feels like she's a terrible player and should quit the team. Ask the dream team if they've ever experienced a strikeout (of course they have!) and how they would advise her to think past the disappointment to the truth: The most important play is your *next* one. If your child is struggling with fear about school—bring together her favorite teachers and see what they would say about the current challenge. They might remind your child that she is just having trouble with *this* paper because it's hard, or because it's a new type of challenge, but none of that changes or takes away from the fact that she is a strong student overall. Young children can assemble their favorite superheroes to weigh in and instill bravery and encourage them to boss back their worries. Next time your child is struggling with worry thoughts, don't ask her to take your word for it. Suggest that she turn it over to the panel.

STRATEGY: Separate the Situation from the Stress

You may be hearing your children, especially teenagers, say things like: "I'm so stressed about my work!" And they may be spending hours "working." But many of those hours may be spent procrastinating—worrying about how much they have to do! It may be that the situation is more manageable than they think, and you can help them narrow it down to the steps required to get the work done. Ask them what percentage of stress comes from the situation itself (the term paper, test, dance, college applications) and what percentage comes from worrying about it (thinking about how hard it will be, what will happen if they don't do well, what this means about their future). Help them see that it isn't the work that's tipping the scales for them, it's the worry, and if they can put the worry aside, the work will become much more manageable. Help them estimate how long it will take to do the work—when they stop worrying and assess the situation, they may be surprised. If need be, get them to separate their "work time" from their "stress time." They can set a time limit—three minutes—on the worry a couple of times a session, then get back to work!

STRATEGY: Think in Parts: One Part Is Nervous; What Does Another Part Say?

I'm nervous! I'm scared! These are usually the first things out of an anxious child's mouth when facing a new situation. Validate and reflect back your child's experience for what it is: "Yes, part of you is nervous, but let's get another part on the job. Let's see, who else do we want to hear from? Your worry part is saying it's scared; what about your smart part? Your curious part?" Once you've helped your child lay out the possibilities, usually he has already moved on from the scared and is already thinking about how he is going to approach the situation. If necessary, you can help your child do these side-by-side comparisons: "Okay, let's see, which part would get an A in school for getting the right answer? Which part would win the million-dollar question?" As usual, you aren't convincing your child to stop thinking one thing; you are helping motivate the natural chooser in him to find another way of thinking.

Janet is heading into high school, and like any student in a transition, she is nervous. I explain to her that it's normal to be nervous, and that the nervous feeling is just what surrounds something that is new or unfamiliar to us. But we shouldn't be alarmed or detoured by it, shouldn't get overly flustered by it; in fact, we should expect to feel that way, and know that it's only part of what we feel. It's kind of like the bubble wrap or packing material that surrounds the iPod or new sneakers that we get in the mail. When we open a package we don't say, "Uh-oh, what is all of this?!" We know and expect that stuff is going to be there, and we keep digging for what we really want in that package. It's the same with worry. It surrounds a new experience, but there are other feelings that we have about that experience. When we can unplug worry's microphone, we can hear from other parts. After Janet talked about her scared part, I asked her to think about what *other* parts are thinking about high school. What does the excited part say? The curious part? The I-want-new-friends part? The I-know-I'll-get-used-to-it-in-a-couple-of-weeks part? Without having to be convinced or cajoled, Janet was able to balance the picture and see worry as one small part of the picture, and that small part was quickly getting crowded out by other, more reliable parts.

STRATEGY: Change the Emotional Tone: Make It Silly, Not Scary; Do a Monster Makeover

Images from movie previews that children shouldn't see, images from movies that were scarier than kids thought they would be, scary superstitions told around the campfire, or simply the monsters that are born from their own imaginations—these are things that stay stuck in a child's mind, follow them up the stairs, hide under the bed, and are ready to jump out from any dark corner (or so their imagination tells them). To help kids use their imagination for themselves rather than against them, suggest doing a monster makeover. Either with words or with drawings, turn the scary into silly. Add funny props and wardrobe items so that what was once frightening is now slipping on a banana peel, juggling pies, while balancing on one foot and wearing a tutu. Have your child create her own new monster to reinforce the idea that it's all made up. Also, see Chapter 18 for more scary monster interventions—especially at bedtime.

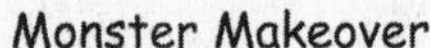

STRATEGY: Get Used to Uncertainty: Learn What to Do When It's a "Maybe"

Children with anxiety don't like uncertainty. They don't like answers other than yes or no; maybe's are especially hard for them to process; and anxious kids may keep coming back to you to get the definitive word. But what if there isn't one? Either because it's a question like "Will I ever get cancer?" or "Will anything bad ever happen to you and Dad?" Or, on a more mundane level, "Can we go get my new video game today?" when you're really not sure there will be time. Either way, being able to let unanswered questions be, to proceed with their lives without having all the answers, is essential to freeing them from worry.

Instead of withholding ("I refuse to answer any more questions!"), which will only ramp up the amygdala, empathize: "I know it's hard for you that there isn't a yes or no, but there isn't. If there were, and when there is, I will tell you. What do you want to do now to help your mind shift gears?" Rather than focusing on the one thing they don't know, help them focus on what they already know or what they can control. Being able to embark on something without knowing exactly 100 percent for sure what the outcome will be—this is how we master anxiety.

STRATEGY: Set Up a Worry Time

Spending more time worrying doesn't protect you; rather, like listening to a sales pitch that preys on your fears, it only leads to more worry. To set limits on worry, teach your child to limit the amount of time and attention she gives worry. Decide how much time your child will devote to worry and schedule it. For example, decide on a five-minute block that is "worry time." Then, the rest of the day when worry thoughts come up, she can tell those thoughts, "It's not time yet." At worry time, she should start with the worry story. She can talk about her concerns or write them down on one side of a piece of paper. Next she should rate how likely they are to happen, from 0 to 100 percent (or simply low, medium, and high), then write in what the logical alternatives are. Write the more realistic conclusions on index cards. She can carry them with her and refer to them as needed during the day when worry tries to pull her back to the scary story.

STRATEGY: Define the Problem: Get Specific and Narrow Down the Worry to the Thing That Counts

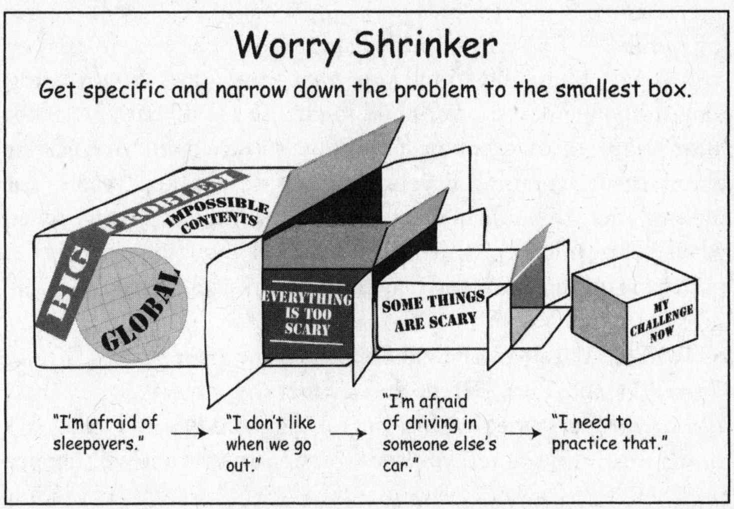
Worry Shrinker
Get specific and narrow down the problem to the smallest box.
BIG PROBLEM
IMPOSSIBLE CONTENTS
GLOBAL
EVERYTHING IS TOO SCARY
SOME THINGS ARE SCARY
MY CHALLENGE NOW
"I'm afraid of sleepovers."
"I don't like when we go out."
"I'm afraid of driving in someone else's car."
"I need to practice that."

Children say, "I'm scared," and a dark shadow falls over their face. They can't think clearly; they are just all fear. It can be hard to find out what is bothering them. Often children will respond with "I don't know!" And they may not! But you can help your child untangle his or her fears by walking through the experience with them step by step. "What happens first, next, next?" Not only will this process help you pinpoint where the problem is, but the detective work involved may help your child to realize there is only *one* thing that is really worrying them in the whole clump of worries—and many, many parts that they feel competent about. Once you've identified the real concern for them, you can get started on putting the worry to the test. For example, one child who was going on a camping trip with her school discovered that the only hard part for her was falling asleep at night. We could focus on strategies for falling asleep. This investigation also helped her see something that hadn't occurred to her in the spin of worry: Every other part of the trip—the bus ride, the activities, the meals—was fine! Her e-mail to me after the trip confirms that her hard work paid off: "It was so fun. I actually think it should have been a longer trip." When worry starts out big, use the Worry Shrinker boxes to help your child first put the problem in the smallest box: That's the problem she can easily solve.

STRATEGY: Re-record the Message:

Ask your young child to tell you what worry says about his fear (dogs, cats, bees). Ask your child to choose a different part of the brain to give the microphone to: Is it the science brain? The teacher brain? The true brain?. Let your child choose and then "record" the message that this other, wiser, part of the brain is saying. Later, when your child begins to express fearful thoughts, ask him to push Stop on that part, and play the new message. What did it say?

STRATEGY: Tell a Different Story: Tell the Worry Story, Correct It, and Then Tell the Smart Story

Children love stories with a beginning, middle, and end. Ask your young child to tell you the worry story of what will happen at the swimming pool or on the first day of school. Ask questions about the parts that worry is exaggerating or getting wrong. Now ask your child to tell the story again, making it the true story. Your child can dictate this new story to you, you can write it down or type it, then your child can create drawings or decorations. For each subsequent worry, you can suggest she make a new book, or, because the idea will be familiar to your child, you can just hold your hands out and mime as if you are turning the pages of a book, and say: "I think we're reading from the worry story book. Let's put that one down and read the *real* story of what will happen."

DO IT TODAY: ASK, DON'T TELL

When your child says, "I can't, I'm too scared!" your parental instinct is to fix it for her—tell her it's okay, or that you'll take care of it for her, or even that she doesn't have to do it. Remember to think twice: Your second parental instinct is to help your child grow. That's the long-term goal, and you can work on it in this very moment by asking questions rather than giving answers. Our answers slide right off our children's minds because they don't have to do anything but listen (or pretend to listen) to us. They stay in amygdala overdrive. Asking questions shifts their internal program to thinking mode: They are up in the cortex solving problems like they do in school. Children grow through the questions we ask, so that they can be the hero and discover the answers for themselves. Help them move on from their worry by asking good questions: "What would be the million-dollar answer to what's going to happen on the test? What do you really think will happen? Let's do the side-by-side comparison of fears and facts and see which one would get the A in school. Let's ask a different part of the brain for the answers." By asking good questions you become an essential part of the thought-shifting solution, a solution that over time your child will be able to work through for themselves.

WHAT WOULD YOU RATHER DO BESIDES TALK ABOUT WORRY?

Some children feel the need to report to you every single fear they have . . . and for hours! What can you do with the daily download of worry? Even though worry may think that "everything" is a big deal, and super important, help your child to learn to sort and prioritize.

Ask your child to think about what is small, medium, and large about her day. Have your child tell you just the headline news or the "large" items. Ask your child: "Big deal or little deal?" Help her make her own examples for those sizes; for example: Got in a fight with a friend—big deal. Didn't get to sit with a friend on the bus—little deal. Lost a book at school—medium deal. If she feels a burning need to process the little things, she could write them in a journal rather than talk to you about them, which is one step toward autonomy. What's in it for your child? Training the brain to filter out the small stuff, and . . . if they're spending less time with you on the daily report, there's more time for fun, more time with the amygdala on standby rather than on alert. Ask your child, in fact, what she'd rather do instead of rehashing the day, and how much time she wants to give to worry. By teaching your child to work the "filter," you will help her to be happier, and you may find the "evening news" gets shorter every day.

Chapter 6

HOW TO CALM THE BODY AND UNPLUG THE ALARMS

THE BODY ELECTRIC: WHEN THE BODY'S PROTECTION SYSTEM IS THE PROBLEM ITSELF

For some children, worrying seems to be "all in their head." It's all about thoughts, and they don't have any physical signs of anxiety. Other children are so physically tense that it's written all over their faces and is coursing through their veins. They can't eat, they can't sleep—sometimes they are so tense they can't sit still. They may have a constant stomachache and suffer tension headaches. Pacing around, they think: "What's going on with me? What's happening?" Even if they can't express particular worry thoughts, the feeling of anticipation in their bodies makes it hard to concentrate on anything else.

Sometimes these children can articulate that worry is making them feel this way, but for some children, worry seems to bypass their thoughts and go right to their bodies. Sitting in class, the teacher mentions a test and it's straight to the nurse's office. It may be because they have a headache or a stomachache, feel dizzy, out of breath, have a racing heart, tingling in their limbs, feel hot or cold, feel faint or nauseous, feel angry or tearful. If you ask them why, they might not make the connection. They just know they aren't feeling good. We call these kids "somaticizers."

These physical symptoms are often very scary for children. You can help your child accurately interpret the physical symptoms he is experiencing and know that even though they are uncomfortable or even alarming, he is completely safe. You can explain why these symptoms are happening: The amygdala got triggered, sometimes for no reason, but it's following its program—prepare for fight or flight—and mobilizing to protect him. But if your child wasn't in danger in the first place, this internal security system becomes the problem itself. The goal is to disengage the survival program that has been unnecessarily engaged, put it back on standby, and switch back to neutral. Your child's body is running away from him (or making him feel like he needs to run away), and you need to help him to slow down, so he can come back to his senses where he belongs.

In this chapter, we'll take a look at how the body gears up and how to calm it down. Teaching your child how to calm the body on a daily basis will provide a good buffer between him and his stress. We'll see in a minute how you can help your child monitor his fear temperature—his subjective rating of the level of fear he experiences. Some kids may prefer to call this a stress temperature or a worry temperature. Any name is fine; what matters is knowing how to keep the temperature as low as possible. If your child starts his day with a fear or worry temperature of four out of ten instead of an eight out of ten, little things won't put him over the edge so easily. He will feel less stressed and less of his attention will be taken up by the storm that's happening in his body—in fact, there won't be a storm at all and that's the point. He will be able to focus on the real things happening in his day. That's why we need to teach children how to shut off the alarms and calm the body down. Here's how.

THE BACKSTORY

As we saw in Chapter 1, our body's early-warning system saves us from danger—anything from touching a hot stove to darting into traffic—but there are some downsides. This defense was built in a time when life-threatening physical danger was a daily reality, but now, thousands of years later, we are still operating with the same equipment. Our worries are about things that aren't a matter of life or death, such as a test at school, saying hi to someone in the hallway, or walking down the basement stairs. Though we can't do a system upgrade for our antiquated emotional equipment, there are many things that we can do to override it when it gets set off in non-emergency situations. What follows are some lessons in how to be smart about the machinery we've got.

LESSON: Worry's False Alarms—Protection That Becomes the Problem

When the body's alarm system is mobilized without any immediate threat, you have anxiety. Unless you have been told that your body can create false alarms, you will continue thinking there's a real danger. In other words, *if the situation doesn't scare you, your body's reaction to it will.* When kids understand why certain symptoms happen in the body, they are no longer afraid that those symptoms signal a problem; they understand that the symptoms actually signal that the body is amping up a solution, albeit an unnecessary one. Kids are fascinated to learn why their heart races and their palms sweat. They are reassured to know there's nothing wrong with them and may even find the antiquated functions funny. The next time they start panicking, they have a new circuit to engage—"That's just my brain sending out the wrong signal. False alarm!" Learning about the physiology of anxiety also reassures children that as anxious as they may feel, their symptoms are not dangerous; the body knows how to cool down and reset, and we can help it do that.

Body Check: Where Is Worry Hiding?

To understand where to target your relaxation exercises, have your child tell you where they feel worry in their body. You can have them draw a simple outline of themselves, and then X marks the spot where they feel bad or uncomfortable when they are worried. Then, you can make sure you address your child's particular symptoms, reinforcing that these symptoms that feel strange now would be helpful and not noticed in a real emergency.

The nervous system is made up of the sympathetic nervous system, which mobilizes the fight-or-flight mechanism, and the parasympathetic nervous system, which restores the body back to normal. When the sympathetic nervous system is going full tilt, kids and adults alike experience a lot of strange and sometimes uncomfortable symptoms, which are entirely safe:

Racing heart: The sympathetic nervous system makes your heart beat faster. Why? To speed up the blood flow to the legs and arms so that you can run or fight, and away from the fingers and toes (peripheral locations that can be punctured most easily). Kids may notice that their hands and feet feel cold, prickly, and numb, and that their skin looks pale when they are afraid.

Dizziness: In preparation for protecting you, breathing speeds up. You may feel like it's hard to breathe, and even that there's a tightness in your chest. You may feel dizzy because the blood supply to the head is slightly (but safely) decreased.

Sweating: You sweat so that the body won't overheat. It's like a cooling system. But when you sweat your skin also gets slippery. Back in prehistoric times, slippery skin would make it tougher for an enemy to grab hold of you.

Temperature changes: Your body is like an engine heating up, kind of like when you use your computer for a long time it heats up. So it's normal to feel hot—in your face, your cheeks, your chest—when you are anxious. Then, because your body is always working on your behalf, it will cool down—so you may feel cold at other times, and even sweaty.

Light-headedness: In order for you to run fast and be strong, the blood needs to go to your arms and legs. When that happens, with your heart pumping to get the blood all the way to your extremities, you can feel a little light-headed. It's not dangerous at all, and it's temporary.

Feeling disoriented or unreal: Sometimes children can get very disoriented from being scared. Sometimes this is from crying, but often this is a result of the brain focusing on one point (the proverbial tiger) so intently that you begin to feel strange. Things feel unreal or like you are in a dream. You may feel disconnected from your surroundings. Think about what happens when you say or look at a word over and over—you start to lose perspective and have an odd feeling as you question if it's really a word. Suddenly, what is ordinary feels unusual and unfamiliar.

Feeling out of breath: As your lungs are pumping to help your body run fast, to be most efficient, you take fast, shallow breaths. It isn't dangerous, but it can feel uncomfortable.

Feeling agitated: Adrenaline is pumping through your child's body to ready him for an attack. Adrenaline keeps you charged up and anxious, but it is also what you feel when you are angry. So for some children, the way that they express anxiety may look more like anger.

Stomachaches: The digestive system shuts down abruptly because when you're under a proverbial attack, there's no time to think about food! Unfortunately, the result can produce nausea, stomachaches, or even constipation.

Trembling: The big muscles, such as arms and legs, are tensing up, ready to fight; this can result in an aching feeling in the extremities and even trembling.

Next time your child comes to you afraid because his heart is racing and his stomach feels funny, help him to take a deep breath and reset the system back to normal. There is no emergency; it's just a turbocharged overreaction to an uncertain situation.

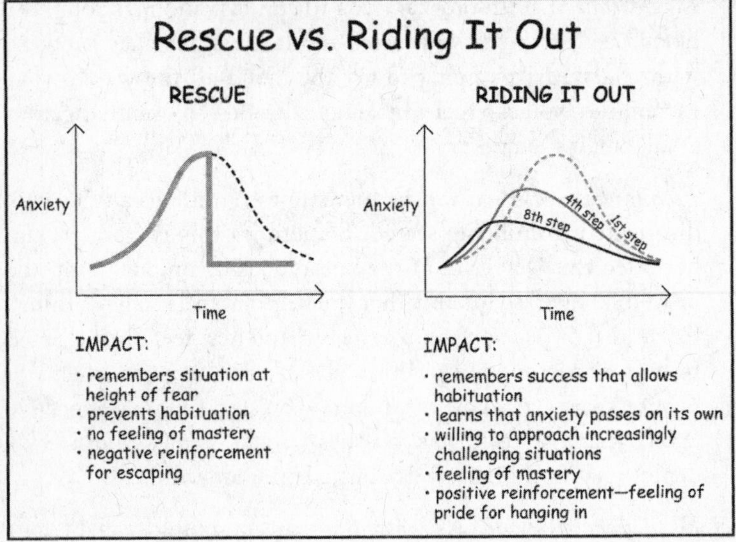

LESSON: What Goes Up Must Come Down—Anxious Feelings Will Pass

Our nervous system reacts strongly to novel experiences and changes. Given a little time, however, it will also get used to things. That's the lesson that kids need to learn about approaching anxious situations. At first something new will feel uncomfortable, but then it will get easier. Ask your child to think about a swimming pool. When you first get in it's cold! But does it stay that way forever? If you stay in the water you know you get used to it, but if you get out immediately, you will be stuck thinking that the only way to survive the cold is to get out. Rescuing children from scary situations at the height of their anxiety (as shown in the "Rescue vs. Riding It Out" drawing above) doesn't allow them the opportunity to see that the situation would have become manageable given a little time; rescuing them also reinforces the tendency to seek escape rather than riding out the temporary discomfort that being in that situation generates. Help your child think of other situations in which he had strong reactions at first and then got used to things, whether it was getting out of a nice warm bed in the morning (it's the first few seconds that are the toughest) or into a nice warm shower (which feels cold when you first get in), or even trying a piece of gum—it seems too spicy at first, but if you keep chewing it's not as strong.

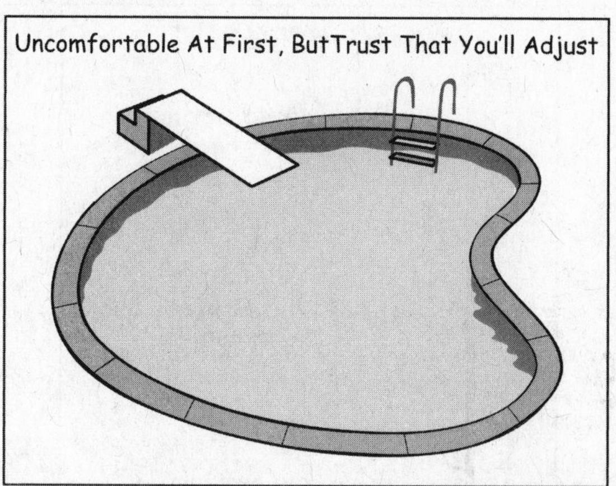

Uncomfortable At First, ButTrust That You'll Adjust

Just like a roller coaster, you will find that anxious feelings go up, but they always come down. Ask your child if he has ever experienced a time when his anxiety didn't come down. With the "Get Used to It" or GUTI exercises that you will find throughout the book, you are giving his nervous system a chance to get used to and overcome the initial fear and adjust.

An important tool in the GUTI process is using a "fear or worry thermometer" to track changes in your child's degree of anxiety. Taking your child's fear temperature every few minutes while he is approaching a tough situation will help him to witness a decrease in his anxiety as he hangs in with the situation. Just ask him what his fear level is from 1 to 10, where 10 is the highest or most fear. For younger children you can create a simple scale by raising your hands in the air: low, medium, or high. Ask a few minutes later so your child can watch the numbers go down. You can also use the fear thermometer when you're doing any of the thinking exercises; for example, if your child is doing the side-by-side comparison of worry to wisdom, ask what is his fear temperature when he's listening to worry, and what is his fear temperature when he's listening to his smart thoughts. That way he can measure the effectiveness of a strategy based on how it affects his anxiety level, and it's a clear choice.

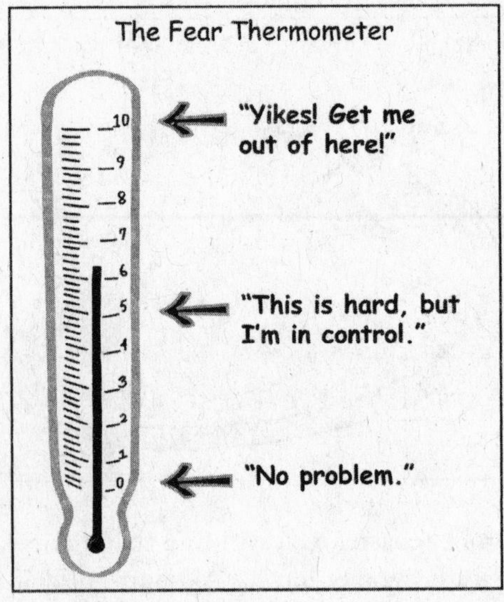

LESSON: Anxiety Keeps Building Up: Keep Your Baseline Low

It can be confusing to parents when their child's anxiety snowballs; one worry seems to make her more likely to get upset by other things—even things that didn't bother her before. But there is a logical explanation for this. If a child starts having a specific fear or panic attacks, for example, the baseline level of anxiety—how they wake up each day—goes up. This happens to adults as well—when we are stressed about being late for work, and then we drop something while leaving the house, or miss a turn, we are much more upset than we would be if it had happened on a calmer morning. We are on the defensive or on alert, so we interpret neutral things as more threatening. The result? More stress. Think of it as an anxiety bucket: When kids get nervous, the bucket gets filled up, and it only takes something small, even something that had been familiar and fine before, to make the bucket overflow. When it overflows, the whole scene is more than your child is able to cope with, and you see symptoms of anxiety. The exercises here will help to "empty the bucket" for your child. The lower their stress level is, the less likely they are to misinterpret neutral cues as threatening.

STRATEGIES FOR CALMING THE BODY

Making the Connection: Take Your Child's Calmness Temperature

Whenever you do relaxation exercises with your child, help them to monitor their anxiety level before and after. You can also monitor their calmness level if they prefer: Give them the choice. This reinforces children's competency in telling their body that it's okay (and desirable) to calm down now. If they register that they are able to lower their anxiety temperature several points just by doing a few stretches or a few deep breaths, then you won't have to sell them on that technique: It will sell itself.

STRATEGY: Take Five Deep Breaths

Just as shallow breathing (hyperventilating) is a sign of anxiety and signals the body to be on alert, slow, deep breathing is the all clear signal. When your child is acutely upset, help him breathe with you, slowly and calmly. This helps the body switch from the danger program to the calm program, or at least standby. There are many different specific breathing techniques, but don't worry about the details. Breathing is natural for us. The important thing to know is that just breathing slowly from the abdomen will help.

Sometime when you're not in the heat of a worry moment, do an experiment with your child. Both of you breathe in slowly and from the abdomen a few times and see how much calmer you feel. Now try something a little different: First stretch your arms over your head and let them drop slowly, then stretch them out to the sides but slightly behind you (picture a bird spreading its wings behind it). Then let them drop slowly. Now take a few deep breaths again.

See if you and your child notice a difference. For most of us, it feels better and easier to breathe deeply when we've opened up the chest muscles, since the lungs can expand and the breath can be more satisfying. Because we are programmed to protect our chest most of all—all the vital organs are there—those muscles store a lot of our tension. Opening up the chest muscles may be the fastest way to loosen things up. At home or discreetly in class or even in the bathroom, kids can learn how to do this easy two-second stretch, which will enable them to breathe more deeply and calmly, instantly lowering their stress temperature.

Because hyperventilating or overbreathing keeps the body in a state of tension, train your child to do normal breathing. Coach him with the following script: Lie on your stomach, chest flat against the floor. Breathe in and out, slow and low. In this position you will be doing belly breathing, which is the kind of breathing we do when we are relaxed. After you get good at doing this lying down on the floor, you'll be able to find those same muscles when you are sitting up. Make sure that when you breathe in you don't hold your breath. Keep your breathing even; breathe in through the nose counting one, two, and out through the mouth (one, two). If you say the word "relax" or "calm" when you exhale, even picture the letters "r-e-l-a-x" floating in front of you, this will be an additional cue to your body that when you hear those words your body will more quickly be ready to transition into a calmer state.

Encourage your child to practice a couple of times a day, and within weeks she will be able to do this belly breathing inconspicuously whenever needed. She can focus on a pleasant scene—a serene, gentle waterfall, a beautiful spring day, or her cozy bed. Your child can imagine the sights, sounds, smells, and textures of that scene. If your child is distracted by other thoughts, rather than despair or fight the thoughts, just tell her to set those thoughts on a sailboat, let them pass, and know that she can pick them up later when the exercise is over.

Some kids have difficulty relaxing—it isn't active enough for them; they need a more structured exercise to guide them. For these children, the following script can be used:

"In bed, start your breathing and imagine that with each breath you are blowing up a balloon. Then track the flight of the balloon. Watch it fly up above the treetops, above the buildings, into the clouds. Then 'blow up' another balloon and track its ascent. Watch as the sky fills up with balloons, a rainbow of different colors, one by one."

Your child can choose whatever repetitive image suits him best.

It is most effective to practice these exercises every night before bed—five minutes is more than enough time to do so. It takes about three weeks to establish a new habit, so think about devoting a few minutes of your nighttime ritual for the next month to the pleasant practice of relaxation exercises. It will help your child settle in better at night, and he'll be building up his "relaxation muscles," which will help him during the day. Increase your child's interest and motivation by sharing the job with him. Ask your child to lead the breathing, decide which color balloon to blow up, and decide where you will be floating those balloons—over the Eiffel Tower in Paris? The zoo? The Pyramids in Egypt? Any place will do—no airplane ticket required, only a good imagination.

For young children: To keep your child's attention for deep breathing, enlist her imagination: Is she an animal, a superhero, a princess, an astronaut, a firefighter taking a deep breath? Let her choose. Props can help, too. It is generally easier for children to imitate you when you're doing a big inhale, than a big exhale. They can look in the mirror to see how their chest and shoulders stay relaxed (i.e., not jumping up with each breath). To emphasize what it feels like to exhale, you can use props such as exhaling by blowing soap bubbles through a wand, or blowing out (parent-supervised) candles, or just pretend to blow out candles on a cake, or blow up balloons, or blow on a feather.

For older children: You can explain to older children that diaphragmatic breathing has been proven to lower your heart rate and your blood pressure, so it's good for your health. If you practice this breathing regularly, your body will learn this new program or gear to downshift into, so when you want to shift into it in an anxious moment, it will know how to do it faster. And the sooner you shift into it, the better you'll feel. Use a technique similar to that used with younger children: Place one hand on the chest, one hand on the abdomen, and let the breath come from the abdomen. Children can choose a calming picture to focus on—and imagine that they are breathing in calmness and breathing out their tension. They can also use self-talk, saying things like the following: "I am safe. I am calm. I am in control of myself." Use visualization to put yourself in the place that you want to be—and notice how different your body feels when you are in that place. You can imagine that with each breath you are making the image of your calm place more vivid—you can see the blue of the sky or the ocean. You can imagine yourself rocking in a hammock. Experiment with different images and see what works best for you. Once you learn how to do this breathing, it can be "on call" for you when you need it: before a test, an interview, a sports event. The more you practice, the more your body will know the code for disarming the alarm system so that you can put it on the setting where it belongs—on standby, no extra effort from you required.

STRATEGY: Practice Progressive Muscle Relaxation

The idea behind progressive muscle relaxation is that in order to relax a muscle you first have to "locate" it by tensing it up. Rather than telling a child to relax his hands, with progressive muscle relaxation, one instructs a child to make a tight fist, and then by letting the fist go, his hand naturally relaxes.

For young children: To keep your child's attention, enlist his imagination: What animal does he want to be learning how to s-s-t-r-e-t-c-h and relax? A young child can imagine that he's a cat or his favorite animal and can play Simon Says or follow the leader, imitating the stretches that you do. For younger children, it may help them to picture a fairy sprinkling magic dust on each body part to help them relax, or the friendly king of Sleepland who leads the relaxation exercise by pointing his scepter. The sky is the limit. You and your child will come up with the story that works best.

For older children: For older kids, focusing on muscle groups is most effective. So, for example, you can coach your child: "Begin with your toes. First stretch your toes. Feel the tension, and give it a color—is it red? Then hold the tension to a count of three, then let the tension go. Feel the relaxation in your feet, and see the tension break up and dissolve. What's the color of relaxation for you? Is it a silvery blue, a healthy green, a warm yellow like from the sun? Choose a color."

As you continue up the body and repeat this sequence through legs, pelvis, stomach, back, chest, shoulders, arms, fingers, neck, eyes, and face, make sure that your teenager is seeing the tension color dissolve like sand and blow away, to be replaced with the color of relaxation.

STRATEGY: Get Moving!

Relaxation exercises are one way to calm down the adrenaline pumping through your child's system, but there's another way: Get moving. If your child is getting worked up with homework stress, or has built up a lot of worry from her schoolday, sitting still and doing deep breathing may not be the best way to relax. Burning off the adrenaline by getting active—running with your dog, shooting hoops in the driveway, riding a bike, playing freeze tag in the backyard or freeze dance in the living room—will have a similar effect. Why? Because exercise produces endorphins—the brain's feel-good neurotransmitters that elevate mood; exercise also helps your child to zoom out and switch gears away from their worries by getting engaged in other (more fun!) sights, sounds, and experiences. Afterward, when they come back to the homework, test, or challenge, it no longer seems so daunting.

DO IT TODAY: PARENTS NEED TO CALM DOWN, TOO!

There are many opportunities for our children's anxiety to keep us honest about our own. If we are going to teach (sell) the lessons effectively, we need to be practicing them ourselves. Consider weaving a few minutes of quiet, calm breathing and muscle relaxation into your bedtime routine. You'd be amazed what a difference two minutes can make! If your children are young enough that you are still tucking them in at night, this can be part of your bedtime routine. If they are older (*especially* if they are older), they will be the first to point out a double standard, so be honest—take on the three-week challenge of doing a breathing or relaxation exercise at night. Notice how you can refresh that feeling by going back to it during the day. Notice too how over time, when you just think about doing a breathing exercise, your body begins to anticipate the positive feeling, and you're already halfway there before you've started. As you see the benefits, you will be a more convincing salesperson to your teen, and they'll know that you actually believe in the product you're endorsing.

Chapter 7

HOW TO CHANGE ANXIOUS BEHAVIOR AND HELP YOUR CHILD TO FACE THEIR FEARS

I feel so sad when I have to leave a party or baseball because of worry. My stomach hurts so much, but then when I get home, I'm always fine. I don't want to have to leave, but I don't know what to do.

We feel trapped in our home. My daughter doesn't feel safe when we go out. We can't leave her with a sitter. She won't let us go in the backyard without her.

As parents we can try to convince our children that everything will be fine, but nothing replaces direct experience for doing the "convincing" job for us. This is how our children learned how to walk, and how they achieved every accomplishment after that. It may not have been easy, it may not have been comfortable, but it was totally worth it! So it is with anxiety. Seeing is believing, but that's easier said than done. This chapter is all about how to find and create opportunities for the second part of the "shrink and approach" formula for overcoming fears. By *approaching* your child at the right time, in the right place, with an exposure geared to the right level of difficulty, you can help your child learn "yes I can!" And once they have, they'll be glad they did.

THE BEST WAY TO OVERCOME FEAR: DOING EXPOSURE EXERCISES MEANS BEING UNCOMFORTABLE ON PURPOSE

Scientists know that the best way to prevent pet allergies is not to keep babies away from pets, but to gradually expose them to allergens to make sure the immune system is prepared to do its job when it's time. The same principle applies to dealing with fears, worries, and frustration. If you want to protect your child from being overwhelmed, you can help her to build up her "worry management muscles" a little at a time. This is how "GUTI" (Get Used to It) happens best. The more your child puts herself in anxiety-provoking situations (that are perfectly safe—like raising her hand in class), the more she proves to herself that worry's interpretation of the risk was wrong and that she really can tackle and overcome the challenges she faces. This is a secret you want your child to know.

Experience, or what we psychologists call "exposure," teaches kids that they can count on themselves to manage and ultimately master situations; that bad things don't come true just because we worry about them; and that fear goes away by being in a situation, not avoiding it. Systematic desensitization is a process wherein a child gets gradually closer to a feared situation, either by picturing himself approaching it (imaginal exposure) or by actually approaching it (in vivo exposure). Essentially, exposure gives children planned practice with the things that are most difficult for them; it gives them an edge. A child who is afraid of sleeping alone first has a parent in bed, then next to the bed, then next to the door, then out in the hallway, then downstairs. By chunking the challenges, as the child rises to the occasion and adjusts gradually to each step, they are ready for the next. The child learns that calm breathing and realistic thinking make it easier to take on the challenge. By hanging in through their discomfort, kids are able to change their anxious association with the situation and replace it with a sense of competence and possibility. Using the fear thermometer as a guide, the child stays in the situation until the fear comes down at least two degrees (out of ten), but preferably 50 percent or more. Exposures should be repeated until they become boring or too easy; then the child is ready to climb to the next challenge on his list.

Where do you start? Find your child's starting point by asking, "What part of this are you ready to do now?" Any task can be broken down into smaller steps; find the one that is just outside your child's comfort zone. If your child is having trouble with this, you can ask him, "What would you like to do that you can't do now because you're scared or worried?" Make a hierarchy of fear challenges, ranking them from easiest to toughest using their fear or worry thermometer.

It can be a good idea to practice these challenges first, role-playing how the child will handle the situation, before tackling the exposure itself. GUTI exercises are best done frequently. Fear muscles, just like other muscles, are built best with regular practice. If a child has infrequent exposures, he is likely to forget his success in the situation and revert to his previous fearful association.

How many times does it take to get used to things? Share the job and get your child thinking about that, too. Ask your child: "How many times do you think you'll need to get used to it? How do you think you'll feel after doing this three times?" Is this challenge easier or harder than a previous challenge she's mastered? Ask how she mastered that challenge; when she answers: "I got used to it," ask how and listen for the word "practice." Set the positive prediction that somewhere over the rainbow—over the three times of exposure—skies are blue.

ACHIEVING BUY-IN BY COLLABORATING ON A PLAN TO REACH YOUR CHILD'S GOALS

"Okay," you may be thinking, "this sounds great, but do I just force my child to do things? He won't do them on his own." We could force our children to do things they aren't ready for—but that approach is double trouble. Not only will a child's amygdala switch into defensive mode because he is having to tackle his fear, but the child will feel unsafe because you're forcing him to do something. So even if your child is able to get through the exposure that you choose for him, he won't feel more confident in himself, and he will feel less trusting of you. Forcing things is a lose-lose.

Fortunately, there is a powerful alternative: collaboration. Think of you and your child as being on the same team, working to find a win-win solution, creating a methodical plan for tackling the easiest goals first and then building on those successes. It may take a little longer, but it's worth it. Your goal is to create lasting change that your child can feel confident about, rather than short-term compliance because he's afraid of you getting angry at him. Always tie it back to what's in it for your child. If he wants to be able to go to sleepovers, or play with his toys in the basement, ask: "What are the things you need to practice and get good at before you can do that?" Then you're well on your way to a game plan.

If you as a parent are in the habit of expecting your child to take responsibility and collaborate with you, your child will rise to the occasion. Note that collaboration doesn't mean that you'll agree to anything your child asks. If you aren't able to go with your child's suggestion, thank her for making it, but let her know that's not going to work and why. Give her another chance: "Let's keep trying."

If your child says "No!" to the plan, you'll say, "That's fine, but now you need to find a goal that you can say yes to." Even before you get to that negotiation table, though, remember we shrink (the risk) before we approach (the situation). Make sure you've done the previous steps to rethink and shrink the risk of the situation down to size, because it may be that once your child sees the situation without worry's distortions, she'll be ready to approach it anyway.

GETTING STARTED ON EXPOSURE EXERCISES AND BUILDING THE STAIRS OF LEARNING

A parent asks a child with panic disorder to go on a two-hour trip to the city. The child yells, freaks out, and refuses to go. The parent thinks: "But I'm the parent, I planned this trip, and we're going!" Chaos ensues. Though the trip is a few weeks off, the parent and teen spend the next couple of weeks arguing about this, and on the day of the trip it is clear that the teen won't (and truly, can't) go. The parent, frustrated, cancels the trip; the teen feels bad that her parents are mad at her. This is what we call a collaborative failure. It's nobody's fault, but flexibility on all sides would have made things better.

How do we turn this situation into a collaborative success? The challenge was too big for where the teen was at that time; rather than arguing for weeks, both the parents' and child's time could have been spent looking for the smaller steps to get her ready to go from point A to point B. That is the road to GUTI—staying in line with or just a little bit ahead of what our children are ready for.

Finding the Behavior Sweet Spot

There is a clear relationship between stress and performance, and it looks like the illustration below.

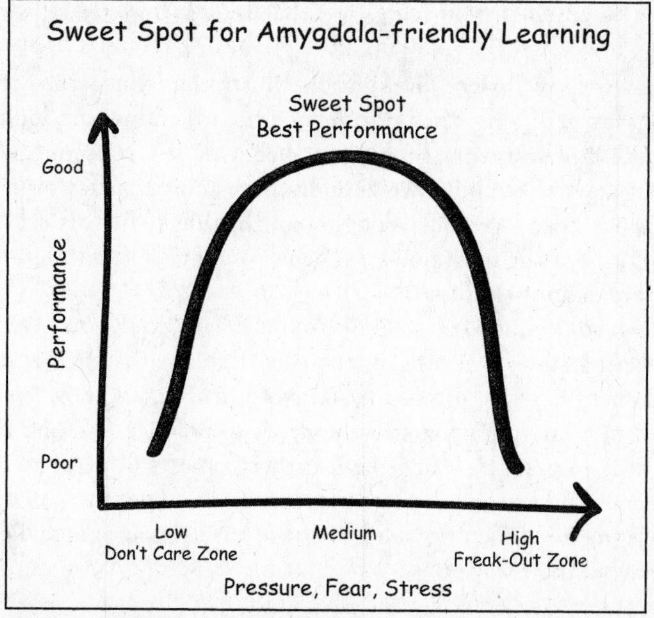

If a task is too easy, your child isn't stressed or challenged at all, nor is she motivated to try, and as a result her performance is low. But when children are challenged too much, they get so stressed that they aren't willing to try either—the stakes are too high—or they are too scared to evaluate the stakes; they just need to protect themselves. A child's performance is low then, too. The sweet spot for optimal learning and peak performance is right in the middle: just enough fear to make it worth your child's while, but not so much that she's too stressed or scared to focus on the task at hand. This is the essence of amygdala-friendly learning and the road to GUTI.

How to explain the "sweet spot" to your child: Ask your child how it would feel to sit in a class where the work is too hard. They'll say stressful—that's the danger zone. Next ask what it would be like if they went to school and the work was too easy—that's the bored zone. They may say boring or frustrating. Explain that it's the same with worry work. The goal is to find the step that they are ready to take that's hard but not too hard. This way, they won't feel stressed, but they'll also feel like it was worth their time and that they accomplished something.

As we saw in the brain train illustration, once the worry thoughts get going, the body gets on board, and we are looking for the quickest exit. Though our behavior is a consequence of thoughts and feelings, we actually have more control over our behavior than over our thoughts and feelings. In this section, we'll look at the most powerful behavioral principles for mastering an anxious situation.

Ask your child what he'd like to be able to do if worry weren't bothering him or getting in the way. Explain that this accomplishment is at the top of the stairs of learning, and now we just need to figure out what steps he needs to practice to climb from point A to point B. Using the fear thermometer from Chapter 6, ask your child to give each item a fear score and put them in order of degree of difficulty; start with the easiest courage challenge and work their way up.

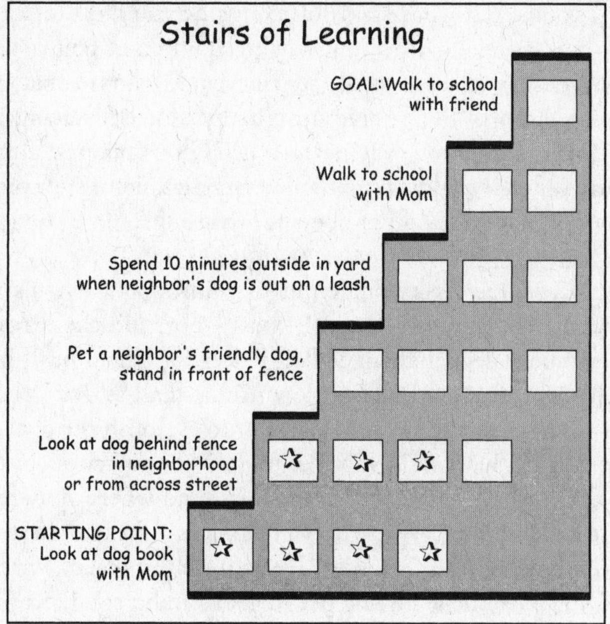

Creating the Stairs of Learning with Your Child, One Step at a Time

I'll never be able to raise my hand in class! I'll never be able to touch the sink faucets! I'll never . . . All the things that feel out of reach for your child now—these are the very things about which to say, "Hey, right, that's what you'd like to do. Let's put that at the top of the staircase. And where you are right now, the kinds of things you can do now, let's say you are at the foot of the stairs. Now let's think about what kinds of things you need to do and practice to get from the bottom of the stairs to the top."

For young children: You can show worry who is the boss. You might say, "Let's practice the things that worry says you *can't do*. We can practice it in steps. Every time you don't do what worry says, you weaken worry and make yourself stronger. It won't keep bothering you!"

Ask your child what kinds of things he could do to feed the worry bug (listening to worry, staying home, not trying things, missing out), and what small step he could choose that would shrink that worry bug (going upstairs by himself, staying in his room for five minutes, waving to a neighbor's puppy). Take the pressure off your child: It's not about him; it's about smushing (or simply outsmarting and not obeying) that bug!

For older children: Ask your child to think about what kind of learner she is. Think back on the past—how did she learn how to overcome a new challenge? Is it better for her to push herself and "just do it" or to break it down into small steps? Whatever her answer is, use the stairs of learning to establish the goals. You might ask: "What would you like to do when worry is out of the way? Okay, that's the top of your stairs, and where you are now with it is down here. What do you think is your best strategy to get from one point to the other? If you were the coach, what steps would you have the team practice to get from here to there?" Now the goal has changed from an overwhelming jumble of fear and failure to something they can tackle.

If your child is wavering, go back to GUTI.

For young children: Ask how they learned to write their letters, tie their shoes, build a tower. Could they do it right away? How did they get better at it? Right, they had to practice.

For older children: Remind them of how they learned how to do the complex math that they are doing now, or the elaborate moves they have mastered in sports. They had to start small and build up. They got more confident and skilled *because* they practiced. You don't wait till you feel confident to get started.

Use the Anxiety Equalizer to Create Your Hierarchy of Fear Challenges

If you are driving somewhere new, is it easier to go in the daytime or at night? If you're giving a sales pitch, is it easier in your hometown or across the country? As it is for adults, so it is for kids—there are some common variables that affect the degrees of difficulty for doing "exposures." Rather than just blindly insisting that a child tackle the situation, work together on what variables turn up or down the stress temperature.

Use the following Anxiety Equalizer graphic with your child to create your exposure hierarchy. Ask your child to identify any factors she thinks may make a difference. The idea isn't to avoid a factor if it's hard—for example, doing exposures at nighttime—but to recognize what work needs to be done to build up competency so that the tough variable won't be such a reach anymore.

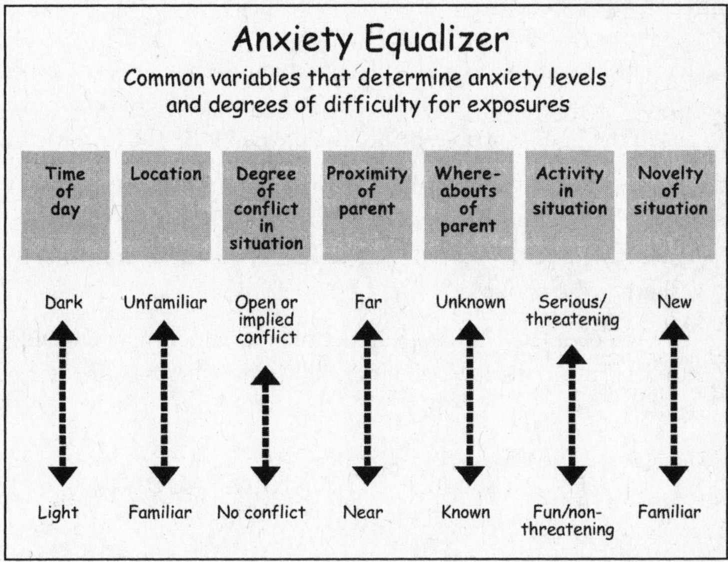

Your child may want to add her own variables, but use this tool by asking: "What would make it easier? What would make it harder? Would it be easier if it were in the daytime? Would it be easier if Mom stayed home and you went out?"

Here are some examples of how the variables can be manipulated to create amygdala-friendly learning for your child:

If a child is afraid of going to the dentist, take them out of the "hot seat": Visit the dentist when it's not their turn. See if you can borrow some tools to practice with at home.

If your child is afraid of flushing the toilet, have them practice when they aren't using it. Have them flush candies, or trace their feet on a big piece of paper and move the mat closer and closer to the toilet when *you're* the one flushing it.

Afraid of dogs? Have them observe sleeping dogs first, which limits the unknowns of what the dog might do.

Having test anxiety? Give them a test about flavors of ice cream first (or the material they've already mastered) rather than hard math questions, to have a chance to practice the mind-set for test taking.

Trouble going to the movies? Take them to the movies to buy a snack, or go to the arcade, not to a movie itself. Go to a movie when the lights are on—before the previews. Be the first one in.

Watch someone else do the thing they're afraid of to see how it works. Afraid of diving? Watch a video of someone diving off the diving board, observe their sibling or parent diving, observe others at the pool.

Say words related to the feared situation which may engender anxiety and avoidance (thunder, lightning, clouds, rain, storm, wind).

WHAT YOU NEED TO KNOW ABOUT BEHAVIOR CHANGE

LESSON: Don't Expect It to Feel Good at First, but Trust That You'll Adjust

How can children be willing to "get used to it" (GUTI) when the beginning of that process can feel so uncomfortable? Why would they sign on for something that feels bad without any hope of its feeling better or different? They wouldn't, and neither would we. But the news is good: That's not at all what they're stepping into. To explain how things will be hard at first and then get much easier, you can always turn back to the example of a swimming pool (from Chapter 6). Help your child understand that it's natural to feel uncomfortable at first in a new or challenging situation, but that he has the ability to adjust and warm up if he just gives it some time. He shouldn't misinterpret that initial discomfort as a sign that he should stay away (get out of the pool). Also, the more your child practices facing challenges, the more she will begin to anticipate feeling better sooner, and that will generate less anxiety in the first place. This means she will feel less discomfort with repeated exposures and they will resolve faster.

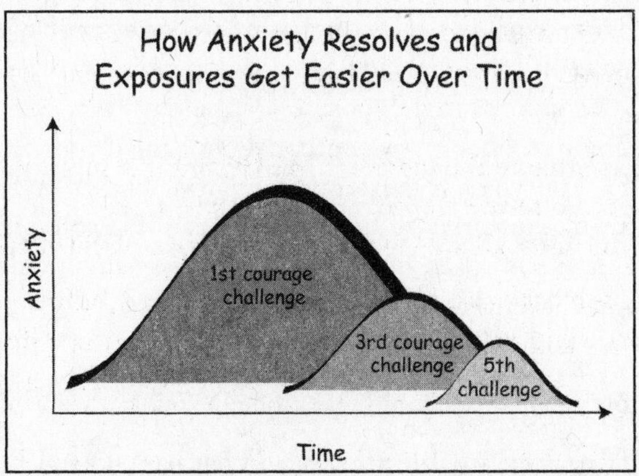

How long will it take to get used to it and adjust? Ask your child to estimate. By starting to picture her success, and your entrusting her with the task of estimating how long it will take to achieve it, she'll feel empowered in the situation, rather than just passively taking your word for it, and most of all, she will begin to see the relief as a possibility around the corner.

LESSON: End on a Good Note of Success, Not Escape

Remember from Chapter 1 that "escaping" or avoiding a feared situation reinforces anxiety? On a physiological level, when your child is at the height of anxiety and you scoop him up and whisk him out of there, this is called "negative reinforcement," and it is very powerful. You are reinforcing the behavior by removing what is negative or aversive: the fear! It tells your child—be anxious, because then your parents will back down and let you off the hook! This is not the message you want to be reinforcing.

If your child is really struggling in an exposure, or even just a naturally occurring situation, such as being overwhelmed at a sporting event or birthday party, you may need to be flexible and shorten the excursion, but not immediately. While being compassionate to your child's struggles, try not to just run out of there at the first sign of discomfort. The best way to make the change your child is requesting—like taking them out of a situation—is when they have calmed down. You may suggest taking a few steps back, having a powwow in the bathroom or a similar place, to help your child take her anxiety down a few notches—even if she's had enough of that exposure for the day. That way anxiety isn't calling the shots, but you are, having gained your child's cooperation. You want to be reinforcing your child's self-control, not rewarding her anxiety. This doesn't mean that you ignore your child while she is upset, but your messages are about helping her calm down rather than negotiating about escape.

Here are some things you might say:

"I know you're upset, and I want to help you. Let's slow it down."

"What part feels hardest to you? What part do you think you can do? What part do you want to master most?"

"I want to help you. We need to work together here, when you can slow it down a little, then we can talk about next steps."

"I want to help you feel better. Let's figure out together what's going to help you now. Let's slow down the breathing together."

LESSON: Talk About Exposures as a Matter of Fact, Not a Matter of Fear

"You'll be fine—I promise! Nothing bad is going to happen! You can call me ten times. I'll be right at home and I won't move!" At first glance these seem like reassuring words to speak to your child, but take a closer look at what's happening and wait. Whose side are you on? Worry's or your child's? If you're on your child's side, then ask yourself, What would the message sound like from a worrywise perspective? What would you say (compassionately) if you were not buying in to worry's version of the story? It would likely sound more straightforward. Researchers have identified that parental "warmth," the quality of parent-child interactions and the spirit in which information is conveyed, is an important anxiety-proofing factor[7] (more about that in Chapter 10), so straightforward doesn't mean "mean" or "strict" and a little warmth goes a long way: "I'm going up to do the laundry. Be right back. Hey, have fun!" If you never provide these opportunities for exposure/learning, your child misses out on important practice, but something else happens too. We send the wrong messages.

It's clear that when parents pinky swear, promise up and down that they'll be right back, or reassure—all the doors and windows are locked and everything's fine!—it sends a message to the child (paradoxically) that these situations (or your child) need shoring up because otherwise they wouldn't be okay. That these ordinary situations are too hard or threatening, or even dangerous. There are self-fulfilling prophecies of different types. Generally, we think of the negative: If we don't believe our children can do something, and we verbalize our doubt, they will likely prove us right (unfortunately) and not even try to take on the challenge, because they've gotten the message from us that we don't think it can be done, or that they can't do it. Work the other side of the street: the positive prophecy. Children pick up on our confidence too: Be excited for your child's progress; don't focus on reassuring details about the situation. Remember, there was never anything wrong with it in the first place; that was just worry giving unreliable data.

LESSON: Avoid Avoidance!

Avoidance feeds anxiety. If as parents we "make" our children do things they don't like, such as cleaning their rooms and eating vegetables, but we're letting our children avoid dogs, it must mean that dogs really are dangerous, or maybe even that Mom and Dad are afraid, too (that idea is very powerful). But most of all, Mom and Dad appear to think their children can't cope—so a child will conclude: I guess I can't. Parents struggle with insisting that their child go or insisting that they stay. The point is that you want to help your child see that there's nothing wrong with them or where they are; it's that worry is telling them a story that's making them feel scared. Help them to interact with and get as close to that situation as possible, while staying in an amygdala-friendly zone.

LESSON: Take "I Can't" with a Grain of Salt

Even when kids really understand the idea of exposure, they might still make sweeping statements in a moment of frustration or fear: "I just can't!" We have to see past the frustration or fear talking. Many children have told me that when their parents have let them off the hook about something they said they couldn't do, they are surprised. It would be as if your child fell off his bike and said, "I don't want to do this anymore!" and then . . . you gave away the bike. Just as we might exclaim, "I've had it!" when we're on our last nerve, respect that your children may *feel* like giving up in that moment, but another part of them doesn't want to. Align yourself with that healthier part. Empathize with the frustration and ask them what piece they can do, or when they think they'll want to try again.

LESSON: Burn Out Your Worry with Competing Emotions—Anger, Relaxation, Humor

There is a popular commercial that says, "When banks compete, you win." Well, when emotions compete, you win too. It's a process called reciprocal inhibition. When relaxation, amusement, or even some righteous annoyance competes with anxiety, one of them will win out over worry. Feeling mad, relaxed, or goofy inhibits your ability to feel scared. Basically you can't be in two places at once emotionally, and fortunately the brain will favor the positive over the negative emotion. Your child won't feel as afraid if he is feeling annoyed by his fears. Fear and annoyance are two different programs in the brain. What can your child do? Encourage him to make a rap song out of his fears, stick his tongue out at the bugs that bother him, or play catch with a shoe that feels "contaminated." Switch the emotional tone out of scare mode and into something that feels more familiar—goofy, righteous, fun.

Note that this fun is at the expense of the worry, and it should never become making fun of your child. Sometimes kids are not ready to poke fun at the anxiety. Follow your child's lead. When your child is ready to use some healthy humor and sarcasm, he'll let you know.

LESSON: Don't Just Distract Your Child from Worry; Dismiss It Altogether

Many well-meaning people have probably told your child to simply distract himself from worry. Any child will tell you that doesn't work, and he is right. Distracting yourself from a bat in the room won't reduce your anxiety. Seeing that that bat was really just a shadow all along will. Of course, if there is actually a bat there, distraction would really not help! You must help your child to identify his worries as mistakes his brain is making that are not worth his time, so that it will be much easier for him to discredit them, dismiss them, and get involved with what matters more. But still, it will take a few minutes for the anxiety to pass while he recovers from thinking he was dealing with a real threat. In that moment, it's best to get busy with other things. When you are fighting worry, the best choices are active ones. Sitting and reading or even playing a computer game still leaves your child's mind a captive audience for fear. Play a fast game of catch or hot potato with a softball, walk the dog, sing, or dance—all these activities help your child move out of worry mode and engage a healthier part of his brain.

LESSON: Do One, Teach One

We've seen that you can fight worry with silliness, but another way is to fight it with competence. Fear is all about *not* knowing; competence is all about finding out the facts. Become an expert. Have your child do research about the topic of their fear—the habits of dogs or bees, for example—or even how common that fear is. Have your child create a lesson, a PowerPoint presentation, or a true/false quiz and teach a grandparent or the family at dinner what he's learned.

LESSON: Leave Less to the Imagination, Give More Confidence for Your Child

Anxious children have to mentally push through the unknowns, but sometimes they can't. At those times, there's *imaginal exposure.* This refers to interacting with the feared situation through role-playing: pretending to call a friend; or asking for help at a store; or simply by running through a scenario in your imagination: what would happen first, next, and so forth. Think of imaginal exposure as a dress rehearsal so your child can practice his lines and see how manageable the situation really is before he tackles it head-on. The more he knows what to expect by going through the motions, the more confident he will feel going into the situation.

Previews: Make the imaginal exposure as realistic as possible by looking at pictures on the Internet of the place he'll be going, or visiting the situation (school, restaurant, friend's house) before the day of the event.

Be the first: As much as anxiety may delay getting your child out the door and where she needs to be, it is greatly advantageous to get there and settle in early and gradually. There's an enormous difference between entering a room full of people, a blur, a buzz of activity and being the first one, having other folks enter one by one.

LESSON: Make Every Action Count

Though we may be tempted to just keep track of the big steps—a child sleeping in his own bed, or a teen being able to stay at the mall for a long time—any success, however small, is a significant building block as your child works toward the big shifts. Don't wait until your child is ready for the "bull's-eye" exposure. Those big-ticket items may not happen for a long time, and your child will likely be angry or give up if your stance is "go big or go home." Instead, keep an eye out for opportunities to take small steps that might not hit the target but "hit the board," and reinforce the importance of those small steps! On the other hand, if your child is insisting on the "off the board" moves only, i.e., exposures that are too easy for him, it's time to reinforce the idea that you are there to make your child stronger, not to strengthen worry, so you need to figure out the next couple of steps to put your child in charge. Look to the Anxiety Equalizer (on page 131) together for ideas about how to make the next step more in reach.

Problem	Bull's-eye	Hitting the Board	Off the Board
Separation anxiety	Child goes to sleep in her own bed	Child falls asleep in parents' bed without parents there	Child sleeps in parents' bed all night
Fear of bees	Child picnics outside with friends	Child eats lunch in the car, but comes out for dessert	Mom and child sit in the car for the picnic, or stay home!
OCD: Contamination fears	Child touches computer, doesn't wash hands and has a snack	Child touches computer with tissue and has a snack without washing.	Child will only touch computer with a tissue, washes hands for several minutes
Panic and agoraphobia	Child plays sports in the hot sun, though has a fear of fainting	Child plays sports but has a pass to sit out for a few minutes whenever needed	Child skips practice if not feeling well

LESSON: Don't Let a Slip Turn into a Slump: How to Prevent Relapses

Once your child overcomes a fear situation, celebrate her success! Also be prepared for anxiety to try to sneak in again, particularly at times of stress. It will be different this time, because your child knows how to handle the problem. If you see anxiety and avoidance returning, revisit the fear strategies at the first signs of a problem. Pull out the fear hierarchy and redo the necessary steps to get that fear-fighting muscle back in shape.

LESSON: Make a Stuck Moment into an Opportunity to Make Progress

Connect with what matters to your child and think in parts:

I won't go to bed unless you stay with me the whole entire night! I'm not going to school unless you walk me in!

When our children say "no," *we* start to panic. "If they can't do this, they'll never be able to do anything in their lives independently!" We think: "I have to get them to do this, or else!" Slow down. Fact-check your own worry, and narrow down the problem. It's not their whole life that's at stake here—it's this one moment. Use your flexibility to take the long view and be willing to think in parts and partial successes. Make getting unstuck into a collaboration, and enlist your child's input. Something needs to happen for forward movement, but you're going to be flexible about what. Tie the task to their goals, not yours: "I know you really want to do sleepovers someday. This can really help you get there," or, "You've been working hard not to let worry ruin your time at parties. Don't stop now."

If the step your child is willing to take is just to put a pinky in the proverbial swimming pool and not his whole foot, resist the urge to let your anxiety speak. Instead of saying, "That's not enough!" ask, "You could do that, but I'm just wondering, will it feel worth it? If it's too easy, it might not feel good to you. What's one step more that will feel hard but not too hard?"

> *What part of this can you do?* "It feels too hard to go to that party because of social anxiety, but I know that part of you wants to go. What are the options? What would help? Yes, going in with a friend, that sounds good, and what if you just went for part of the time, and what if you offered to help with the music? If it's really not fun, you can leave, but this way you can find out."

> *Can you think of a way that you and I can share this job?* "You are afraid to go upstairs to take a shower by yourself, but Mom has

to do dishes. How can we make this work for both of us? Yes, I can walk you up and then check on you once."

IS IT OKAY TO GET ANGRY AT ANXIETY?

Sometimes kids (and parents) get frustrated at anxiety and say things like the following: "I want to kill my anxiety!" Or "I'm going to shoot it!" As understandable as the frustration is, this approach fires up the amygdala just like anxiety does, so it is counterproductive. You don't want to get angry at your child for saying things like this, because that will only compound the problem. Instead, to keep the amygdala in the standby position, redirect your child's frustration: "I know you are really mad about your worry. Let's show it who is the boss. What's one thing you can do now to show that worry isn't invited to the ball game or concert?" Or redirect the anger into authority: "Let's teach worry a lesson here. Shake your bossy finger at worry and tell it why it's wrong!"

GOOD EXPOSURE CHECKLIST

- Amygdala-friendly challenge (a five out of ten on the fear thermometer)
- The child has chosen challenge because worry is in his way.
- The child has done the "rethink" already to shrink the fear and has lines ready to boss back or correct worry's mistakes.
- The child stays in a situation until anxiety comes down a minimum of two points, bur preferably 50 percent or more.
- The child and parent decide what the parent's job is—whether to be involved (or not).
- Encourage playfulness and creativity wherever possible: the child acts as tour guide of the basement if he's afraid of the dark; the child is teaching a class on dogs if he's afraid of dogs; the child names a bee "Ms. Buzzy" and "interviews" her for the news because she's afraid of bees.
- If the child is struggling, step back but don't leave. Regroup

and reapproach the situation so that your child can end on a good note of bravery and competency.

Courage challenges don't have to be boring. Introduce the element of surprise by having your child write down the challenges that he's ready to take on. Each day have your child choose one mystery exposure out of a basket.

DO IT TODAY: BUILD A SENSE OF COMPETENCY WITH CHORES AND OTHER NON-ANXIOUS TASKS

For parents: You want your child to take action to confront anxiety, but your starting point may be disadvantaged by the fact that you can't get your child to comply with the "low stakes" tasks that establish basic cooperation (and have nothing to do with fear!): e.g., carrying his backpack in from the car, putting his plate in the dishwasher, helping water plants or feed the family pet, getting his own snack after school (hint: move snack foods down to cabinets within their reach). Giving your child a sense of competence with the easier tasks will boost his confidence in tackling the tougher ones. Review a typical morning and evening in your home, identify two or three tasks that you're doing for your child that he could really do for himself, and talk to your child about how he can best accomplish them himself: What tools or reminders (or stepstool!) does he need to be successful?

Chapter 8

PUTTING IT ALL TOGETHER

The Master Plan for Taking Charge of Anxiety

I always felt so bad when my daughter was scared. All I could think of was I need to tell her whatever she needs to hear to make her feel better. I know it didn't work, but I never realized that the real way for her to feel better was not by telling her things to reassure her, but by asking her questions so that she could see the situation differently herself.

In Chapters 4 through 7 we looked at the mechanisms of anxiety—why we need to challenge anxious thinking, and how to do so, along with strategies to manage physiological reactions and use gradual exposures to begin to approach fearful situations. This chapter gives you scripts and a step-by-step action plan for the heat of an anxiety moment and explains in general how to rewire your child's anxious thinking and teach them to expose themselves to uncomfortable situations, because that's how they'll get comfortable!

The master plan puts your child back in charge, helping him reconnect with how he would see the situation if worry weren't calling the shots. In the short run, this plan will build your child's competency and confidence. In the long run, your child will have a foundation of anxiety-management skills that will be ready at hand, whatever comes his way, for today and always.

The master plan has sample scripts and exercises, which are presented in most instances for three age groups: very young children (under age six), those in middle childhood (ages seven to eleven), and adolescents (age twelve and up).

THE PARENT'S MASTER PLAN FOR ANXIETY

Step One: Empathize with what your child is feeling
Step Two: Relabel the problem as the worry brain
Step Three: Rethink and shrink worry down to size
Step Four: Get the body on board—turn off the alarms
Step Five: Approach the worry on purpose and practice getting used to it (GUTI)
Step Six: Refocus on what you want to do
Step Seven: Reinforce your child's efforts at being courageous!

You won't always need to use each step every time. At first it may help to follow the steps in order, but over time the concepts will become second nature and you'll go right to the one that's best suited for the situation your child is in.

STEP ONE: EMPATHIZE WITH WHAT YOUR CHILD IS FEELING

The best way to approach your worrying child is with empathy. Rather than immediately trying to redirect him or correct him, lean in and meet him where he is. When we make a connection, there's trust and a willingness to listen. So resist the temptation to tell your child to stop worrying, or to reassure him that there's nothing to worry about.

How do you do this, exactly? First, acknowledge what's going on for her. You're not agreeing with it, but you're acknowledging that this is how she feels. This can be done with words, with a gesture that lets her know you are on her side: a hug, a knowing look that says, "I know you are sick of this." Kids will appreciate your candor, so if something "really sucks," don't be afraid to say so. Your empathy doesn't mean you're going to get stuck in the quicksand that they are experiencing; it means you are going to join them and lead them in a new direction. You can do this compassionately by converting their *permanent* pronouncements ("This is impossible!" "I can't!") into *temporary* frustration.

Make the Terrible (or Terrifying) Temporary

When your child is upset and telling you that things are too hard, or impossible, this is your opportunity to do the "red pen edit" strategy, but invisibly. Take your child's feelings that he's stating as if they were facts, and reflect them back to him minus the permanence. He won't have to fight you, because you aren't trying to convince him out of his feelings; you're just restating them in a more workable form.

YOUR CHILD SAYS:

"I can't do this!"

"I'm too scared!"

"This is too hard!"

"Don't make me!"

YOU SAY:

"I know this is hard right now. *I want to help you make this easier."*

"Worry is making this seem *really impossible* right now."

"You are really feeling *like this is too scary* right now."

"You really don't want it to be like this right now."

"You are really having thoughts *that* feel *overwhelming* right now."

STEP TWO: RELABEL THE PROBLEM AS THE WORRY BRAIN

Worry thoughts don't come clearly labeled "unreliable" and "unrealistic," but once you get to know them, they do have a familiar ring: *You can't! What if . . . ? Oh no! It's going to be a disaster! Someone will get hurt! Don't take a chance!* They are the brain's knee-jerk response to any risk or uncertainty. They tell us everything about our primitive wiring and very little at all about the actual situations we find ourselves in. Ask your child if worry is calling on the phone, how can she tell that it's worry? Does she really want to hear what worry is saying? If not, hang up! Or invite your child to list his worry thoughts and then "stamp" them with his thought stamper: what is true, what is unlikely, or even what's preposterous!

Do You Know Who's Talking to You?

The power of relabeling is that it separates the worry from your child: Instead of just following worry's orders, the child pauses and considers: "Who is asking me that question? Do I need to listen?" Parents doing the relabeling is strategic and can at times lighten the mood: "Worry, is that you again? Michael, I know you're in there. I hear what worry is saying, but what do you think about this situation?" This takes your child out of the hot seat of being the problem, frees him from having to defend the reasons that he's worrying, and also gives his mind the opening to get into smart mode and analyze how to master the situation rather than continue to work to avoid it. With worry labeled as the real problem, parents and kids can join forces to take charge of the anxiety instead of fighting each other.

Relabeling Techniques

WHAT YOU CAN SAY:

"This sounds like worry talking to you."

"This is exactly what worry brain would say."

"Worry is up to its old tricks, isn't it?"

"What's worry bugging you about this time?"

WHAT YOU CAN DO:

Ask your child: "What do you want to call your worry?" Give the worry a nickname, like brain bug, Mr. Panic, Mrs. Watch-it (let your child choose). It helps your child to externalize the problem, get him off of the hot seat, and distinguish his rational thoughts from worry thoughts.

Draw a picture, or make a puppet, doll, or figure, of the brain bug.

Give fears a voice of their own. Say them with a silly voice or sarcastically to keep them from sounding scary. Sing them like Elvis, or Rihanna; say them like Homer Simpson or Sponge-Bob. Feel no obligation to respect the voice of anxiety.

Stage an impromptu worry talent show. Do impersonations of the worry voice. Which version is it easiest for your child to dismiss?

EXERCISE: INVITE YOUR CHILD TO NAME AND ROLE-PLAY THE DIFFERENT PARTS OF THE BRAIN

Have your child create characters—these can be game tag avatars (the icons kids use to represent themselves in video games) if they prefer, or just characters for children who don't play video games: fun guy, smart guy, worry guy, hungry guy, sports guy. See what those different characters would say about the situation at hand. Give each of them a voice. Which thought belongs to whom? The Defender, the Genius, the Fun Guy, the Worrier, the Planner. Have your child look at the Portrait Gallery drawing in Chapter 4 to get her imagination flowing.

Relabeling Worry with Very Young Children: A Script

Parents can use puppets, stuffed animals, drawings, or a silly voice to differentiate worry thinking from smart thinking. In the context of a game or role-playing, worry can be a bug buzzing around, scaring a stuffed animal, say an elephant. The elephant is afraid of everything, but only because the worry bug keeps saying mean things in his ear, such as "You can't play with the doggy. You are too afraid. Doggies bark and are too scary." Then you can turn to your child and say, "Wow, that worry bug is mean, and bossy, and I don't think he's right. He says that all doggies are mean. Let's see if we can prove him wrong. What about that doggie that we saw in the park running after the frisbee—did he look mean? No, I don't think so. He didn't want to hurt anybody; he was a nice doggy. Let's teach the worry bug a few things about dogs. Let's use a strong voice and boss worry bug: 'Hey, worry bug, doggies are the best friends of lots and lots of children. They bark when they are happy or surprised, but that doesn't mean they want to hurt me!' Let's sing a song: 'Worry bug, go away. I just want to go and play!' Next time when we see a dog, it will be easier because you won't feel so scared." Repeat the role-playing, letting your child decide if he wants to play the worry bug or the brave child who bosses back worry bug.

Relabeling Worry with Older Children: A Script

"When you worry, it's your body's alarm system starting to backfire, setting off false alarms about situations that are not as risky as your brain junk mail is telling you. But you can decide that you're not going to fall for that trick. What do you want to call the brain trick? It helps to give worry a name—Brain Bug, Worry Glasses, Exaggerator Man, Repeater Reptile, Tricky Guy, Question Man, Bratty Brain, Drama Queen, Disaster Guy, The Exaggerator—so you can start to boss it back.

"The more you start to talk back to your worry and correct the mistakes it makes, the more your brain will learn to alert you to only the real risks. Let's draw a picture of your Worry Guy and do some role-playing to practice bossing him back."

Relabeling Worry with Teenagers: A Script

"You know the kids at school who create drama? There's someone who exaggerates a lot or starts rumors—and you tune them out because they are unreliable and don't tell the truth? Do you like hanging out with them? Do you trust what they say? Would you consult them if you were studying for a test or trying to find out what *really* happened at a party? Right. Think of anxiety as the drama-maker in your mind. Is that who you want to rely on in important moments of your life? Turn off their microphone, think of someone else you trust, and rewire with your wisdom."

Or, "You know how you get spam in your e-mail? A message that says that you need to update your private information, or that you need to save someone who was pickpocketed in a different country? Maybe the first time you saw those e-mails you were confused, but from then on you could tell right away that those just *seemed* important—but they weren't. Your worry does the same thing. It sends you urgent warnings, but after the fact, when you go back and see what actually happened, what is worry's track record? The warnings really had nothing to do with your life—those things didn't come true. Save yourself a lot of grief by recognizing and dismissing worry messages rather than absorbing them."

QUICK HINT: IF YOUR CHILD REFUSES TO RELABEL AND INSISTS THE PROBLEM IS "HIM"

Some children don't like to relabel. They insist that if they're thinking a thought, it's part of them and they have to listen. Without getting into an argument about it, show your child that it's okay not to listen. We have other messages that we don't listen to—because we decide that they're not important. An air conditioner, a lawn mower, traffic sounds, even the "I'm hungry" or "I need to pee" or "I'd really rather be home playing video games." We ignore those signals even though they are our own. The brain is an information processing center. We decide which information to prioritize, and what can wait or be discarded. Worry acts like an emergency, but we need to recognize the telltale signs and throw it in the recycle bin. The key is to decide which is the best part of the brain to be in charge at this moment, and worry brain is not going to get chosen for the job.

STEP THREE: RETHINK AND SHRINK WORRY DOWN TO SIZE

While you may be tempted to just tell your child the "right" answers—what they *should* think—always start with the worries or fear thoughts first, because that's where she's stuck. In order to help her correct the worries, we first need to know what they are. And she needs to tell you, because every child's worries and fears are different. Ask your child what worry is telling her. Then use the thought-shifting strategies that we saw in Chapter 4, listed on the next page, to have your child "fact-check" worry, get the other side of the story so your child can then compare the facts side by side to the fears and choose what is most accurate. Remember: While anxiety will choose the most *frightening* scenario, you can help your child generate the other side of the story, the most *likely* scenario, by asking: "What do you think will really happen, and why do you think that?" Once the child has determined that worry is wrong, she can be encouraged to "boss back" the worry, telling worry how it has it all wrong and that she's not going to listen.

Like buying a refrigerator or a video game, you want your child to be an educated consumer when it comes to studying the thoughts that come up in his mind and comparing and contrasting "features" (i.e., the facts), before deciding which are the best thoughts to carry with them into a situation. Having created the choosing moment where the child can see the two versions of the situation side by side, ask your child:

"Which version is more accurate or true?"

"If you had to take a test at school, which side has the right answers?"

"Which version feels better to you? Which one would you like to hear?"

"Which one will be more helpful to you so you can be successful in that situation?"

"Which one do you think your friends think?"

"Which one would you choose if worry weren't talking to you?"

"Which one keeps your worry temperature lower?"

"Which script would you want to bring into that situation?"

If they are not convinced that it's okay *not* to listen to worry, use the long-distance learning technique that we saw in Chapter 4. Take something your child feels confident about—a sport or other situation they don't worry about, but that others do. Ask them: What does your friend say about basketball? ("That's too scary, I'll get hit!") What do you say? ("I love basketball. I might get hit, but it's rare."). Ask them if they want to think about getting hurt in basketball—they will say no. Point out how well they are able to filter out their worry thoughts and function well by focusing on what is most likely. This helps them know that worry thoughts are unreliable and they don't need them! Then help them transfer that skill to the current fear challenge they are facing.

RINSE AND REPEAT!

Given how ingrained the worry response has become, your child needs to repeat a realistic comeback many times—and with feeling! Worry thoughts have dominated the airwaves in your child's mind; as a result, hearing themselves say the confident, realistic thoughts is a powerful new experience. Have them write their smart thoughts on an index card, and keep it in their backpack, pocket, or bedside table. Repeat often!

Rethinking with Young Children: Bossing Back the Fear

Rewiring is about reconnecting to more realistic circuits and taking the power back from anxiety. Children need to find their "boss back" voice, the strong voice inside them they use to let people know they can't be pushed around. In order to tap into this mind-set of defending their emotional turf, kids can be asked to think of the voice they use when a bully or a sibling is trying to take their stuff or boss them around. Children can think of what a favorite superhero would say in that situation—because, after all, as one very vocal five-year-old recently told my husband, "Superman never worries!"

EXAMPLES OF BOSS BACK TALK

- "You are not the boss of me! I decide what to think!"
- "If this were really important, my parents would be helping me worry, not helping me stop!"
- "You don't know anything about this, Brain Bug. Go back to school!"
- "You are just a false alarm. You don't know what's going to happen!"
- "I don't have to listen to you. I'm changing the channel."

RETHINKING TOOLKIT FOR YOUNG CHILDREN

- Make a thought sorter and separate out your child's thoughts: worry or smart, silly or true.
- Stage a puppet show debate between worry and smart thoughts. Create thought bubbles for Worried Walter versus Smart Samantha.
- Look through the worry glasses versus the smart glasses.
- Use the possibility panel: What would your favorite superheroes say versus what worry says?
- Think in parts: Ask what protector brain says versus smart brain.
- Use your remote control: Switch the setting to "truth." What does the movie look like then?
- Do a "monster-makeover" by adding curlers, hats, roller skates to the worry and turning what feels scary into something silly.

WORRY GLASSES
We're doomed!
What if the basement floods?
What if the house catches fire?
What if the lights go out?
Fear temperature 10+
SMART GLASSES
We are safe. Thunder
is loud but not dangerous.
Rainstorms are part of life.
I can handle it.
Fear temperature 3

OTHER RETHINKING STRATEGIES FOR YOUNG CHILDREN

- "Worry is saying all the things that are going to go wrong. How do you think the story is going to end? When you're home in your bed tonight, what will you say happened?"
- Demystify the scaries: Take something your child is afraid of, such as monsters, and help them see how they really work. Monsters are made up. Ask your child, "How many have you seen?" Use levity: "Let's make up our own monster. How about a monster who doesn't know how to say 'boo,' but says 'broccoli' instead? Maybe the monster is afraid of his shadow because it's so big! The monster wants to play the guitar, but no one will teach him."
- If your child is not ready to face a situation directly—for example, approaching clowns, dogs, dance class—they can do "research" and watch how other kids manage in that situation and then report to you what they learn.
- Act out a scene with worry, rhyming the words or using silly words to make fun of worry: "You think I'm going to fall? What? You said I'm very tall? Oh, haha. Thanks, worry." Or, "You want me to think about getting sick? What? My pet dog has a tick? What? You think I'm very quick? Haha, thanks, worry."

Rethinking with Older Children

Older children don't like being told what to do, and they don't like being scammed. Though they may come to the exact conclusion that you'd hope, being able to discover the truth for themselves (with the help of your questions) is much more reinforcing and convincing than your telling them what to think. The key is finding out exactly what your child is worried about. Let him tell you. Be careful about guessing—you may guess wrong and inadvertently introduce a new worry angle to the problem. By going through these steps your child will feel better, and the bonus: It's all true. We want your child's mind to be more truthful with him. Put it to the test.

Have them do the side-by-side comparison of what fear is telling them and what the facts are. Ask your child what she wants to name the other thoughts—smart thoughts, calm thoughts, or simply reality. Have your child read both descriptions, taking their worry temperature after each one. Ask them: Which description is better? Which makes more sense? Which one do they believe? Have your child write the realistic script on an index card and carry it with her into the fear situation so she can consult the facts when necessary.

If you put your mind to it, you will be able to come up with more creative choices for helping older children and teenagers with rethinking. Here are some ideas:

- Use the brain train illustration (see Chapter 4) to talk about how the worry thoughts lead to certain feelings and behaviors, and how differently a situation can turn out if you just change your thoughts about it.
- Use the pie charts in Chapter 4 to color in how much your child thinks the worry will come true versus how much he feels afraid of the worry. Feeling something doesn't make it true. Feelings change; the facts stay the same. Help your child put his thinking part in charge. Remind him that when something is a small risk, he doesn't have to plan around it. (Isn't there a risk that he might get hurt in sports, but doesn't he still play? That's when he is in charge and the worry brain is quiet.)
- Ask your child to write her worry thoughts on cards and put them in a hat. Have her pull out a card and name two coping thoughts that will reduce the anxiety surrounding that thought. Then parents take a turn doing the same.
- Have your child imagine she is a detective, or a lawyer in court, and she has to prove her worry case with the facts. Ask her to explain how she would go about it. Could she prove any of the worries, or are they really unlikely?

QUICK HINT

If you need to do this quickly in a pinch and don't have time to go through writing it down, just say to your child: "Let's 'side-by-side it.'" Or, "What's the answer to the million-dollar question? Do you think worry is really right?" When he is reminded that truth is not only an option, but the best option, your child will be able to make the quick pick to get the answer right.

RETHINKING TOOLKIT FOR OLDER CHILDREN

- *Ask your child the million-dollar question.* If he could win a million dollars by guessing what's going to really happen—what's the right answer?
- *Bring in the possibility panel.* Have your child assemble her "trusted advisors," and in her imagination, have her ask them to weigh in about what is really happening in the situation.
- *Turn the worry into a question.* Don't take worry at face value. Take each worry statement, turn it into a question, and answer it.
- *Do the side-by-side comparison:* Have your child list the fears and the facts about the situation at hand. Read them off—choose the more accurate side.
- *Do the red pen edit:* Edit worry's version of the story; when it says something could really happen, correct it and say it's unlikely. Edit in the fact that you are feeling scared but that you are not in danger.
- *Put the problem through the Worry Shrinker boxes (page 105):* Worry starts a big warning that everything bad is going to happen. Narrow it down and see if there is something that you do need to worry about or plan for. Or does worry have it all wrong?
- *Fast-forward to the end—what really happens?* What are you going to be saying to yourself the morning after? Did you fail the test, make a fool of yourself, or is everything going to turn out fine?

STEP FOUR: GET THE BODY ON BOARD— TURN OFF THE ALARMS

Okay, your child has done his relabeling. He still might need to pause to shift his body out of the amygdala's threat-protection program and into calm, clear thinking. There are different ways to make that shift. Deep breathing helps some children center (see strategies in Chapter 6). Don't just say, "You need to take a deep breath!" Your child is so anxious that one more instruction can register more like a threat than a helping hand. Instead, make this a two-person moment and ask your child to breathe with you.

If your child is in the throes of an anxiety moment, he may not be able to start slowing down his breathing right away. Put out the expectation and suggestion that in a few minutes when he is ready he will be able to slow everything down. With younger kids you can hold their hands and have them match their breathing to yours. For older kids, have them focus on counting, breathing in 1, 2, and out 1, 2, without holding their breath at any point. Kids' bodies also get revved up when their behavior becomes agitated, regressed, or disorganized. Calmly but firmly instruct them that their job is to try to slow things down when they are ready.

- Remind your child that anxiety always passes, but he can help the calming effect along by slowing himself down.
- Take your child's worry temperature on a scale from 1 to 10, or simply have the child rate her fear as low, medium, or high. This will help your child see that even though she may still feel anxious a few minutes later, the anxiety actually has started to decrease through her own efforts.

For some kids, breathing and relaxing is the last thing they want to do; they need another way to burn off the adrenaline that worry is pumping into their system. Movement is good—play a quick game of catch, play freeze dance or freeze tag, walk the dog.

STEP FIVE: APPROACH THE WORRY ON PURPOSE AND PRACTICE GETTING USED TO IT (GUTI)

It's not enough for your child to just correct worry and think differently; he has to prove to himself that he can resist the warnings of worry and act on what he knows to be true instead. Seeing is believing! This means finding a starting point with the fear or worry situation and beginning the gradual approach and desensitization.

Ask your child what he'd like to be able to do if worry weren't in the way. Then ask him to make a list of feared or avoided situations that he needs to master in order to reach his goal. Have him rate his fear temperature for each challenge, then rank the steps and create a hierarchy or stairs of learning (see Chapter 7), putting the easiest on the bottom step and the final goal at the top. Plan a series of "courage challenges," which are small exposures or GUTI exercises where your child will practice facing his fear. Your child can start from the easiest, right outside his comfort zone, and then, with frequent practice, begin to conquer that specific fear by approaching the situation. Help your child choose a challenge that is not too big but not too small. Remember, if it's too hard, he will fail; if it's too easy, he won't have a sense of accomplishment. Your child can progress to the next step when he no longer feels significant anxiety from the current challenge.

For younger children, GUTI exercises can be opportunities to show worry how wrong it is, and in small reasonable ways, get even with the trouble worry has caused. You can take the straightforward approach of asking, "How are you going to work on this?" But phrasing it by saying something like "I think I'll bug my worry with this" or, "It will really bug my worry if I do this" may help harness your child's motivation.

In Chapters 11 through 17, you will find sample GUTI exercises for your child's particular type of fear or worry. Remember, there are some common variables that affect the difficulty of a certain exposure (such as going somewhere at night versus during the day). Older children may be able to articulate these factors; younger children may not. Consider the factors illustrated in the

Anxiety Equalizer on page 131, and see which ones are relevant to your child's fears.

STEP SIX: REFOCUS ON WHAT YOU WANT TO DO

Once your child has bossed worry back and corrected its mistakes, it is time to dismiss the worry and move on. Because the anxious feelings can take several minutes to pass, it is best to get busy with something else. With this step you are not simply distracting your child—you're showing him how to pick up his mind and put it where he wants it to be.

Ask your child, "What would you want to be doing—right now—if you weren't feeling worried? Let's get busy with that and your brain will learn to jump the worry track and stick with truth." If your child isn't ready to switch gears to a preferred activity, he may need a transitional activity to get unstuck and get the wheels of the mind turning in a new direction.

Physical activity is best; for example, throw a ball back and forth (a pair of socks will do in a pinch), go for a run with the dog, dance, sing, or play tag. If physical activity isn't possible (i.e., if you are in the car), play a quick game of categories. Name all the movies you saw in the last few months, name all the foods that begin with the letter *P*—do something that gets your mind busy thinking and is a fun and better use of your time. Remember, sedentary activities will likely not offer as much relief, because your child may still be thinking about the worry while doing the activity.

STEP SEVEN: REINFORCE YOUR CHILD'S EFFORTS AT BEING COURAGEOUS!

Praise your child for getting through a tough situation and strengthening those good circuits! Use tangible reinforcers and rewards to increase a child's willingness and drive to fight the worry. Rewards such as stickers, small treats, special time with parents, and yes, even toys, are not bribes but acknowledgments of a job well done. Make sure that you convey that message to your child. Don't say, "If you stay in bed and don't call out for the next five nights, I'll buy you a new doll." Instead say, "You are going to work hard on staying in bed and using your 'boss back' talk and your nighttime journal if you are scared. Is there a special treat you would like after you've had five nights where you met your goal?" Another advantage of rewards is that they change the tone of the work from serious and fearful to something positive—working toward getting pancakes for breakfast, scoring a free pass from taking out the trash, or having the privilege of borrowing the car.

The Two-Jar Technique

Take two jars, and write your child's name on one and "Worry" on the other. Fill up the worry jar with pennies, buttons, clothespins—whatever you have on hand. Every time your child completes a courage challenge, or practices their exposures on their stairs of learning, or simply does something spontaneously courageous—give them credit! Have them take one item out of worry's jar and put it in their own. You can do a special celebration every time your child has five or ten items in their jar. Keep the association with this process and the jars positive; never punish your child or threaten to take items out of their jar. Your child's successes are

what will propel him forward; if there are difficult moments, don't punish; instead, break the challenges down into smaller chunks to make them work.

HINTS ABOUT INCENTIVES/REWARDS

- In general it takes about three weeks to establish a new behavior, so continue rewarding your child until the new behavior is established.
- Highlight successes in coping. Don't dwell on unsuccessful moments.
- Be specific about the target behavior: the amount of time involved or the specific behavioral challenge. For example, stay in bed for ten minutes without calling out or crying out; go to the convenience store and ask one question; retie your shoes one time instead of five; make calls to three friends.
- Don't just look at the bull's-eye; reward any behavior that hits the board. Change the reward to an agreed-upon compromise if the child is able to partially complete the task.
- Don't look for consecutive successes (e.g., staying in bed five days in a row); instead go for cumulative successes (a total of five days). Progress is often two steps forward, one step back.
- Gradually fade out rewards for success with a given behavior as the task gets easier, then switch the reward to the next challenge on your child's stairs of learning.
- Remember that behavior changes before thoughts and feelings. Kids will continue to say, "I can't. I'm scared." Don't wait for anxious feelings and thoughts to go away as a sign that your child is ready to change his behavior. Encourage your child to work on correcting his thoughts, and then work on what he *can* control—the behavior.

GENERAL DO'S AND DON'TS FOR ALL THE STEPS

- Do let your child know it's okay to be afraid.
- Do get your child's input—what's on her worry list, why does she want to fight it?

- Do help your child define his comfort zone and move out of it step by step.
- Do talk your child through the situation with pleasant, calm language.
- Don't avoid the feared situation.
- Do reinforce and encourage any interaction with a fearful situation—talking about the situation, drawing it, reading about it, role-playing with it.
- Don't aim too high or your child will feel overwhelmed and will either resist or not learn.
- Do give kids a feeling of control by letting them help you decide what steps they are ready for. The more they are involved in the planning, the more likely they will cooperate with the implementation.
- Don't force your child into a situation that is too scary; see what variable you can change to make it feel safer. Remember, kids grow from a place of security, not from a place of fear.
- Do at least some of the challenge to end on a good note. Remember, it's not a race!

HUMOR AND LEVITY, PLEASE!

Whistle while you work? Maybe that's going too far, but any opportunity to make this worry work lighthearted, provided it's at worry's expense and not your child's, can go a long way toward changing the tone, connecting with your child, and making the process more pleasant.

When your child with social anxiety is afraid to order in a restaurant and is practicing with you at home, pretend to be the waitress and say something like this: "No! Not the hamburger with fries! Oh no! I can't take it anymore!" This way you and your child can have a laugh at worry's expense. Or, if you're encouraging your son with OCD to touch a doorknob, use a dramatic rendition of the "I'm melting" scene from *The Wizard of Oz* to show how you're squashing the brain bug: "I'm melting. You've squashed me. Oh, no, I guess I can't bug you anymore . . . . Mommy!!!" Or, for an exposure challenge with a child who is afraid of dogs, pretend to say what the dog is thinking: "Hmmm, where's the nearest fire hydrant? Can't anyone get a decent bone anymore? Boy, would I love to chase a cat right about now."

You may be thinking that these are hardly knee-slappers, and you're right. That's okay. What I have found through working with thousands of children over the years is that even if you're not funny, and your humor is what kids would call "lame," you are helping to lighten the mood and handing them a gift: They can (respectfully) tell you how you're not funny at all. This confidence comes in very handy in that moment and will help them compete with the fear. Remember, always make it clear that you are poking fun at anxiety, not at your child. You are making anxiety look like the unreasonable, bossy and soon-to-be-defeated opponent that it is.

In this chapter we've laid out the steps to follow in teaching your child to reduce the amount of time, distress, and brain circuitry devoted to worry and anxiety. By learning to relabel worry, kids begin to devalue its logic (or lack thereof) and develop more realistic ways of looking at fearful situations. Over time, through these reasoned thoughts, healthy circuits will become more accessible to your child. The path to tempered thinking, greater options, flexibility, and more accurate reasoning will be paved by your child's practice and skill. With pride and relief you will step back and watch your child go!

WHAT IF THE THOUGHTS ARE STUCK AT BEDTIME?: THE DOORS EXERCISE

If your child has done everything you've said but they are still being bothered by the thoughts, help them to move on to something else. Use the doors exercise. Tell the child that after he bosses back his worry, he might try giving his mind somewhere else to go. Ask your child to think of four things he'd *like* to think about: birthday parties he wants to plan, celebrities he'd like to hang out with, animals he loves, Legos projects he wants to build. Have him draw four doors and label them with these topics. Have your child tell you which door he'd like to explore. Tell him he is always free to explore what's behind another door and he can share his explorations with you at breakfast the next day. To keep it interesting, have your child change topics frequently!

WHAT IF YOUR CHILD HAS ALLERGIES OR OTHER REALITY-BASED FEARS?

If your child has a food allergy or other reality-based fear, the master plan still applies, because worry always exaggerates risk—even when some exists. Your child's protector brain may still be in overprotection mode and be holding them back from doing things that even their doctors and parents believe are safe. Do the side-by-side comparison.

Fear	Fact
You have an allergy! You can't try it! You'll get sick!	I do have an allergy. My doctor says it's okay to eat foods with that label.
Don't take a chance; it's better to be safe than sorry.	This is a safe risk. I'll never know if I don't try.
Listen to me! Never take a chance!	My parents and my doctor are telling me it's okay. They know more than my worry does.

Ask the million-dollar question: "What do you think will really happen if you ate that (doctor-approved) food?"

Consult the possibility panel: What do other people who have the same medical condition do? Finally, approach the exposure on purpose: Help your child to be scientific and collect data. Try a safe but avoided food and graph their anxiety symptoms and any physical reactions every minute or two. Repeat the experiment several times with the same food till your child is confident that it is safe. Start the experiment at home, and then generalize to eating that food outside the house as your child feels more comfortable.

Create a stairs of learning for going to friends' houses, first going over without eating, next going over and bringing their own snack, then eating a snack that is parent-approved, with their parent nearby, then doing the solo playdate: eating a snack at the friend's house without Mom or Dad. Your child will learn that worry *isn't* what he needs to take with him to be safe!

DO IT TODAY: BALANCE THE PICTURE—NOTICE WHAT'S NOT WRONG . . . AND EVEN RIGHT IN YOUR LIFE

Children with anxiety have many more negative thoughts traveling down the circuits and pathways of their mind. The worry is maximized on their screen; the joy or even the ordinary is minimized and off their radar. To create a sense of true mastery, we need to encourage our children to get in the habit of noticing and spending time with the things that are going right in their lives—the pleasant moments, the successes they've created but have overlooked or dismissed as unimportant, the surprises, the connections, the joy. Researchers have found that the positive experience of gratitude has many physical, psychological, and social benefits, including reducing anxiety and stress, increasing optimism and positive emotions, and making people feel more forgiving, outgoing, and connected.

How can your child help balance the picture in his mind? Every night before bed, ask your child to list out loud or write down at least five experiences that were positive that day: happy, surprising, funny, interesting, or things he is grateful for. This exercise will work best if you do the exercise, too, to model this behavior for your child. So before bed or at dinner, it's "Give Me Five" time. Over time, the brain will find more of a connection to the positive, and your child won't have to scramble to find those experiences—they will be more visible on his screen.

Chapter 9

THE PROJECT

How to Make the Process Work

Worry is getting weaker because I'm doing more of the things I'm afraid of and seeing that it gets better.

—A TEN-YEAR-OLD WITH PANIC DISORDER

Now when I do OCD rituals I don't feel better anymore. Which is good, because I don't want to do them. I see that they are fake. I can be more brave. It's helping me stop.

—A TWELVE-YEAR-OLD WITH OCD

I've learned to do flooding before I go into a situation. I think of all the ridiculous things that could go wrong, but won't. But since I'm thinking them instead of my worry telling me, I feel strong.

—A FIFTEEN-YEAR-OLD WITH SOCIAL ANXIETY

When talking to children, I refer to the work we do in therapy as "the project." I don't talk about it as treatment or therapy. These terms are often unfamiliar to children—and if the terms are familiar they may have negative connotations. Projects, on the other hand, children understand. From school or around the house, they know that projects take work, have a goal or endpoint, and give a sense of accomplishment and ownership when they're done. Whose project is taking charge of anxiety? Your child's. But it's up to you to present it. In this chapter we look at the top questions that parents ask about the nuts and bolts of making this project work for you and your child.

WHAT EXACTLY IS THE PROJECT? CHILDREN'S SECRET MISSION TO BE INDEPENDENT

Children inherently want to grow and be independent. Yes, they also want us to make their peanut butter and jelly sandwiches for them, but that's only because there are more exciting things that they want to do instead. If we step in and do something that they can already do, we've snatched away their victory. The natural state of human life is to grow toward greater mastery and autonomy. Keep this in mind as you approach the anxiety project. Your child doesn't want to suffer; she wants to succeed—on her own terms and at her own pace.

Now, if you've been dealing with an anxious child for a while, this secret mission of theirs may look *extremely* secret right now, given how much they are regressing and leaning on you for anything and everything. In fact, it may seem as if your child's mission is to do anything but venture out into the world. But your child is not himself right now. Remember, if your child is in an anxious state or stage, he is being controlled in part by the amygdala. When a child is amygdala-driven, things like growth and stretching don't seem possible. They feel like luxuries. Your child just thinks he needs to survive and that his survival is in question as he goes about the challenges in his day. Fortunately, growth awaits on the other side of fear.

The goals of the project are as follows:

- To teach your child to see how worry is the problem, not the challenging situations themselves, and to encourage him to interpret those moments more accurately by seeing what his choices are.
- To get your child to interact with what feel like scary situations more often and more independently in order to desensitize himself, wear out the fear reaction, and build mastery.

The steps your child will learn by taking on this project will serve him well whenever he faces new situations or fears throughout his life. This project isn't a luxury; this is standard equipment for thriving in today's world. Here we go!

STARTING THE PROJECT: WHAT'S THE HOOK? WHAT'S IN IT FOR YOUR CHILD?

Jay's mother gave me a very skeptical look as her son walked in for his first session, a look that said: I really doubt he's going to talk to you. I said to Jay: "You know what I help kids with, right?" "Worries," he replied. "Right," I said. "Is there anything on your list that I can help you with?" "I don't know." "But the things you think about bother you, right? And you'd like not to have to think about them, right? They are stressing you out at nighttime when you want to be sleeping, right?" "Yes," Jay replied. "I can help you." With that one-minute exchange, we were launched into a great session of planning the project of eliminating Jay's bedtime rituals.

What's the "hook" to get your child started on the anxiety project? You might think it has to be a new toy, a pair of sneakers, or an ice cream cone—and there's no problem with sweetening the deal with those items along the way—but deep down what your child wants is to eliminate his worries and be able to do things that other kids do without being upset. So rather than take out your wallet, the first thing you need to do is step into your empathy.

Remember that empathy is about leaning in and supporting your child. Your child is feeling stuck, scared, and often frustrated because of the limits that he perceives that worry is putting on him. Responding with empathy means separating your child from the worry and framing it as an optional, temporary, changeable (unreliable) interpreter of the situation, so your child can choose to listen or not. Part of that empathy is understanding, too, that your child doesn't *want* to have to do this project. He just wants the problem to be fixed. Understanding this will help you be patient and also not expect your child (even if he is cooperating) to whistle a happy tune or thank you for helping him with this work.

ASK YOUR CHILD QUESTIONS SO THEY CAN SEE WHAT'S IN IT FOR THEM

"What bothers you the most about this?"

"What do you want to be different or easier?"

"What would you like to do that worry is making it hard to do?"

"What would you want to do if worry wasn't talking to you?"

When and How to Start the Conversation

A lot of the parents I work with struggle to find the right time to talk to their children about these exercises or about anxiety in general. The heat of the moment is clearly not a good time to first introduce these ideas. But when things are fine, parents are reluctant to raise the topic and "poke the beast." Some dread raising the conversation because they fear that talking about it will make it more of a "thing"—will make it worse. Others avoid the conversation because they don't know exactly what the goal is, and they don't want their child to feel bad.

Anxiety is not a problem that will go away on its own. Avoiding the conversation makes it worse. The goal isn't to make your child recognize he has a problem, but to focus on solutions. You're going to teach your child that he can live unencumbered by worry if he works at it. He's going to do that by hearing his worry differently, and by approaching and interacting with the situations that worry makes him feel like he has to avoid.

For young children: Find a quiet time after dinner or after school and dive in. The first conversation could be as short as five or ten minutes. Here are some starters:

Let's say your child is having trouble going upstairs by herself or going to the bathroom alone, or sleeping by herself.

"You know how it's hard for you to go upstairs without Mom? And you know how you get scared and want the dog to be there if I'm not there?"

"Yes."

"What is your mind telling you about going upstairs?"

"There are bad guys from the movie I saw, and they are going to get me."

"That is a scary thought. Which movie?"

"The one with the zombies."

"You know, I think anyone would be scared thinking that those zombies were going to come alive, but did you know that this can never happen?"

"Why?"

"Because zombies are made up. Just like you make up games with your brother, somebody's job was to make up the zombies from that movie. The actors had to sit for hours while someone put on their costumes and makeup to make them look like that. For hours! Wow, they must have been really bored! They have no special powers. Underneath the costume they're just people like you and me.

"So, zombies aren't real and worry makes things up. It tells us to be afraid and not to do things that are totally fine. What would you like to do if worry weren't bothering you?"

"I'd like to play video games in the basement by myself."

"Okay, great. Let's make a stairs of learning chart and figure out a few things that you can practice to show worry that you can do these things. If you do a courage challenge each day, how long do you think it will take before you're ready to play in the basement?"

"Maybe two or three weeks."

"Great, let's decide the best time to practice."

For teenagers: Teens don't want to be different. Just having the wrong jeans or sneakers can be enough to set them apart; having to deal with anxiety is a difference too far. But ignoring the problem will only leave room for it to grow and become more problematic for them. So jump in—but thoughtfully. It is best to go in with flexible expectations; if your teen senses your pressure, the conversation will be over. You don't need your teenager to make a commitment at this stage. You just want him to explore the possibilities for how things could be and what he might do to get there.

Be open-ended ("How are things going with school?"). Third-person conversations are often most effective with teens: "I know a lot of kids are really stressed about grades and college. Where are you with all of that?" Or, "It seems like there is so much pressure. What's that like for you?"

Keep in mind that awkward silences can be frustrating for teens. They might interpret silence as pressure or a failure on their part. If this is happening, get more specific: "I see that some things are hard for you, and I don't want it to be that way for you." "Lots of people have stress and worry—millions of teens actually—and adults too." You can share briefly your own experiences here in appropriate terms—even if you don't have an anxiety disorder; everyone has anxiety. "Worry is normal and it's part of life. But when it's making things really hard or stressful or you feel like you can't do things because of feeling nervous, then it's out of balance, and there are things that really work to help. Have you thought about that? I know it's not comfortable to talk about. But it's doable. This is something that you can learn about—and pretty quickly—and you can make things better and easier for yourself. Do you want to read about it? Talk to someone? Look at some websites?"

These days, many kids are already searching the Internet about their panic symptoms or social anxiety or OCD. That's good news: They have already started to take ownership of the project. Suggest that they speak to someone, but be open-ended about that, too: "I found someone you can talk to who specializes in anxiety and worry. You can meet with her and see if what she suggests sounds good to you, and then we'll take it from there." Don't fight the fight now about how many sessions it will be, or whether your child is willing to talk at a session. Truly, if your child meets with someone who is helpful, she will talk. Leave some work for the therapist! Tell your teen that you'd like him to try—if he chooses to talk, that's his choice, but why doesn't he wait until he gets there to decide. Give him a wide berth. Tell him, "You be the judge. See what you think. Let's see how it works for you." Let them be window shoppers with no obligation to buy. Remember the secret mission that children are on: They want to be free; if the shoe fits, they'll wear it.

Look back at Chapters 4 and 8 for scripts for explaining to your teen how anxiety tries to fake you out. If your child says that they don't want to talk with you about it, be understanding and also make your point: "I know this isn't what you want to talk about, and I want to respect your feelings, but I need to tell you this: I want things to be easier for you, and I think they can be. I'm not an expert. If we can get the information, you can decide what you want to do. But I'd hate not to offer you this opportunity and for you to find later on that you wish that you had done something when it wasn't as bad." Focus on your child's strengths and goals: "I know there's a lot that you want to do in your life—playing with friends, sports, doing well in school. If you take care of this now, you can be sure that this worry stuff doesn't get in the way of that." "This isn't who you are—it doesn't define you." "Millions of people have anxiety who are very successful—doctors, lawyers, teachers, athletes, artists—but they've got to take charge of it so that they call the shots."

WHAT IF MY CHILD INSISTS HE'S NOT INTERESTED IN WORKING ON THIS, BUT IT'S CLEARLY A PROBLEM?

Many parents tell me that their child won't admit or accept that his worry is a problem. This is where you need to frame the project in terms of what *does* matter to your child. This is especially common with teens. I often connect with children by asking, "Why do you think your parents are worried? Are they making all of this up?" "Okay, let's say your parents are making some of this up because they are worried—but is there some of it that is true?"

HOW DO I MANAGE THE INITIAL RESISTANCE AND EXTINCTION BURST?

The "extinction burst" is the initial backlash or resistance from your child that may occur when after months of reassuring and accommodating your child's fears (to no avail) you switch goals and instead explain to your child that together you will face the worry head-on. The resistance may come out in a burst of protest, or tears, or demands that you answer questions twenty times the way you always have, or walk her upstairs, the way you always did before. And that's the key: she wants things to stay the same—she isn't ready to give up her worry routines, and likely you as the parent have had a big role. She may suddenly react by saying, "Why are you being so mean?! You are the worst parent in the world. If you understood you would never do this!" She may refuse to cooperate. Like the first nights without a pacifier, or sleeping alone, kids are adjusting to a change of plan. An extinction burst commonly occurs when we set out to change a behavior. It's not how they'll feel forever, and it doesn't mean that the change of plan is wrong. Expect the "burst," ride it out, and don't overanalyze it or take it personally.

I know your heart is breaking. But stay the course. You're doing this to free your child, and sometimes breaking free is thorny and uncomfortable. Hang in there. Even though your child is more comfortable when you are reassuring or letting them avoid facing something, they're not really happy. Just like shots or surgery are *planned discomfort* with a purpose—a better and healthier life—so it is with the project of freeing your child from anxiety. So don't give up in the middle of the process. Believe in your child's ability and be patient; you are riding the crest of an invisible wave. Your child's discomfort will resolve. Rather than tell your child why you are changing course, ask him to tell you. He'll see that even though it might not feel good right now, switching gears is really in the service of what he wants.

WHY IS MY CHILD STILL HAVING BAD THOUGHTS? SHOULDN'T THAT STOP?

As much as we'd like the worry thoughts to stop, and fast, the thoughts are actually the last thing that will change for your child because they are the most automatic. The first thing that your child can change is his behavior. That's under his control. He can choose to approach or avoid situations, learn to check things or resist, and as he learns to ignore the worry messages and prove worry wrong, this will create new, more accurate associations with the target situation. So it's not about stopping those thoughts; it's about deciding how you want to respond to them and how much attention you give them. Just as kids ignore ambient sounds—traffic, the humming of air conditioners, or even important sounds, such as your telling them to turn off the TV—kids can have control over how they experience those thoughts by deciding which messages are important to them and which are not.

DO WE MAKE OUR CHILD GO PLACES WITH US OR DO WE LET HIM STAY HOME?

Our son doesn't like to go anywhere new. He is very structured and doesn't like changes in routine, but also he has fears of getting sick if we are away from home, or at a new restaurant. So his automatic response to any idea is no. Do we just stick to the routine, leave him with a sitter, or make him go?

Parents of anxious children struggle with this question, but it's not an either/or. It's not going to work to push, because he'll push back and then everyone will be too upset and worn out to go anywhere anyway. But conspiring with his anxiety by avoiding situations that are perfectly safe sends the message that he can't handle it or that it is dangerous. Share the job. Get to the collaborating table together through empathy so you can get his head nodding in agreement, and even though things seem easy and even enjoyable to you—respect that this isn't where your child is yet. Your understanding of this will help keep your child at the collaboration table. Consider how you would want someone to approach you about your fears. Compassion is the way. The script that follows gets to the heart of the issue of why a child is avoiding doing the work, and what to do. Use the fear thermometer and the stairs of learning, and if your child isn't ready for the particular challenge that is on your calendar, make other arrangements for your child, or see what part he can do. Make sure, however, that you are creating opportunities for your child to work on this fear so that the next time that invitation comes along, he's ready.

"Nate, you don't like going to new places, right?"

"Right!"

"Okay, right, I know that. What does it feel like?"

"I don't know. I just hate it."

"Nate, remember we've talked about how the worry button always says that bad things are going to happen, but when we test worry afterward—what do we find? Is worry right or wrong? Like when we went to that new ice cream place?"

"Worry was wrong."

"Right—exactly. It's wrong every time. You were a little scared at first and then what happened?"

"I was fine."

"Right—yes! You see, worry doesn't learn from experiences; it says the same thing every time, no matter what. But you learn.

"So the family wants to try some new places for dinner. We like trying new things; sometimes that's how we find a new favorite. Because we know it's hard for you, you can choose the one you're ready for. We can go visit, we can look at pictures and menus online, or just go."

"I can't! I'm too scared!"

"I know worry is bugging you about this, but let's see what we know. Let's do wheels of wisdom and wheels of worry. Tell me five words you'd say about a restaurant if worry weren't bugging you."

"Yummy! French fries! Milk shakes! Dessert! Fun!"

"Great . . . now, what does worry say?"

"Don't go, throw up, sick, bad, sad."

"Which one fits the restaurant better? Which one do you want to believe?"

"The first one, but I'm still scared."

"It's okay to be scared and still go, because after a little bit you'll adjust and what? Maybe even be happy that you went; that's how we're going to prove worry wrong. Let's look at those restaurant websites now."

Notice how you avoided saying, "Don't you remember you were fine last time?" It might be true, but this makes the child feel silly for holding on to a worry that makes no sense. By blaming the problem on worry, the child is not the bad guy. Worry is making all the trouble.

WHAT IF MY CHILD HAS AN "UNSUCCESSFUL" EXPOSURE AND WANTS TO QUIT?

It's all systems go. You've done the prep work and are all ready for your child to sleep in her own bed. Then your child melts down and you can see the long arc of a sleepless night for everyone stretching out ahead of you. You scrap the plan. The next night, you want to try again but your child says, "That plan didn't work, so we can't try it again."

Talk to your child about other times when things have had a rocky start but you kept going (like riding a bike or the first day of school). "Maybe you wanted to learn how to ride a bike more than it feels like you want to learn how to sleep by yourself. But remember your goal? You want to be able to do sleepovers this year. This is the way. Last night was tough, but tonight is a new night."

When your child has difficulty with a particular exposure—let's say he tried to go to track practice but only made it to the parking lot—help him interpret the situation accurately by getting specific. Think of the Worry Shrinker machine from Chapter 5. Your child's first thoughts are likely very dramatic and negative: "I'm a failure. I'll never be able to have a normal life. I can't do anything." Keep asking questions to determine what was difficult about that particular exposure. Perhaps your child will say something like "I was tired," or "It was cloudy, and bad weather always makes me feel more nervous." Keep narrowing the situation down and put the problem in the smallest box. For example, your child might say: "I was game to try, but I wasn't prepared for the bad weather, and the fatigue didn't help." Or even just, "That was one tough day. Other days have been easier, and at least I did try."

WHAT IF MY CHILD REFUSES TO DO THE EXPOSURE WE AGREED TO?

This problem can be easier to handle than you think if you apply some of your own flexibility. My rule for my patients is that it's fine to say no to the exposures I suggest, as long as they say yes to something else that is worth their time. Don't overstress. As long as your child is working, they are making progress. You might say something like this: "Okay, I hear you. You're not ready to do this one. We have options. What *feels* too hard about this one? That will help us figure out how to make it work. Or maybe we could find something else to do until you are ready to do that—something that will help move you toward your goal." Notice the power of suggestion here. Don't reinforce your child's feelings, making them into facts. If he says, "I'm not ready," say, "So something is making you *feel* not ready. What do you think it is? What part of what you're trying to do is a problem?"

WHAT IF MY CHILD CHOOSES AN EXPOSURE THAT'S TOO EASY?

Your instinct may be to say, "That's not a good one. You can already do that!" But it's more effective to say, "That could work. I'm just wondering if that's going to give you a sense of accomplishment and satisfaction. Why don't you take a minute to see if there's another challenge that you are ready for." If your child is really stumped, see if you can do his chosen plan, but alter the time (more time) or the support (have the parent be farther away or come later). Yes, you could get frustrated by the lack of cooperation, and it's fine to tell him, "We really need to work together here." But anchor your ship to their destination—where they want to succeed. It will be a lot easier to navigate that way.

WHAT IF MY CHILD CRIES OR STARTS TO THROW A TANTRUM DURING A COURAGE CHALLENGE OR EXPOSURE?

Think about when your child is tired. He'll say every irrational and angry thing, except that he's tired! It's the same with anxiety. When your child feels stuck or overwhelmed with worry, she may say anything under the sun but that. She may lash out at you and say, "You're the worst mom! I hate you!" Understand that it's not personal; it's self-preservation. She is afraid of doing the exposure, and she's afraid that she's going to fail if she doesn't! Stuck between a rock and a hard place, she may turn the anger on you. Certainly make clear that his or her lashing out and hurting other people's feelings is not okay, but do this *after the fact,* when the child can hear you. In the heat of the moment, it's best to empathize first: "I know this is really hard, or this feels really bad to you. I want to help you. I know it *feels* like if I say that you can leave or if I reassure you that that is going to help you, but it's really going to help your anxiety."

If this hasn't calmed your child down, use your flexibility to back away some (it doesn't help your child's desensitization process to be so agitated during an exposure). Some crying or anger may be par for the course, but if your child is getting to that "point of no return," it's best to back up, tell your child you're going to slow down, and think with him about how to make this better. It's important to keep in mind that you're not backing away *from the project,* but reevaluating the specific goal you had for this exposure.

Be careful not to say something out of your own frustration, such as "If you're not going to work on this, forget it!" Your child will be half relieved, but also she'll be convinced that she is incapable or that simple, safe things are too dangerous for her. Instead, come back and end on a good note. Salvage the work you've done so far, work with your child to figure out what part of the day's goal she can do (or even just *imagine* she can do). This is what we call a partial success. You are not hitting the bull's-eye, but you haven't missed the board entirely. Bigger successes are built on moments like these.

WHAT IF MY CHILD WILL ONLY DO EXPOSURES SHE IS COMFORTABLE WITH? DO I FORCE HER?

The short answer is no. Remember, your goal is amygdala-friendly learning. To help your child stay in control, keep interacting with the project, but be flexible and give her choices of how to modulate her contact. There are always options for doing exposure:

- Do it from a distance.
- Do it with the volume off.
- Pretend with your child that you're doing the exposure, or have your child do the exposure in her imagination.
- Draw a picture of it.
- Pretend you are someone else doing the exposure—a celebrity, a superhero.
- Do part of the exposure.

Ask for your child's help. Remember the rule of thumb: It's fine to say no to an exposure as long as your child can find one that is at their level of challenge and that you can say yes to. For example: If she "refuses" to look at the bugs you collected for her, give her options. You can offer, "Can you look with one eye or from across the room?" In other instances you might say, "Can you watch the video of thunder or vomit with the volume off?" Be flexible with the exposure, because you could spend ten minutes fighting about doing the exposure you agreed on and accomplishing nothing, or you could spend two minutes negotiating what you'll do instead, five minutes doing the exposure, and another three minutes celebrating or moving on to the intended next step.

Rule of thumb: If you are getting stuck and your child is saying "no" to the plan, ask him to figure out with you the challenge that he can say "yes" to.

HOW DO I REMIND MY CHILD TO PRACTICE WITHOUT BEING A NAG?

Rather than sounding like the broken record, saying, "You have to practice now," flip it around. Ask your child how he is going to remember to practice his courage challenges. Would he like to "hire" you (free of charge) to remind him? Give your child ownership and responsibility. If he says that he will remember himself, you can reinforce his taking initiative, but also do a couple of reality checks. First say, "That sounds great. Can you just let me know what your plan is so I can cross it off my list?" Second, you can say: "That's great, I'm all for that. I know it can be hard to remember to do these things, or just simply hard to do them period, so I am your backup. Let's see how it goes this week with you taking on the job of remembering. If it goes well, great! If you have trouble with it, we'll reassess on the weekend. If it was hard to remember, then you can think about hiring me to be your coach and remind you to practice."

Using grandma's rule: Just like you have to have dinner before you can have dessert, it is best to have practice time just before doing something else that is a more preferred activity (watch a television show, play a game of catch in the backyard, or be driven to a friend's house). Looking forward to the preferred activity may give your child momentum to muster the courage and power through the courage challenge.

SHOULD I USE REWARDS?

For some kids, rewards are a great way of changing the tone of the worry work. It's about earning freedom, and earning something else special in their life—extra solo time with Dad, those cool sneakers they want, a new book, and so forth. However, for some other kids rewards feel like pressure: If you do X, then you can have Y; instead of a carrot dangling in front of them, it feels like an expectation, and one that they may fall short on.

If your child isn't interested in specific rewards, offer instead a celebration—something fun to do to mark the occasion of your child's accomplishment. If you do use rewards, keep them small and reasonable, like a small toy or an outing after each week or two of hard work. Remember, this isn't a bribe. You aren't "begging" your child to do this work; rewards are giving credit where credit is appropriately due. Don't demand consecutive days of success; expect that there will be good days and harder days. What's important is the overall trend of steady effort your child is making on the project.

As we saw in the master plan in Chapter 8, a simple reward plan is the two-jar system. Fill one jar with marbles and label it "Worry," and leave the other jar, with your child's name on it, empty (for now). Whenever your child does a courage challenge or meets a goal, take marbles from the worry jar and put them in your child's jar. She can trade them in periodically for a treat or celebration.

BE ON THE LOOKOUT FOR SAFETY BEHAVIORS: THEY ARE A TRICK

Quick: Do you think it helps your child if you carry a plastic bag around with you if she is afraid of throwing up? On the surface it might look like a great idea, but look deeper and you'll see that planning for a problem (and an unlikely one at that) raises anxiety levels, rather than lowering them. Remember, you want to go into tough exposure situations with *less* anxiety, and the best way to do this is to pin the problem on the problem: Throwing up isn't the problem! Worry is the problem. You don't need a plastic bag for that!

Safety behaviors, such as sitting by the door because your child is afraid of having a panic attack or speaking quietly because your child is afraid of making a mistake and hopes this way no one will hear, are based on the premise that something bad is going to happen. Eventually you need to take away these crutches to prove to your child that he is fine either way. Help your child see that using safety behaviors is like predicting, or actually expecting, that things will go badly. Instead, share the job of finding a middle ground: sitting in the aisle seat, but not by the door, or keeping the plastic bag in the locker, but not in your backpack. Eventually as your child gains more confidence, he will understand that these so-called safety behaviors were just making him more nervous by bringing unnecessary attention to the dangers that weren't even real risks.

WILL IT GO AWAY?: REASONABLE EXPECTATIONS AND RELAPSE PREVENTION

This is the million-dollar question for desperate parents who are in the midst of the toughest part of this process (a child who is unable to go to school, or go to sleep at night, or be with friends—you name it). Yes, things will improve and you will start to see your child becoming your child again—laughing, being less tense, and not seeming like they are on the brink of disaster or the edge of tears. But remember, worry is a normal experience that comes in the interim between being exposed to something new and actually mastering it. Worry comes and goes with experience. As a result, with every developmental challenge your child tackles—starting a new school, starting to drive, going on a first date, applying to college—you may see a return of worry and apprehension. Don't panic! Your goal is to keep the conversation open for both you and your child, and try to monitor the line between regular worry (which is accompanied by reasonable precautions and behaviors) and excessive worry (and the unnecessary behaviors that come with it). You and your child are both stewards of his growth. So if either of you sees something that would impede it, you both have an interest and a duty to address the issue.

There are many ways to make sure that you are watching that line, without having anxiety, or anxiety treatment, invade your life. Some families will do monthly "appointments" (without a therapist) during which they just do a check-in to see how things are going. Many families will tell me that they hold on to the index cards (their cheat sheet of good boss back talk ideas) and their stairs of learning charts, and that they occasionally review their past work and do a few exposures to keep their tools sharp.

The most important thing is to catch a problem when it is small. Don't wait and watch your child revert back to their anxious ways of reading a situation. Speak up—supportively; for instance: "I know this project is a big stretch—it's new for you. It sounds like worry is getting kicked up because of that. Let's try to separate the facts from the feelings. I know you're scared about this because you haven't done it before, but how do you really think this will turn out? How much of you knows that, fear aside, you will totally get this done as you have other things?"

But if you and your child find that conversations are not moving your child through the anxiety spike, it's time to get some coaching. Check in with your therapist to get back on track, or if you haven't worked with a therapist before, get some guidance about how not to let this slip turn into a slump.

DO IT TODAY: HOW NOT TO BE JUST THE BAD GUY

All work and no play makes kids think of their parents as grumps, and that's not fair or good for anyone! Imagine if you were trying to make a change in your life—lose weight, get a new job, start an exercise routine—and every family interaction you had was someone asking: "What did you eat today?" "How many jobs have you applied for?" "Have you worked out yet?"! The pressure would become its own problem. If you are working regularly with your child on anxiety exposures, make sure that you balance that role with getting the good times in, too. If you do exposures daily, you can spend some time afterward enjoying each other's company without an agenda: playing a game, going for a quick bike ride. Or save up the time and plan a parent-child date once or twice a month, to celebrate the hard work your child has been doing. Children often accuse parents of only caring about their anxiety. Make sure that in your daily conversations you remember your *whole child.* Engage around other interests and activities—so they can remember the very important fact: They are much more than their anxiety.

Chapter 10

THE PARENT'S STANCE

Broadening Your Child's Base in the World and Expanding the Confidence Zone

These words reveal the child's inner needs: "Help me to do it alone."

—MARIA MONTESSORI

You got to learn how to fall
Before you learn to fly.

—PAUL SIMON

Children with an inherited propensity to anxiety do not just become anxious because of their genes, so what we need are ways to prevent the environmental catalysts—in this case, parental behaviors—from unlocking the underlying genetic mechanisms responsible for the disease.

—GOLDA GINSBURG, PH.D., JOHNS HOPKINS UNIVERSITY

What is your role as a parent? So far we've been talking about this in the trenches, that is, the specific steps to take to free your child from anxiety. But as anxiety occurs in the context of a growing child, in this chapter we take the bird's-eye view, to ensure that the approach you take with your child contains the ingredients that are most crucial for fostering growth and resilience overall: autonomy, competence, mastery, and flexibility.

RESETTING YOUR PARENTAL GPS: BUILDING COMPETENCE, NOT REMOVING STRUGGLE

Is this your parenting?

Dylan gets so stressed about school and homework, our whole lives revolve around making sure it gets done. Every night I sit down and tell him what he needs to do. He gets mad and won't listen to me, because he says I stress him out. But I'm the parent, and I know that if he doesn't do it and he's up late, he'll be miserable and will have a horrible day tomorrow. We spend a lot of time fighting, and then either he's staying up too late to finish, or I end up finishing things for him.

Or is this?

Dylan gets so stressed about school and homework, so every day we sit down and make a plan together. I ask him what work he has to do, and ask him what order he thinks he wants to do it in. He schedules two work time blocks—one before dinner and one after dinner. We use the "menu" approach: start with an "appetizer"—an easy assignment—then get to the main dish—the harder work—then end with a "dessert," an easier assignment. I let him take charge of planning which assignment to do in each block. If I think his plan isn't going to work I ask, "I'm thinking about that idea of leaving the hard thing till last: Do you think you'll have enough energy left?" It doesn't always work, but we've agreed on the system together and that helps us a lot. Some nights he can even do the plan on his own.

In a 2011 review, psychologist Jeff Wood and his colleagues at UCLA identified two primary factors that negatively impact children's sense of competency: (1) parental intrusiveness/overcontrol (giving unnecessary assistance, infantilizing behavior, invasion of privacy) and (2) parent modeling of anxiety (describing problems as overwhelming, irresolvable, or dangerous, and discouraging coping behavior). The healthy alternative: granting autonomy, problem-solving together, giving love and support for your child rather than supporting anxiety.[8]

In the first example, Dylan's mom (with all good intentions to avert a disaster the next morning) is taking over. She is doing the planning that her son could do himself or at least participate in. She gets critical, and her son takes offense. Chaos ensues, and the situation ends with mom overfunctioning by completing Dylan's work. In the second example, Mom sees the homework planning as a joint venture, with Dylan doing as much as he can on his own. Does it take a bit more of a leap of faith to work with your child? Yes. Does it take more time? Perhaps initially, but not in the long run. The more your child participates in making the plan, the more he'll buy in and the less he'll fight it. And the benefits of this process will benefit your child far beyond the task at hand. He will see himself (accurately) as a competent, capable problem solver. This is the resiliency equation and the antidote to anxiety.

Often, in my experience, parents overfunction either for expediency ("There is much to do and it will be faster if I do it") or guilt ("He is struggling so much already; I'll do whatever I can to help"). Sometimes it is impatience, perfectionism, or difficulty tolerating uncertainty and struggle ("I just want it to be done right, so this way if I do it, I know it will be"). But just as children need to see beyond the anxious moment and understand that this discomfort is temporary, parents need to do the same. Get ready: You are going to get braver and wiser through this process too. Call on your best self, and you will bring out the best in your child.

THE SOLUTION: UNDER-FUNCTION STRATEGICALLY: BE A GOOD-ENOUGH PARENT

One parent told me that the clearest advice I ever gave her was when her children were calling out to her that they couldn't find something—their cleats, their homework, the peanut butter—to reply like this: "Look harder!" As a highly motivated woman who was very concerned about being a good parent, it had never occurred to her to wait. Just wait. Maybe even offer support, but from a distance, to see what her kids might be able to come up with on their own. The same goes for an anxiety situation, when your child is desperately saying: "I'm stuck in a ritual," or, "I can't e-mail the teacher," or simply: "I can't do this—can you?" Doing *for* kids convinces them that the task is too hard, that you don't believe they can do it, that it's better to rush to get it done than take the extra time to let them struggle a little and then arrive at a solution. Waiting and encouraging them from the sidelines gives them the opportunity to be the hero. To see what it's like to win, to stand up to the bully in their mind and not get tricked, or scammed, or deprived of what they really want to do. By under-functioning in kind, strategic ways, you enable your child to function "up."

Dr. Donald Winnicott coined the term "the good-enough parent" to describe the best fit between a child's needs and a parent's responses. The best relationship between parent and child, he argues, is one that leaves room for growth by requiring the child to manage some disappointment or frustration. In manageable doses, this frustration gives the child the opportunity to learn tolerance for managing the discomfort that occurs between the need and the relief. Good-enough parents—who don't meet every need, or prevent every disappointment, or remove the source of frustration each time—foster true strength and growth. While behavior therapy is about planned discomfort, parenting is about fielding *unplanned* discomfort—which usually is quite manageable. We can't take away the unfriendly child who says no to your child on the playground, or the B–, or the college rejection, but we can clear the way to teach our children that *they* can handle it.

When our GPS is set to our children's happiness, it requires us to eliminate obstacles, foresee problems, run out at 10:00 at night to get supplies they forgot, stop talking about things they want to avoid—in short, to tiptoe around any chance of disappointment or discomfort. And it means doing all the work ourselves. What kind of message are we sending to our children if they need to passively wait for us to fix problems for them? Waiting for us to make it better deprives kids of a sense of competency—and this can become fertile soil for the seeds of anxiety to take root.

What's the alternative to swoop and rescue? Slow down. Under-function strategically. Create a conversation and ask questions. Share the job of shifting perspective and finding the solution with your child.

In every anxiety moment, you and your child have choices. Choices to see things differently, to separate your child from the fear, to tiptoe into the swimming pool. Making choices makes your child feel successful, included, and *normal*. How do you enable your child to make choices? By asking the right questions and waiting for the answers. There are two questions to keep in your pocket, like master keys to unlock a moment from worry's clutches:

Change perspective: "What is worry telling you about this? What do *you* think about it and why?"

Change behavior: "What part of this do you think you can do? What's the biggest step you're ready to take today to prove worry wrong?"

So when you are about to swoop down and fix whatever your child is struggling with, wait. Pause and center yourself, decatastrophize, and consider this: Is what you are about to do good for your child, or good for their anxiety? Are you building their competence by sharing the job and working together with your child, or inadvertently reinforcing their doubt and dependence by doing things for them that they could do for themselves? Doing something good for your child means you are showing them how they can solve the problems themselves (or at least share in that problem-solving). Good for anxiety means doing something that keeps them scared, passive, and dependent on you. Hanging back doesn't mean that you are withholding support from your child; it's just a different kind of help. Picture two jars: One is the Doing for Your Child jar; the other is the Doing with Your Child jar. If you are only filling up the first jar, you're setting your child up for anxiety because she won't get to learn. If you fill up the second jar, you are scaffolding, teaching your child how to do things, and then little by little you fade yourself out of the picture as your child can do more and more on her own. You know which jar is going to be best to fill up.

HOME IS THE BEST PLACE TO PRACTICE FEELING UNCOMFORTABLE

A huge part of your role as a parent is to teach your child that discomfort is temporary and not something to be afraid of, and to give your child opportunities to feel uncomfortable. Discomfort is a necessary middle step before mastery happens. Families are the best and safest place for children to work on this. We may think that making home safe means working around all of a child's fears and making her comfortable all the time. But the family context of warmth, love, support, and constructive criticism allows children to try out small doses of adversity, to make choices, and to problem-solve. Over time, this base of competency, and a child's identity as someone who counts, expands out into the world.

Look at the options that follow. At the end of the interaction, what's going to be stronger—your child, or his fear?

OVERDOING SUPPORTS FEAR

- Are you doing things for your child he could do himself (ordering in a restaurant, e-mailing a teacher, calling a friend)?
- Are you helping your child avoid (sleeping in parents' room, staying home from school when they have a book report)?

- Are you spending time supporting your child's fear—staying up past your bedtime talking with your child when he is doing rituals or seeking reassurance?
- Are you failing to ask for your child's input and relying solely on your own opinion?
- Are you answering questions your child could answer himself?

SUPPORT YOUR CHILD BY COLLABORATING

- Wait to see what your child can do himself, or ask what he can do, or offer to do some parts, while he does others (he orders drink, you order meal; he dictates e-mail to teacher).
- Help your child approach a problem by breaking it down into small parts, parts he can do himself, parts he needs help with.
- Spend time supporting coping: doing exposures with your child.
- Ask, don't tell: Ask your child what he thinks the answer is to his reassurance question.

HOW TO MAKE THE CHANGE: FROM SWOOPING TO SUPPORTING FROM THE SIDELINES

Many parents are ambivalent about this advice at first. They think that waiting to help a struggling child is mean, or withholding. The fact that your child is accusing you of these things may make it harder to see that this is not the case. It's all in the presentation and your intention. While your heart may be straining, in your head, remember that there is a clear line between setting healthy limits and boundaries and ignoring your child or saying hurtful, uncaring things. Your purpose in holding back is to give your child the chance to build her own sense of competency; in order to do so, you have to make room for it. You are going to "under-function" using kind, clear, firm language like this:

- "I want to help *you,* not your anxiety."
- "Your anxiety isn't being fair to you. It may seem like it's protecting you, but it isn't."

- "I know this is hard, especially at first, and I want to help you. The only way that can happen is if we are both working together."
- I support you 100 percent. If I support the anxiety and what it wants, I'm not supporting you."
- "Let's figure out together how you can move forward. Any steps you take are good."
- "I am here to help you work and get better. You are my top priority. I know you can do this."
- "I will work with you. Let's do this together. What part of it can you do now?"

As we saw in Chapter 9, "The Project," there may be an initial backlash or extinction burst when you change your approach. Hang in through the protests and accusations that you are a mean parent. You know why you are doing this. Your child won't thank you, but seeing his progress will be thanks enough.

THE PROBLEM WITH REASSURANCE

So many parents start off their meetings with me explaining how they've responded to their children's concerns. They've reassured their child up and down that the thunder won't hit the house, or that the dog will never bite, or that they won't throw up at school, but clearly the fact that they are sitting in my office tells me this strategy hasn't worked. It's not that these parents have done anything wrong. The instinct to reassure is totally natural. But if it doesn't work right away, you've got an anxious child, and rather than your words lifting your child's burden, you seem to be pouring reassurance down the drain.

Does this mean there isn't a role for parents? No. There absolutely is. An even more powerful one—you are going to find the teachable moments and keep your child in the growing zone.

ACCOMMODATING, ENABLING, CAVING IN: WHAT'S THE DIFFERENCE?

"We just think that we are caving in to the misbehavior if we change our plans because she's not comfortable. She should just behave!"

Anxious behavior isn't *misbehavior.* Misbehavior is intentionally doing things that you know are wrong. Avoiding, doing rituals, or being scared is not a choice your child is making. The more you think of your child's behavior as volitional and respond to it as such, the more your child will misbehave—because she'll be angry and feel she has to keep showing you how bad things are until you get it. Your role is to teach her to communicate effectively. If she is having trouble, rather than getting angry or acting out, she can learn to say, "This is too hard for me," or, "This makes me so angry," or, "I'm not ready yet, can you help me?"

What does it mean to accommodate and how is that different from "enabling"? Accommodating means adjusting your expectations so that they are in line with your child's current abilities; enabling, on the other hand, means that likely your child is capable of doing more, but with both of you believing that anxiety is right, you adjust plans for them to do less. When enabling happens, parents feel resentful and defeated and kids never get to see what they are capable of. It's a lose-lose. With this understanding of enabling as enabling the anxiety to live unchallenged, the antidote to enabling is collaborating on the project. For example, if your child is having trouble going to bed at night, accommodating means working out a plan where you each have a job: your child is going to work on coping at night, for example, doing the doors exercise (see page 163), doing her side-by-side comparison of nighttime fears versus facts, and her boss back talk. You are going to accommodate the fact that she's not quite ready to fall asleep without your support, so you agree to check on her every five to ten minutes till she is asleep.

Enabling means enabling the anxiety to live happily in your child and family, rather than challenging its presence. In this scenario, camping out in your child's bed keeps the fear intact. It is agreeing that the situation is too hard or too scary for your child and shouldn't be challenged. Other examples of enabling would be if your child is afraid of making phone calls, making them for him; if he is afraid to eat food you've cooked, buying only packaged food.

THE PLACES YOU GO WHEN YOU'RE AFRAID TO SAY NO: BEING THE ONE WHO KEEPS REALITY IN THE PICTURE

When parents come in to see me, they are often relieved to be able to finally vent to someone about how ridiculously turned upside down their lives have become because of their child's anxiety. A child with OCD has herself trapped in her room because of contamination fears and has the family members trained to take off their shoes and change their clothes before entering her room or none of the family is "allowed" to sit in the kitchen chairs because they are contaminated; a child with a panic disorder dictates that the family have no social life; a child with a bug phobia is sleeping under layers of blankets in the summer, to make sure that nothing gets her; a child with separation anxiety is sleeping in Mom's bed and has relegated Dad to the family room couch. What's wrong with these pictures? These children aren't trying to manipulate and destroy order in your household, but their anxiety may well do that job for them.

Remember GUTI—getting used to it. Feeling uncomfortable (especially in low-stakes small doses, like eating the wrong kind of cookies, not being able to watch on the "good TV" all the time, or using the wrong color pens) is exactly the kind of discomfort anxious kids need to practice on to feel *more* secure, especially when it comes to the truly demanding anxiety challenges.

If you don't need everything to go exactly right—it gives you a lot more breathing room and buffer when things go wrong. So while your child's distress and protests may suggest that these are unbearable circumstances, remember, compassionately, that they are not.

It's essential that someone in the family remain reality based.

Anxiety is greedy and can gobble up your child, your family life, and your marriage if you let it. Worry will get bigger and bigger unless someone—usually the parent—functions as the reality check. The reality checker needs to present his or her findings in a clear but amygdala-friendly way. You're not going to say: "I refuse to do this for you; I'm the parent!," or, "Deal with it yourself!" You will state the facts: "This is not working for anyone. No one is sleeping. We have to make this work for everyone. We will help you with your anxiety, and you need to help us, too."

Collaboration: If something is wrong—figure out how to make it right, together. Enlist your child's help in figuring out a better solution for the whole family: "Everybody needs to sleep. If you're calling out, you're waking up the other kids. It's okay if you need our help, but we have to figure out how you can manage without waking everybody up." Notice, too, that when you are *asking* questions rather than giving answers, kids are using their "smart brain" or thinking brain. They are also more likely to stick with a solution that they had a hand in authoring.

GET USED TO SEEING SOME SIGNS OF ANXIETY

"When I see him skipping sports practice, I feel like he's a kid touching the stove—he's going to get burned, and I have to stop him. I know that missing out on things will only hurt him down the road."

While this well-intentioned dad has a point, you have to be realistic in your expectations. Even though you'd feel better if your child never gave in to anxiety and you could banish it from your house, that would be unnatural; this is going to be a process. When parents become the "anxiety police" and get upset every time their child exhibits anxious behaviors, it just puts more pressure on the child. If he feels that he's letting you down, he gets detoured from the *real* project; he'll be feeling like he has to take on the project of pleasing you or not making you angry.

So lower the intensity, accept that your child is going to feel and look anxious, and focus on your goal of working together. You and your child are on the same side against the anxiety, and together you can figure out how to challenge anxiety's rules gradually. After talking with his son, this father was able to change his tune and say: "Worry is really trying to fake you out about practice. It's saying you're going to get sick. Let's do the side-by-side comparison. What do you think is really true? What part of this do you think you can do?" His son felt better that his dad understood that he really felt scared and was helping him take charge of the fear, and the dad, even though he still had to be more patient than felt natural, felt good knowing that he was part of the solution instead of part of the problem.

BEYOND ANXIETY: HELP YOUR CHILD BECOME ACCUSTOMED TO UNCERTAINTY, DISAPPOINTMENT, AND OTHER UNCOMFORTABLE EXPERIENCES IN EVERYDAY LIFE

There are lots of skills your child can develop that will help them thrive in the world beyond their fears and worries. The components that make up a healthy emotional diet for your child may not be what you think. Here are a few new ingredients to get you started.

Uncertainty Training: Wait, Wait, Don't Tell Them

"She doesn't like 'maybe.' 'Maybe' feels like an emergency in our house."

All kids ask questions. But anxious children's questions are persistent—there is more than curiosity riding on their words, and it can feel like a life-or-death situation. They can't handle "maybe;" they don't like "I'm not sure." When your child is afraid, his mind is saying, "What if this happens? What if that happens?" Feeling that the uncertainty is intolerable, he is looking to you for the final answer to stop all of his doubts, the ultimate reassurance to say he will definitely not fail the test or throw up tomorrow.

Anything short of a definitive answer, any trace of doubt may leave him feeling frantic. He needs to learn that the presence of some doubts and uncertainty doesn't detract from the facts of his realistic thinking. While being compassionate to how your child *feels,* you want to help him see that not knowing "for sure" is normal and manageable and certainly isn't an emergency. Given the fact that we can't know everything, this is good resiliency training for life.

Here are some tips for how to work on this at home:

Be honest. If you aren't completely sure about something, say so. Emphasize that not knowing everything for certain shouldn't stop you from acting on what you think is more or most likely.

Share mixed opinions. Your child may demand the right answer, like on the game show: *Is that your final answer?!* But some questions are more complex. Explain that part of you feels X, and part of you feels Y. It's not wishy-washy; it's just real.

Leave some questions open. Even though some questions feel like an emergency to your child, you know they're not. If you are in the middle of something and really can't talk at that moment, don't perpetuate the emergency classification of the question by answering things that you can't or answering them right away. Help your child learn how to wait, or manage that "I don't know for sure" feeling for a little while. Let him know when you'll be able to get back to it and suggest that he move on to other things. If he doesn't know what to do, have him make a Things I Can Do Alone list (in a calm moment) and consult that.

Give Your Child the Gift of Flexibility

You can't always get what you want.

—MICK JAGGER

"Only I can put her to bed—she refuses to let anyone else." "He will only ride in my car; he won't go with anyone else." Yes, children have preferences, and, as we've said, we want to encourage the "chooser" in our kids, but we do our children a disservice by not giving them the opportunity to practice changes of plans or disappointment from time to time, especially in the safe comfort of their own home, so that they'll know what to do when they have to face disappointment out in the world.

Here are some suggestions for how to work on this at home:

If you're out of their favorite cereal, don't run to the store. Sometimes not getting what you want can be the very best thing.

Switch it up. Make a new plan (coinciding with a new season, a new school year, or even just a new week): "Dad will be putting you to bed a couple of nights a week" (when the child prefers Mom). "He wants to spend time with you, and you and Dad can figure out your own special bedtime routine."

Let someone else choose. Many families work around the choices of the anxious child—for what to watch on TV, what to eat, where to go—at the expense of the rest of the family. If you have other children, make a rotation that allows everyone to take turns choosing the restaurant or the movie, or which side of the car they sit in, and so forth. Protests aren't permanent. Disappointment wanes.

DISCIPLINE AND THE ANXIOUS CHILD: USE YOUR BEST SELF TO TALK TO YOUR CHILD

Parents often come to sessions in tears because another sibling has spoken the truth: "He gets away with everything. You spend all your time with him. I do everything right and no one even notices." This gives parents a bad feeling in the pit of the stomach. Like any child, the anxious child needs limits and discipline. Being clear about rules and expectations helps maintain a sense of order, structure, and control. Children feel safer with this clarity (though they won't tell you this!) because without it, there is a sense that no one is in charge. Remember too that discipline is about learning, not about punishing.

If a child with anxiety is yelling, cursing, or acting disrespectfully, ignoring that behavior can amount to condoning it. Setting limits doesn't mean that you are going to get into a fight by immediately threatening consequences or time-outs. And you should never punish your child for being anxious. But you *should* intervene if your child is being disrespectful, dangerous, irresponsible, or insensitive. This may happen when a child is feeling stressed and anxious, but you need to respond clearly: "I know you're anxious, or stressed, but it's not okay to talk to us like that. That's not what we do in our family. We need to figure out a different way." You can accept the feeling that your child is having—anger, frustration—but put limits on the behavior:

- "This isn't okay with me. This isn't how we treat each other."
- "This isn't how I want to be talking with you, and I don't think you want to be talking this way to me."
- "We need to do things differently. It's not working out for the family this way. We need to work together to make it better for everyone."
- "I know you want to say something to your brother, but you need to try that again with different words."

Over time, as your child learns that everyone is accountable for their behavior (that means you, too, apologize when you make a mistake, and that you are sensitive to others' needs), your child will know those house rules so well that when he is misbehaving you might simply be able to say: "What do you think I'm going to say here?" Or, "What do you think needs to happen?" You don't need to be the one giving the discipline, or the answers; it's even better when your child can fill in the blanks. She will feel respected and responsible when you give her the chance to show what her better self would do in the situation, even if it's in the "take two."

ARE YOU MODELING ANXIETY OR COPING?

Children, especially those who are vulnerable to developing an anxiety disorder because of genetic or other factors, are constantly on the lookout for cues about what is dangerous and what is not. A parent can inadvertently prime the anxiety pump for a child in two major ways: first, by describing situations as overwhelming, too hard, or too scary; and second, by avoiding certain situations. A parent who says, "I don't want to go to that meeting or party; there will be too many people there, and I can't deal with that" teaches their child that uncomfortable situations or experiences are unmanageable.

What if these *are* your feelings? You have at least two important reasons to rethink them: your own freedom and well-being, and your child's. You probably know how unpleasant and challenging it has been for you to carry these negative expectations for many common experiences in life. This is your chance to help your child have a different path. Here are some do's and don'ts to get you both started on that new path:

HOW NOT TO MODEL ANXIETY

Do's: Keep your fears to yourself, or share them with your spouse, a friend, or a therapist, not your child. Encourage your child to draw his own conclusions about the relative risks in a situation. Approach a situation by preparing him to master it. If there is some teaching you need to do, state these lessons in terms of how to be safe, rather than how dangerous something *could* be.

Don'ts: Don't confuse your fears with the facts. For instance, if you are afraid of germs and contamination, don't say: "Don't touch that! [for instance, a pen at the bank]. Who knows who touched that?! You'll get sick, and you'll get the rest of us sick." Instead (assuming that the risk is just in your head), try not to say anything, or if you do speak, say: "Dad is working on his own brain bug here. Help me boss it back! We both know it's okay." Don't create a negative self-fulfilling prophecy by describing neutral experiences that you are not comfortable with as dangerous, or irresolvable other than through total avoidance.

WHEN PARENTS DISAGREE ON APPROACH

"My husband thinks we are caving in by working on these things step by step. He resents the time that it takes, and that it takes away from the other kids. I feel that way, too, but I just don't think she can do this without our help. What do we do?"

A couple is a unit, and often even unconsciously they balance each other out: If one is going too far in the direction of making room for the child's fears, not challenging them, the other parent may come in to compensate by pulling in the other direction. Find the middle ground. Make it safe to acknowledge that you both are upset about what's happening for your child, and you both want things to be better for her. Be willing to take a step out of your comfort zone—whether that is under-functioning a little or being more supportive. It's okay for parents to have different roles as long as they don't cancel each other out. And remember that it's not all on the two of you: Your child is part of the solution too.

IN TOUGH MOMENTS, ANXIETY IS NOT AN EXCUSE FOR UNACCEPTABLE BEHAVIOR

Discipline with Love

Phoebe, age nine, suffered from panic attacks and separation anxiety. Going to school, driving in the car, going out to unfamiliar (or even familiar) places were all challenges that left Phoebe begging her mother to let her stay home. Often Phoebe's protests were expressed through anger rather than fear: "You aren't helping me! You make things so hard for me! I can't do this! You don't care about me!"

After a couple of months of working on the project of bossing back and correcting her worries, Phoebe was making headway. The shift had happened for her when she started to care more about what she was missing out on in life than about listening to worry and "playing it safe." She began to be able to go to school more easily and was ready to tackle the rest of the challenges on her stairs of learning: going to a friend's house, going on errands without panicking in the car, even going to the movies. One weekend when the rest of Phoebe's family was away, she told her mom that she was ready to tackle the challenge of going to a restaurant (which was particularly scary because, like many anxious kids, she had the fear that she would throw up if she ate away from home).

They went to the agreed-upon restaurant and waited in line. And waited. Something they hadn't counted on. The longer Phoebe waited, the more time she had to think and overthink, and she began to panic about getting sick. Feeling out of control and exposed, she begged her mom to leave and started out the door. Phoebe got scared when Mom didn't immediately follow, so Phoebe came back in. Upset, Phoebe started to lash out at her mom: "Why did you take me here? I hate this restaurant! Why are you making me stay?!"

Layne, Phoebe's mom, calmly but firmly told Phoebe that she would help her, but that she couldn't continue to talk like that. The behavior continued. Phoebe was whining and refusing to calm down. At first, not wanting to let anxiety win, Layne insisted they stay. As time went on, however, and Phoebe refused to cooperate with her mom's instructions, Layne knew that even if things improved, she wouldn't be able to enjoy a meal at the restaurant. She was too exhausted emotionally to stay, and also felt that Phoebe was not deserving of the opportunity to eat out because of her misbehavior. Layne said, "It's time to go," that they would try again another time in happier circumstances. Seeing her mom being firm, Phoebe started to calm down and begged her mom to stay at the restaurant, but things had gone too far. They left. Layne didn't get angry or punish Phoebe, but she clearly told her they would try again another time, and that Phoebe could not behave like that again.

That night Phoebe wrote her mother a note. She said, "Mommy, I am truly sorry for not staying at the restaurant with you tonight and for the way I acted, and I would like to make it up to you." She had a written invitation behind her back and gave it to Mom. It said: "You are invited to have brunch with Phoebe—a gift paid for by me! When: 11:00 a.m. tomorrow. Where: Bob Evans. Please accept this invitation so I can show you how sorry I am for my behavior last night." She had drawn a check box next to the words "yes" and "no." At the end of the invitation she used sparkled nail polish and painted a big pink heart at the bottom of the page.

The breakfast happened, and Phoebe, though she had to wait for the success and it was a rocky road getting there, enjoyed it in spades that morning. Anxiety or not, parents need to help their children be accountable for their behavior. Even though it may take longer to get to the triumph—it's worth the wait.

GENERAL GOOD PARENTING STRATEGIES FOR GRANTING AUTONOMY RATHER THAN BEING CONTROLLING OR INTRUSIVE

Do's:

- Let your child do for himself the things he can: choosing clothes, choosing food, making social plans.
- Help your child when it is appropriate and when they ask. Approach that help with a job-sharing stance.
- Encourage your child to ask questions for themselves, order in restaurants for themselves, approach and interact with peers.
- Respect privacy no matter the age of the child. Include your child in decision-making when appropriate (what clothes they want to buy, which friend they want to have over).
- Elicit your child's input and opinions in conversations to make clear that they have a voice.
- Give your child choices in schedule making where appropriate: Rather than micromanage every minute, set parameters for when they need to be ready for bed or finished with their homework, giving them room within those limits to choose how they will use that time. Check in as needed to ensure that they are staying on track.
- Give appropriate chunks of responsibility to your child (ask them what they think they can reasonably take charge of) and let children hire you to be a "reminder" (versus a nagger) as needed.

Don'ts:

- Don't get involved and do for your child what they can do for themselves—even if it is faster or easier for you to get it done.

- Don't use baby talk or refer to your child as a little boy or girl when they aren't babies.
- Don't invade their privacy (not knocking before walking in, looking at your child's journal or phone without asking or warning, insisting that a child talk about a personal matter if they aren't ready).
- If your child is in a new or uncomfortable situation, don't rub her shoulders or soothe her, as this cues their fear rather than their competence and will send the message "You should be anxious and needing reassurance in this situation." Instead, give some space and provide that assurance when your child asks for it.
- Don't be critical. Avoid a negative bias in your interactions: Make sure that you notice what your child is doing well. When you need to correct your child, make it a collaboration. Ask: "Can you guess what I'm going to say here?" Often anxious children, so eager to please and be rule followers, know very well what is wrong, and if they can tell you first, without your needing to correct, all the better.

SHOW WARMTH!

Anxious children, more than other children, are constantly on the lookout for signs that people are angry or disappointed with them, and they often interpret neutral affect (a teacher with a neutral expression) as anger. Studies have shown that low levels of warmth in parents—not smiling, exhibiting positive affect, or offering loving gestures—are associated with anxiety in children. Find a way to express your enjoyment, pride, and appreciation of your child. It doesn't have to be with hugs and kisses if this is not your family's way; sharing a sense of humor, a knowing smile, signals to your child that all is well.

DO IT TODAY: MAKE SURE YOU ARE GIVING YOUR CHILD OPPORTUNITIES TO GROW

Take a minute to write down three ways that you are supporting your child's anxiety and three ways that you want to support your child. Have your spouse (or a grandparent, babysitter, or teacher) do the same. Compare notes and give credit for resisting the urge to "do for" your child. The golden rule for anxiety: Only do for your child what he can't do for himself.

Part III

ALL WORRIES GREAT AND SMALL

Common Childhood Fears and Worries and Problem Anxieties

No two children are exactly alike, and children with anxiety are no exception. Children's anxieties are a unique combination of genetics, temperament, and experience in the world and the specific things that they fear are a reflection of those combined factors. What can be very reassuring to children and parents alike, though, is that there are common underlying patterns in the way children's anxiety manifests itself—supporting the idea that these glitches are nobody's fault.

In this section we will examine the most common subtypes of anxiety that children experience, and each chapter focuses on a specific diagnosis and ways that it is treated. It is not possible to address every worry or anxiety situation in this book (though believe me, I've tried!), but you will at least find close cousins of your child's situation and be able to apply the principles outlined here to your child. If your child has symptoms of multiple diagnoses, as many children do, you can jump around among the chapters to get the information you need. And even if your child does *not* meet the criteria for a diagnosis, the strategies in these pages will give you a behind-the-scenes look at what the symptoms are all about, and ideas about what to try at home. Familiarizing yourself with how worry works and how to best address it will prepare you to be a wonderful (and effective!) coach for your child.

While there are very specific strategies for some diagnoses, the underlying ideas are always the same: See worry as separate from your child, help your child identify the mistake the brain is making and why, teach your child to retrain the brain by under-reacting to unnecessary signals, and, finally, break worry's rules—have your child do what feels uncomfortable at first and watch the discomfort pass as you see all the good things that happen when your child is not missing out on life! GUTI (or "Getting Used to It") with small steps using the stairs of learning is the way your child will prove to herself that she can do things just like other kids, even if her mind is telling her otherwise. Remember that it is never too early to teach your child to manage her worry thinking—and likewise it's never too late. Try these strategies on yourself when you recognize your worry racing ahead or find yourself spinning in a wheel of "what-ifs." Verbalize, analyze, and get your smart brain working to rewire your anxious moments. You'll be that much calmer when your child comes to you for help.

Chapter 11

FROM EVERYDAY WORRIES TO GENERALIZED ANXIETY DISORDER

A good imagination is good; too much imagination . . . that can be really awful!

—A SIX-YEAR-OLD WITH GAD

I worry so much about the future. I don't even have time to enjoy what's happening right now.

—A TWELVE-YEAR-OLD WITH GAD

Nina worries about everything. Sometimes I think that the world is just not made for anxious kids. People say things all the time that they don't mean, but Nina takes it all to heart. Her teacher says to the class, "You'll never go home unless you quiet down." Nina immediately starts worrying about staying at school forever. These things happen all day long.

Mitch puts so much pressure on himself. We don't know where it comes from. We don't pressure him about grades; in fact, we are trying to convince him to stop working so hard. It sounds backward, but he makes himself sick needing everything to be perfect.

WHAT IT FEELS LIKE FOR YOUR CHILD: NO DEGREES OF SEPARATION BETWEEN CATASTROPHE AND YOU

Although many kids have worries that come and go, children like Nina and Mitch have worries that take on a life of their own. Any snippet of information is immediately processed for what could go wrong. Even the best of situations—like a birthday party—is gutted by worry: Will we be late? What if people don't have fun? What if I mess up? What if we run out of cake? What if it rains? The anxiety is at once effortless and automatic, and incredibly draining. And worry also barges in when undesirable situations occur: if a child learns of a fire, a layoff, or an illness affecting someone else, even someone he doesn't know, he immediately thinks, "Will this happen to us?"

It's not the *content* of the worry that's unusual. After all, any child might have concerns when hearing about something unfamiliar or frightening. But for most children, these fears are a passing thought and are easily allayed by parents' explanations, or are simply forgotten over time. For children diagnosed with Generalized Anxiety Disorder (GAD), there is no forgetting, there is only anticipating, and anticipating the worst, whether it is about health, finances, or academic or athletic performance. Generalized anxiety disorder is characterized by excessive worry that is constant and feels uncontrollable. Though their fears are typically remote, children with GAD live "as if" the catastrophes have already happened or are on the verge of happening.

Being unwittingly locked into disaster mode makes kids mentally exhausted, and it takes a toll on the body, too; another cardinal symptom of GAD is the inability to relax. Children may have difficulty sleeping and suffer from headaches and stomachaches. Constantly firing up the emergency "fight-or-flight" equipment, the brain of the GAD child eventually assumes that it is necessary to stay in high-alert mode. Everyday concerns—being on time for the bus, having people like them, completing homework—register to these children like mission impossible. Given how they approach these situations as if they are hanging on by their fingernails, one might be surprised to learn that most kids with GAD are excellent students, entirely responsible and successful—not *because* of their worrying, but *in spite* of their worry. Nevertheless, their competencies and excellent track record bring them no relief. Even though they've done everything handily many, many times before, the thought plagues them: "This time *could* be different." Life is a cliff-hanger.

Every day children with excessive worry and GAD feel how we might feel when we receive bad medical news, or an unexpected bill, when no amount of reassurance can release us from worry's grip. Powered by a supersonic imagination, the worry radar stays on all the time. Whereas kids with fears and phobias have excessive fears about a specific situation—dogs, insects, thunder—for kids with GAD, worry is pervasive, a free agent that can latch on to any passing situation. Children with GAD can pick up the weakest signal, the most inconsequential aberration, and misinterpret that signal as something urgent and inevitable. Kids with GAD live on "borrowed worry," spending endless time struggling with concerns that really belong to other people.

Take Elizabeth, for example, a straight-A student in school with impeccable behavior who wouldn't so much as blink an eye if it were against the rules. Yet she sits in front of me, wringing her hands, explaining why she is up until midnight every night worrying. She can't stop worrying about school because she doesn't want to go to the principal's office. She explains, "He has a mean face. When he gets angry he yells until he turns red." But it's not just the principal; it's also the teacher. "She's stressed and she gets mad a lot and yells. And if we don't finish our work in school, we'll have to stay after. If we talk in class, we miss recess. If we get in trouble more than once, we'll have to go to the principal and we'll get detention. If we don't write our name on our papers, we don't get credit. If we put our name in the wrong box, we get an F. And cheating—don't even ask, we get our tests taken away." At night Elizabeth is so keyed up that she spends from nine p.m. to midnight trying to figure out what she might have possibly done wrong at school that day to make sure that she won't find out the next day that she's in trouble. She is beside herself with worry.

We could say that Elizabeth has had her worry wires crossed with the proverbial kid "in the back of the class," the child who doesn't listen and breaks the rules. This is the child whom the teacher is *really* directing her comments to, not to the Elizabeths in the class. If only the teacher could flash the message (in bright lights) that Elizabeth's brain is missing: "This isn't about you."

THE DIAGNOSIS

Generalized anxiety disorder is a condition that afflicts anywhere from 2 to 19 percent of children and adolescents. For someone to be officially diagnosed with GAD, the worry and associated symptoms must be present for at least six months. Children with GAD wiring struggle with a system that is overprogrammed to find the element of fear or potential for problems in any situation. Rather than there being six degrees of separation between kids and any catastrophe, the worry insists it is a clear and present danger. These are not just children who wonder "what if?"; they are braced for it every day. A key sign of GAD is that the worry is many steps removed from the initial situation. A child gets a ninety-four on a test and is worried about how this will affect her college career and future employment; when the grill chef at a Japanese restaurant is poised to (skillfully and carefully) "throw" food into his customers' mouths as part of his thrilling performance, she's sure she will go to the hospital choking, or maybe even die. Here are some indications that a child may be suffering from GAD:

RED FLAGS

- Always has a list of worries (topics can change daily)
- Needs to know details ahead of time and has pressing questions about logistics
- Takes offhand comments literally and seriously

- Future orientation (elementary school kids worrying if they will be good drivers, high school kids worrying about a job after college)
- Doesn't like things unfinished (can't take a break unless homework is done)
- Can't have things "on hold" (has to study for tests right away)
- Has performance fears: perfectionistic, always seeking assurance, very afraid of failure or getting in trouble
- Has social/interpersonal fears: worries that friends don't like them or are mad at them
- Carries concerns about family: keeping constant tabs on the status of parents' marriage, worrying that parents are going to get divorced
- Has fears about illness: an insignificant symptom may be a sign of a serious disease: "My mouth tasted like pennies today. Is that a sign of a stroke? I saw it on TV."
- Has an excessive need to know about finances and financial repercussions, how much things such as groceries, household repairs, and doctor's visits cost
- Suffers the consequences of stress: always on edge, looks tense, is difficult to reassure, has difficulty concentrating and sleeping, suffers from headaches or stomachaches, is distractible and unable to enjoy things, is overwhelmed by their schedule
- Worries on Sunday night about trying to imagine and feel secure about everything that is going to happen in the week

THE TRICK AND THE GOAL: NOT EVERY BELL TOLLS FOR THEE: FROM STATE OF ALERT TO STANDBY

The child with GAD falls prey to two brain tricks: First, there's trouble out there and you need to be on alert, constantly, to find it, otherwise you are irresponsible and that leaves you or others you care about at high risk for bad things happening; and second, if you hear about any trouble (a neighbor's heart attack, a burglary on the news), it pertains to you directly and you need to do everything to prevent it. The key to overcoming GAD is for the person to learn that even though they *feel* like something bad is about to happen, there's no trouble—the alarm is malfunctioning and they need to reset it. Being worrywise means learning to separate their body's automatic reaction to those ideas from the actual risk and downsize it, concluding, "I've got this covered," or, "This isn't about me," or, "Everything's fine."

The best way to do this, as we've seen, is to help your child retrain his brain by not taking worry at face value, and instead creating a new habit of side-by-side comparison to put worry to the test. When worry gets the facts wrong again and again, like a bad teacher or friend who exaggerates, your child will learn to distrust and dismiss worry thoughts when they come along. Coach your child to first state the worries, then what he believes is most likely to happen. Remember, the worry brain and the thinking brain ask very different questions. Worry asks: "What's the worst thing you can think of that could possibly happen here?" Wisdom asks: "What's the thing you really, truly believe is most likely to happen in the situation?"

After shrinking the worry in the step above, the next goal is getting the action going in the right direction. Your child's mind is currently programmed to think of every eventuality, to overprepare, to worry about their performance even when it's great. They don't know where the off switch is—and they aren't convinced that it would be safe to use it even if they knew where it was. We teach children why it's okay to "break" worry's rules and not live on a "just in case" basis, by practicing eliminating unnecessary questions, apologizing, perfectionism, and so forth. By forgoing the "just in case" safety maneuvers, children with GAD learn that worrying less does not make bad things happen, that they aren't being irresponsible or unprepared, and in fact worrying less will greatly improve the quality of their life. You can assure them that it's okay if it feels strange at first. Worry has become the familiar, default mode. But through repeated opportunities to approach things a different way and let the worry calls go on the machine, they can GUTI and feel much better. They can learn to count on themselves to be prepared—because of what they do, not because of how they worry.

HOW YOU CAN HELP: SEPARATE YOUR CHILD FROM THE WORRY; TAKE YOUR CHILD SERIOUSLY, NOT THE WORRY

"We want our child to trust us more," a father of a ten-year-old tells me. The more we talk, I see that this father feels upset, offended, and confused by his son's refusal to just *believe* him—that he did sign the permission slip for school, that the gas tank is full, that they'll get to school on time. The problem for GAD kids, though, is not that they don't trust their parents. It's that worry keeps on bugging them with "what-ifs," not letting them listen to the facts, and instead making them focus on the doubts. The best thing you can do is not to run around double-checking things, as your child is insisting, or take his or her "distrust" personally, but to make this a choosing moment where you speak to your child's smart brain, ask him the "million-dollar question" to decide if these extra steps are necessary or if he really already knows the answer.

Another important way to help is not to be dismissive of your child's concerns even though they sound so far-fetched. Worry and fear are in the eye of the beholder. Children suffer greatly when no one knows they are worrying. This is where separating your child from the worry is most effective. Instead of saying (critically): "Why would you ever think that? That makes no sense!" you say: "Wow, listen to what worry is making you think about! Can you believe how far out worry goes?!" Your child gets distance from worry, and gets to be the good guy pointing out worry's shortcomings, rather than defending himself from feeling like you've just pointed out his own flaws.

So many parents ask me, "Aren't I enabling my child if I drive back to school, recheck this and that, or go to the doctor every time something hurts?" Almost, but not exactly. Something is being enabled—but it's the worry, not the child. Parents need to take their child seriously by asking different questions and showing them how to look for ways to challenge their worry. So rather than running to the doctor if your child is afraid of an ache or pain that they are convinced is serious (supporting the worry), you're going to ask your child the million-dollar question: "Do you really, truly believe you have a heart condition?" Or you'll teach your child by saying: "Worry tries to trick you that pains are signs of a serious illness. Let's put worry to the test. How long does the pain usually last? Right, okay, maybe like ten minutes. Let's decide that if a pain lasts longer than an hour, we'll talk about it; otherwise we know it's just a passing ache, and worry is overinterpreting it." Or if your child is convinced he will fail a test and has you sitting for hours quizzing him on material he already knows—that's supporting the worry. Instead work out a system with your child for him to decide if he's prepared or not, asking: "If you had to place a bet now on whether you are going to fail, would you?" That's supporting your child's smart brain.

THE STRATEGIES: KEY INTERVENTIONS IN TREATMENT

When kids with GAD learn that their risk detector—or yikes button, amygdala, or worry brain—is being engaged at the wrong time, they can begin to reassure themselves that the risks are really not what they seem. Only then can they respond to those worries with skepticism, sarcasm, and maybe even a touch of condescension—"Yeah, worry, that story is really likely"—rather than reacting with their fear. The goal of rethinking with the side-by-side comparisons is to prove that the child is smarter than their worry. And that is a greater relief than any reassurance you can deliver. When well-meaning parents, teachers, and even therapists take the worry at face value and rush to reassure, they are inadvertently reinforcing the idea that these concerns warrant your child's attention. They don't. The GUTI exercises will seal the deal and show them that by "breaking worry's rules," by not over-apologizing, over-preparing, overreacting, they can enjoy their life, like other children do, rather than constantly running safety checks on it. Here are the most important things to keep in mind when helping your child deal with GAD.

Step One: Relabel the Problem as the Worry Brain, Downgrade the Danger!

Teach your child to expect worry, recognize the telltale signs when it comes along, and distinguish it from her other thoughts. By sorting her brain mail, separating what's real from what's "spam" and deciding which thoughts really warrant her attention (see Chapter 5), your child is able to immediately downgrade the authority of the worry and start thinking more realistically.

For younger children: Your child is the boss. Give worry a silly name and voice, use stuffed animals to stage a conversation between worry brain and smart brain, make thought stampers to distinguish worry from wisdom, create "Boss Back Talk" to bring out your child's confidence.

For older children: Your child is the chooser. Ask them to distinguish their inner worrywart from their inner Einstein. Which voice is more reliable and accurate? Which makes a more ideal and reliable coach?

Step Two: Rethink and Shrink: Do the Side-by-Side Comparison: Don't Go by Your First Reaction; Think Past the Worry to a Second, Realistic Reaction

Worry has power over us when it is left unchecked. Once we "verbalize and analyze" by saying our worries out loud or writing them down, we begin to shift from amygdala mode to thinking mode, and already, the worries start to sound unrealistic or sometimes even silly. This is exactly the moment you want to create with your child. You don't have to tell her to stop worrying—when she really hears her fears, she'll be ready to dismiss them herself. The questions that will be answered by the side-by-side comparisons include the following:

- Is this fear really about you?
- Is thinking about this necessary or important right now?

- What's the truth about you and this situation? Do you have it covered already?
- Is the real problem that worry is bugging you about unnecessary things?

STRATEGY: Do the Side-by-Side Comparison to Outsmart the Worry Brain Trick

Use the variety of methods in Chapter 5 to enhance realistic thinking and generate alternatives: Ask the million-dollar question; stage a debate between worry and your child; make a true/false quiz for worry; sing the worries and say the truth.

Once you and your child have set up these thinking options, analyze the worry thinking and identify the brain trick—the way that it's getting the story wrong. When your child sees the trick, he will be confident that it really is safe to let the worry story go. Remember, the two most common thinking mistakes are focusing on how awful a situation could be, rather than how unlikely that scenario is, and letting your feelings about a situation (how scared you feel) color the facts (you aren't at risk).

STRATEGY: Separate Facts from Feelings

Teach your child how to do risk assessment to counteract the way worry confuses facts with feelings. Look again at the pie charts from Chapter 5. Have your child map a circle representing how much she feels afraid that something will happen—a robber will break in—and then another circle showing how much she actually believes that the bad thing will actually happen. She will see that even though she is 100 percent scared, she knows deep down it's not likely (.5 percent). Let her know that it's normal to feel scared when thinking scary thoughts, but feeling scared doesn't and can't in any way make the feared occurrence happen and she needs to repeat the facts in her head instead of the fears.

STRATEGY: Schedule Worry Time

Kids with GAD have a running worry dialogue throughout the day. Help them get more control by compartmentalizing the worry to a given time each day. If it's not worry's appointment time, your child can say: Take a number, you'll have to wait. See Chapter 5 (page 105) for more details on how to do this.

STRATEGY: Deal with Now, Now and Later, Later: Make Appointments in the Future

A cardinal feature of GAD is that worry feels uncontrollable; just because kids could worry about something, they feel they must. Similar to the idea of worry time, kids can take charge of the future-oriented worries that worry tricks them into thinking they need to worry about and settle now, by making an appointment for a future (and more appropriate) date to think about these things. For example, a middle school boy was worrying about colleges because his brother was applying. A ten-year-old girl worried—after hearing about an accident—what if I'm not going to be a safe driver? Making a date on the calendar for when these topics would deserve kids' attention helps them feel more in control, puts worry in perspective, and takes these faraway issues off their immediate "to-do list." Do kids need to "keep" their appointments? Probably not—once kids set it, they can forget it. But even if they do keep it, it will be on their terms.

STRATEGY: Lower the Stakes, Not the Standards: Change the "I *Have* To" to "I *Would Like* To"

"I have to do well. I have to get an A. I have to do everything perfectly!" Help your child separate themselves from the worry. Ask your child, "What is worry telling you? How do you feel about that message? Do you think it will help you?" Have some fun doing the long-distance learning: Ask your child to be the voice of worry pressuring you about how *you* do your job: "You have to be the perfect parent! No mistakes are allowed! Everything counts! Having takeout instead of cooking—unacceptable!" Ask: "Is that going to help you do better, or stress you out?" Help her re-record a new message of what she would like to hear, a message that takes into consideration her effort and the parts that she can control, for instance: "I *want* to do well, and I usually do. I do that by working hard, studying, keeping a good perspective, getting enough sleep, and not listening to my worry brain!"

STRATEGY: Unchain the Catastrophe: Think in Parts

Children with GAD catastrophize—they are one step away from disaster. Their worry puts their problems in a big box. When the problem is "everything" (as in "everything is wrong"), or "nothing" (as in "nothing is working"), we know the problem is worry. If I don't get the A on this test, then I won't do well in the class, then I won't get into the right college, then I won't get a good job, get married, and I'll end up homeless—whoa! Slow down there! It is important to help your child do their detective work and narrow down the consequences to what they really think they will be, or narrow down the worry to what it's really about by using the Worry Shrinker boxes (also found in Chapter 5). Ask your child what's the worst thing that they are afraid will happen. Then, fact-checking, help your child narrow down the fear to the smallest box.

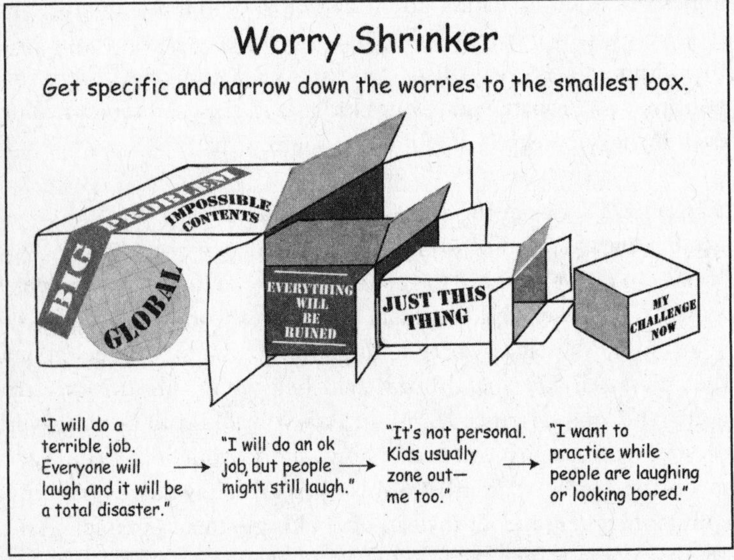

Worry Shrinker
Get specific and narrow down the worries to the smallest box.
BIG PROBLEM
IMPOSSIBLE CONTENTS
GLOBAL
EVERYTHING WILL BE RUINED
JUST THIS THING
MY CHALLENGE NOW
"I will do a terrible job. Everyone will laugh and it will be a total disaster."
"I will do an ok job, but people might still laugh."
"It's not personal. Kids usually zone out—me too."
"I want to practice while people are laughing or looking bored."

STRATEGY: Create a Test Strategy: Are You Already Prepared?

Kids with GAD get frantic at the mention of a test and immediately start preparing and keep preparing up to the last second that the test happens, studying (or worrying) in every spare moment. But do they actually need to? Worry will never tell you: "You've got this." So have your child do a quick "needs assessment," using the million-dollar question: If I had to place a bet, am I ready to do well, or is there something left I still need to study? This will help eliminate the unnecessary overstudying that anxiety will insist is essential.

STRATEGY: Help Your Child Script Out Replies to Frequently Asked Questions (FAQs)

Lucia, age twelve, was always worrying about school. "Will I do well? What will that mean for my future?" Jesse, a seventeen-year-old, came into a session with me with a list of concerns. "How will I know if I'm going to get into college? How will I choose my major? What if I don't like what I choose? What if there are no jobs for me? How will I pay back my student loans?"

Though for both children these questions weren't new, every time they came up, it felt like it was back to the drawing board. Many kids with GAD have to reassure themselves over and over again—they don't retain any of the comfort or confidence from the last time worry struck. Just like websites have FAQs that let you know that your questions are common and answerable, you and your child can create scripts for each of their common concerns. For example: "Do my friends like me?" "Are people mad at me?" "Will I do well in school?" That way they can just refer to the list of answers you generate (based on the facts!), rather than panicking or going back to you day after day, night after night with the same questions. Take out the FAQ sheets whenever you need to—though I find that just mentioning them can do the trick for many kids: they remember, "Oh right, I don't need to keep that on my worry list!"

STRATEGY: Matter of Fact versus Matter of Fear: Choose One

Prove to your child how "offbase" the worry brain is. Take a topic that your child is afraid about (let's say a sleepover). Ask your child to "free-associate" about that word, first from the worry brain side, and next from their smart brain, or fun brain, or science brain. Free-associating means naming five or six ideas that come to mind about the topic. Then ask your child: "Which do you think is more true? Which do you want to think?" When I asked Chloe to do this about sleepovers, she was able to prove to herself how strange the worry thoughts were—how they really didn't belong. It helped her to see that she didn't have to trust her worry anymore.

SLEEPOVERS

What does worry say?	What do you really think?
Dangerous. Bad. You can't do it! Something bad will happen. Scary. Don't go!	Uncomfortable. New. Not used to it yet. Need more time. Could be fun. Fun to be with friends. Want to try it!

STRATEGY: Show Your Child How They Filter Risk

Children with GAD fixate on a risk and can't move forward. If they *could* get hit by the ball in baseball, they won't try; if they *could* mess up in orchestra, they'll quit. You can remind your child of the risks they take without knowing it by turning the spotlight off their fears and onto someone else's, maybe even yours. My patient Ellie is very afraid of driving in someone else's car, but when I role-played being afraid to go out on a boat—"I'm going to capsize. I'll get soaked. My swimming isn't all that great. What if I can't get up to the surface? I'd be stuck in the water. Who would help me? What if I didn't make it?"—she started to smile. I asked her why. She said, "Because it's not going to happen. First of all, you wear a life jacket, so you might get wet, but so what!" Ellie loves to go kayaking and has no problem taking the risks associated with it. We agreed that in terms of kayaking, her worry brain is behaving, not pushing the worry button just because the risk exists. We were then able to apply this discovery to her fear of driving in someone else's car.

Step Three: Get the Body on Board: Turn Off the Alarms

Even if kids with GAD don't complain of headaches or stomachaches, you can usually read on their faces or their bodies that they are tense and on edge. Because the mind and body play off each other, it helps to get both working toward greater balance. Kids, especially older children, may be afraid to take the time to relax—even though without any wind-down time, it's harder to sleep, which only compounds the problem of feeling on edge and having difficulty keeping things in perspective. To be worrywise, kids need to have sustainable habits and take care of their body, too. They need to believe that this isn't wasting time; this is the way they are going to be able to stay in the game long-term. Challenge them to try for two weeks winding down fifteen minutes early and doing some breathing exercises before bed, or listening to relaxing music. Ask them what they notice. When they see that they can fall asleep more easily and feel even better the next day, the practice will sell itself. Look at the breathing and relaxation exercises in Chapter 6. Also see Chapter 18 for ideas about what to do when worry strikes at bedtime. Having your child keep a pen and paper by his bed to write down any last-minute worries will keep him from having to cycle these thoughts through his mind all night to remember them. After making his to-do list, your child could make a Done! list to appreciate the things that he's been able to accomplish. Focusing on what is finished, as opposed to just what lies ahead, will help reinforce his sense of competency and self-mastery, which will help the amygdala stay in neutral rather than on alert. Finally, after your child has put the day to rest with to do's and dones, he can turn to the doors exercise we saw in Chapter 8, page 163, to leave worry behind and head through a different door.

Step Four: Approach the Worry on Purpose: Expose Your Child to *Not* Planning and *Not* Finishing Things Immediately

In this final step, your child is going to learn that not overthinking, overdoing, or over-preparing is safe, more sustainable, and more fun. How do you get your child who doesn't want to take risks to do so? For a younger child, the buy-in is all about who has the power: Help your child see how he can have more power by doing the opposite of what worry wants! You might say something like this: "Let's show worry who's boss! Why don't you choose something that would make your worry kind of frustrated because it just wants you to do it that way, even though you don't need to?"

Approach your older child by connecting with the fact that they want to be successful—they want to be a good athlete, a good student, a well-liked classmate. So have them think with you about what successful people do. They might target older students they admire, famous athletes, or respected relatives. Have your child imagine (or even ask them) how they prepare for a test, game, or important presentation at school. Ask if your child thinks they worry, and what they do with their worry. The goal is to normalize that some worry is okay, but that worrying too much or over-planning just adds a lot of extra steps and is counterproductive.

STRATEGY: Imagine Taking Risks on Purpose, and Then Take Them

As we've seen, the best antidote to fear is experience; you've got to see it to believe it. Your child has avoided being unprepared by being over-prepared—meanwhile, he never gets to see how well he would do if he hadn't! Whether it's imagining what would happen if you got a B-, or what would happen if you forgot a book, or even an assignment, kids with GAD need some exposure to these harmless, albeit undesirable, circumstances to see how survivable they really are. Have your child stage a mini-mistake in their mind and tell you the story step by step of what will really happen (or what won't!). Then make a plan for creating that scenario—or some version of it—in real life (turning in a paper without triple-checking it, forgetting a book or assignment, forgetting their sneakers on gym day) to see how the consequences are small if any; by figuring out how to handle mistakes they can finally see a growth spurt in their resourcefulness.

STRATEGY: Use Getting Used to It Exercises to Move from What If to Wait and See

For children with GAD, the GUTI exercises are about not taking the precautions they fear they should. Sometimes that means not doing things perfectly, and other times it means not apologizing or asking someone if they are mad. As with all other fears and worries, work with your child to create a worry hierarchy, and use the stairs of learning to practice and build gradually toward tackling the things that generate the most anxiety. The chart that follows shows an example of what a child with GAD may need to address. The goal is to be able to handle imperfection or mistakes so that worrying about them and trying to avoid them doesn't run the child's life.

One important note: When school-related challenges are involved, the teacher should be told that the child is under a tremendous amount of stress from anxious thoughts, and that she needs some practice making small mistakes so she can learn to handle those situations. Having the teachers reinforce the idea that everyone makes mistakes will support the child's GUTI challenges and make these exposures more manageable.

Challenge	Fear Temperature
Don't double-check homework with Kimmy.	50
Don't ask a friend if she's mad at me.	60
Don't recopy notes that were sloppy.	65
Forget a book at home.	78
Forget part of gym uniform on purpose.	80
Forget to do one homework subject on purpose.	100
Make an annoyed face in class when teacher is looking at me.	100

STRATEGY: Performance Worries: Fire Mr. Perfect

Children with GAD are perfectionists and keep a running tab in their head of how they are performing, how they compare to other people, and what the consequences would be if they didn't do well. For a child with GAD, not doing well means scoring a 99 when they could have gotten a 100. Teaching your child to rethink perfectionism enables them to free up brain space that could allow them to focus squarely on what is actually happening (and enjoy their successes). Because GAD kids want to do well, they are often loath to give up the comparing and contrasting of their performance to that of their peers. This is where it helps to bring in the experts. Experts—professional athletes, actors, musicians, successful students know this: Success is about focusing on how to keep improving, not about proving or scoring yourself every second (more on that in Chapter 21). This is like trying to be two places at once. Either you're in the game, or you're on the sidelines evaluating your performance, but you can't do both. There's a time and place for everything; if you want to evaluate your performance after the fact, that's great, but trying to predict ahead of time, or worse, trying to evaluate yourself while you're in the middle of your task, will only break your focus and make it harder for you to succeed.

Use the possibility panel exercise that we saw in Chapter 5: If your child is worrying about sports, ask them to think of their top three favorite athletes—what would those athletes tell you to focus on? If you look at the most successful athletes and listen to what they are saying before a race or competition, they aren't saying things like this: "If I don't get this, I won't get into the finals," or, "My fans and family will dump me and be so disappointed if I let them down." No, they have their head in the game. They are saying things like this: "I'm really going to focus on my swing [in baseball] or my form [in gymnastics]." Fire Mr. Perfect and help your child create the script they want to hear. If it's good enough for these giant talents to get specific and let the rest go, it's bound to be good enough for the rest of us.

Have your child identify the specific behaviors that he wants to focus on to improve in sports or school. It's not only okay to identify areas that need improvement; it's actually how you make sure that the improvement happens.

ON THE HOME FRONT: STRESS, ANGER, AND NOT OVERLOOKING REAL SOURCES OF FEAR

There's a bumper sticker slogan: If you aren't outraged, you aren't paying attention. Children with GAD often feel angry at others around them—family members in particular—for not being keyed up about the things that possess their minds, or for not simply doing the things that would alleviate their worry: keeping the gas tank full, taking their temperature, or bringing them to the doctor every time they're afraid they are sick.

"Did you write that note to the teacher?"

"For the hundredth time, I'll write the note after breakfast. Stop worrying!"

"But what if you forget? Then she won't know that you're picking me up early. You are picking me up early, right?"

"Peter, you know the answer. Yes, I'm picking you up early!"

"But you might forget. Just write it down so you don't forget."

"That's it, Peter—stop worrying! It's fine, just like it's been every time!"

"But what if you do forget? Can't you write it down?"

"Peter, stop it, that's enough. I'm the mother and I'm in charge!"

As the dialogue above illustrates, worry leads to overplanning. Parents see kids trying to control them. Kids with GAD don't necessarily have a premeditated plan to drive you crazy by controlling you, but they do have a pressing need to know what's going to happen next. The greatest challenge for parents is not to lose patience with their worrying child. The more you take it personally, the more your child will dig in. Be confident in your knowledge that just giving in to worry's demands won't help your child get to the root of the problem. At the same time, remember that your child doesn't want to be feeling this way. Try to remember that your child is in a sense being held hostage by the worry brain, so you can be unified against a common enemy. When your child leans over and wants to know how much is in the checking account, who is calling on the phone, and what were you just talking about, try to use some levity while relabeling what is going on: "Who wants to know—you or your worry?" Let your child know that he is off duty, and tell him to let the worry bully know that he isn't allowed to start worrying about those things until he is an adult.

Another challenge for parents is to not dismiss your child's worries just because the situations don't seem scary to you. Worry and fear are in the eye of the beholder. Listen carefully to your child's fears and worries, because hidden within there may be some misconceptions that you can help correct, and in the process, alleviate much suffering.

Six-year-old Will was having difficulty going to school. Each morning he would cry, delay getting dressed, try to hide, and do anything not to go. His parents were confused and concerned, but as any parent would do, they thought that these were just some school jitters, or maybe even plays for attention, and moved him along to school. When Will's mother, Sydney, was able to ask him what was in his worry "thought bubble" when he was getting ready for school, the story came tumbling out. He was very afraid that an older girl at school was going to "kill" him for winning a game because she had said so (jokingly) when they were playing a game at recess. Will was thinking, "How is she going to kill me? Is she going to strangle me? Is she going to do it in the closet at school?"—being preoccupied with the situation far more than another child would be. Though thinking of being killed clearly is frightening, and should not be joked about, instead of this thought passing through Will's worry net, it was stuck, and the longer it stayed, the more it consumed him. With the kernel of the story uncovered, Sydney could help Will understand what had happened, reassure him that he was okay, and help him to put some new information in his thought bubble—the truth!

ELIZABETH'S STORY

Elizabeth, whom we met earlier in the chapter, had a school camping trip coming up in four months. Afraid to be apart from her mom or try anything new, she never went on any class trips. But she was tired of having to make excuses for missing out on things and was ready to tackle this challenge head-on. She was afraid of the food, of not being able to fall asleep—that she would starve and be up all night! Climbing up her stairs of learning (see the illustration below), when she bossed her fear back she felt better, not because the situation changed, but because her thinking changed. With the trip only three days long, Elizabeth knew that she wouldn't starve, that even if she did stay up at night, she could live with that, that her teacher would be there to help—and overall, that her worry bug was making all of this seem like an awful situation, when truly if she turned down the volume on that, the trip was a great chance to be out of school for a few days, be with her friends, and prove to herself that she could do this.

Her e-mail two weeks later says it all:

> I DID IT! I have completed my mission, defeated my worries, conquered them! I went for 3 days 2 nights at Victory Camp—NO PROBLEMS!!!!!!!!!!!!! I am truly proud of myself! Guess what? I didn't call home either! I am proud!
> —Elizabeth

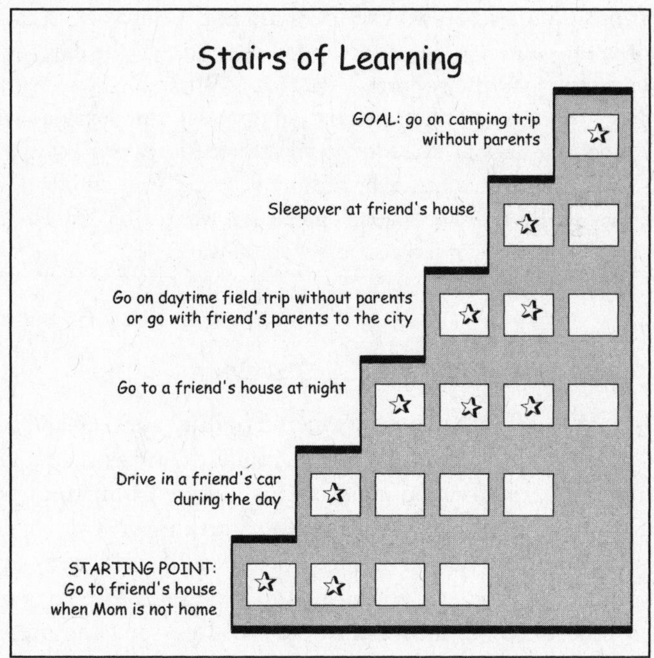

IDEA BOX

- *Overplanners:* Be spontaneous, change a plan, go out without a destination, give your child "wing-it" points for "mix-it-up" days.
- *Certainty seekers—won't take maybe for an answer:* Practice "maybe" tolerance, get points for handling "maybe" answers (versus definite answers).
- *Catastrophizers:* Develop a code or phrase to denote just how "far out" the worry is—Flying Pig Alert, or Brain Bug. Something that says, "That one's over the top, even for you!"
- *Chronic worriers:* Singing the worries to a tune like "Row, Row, Row Your Boat" is guaranteed to reduce the authority of those thoughts.

DO IT TODAY: DON'T BORROW AHEAD ON WORRY, FAST-FORWARD TO THE END

Don't borrow ahead on worry. Ask your child to pull out an imaginary remote control and fast-forward to the end—of the day, the experience, the test, and so forth. Ask him: "What do you *really* think is going to happen? What are you going to say the next day when you're looking back at it? How do you think things will really turn out? Will worry's predictions be right or wrong?" Your child will find that, thankfully, nothing "bad" happened; it was the big "so what!"—which in this case is exactly what he would want.

CHARLES'S STORY

Charles was a high achiever, a perfectionist, a sweet and kind straight-A student, and a worrier. Despite the support of a great family and great friends, none of this buffered him from what worry was telling him about himself. Starting every day with a zero scorecard, he felt he had to prove himself with every interaction, every grade; everything had to go right, or he felt upset, like a failure, embarrassed, and like a bad person. The pressure that worry was putting on him to be perfect was so extreme he was starting to throw up before many events. Before a swim meet Charles was getting stressed, so we talked about how worry was making him focus on all the wrong things, and that worry was just plain wrong. We did the side-by-side comparison and Charles found the facts: "I'm a strong swimmer. I just need to do my best and not focus on winning—that's a distraction." Focus on swimming your best (and for levity: think about the sandwich you're going to get after the race). I told Charles about an Olympic figure skater who advised that in sports you have to turn off your head, not think about what you're doing, trust that your body knows what to do, and "skate stupid."

Charles ended up getting two first-place medals in that swim meet, but the best part? When he ran up to see his mom after the meet, the first words out of his mouth were that the strategies worked, that he didn't throw up or keep going to the bathroom, that he swam "stupid" and it really helped! Mom and Dad were most proud that with worry out of the way Charles was able to perform well in the race and feel really good about himself.

Chapter 12

FROM THE MINI-SCARIES TO REAL PHOBIAS

I wish they would just build a bug house outside for all the bugs so they would all stay in one place and never bother me.

It's gotten to the point with my son where I don't even know how to answer his questions. Sometimes I'll lie to him—"No, there won't be any dogs on our walk"—just so he'll stop asking. I know it's wrong, but how else can I get him out the door?

Some children become paralyzed with fear in the face of a situation that their peers wouldn't even register as a challenge. How can it be that one child clutches at you for dear life at the mere sight of a dog on a leash, while another happily pets the friendly animal? It's all about how that situation is being interpreted. The anxious child is focusing on and magnifying the most potentially frightening aspects of the situation (look at the dog's sharp teeth; he is going to bite me), while other crucial information that the excited child perceives (the dog is on a leash; look at his tail wagging happily) is entirely overlooked. With worry glasses on, anxious kids are seeing a different dog. The stimulus "dog" has been filed in the "dangerous" category, and as far as they are concerned, that's a permanent classification. With the amygdala in overdrive, anxious kids go into survival mode and begin to organize their lives around avoiding that threat.

A parent's first instinct is to keep the child away. The only problem is that there isn't a danger, so by avoiding a situation we are reinforcing the wrong message. Instead, we need to look for opportunities to make the situation manageable by challenging worry and making the picture more realistic by providing your child with (repeated) exposure and contact that will prove to them that this stimulus can be reclassified as safe or manageable. In this chapter you will find the formula for success in treating specific phobias through thought sorting, GUTI, and gradual exposures.

WHAT IT FEELS LIKE FOR YOUR CHILD

Imagine your child going about his day just fine, laughing with his friends at lunch. Suddenly someone mentions thunder, or a bee makes its way into the cafeteria. The color starts to drain from your child's face, and they are suddenly no longer the competent, happy child they were two seconds earlier. Their primitive defense program has taken over and adrenaline surges. The amygdala has hijacked lunch. Given the surge in anxiety, even if the bee is killed, or the conversation topic is changed, your child won't immediately return to normal. His body feels like it's gone through a life-or-death experience.

When dealing with kids with phobias, it's important to remember that they aren't trying to be difficult or rigid. They really are panicked and feel they must ensure that the situation never happens again. This is where cognitive restructuring and exposure, or our "shrink and approach" method, is the best way to reestablish a feeling of safety and security for your child.

THE DIAGNOSIS

To be diagnosed, a phobia must be present for six months. What distinguishes a fear from a phobia is not the content or type of fear, but how extreme or disruptive the reaction is.

Red Flags for Phobias

In addition to avoidance and interference with normal activities, other red flags for phobias include the following:

- *Fears that are out of synch developmentally:* Your child is struggling with issues that are typically resolved at an earlier stage (a teenager who is afraid of the dark, a ten-year-old who is afraid of dogs).
- *Loss of perspective despite knowledge:* Your child loses perspective about the feared situation and her ability to cope. She thinks bees want to sting her and that she'll have to go to the hospital.
- *Sensitization with exposure:* Your child becomes increasingly distressed and disorganized when you try to work through the fear, rather than being reassured.
- *Anticipatory anxiety (planning ahead):* Your child asks too many questions ahead of time—"Will there be a dog there?" "Do we have to eat outside?" (fear of bees)—and refuses to go places without guarantees.

THE TRICK AND THE GOAL: REWIRING THE BRAIN TO CORRECT THE FAULTY AMYGDALA SIGNAL

What is at the heart of a phobia? The knee-jerk belief that "This is dangerous! Get out!" When the amygdala detects the "this shouldn't be happening" signal, it goes on high alert. The experience gets misfiled as dangerous. Not falling for the trick means retagging the situation as safe, by doing the side-by-side comparison of facts and fears using the strategies from Chapters 4 and 5: the million-dollar question, the red pen edit, the facts versus fears, and so forth, and correcting misperceptions about the degree of risk or danger in the situation. Once the risk has been shrunk down to size, the "get moving" strategies involve building stairs of learning to take a gradual approach to the situation through pictures, words, and closer and more significant interactions with it. Remember—just outside of the comfort zone (a five or six out of ten on the fear thermometer) is the goal. The fear sweet spot is an exposure that is hard, but not too hard. By climbing those stairs through regular practice, your child will proudly come to master that situation.

HOW YOU CAN HELP

The challenge for many parents is that there is a mismatch between their experience of feared situations and their child's. The more that the parent insists "*There's nothing wrong!*" the more the child becomes disorganized and emotional because they aren't being understood. You want them to process the experience differently—but in order for that to happen, your first job is to empathize and help them slow down their reaction so they will be able to begin to absorb your good, reasonable coaching. Remember: Empathizing does not mean that you agree that the situation warrants that reaction. You are leaning in to support your child, not their anxiety. This empathy means accepting inconsistencies—that your child could be so competent in so many areas and fall apart in the face of this fear, or that your child may scream when there is a bee nearby but be fearless when it comes to snakes.

Ask, Don't Tell

If your child is fearful about going to the pool, or the dentist, don't assume you know what the fear is. Instead ask questions to narrow down exactly what the phobia is:

- "What's your worry telling you about [the fearful situation]?"
- "What part feels scary to you?"
- "What are you afraid will happen if you were to [interact with the fearful situation]?"
- "What do you really think and why?"

If you aren't getting any traction, ask your child—"Tell me the story. So in chapter one you see a dog. What happens in chapter two? What happens next?" This construction will help you substitute different plot lines to identify your child's fear.

Kids don't grow out of phobias; they grow into them: Phobias that are untreated in childhood tend to persist into adulthood. The final way that you can help is by being patient and flexible, and not avoiding the project. Find positive ways to replace fear with experience—whether doing research at the library on the habits of bees, arranging safe encounters with friendly neighborhood dogs, or being willing to regale your child (with her permission) with gagging sounds to help her overcome her fear of vomiting.

How to Explain This to Your Child

"We know that your worry brain is telling you all sorts of things about dogs. Your brain is going to make you feel like this is the most important thing on your radar and that you can't focus on anything else. It's going to make you feel like until every bee, doll, needle, and so forth, is gone, you can't be safe. Is that true? Is that what you think other kids think? Is this what you want to think? Imagine if your brain were telling you something different—if you had to take a test in school about dogs. What would the truth be about dogs? That they want to bite? That they are vicious? Or that they are friendly, man's best friend, loyal, good company? Just imagine how you'd feel and what your feet would do if you were thinking that. Right—you might be curious. You'd know that there are safe ways to approach a dog. You don't have to get rid of dogs; you just have to change what your brain is telling you about them. You have power here; you can retrain and reprogram your brain. You can record a new message about the fear and listen to it a lot in your mind. Then, if you want to make this the least important thing on your radar, you need to do GUTI—be around dogs so your brain sees that you know how to be safe; it doesn't have to turn on the alarms. You're teaching your body by practicing staying calm when you are around these things—you're telling your worry brain that you can handle it. Then, instead of your world being all about avoiding dogs, they start not to be so important, and there is lots of room in your mind for other things."

THE STRATEGIES: KEY INTERVENTIONS IN TREATMENT

STRATEGY: Rethink and Shrink the Fear: Get the Facts
Imagine if you were afraid of choking on dry foods and your first step in treatment was someone forcing you to eat. You would be so busy protecting yourself from perceived harm that the only thing you would learn is that you couldn't trust your therapist! When it comes to fears and phobias, you can't "just do it." Because the underlying belief in phobias is that contact with the feared situation will cause physical harm, this belief first needs to be verbalized and then analyzed and corrected.

- First have your child say worry's version of the story; then have them correct it. Your child needs to tell you exactly what they fear so you can target the misperceptions. First, have your child list the fears in a worry thought bubble (or role-play them with young children). Next, see if your child can identify the tricks their brain is playing or, like a teacher, correct the mistakes that worry is making. Look at the suggestions in Chapters 5 and 8 for building realistic thinking.
- Help them prove that worry's warnings are unreliable (and that they get to choose what to think) by using the brain train exercise in Chapter 4 with something they're not afraid of but their friend is. Then run the phobia down the tracks.
- If there has been a previous negative encounter with the experience, have the child walk through the pages of that story. Don't stop in the middle at the tough part; make sure your child tells you how things ended up.
- Most fears have some grain of truth, even if it's a very small grain. But just because a risk exists, that doesn't mean the worst is likely to happen. Being worrywise means understanding that the risks are rare, but also being informed and prepared to handle things competently. Always do research about the fears: look at books, talk to experts—such as vets or pet owners—and learn the facts about how to be safe in the situation.

Do the Side-by-Side Comparison

Use the thought shifter toolbox strategies from Chapters 4 and 5 to create new data about the feared situation.

- Have your child generate the data of facts versus fears. Rate the fear temperature for each. Choose the side that is more true.
- Do research and create a true/false test for parents and relatives.
- Do a red pen edit to correct worry's assessment of the situation.
- Ask yourself the million-dollar question: "If you could win a million dollars by getting the right answer, how would you answer this question: "Am I safe with (X)?" Or, "Do I have to totally avoid (X) in order to be safe?"
- Invite the Possibility Panel—let other trusted people weigh in on the situation.
- Empathy is another way to shift the thinking about the feared situation. For example, learning that certain animals are on the verge of extinction may make children have a sense of concern for them. Learning that barking is the only way that dogs can communicate (and that barking is not a way to be aggressive), or that dogs suffer from anxiety and don't like to be left alone, can likewise elicit a caring, rather than a defending, response from your child.

STRATEGY: Calm Your Body: Turn Off Your Inner Alarm

As you now know, the calmer your body feels, the more your thoughts can stay calm (and accurate) too. Help your child to shape a new behavioral reaction: Don't run. Instead, step back till you are ready to step forward. Do calm breathing to turn off the alarms (see Chapter 6).

STRATEGY: Approach Worry on Purpose: Get to GUTI: Create a Stairs of Learning and Take It One Step at a Time

Systematic desensitization through gradual exposure is the treatment of choice for phobias. This means breaking down the fear into manageable chunks and working your way from the easiest to the toughest challenge, replacing the fear reaction with a different experience that lets your child know she's safe. Starting points vary, as do end points. Many children with phobias are so sensitized that they cover their ears at the mere mention of the phobic situation: For them the starting point isn't an encounter with a spider; it's several steps back. Desensitizing may mean listening and saying the word "spiders," looking at spiders in books and gathering information about them, teaching a lesson to an adult about spiders, practicing breathing and boss back talk with a fake spider, and eventually getting closer and closer to the real McCoy (a spider in a jar with small holes poked through the top for air).

To begin, look for amygdala-friendly opportunities that allow for contact with the feared situation, but from a distance. If your child isn't worrying about protecting himself, he is free to learn more about the situations themselves.

The end point is also negotiable. Some kids want to be able to just coexist peacefully with their feared situation; in that case, the ultimate goal would be to sit and watch TV in a room with a spider without paying attention to it. Other kids want to be able to interact with the object; that might mean having spiders crawl on a stick that they hold. Remember that as your child progresses with this, his fear will decrease, so he may be able to set a more ambitious goal after he has a few steps under his belt.

GUTI POINTS FOR PHOBIAS

- *Any* interaction a child has with a feared situation is a step in the right direction. Be encouraging about even small steps; they will create traction. Slow and steady sets the pace, and wins the race. Don't rush—remember that high levels of anxiety are not conducive to overcoming fear.
- After doing research on the fear, have the child teach a parent, grandparent, or sibling what he has learned about the facts of his phobia.
- Practice! Early and often. Massed (frequent, several times a week) practice has been proven more effective than spaced (once a week, or every couple of weeks). If there are long in-

tervals between exposures, the child is likely to forget that he managed the exposure and revert back to anxious anticipation.

- In the midst of an exposure, do a role reversal: "Is the bee afraid of you? What is the bee saying: 'Please don't trap me or I'll die.'"
- Take your child's fear temperature. Make sure your child remains in the situation until his anxiety comes down significantly. An exposure is successful when a child's fear temperature has dropped about 50 percent. Don't leave early. Ask what facts he can say to himself about the situation to bring his worry temperature down.
- Always try to end the experience on a good note, finding the accomplishment even if the exposure is only a partial success. Keep in mind that there is always the opportunity for more practice later.

PATHWAYS TO CHILDREN'S FEARS AND PHOBIAS

Understanding how a fear developed for your child can help reveal the path you need to take to undo your child's faulty learning. Children acquire a phobia through "single-trial learning": A child who briefly choked on a pretzel at a party worries about birthday parties, because birthday party = pretzels = choke = avoid. Modeling can also shape phobias. For example, fear of vomit may in part be influenced by what happens when a child throws up: There's a look of horror on the adult's face as they snatch up the child to race them to the bathroom as if saving them from an oncoming car. Remember that your kids are watching you as a model of competency or fear. Try to remain calm in stressful situations, or, if you do overreact, go back later and explain what happened.

The power of the picture can also lead to phobias. Children may acquire intense fears of fires, hurricanes, plane crashes, or large animals by seeing them portrayed on television. TV news can lead children to believe that disasters are a common occurrence—that fires happen easily, or that weather is always devastating. As a picture can overpower a thousand realistic thoughts, be careful what your children watch and make sure you deprogram them afterward. Find out what they think of the show, and correct any misconceptions.

THE DSM-V SPECIFIC PHOBIAS

The DSM-V outlines five specific phobia subtypes, which are listed below. The steps I have outlined above will help you tackle any of these fears. While there isn't room to address every phobia, the following examples are the most common.

Animal type: dogs, cats, spiders, bees, snakes, birds, mice

Natural environment type: storms, heights, water

Blood-injection-injury type: seeing blood, injection, medical procedures

Situational type: tunnels, bridges, elevators, airplanes, driving, enclosed places

Other types: choking, vomiting, contracting illness, loud sounds, costumed characters

Fear of Animals (Dogs, Bees)

Rethink and shrink: Children think that all dogs are vicious, that they'll definitely bite, that bees want and are trying to sting them, and that they'll definitely get stung if they're near bees. Help your child learn how to be safe around (and even enjoy) domestic animals. Learn why dogs are "man's best friend." Learn that bees have no interest in them (even if they call to them to come over!), only in pollen, and that bees don't want to sting because they will die (in the case of honeybees) and will only sting if they are threatened.

Boss back talk: Bees: I am bigger than they are, they aren't interested in me. It's not fair that worry wants me to stay inside, and I don't need to! If I stand still and don't run, I won't get h
Dogs: Dogs don't want to bite unless they are threatened.

has it wrong! I can learn how to be safe with dogs; dogs are being friendly when they jump, they're playing, they don't want to hurt me! I can use a strong voice and say "sit!" if they're jumping up.

On-Purpose Exposure: Animals

BEES:

- Observe bees out the window, work your way up to observing from a distance outside. Keep count of the number of bees you see. Give the bees funny names and "talk" to them. Ask the bees to come over and say hi. Notice how bees aren't interested in people, only flowers. Eat a snack outside.
- Have someone catch a dead or live bee and put it in a jar. Play "Red Light–Green Light" or "Mother May I?" until your child gets across the room, where the bee is.

DOGS:

- Observe dogs from a window, behind a glass door or fence, or when the dog is sleeping so that your child can stand closer when the dog is sleeping (more predictable) and work up to observing dogs when they're awake and moving (on a leash to start), eventually observing dogs at a dog park.
- Smaller dogs may seem less scary, but they jump more and are noisy. Find a small, quiet dog, or an older sedentary dog for early exposures. Observe a dog owner petting a dog to watch how it is done safely.
- Ask dog owners about their dogs: "What is the dog's name, is he friendly, does he bite?"

Fear of Thunderstorms

Rethink and shrink: Children think weather shouldn't be happening, that it signals that something is *wrong*—something they need to stop from happening. Help them learn about the weather and know that weather isn't the problem: It may be loud, but it's supposed to happen just like that. The weather is doing exactly what it's supposed to be doing. And your child's job isn't to manage the weather; it's to take charge of the worry that's turning on the alarms.

Boss back talk: Thunderstorms are normal and natural. There is nothing wrong! There's nothing I need to do to control the weather. My job is to control my worry. I don't have to stop the weather from happening!

On-Purpose Exposure to Storms

- Watch storms on YouTube (prescreen the clips for appropriateness). Allow your child to control the volume, how close he stands to the computer, and so forth.
- When a storm comes, help your child to be a good observer. Engage the thinking brain rather than worry brain. Ask questions: "What kind of thunder is that? What kind of lightning? How close is the storm?" Imitate the sounds of the thunder. Let your child know that everything is happening as it should and that there's nothing he needs to do.
- Work toward going outside during a storm (safely), standing by window, on the front step, sitting in the car, and so forth.
- If you live in an area with significant weather events, let your child know what the plan is if there is a tornado; for example, "If we are warned about a tornado we go down in the basement until the storm passes. We'll play games down there." Emphasize safety, not danger, in your plan.

Blood-Injection-Injury Phobias

Rethink and shrink: Routine medical injections are very brief: They are over quicker than you can say . . . this sentence. The needle may hurt, but it won't hurt a lot. Statistically, kids tend to rate the pain as a "4" on a scale from 1 to 10. Priming the accurate rather than the fear pump, children can re-record their self-talk as follows: "I can't control the shot, but I can control my reaction to it. They aren't trying to hurt me. It will be over really quickly. It will hurt less if I cooperate and stay calm."

Many children (and adults) with a blood-injury phobia experience what is called a vasovagal response—fainting at the sight of blood—a response that often runs in families. There is an initial rise in heart rate and blood pressure, followed by a sudden dramatic drop that leads to sweating, light-headedness, and sometimes nausea and fainting. This response is physiological, not psychological. It may be helpful for children with this affliction to look away when blood is being drawn.

Boss back talk: Needles are to help me, not to hurt me. They will hurt less if I stay calm. I can't control the needle, but I can control my reaction to it. This will be very quick!

On-Purpose Exposure to Medical Fears

- Watch videos online of medical and dental visits.
- Borrow medical equipment or use toys and let your child practice being the doctor. Then, when he's ready, be the patient. With supervision he could "inject" a stuffed animal, pillow, or piece of fruit; use a tongue depressor or take a blood pressure reading. Children are often surprised at how thin the needle is and how easily it goes in.
- Have your child time how long it takes to "give" a shot. Ask them to think of something else (pleasant) that takes about the same amount of time: unwrapping a candy bar and taking a first bite; running to first base. They can use this type of planned refocusing to imagine during the procedure to help anticipate how long it will take until it's over.
- Practice with ketchup or water with food coloring to get used to seeing a little "blood."
- Ask the doctor or nurse to tell the child to breathe in just before and exhale just as the needle goes in. This is an acupuncture technique that reduces the experience of pain. The doctor can say, "Can you take a nice breath in, and now out."

- Use positive visualization: With dental and medical procedures, help your child imagine "wearing" more padding. Have your child choose the "thickest-skinned" animal—a whale or a bear. "Okay, put on your whale skin, now your extra pillows. What color are the pillows? How many would you like?"
- See if the doctor or dentist will allow the child to watch a video or listen to music in headphones during procedures.

Parents can do their part by staying calm and being emotionally available, but not hovering or focusing on pain. Think of yourself as the container for your child's emotion. You don't want to be shaking the jar.

Gagging, Vomiting, or Choking Phobias

Vomit phobia is the most common fear in my practice. Children with this fear believe that unless they are vigilant, the very rare occurrence of throwing up is about to happen to them. Therefore, they are constantly "making sure" they *aren't* about to get sick by asking, "Am I okay?" or avoiding eating in public, or eating certain foods. While we can all appreciate that vomiting is unpleasant, this fear is about being caught off guard, being sick away from parents, and the belief that getting sick will be uncontrollable or unbearable, and that while logic tells us that vomiting is rare, worry warns constantly that it is about to happen. Children with this fear don't get sick more often; actually, just the opposite happens—they are usually "not throw-uppy kids." They are *not* the ones who get sick several times a year, or who regularly throw up from overeating at sleepovers, and so forth. They are exemplified by the child who at the age of nine or ten remembers exactly the two or three times they have gotten sick (or witnessed someone else getting sick) in their life and use that isolated event as a template for every day. Worry is talking to the wrong kids, but it is exactly their lack of experience with getting sick that perpetuates the fear.

Rethink and shrink: Kids with vomiting phobia misinterpret feeling full, gas pains, or other normal fleeting sensations as signs of imminent risk. Rethinking involves learning that being full isn't dangerous; it's temporary and normal. My stomach needs time to digest. These children also scrutinize every aspect of a situation for a hint that someone is about to throw up: "Did she look sick? She wasn't smiling? She coughed—or was that a gag? Why did she go home yesterday? Who was sitting next to her?" The more they are on the lookout, the more they perpetuate the fear (and the feeling of queasiness via the power of suggestion; see Chapter 5). To put worry to the test, ask your child how often worry's predictions have been right about getting sick. Do the side-by-side comparison: Do they want to be thinking about throwing up all the time, even though it won't happen? Or do they want to stick with the facts: Fear of throwing up doesn't make you sick; it just makes you scared. Help your child accurately interpret the signals of what is going on in their body by asking these two questions:

KEY QUESTIONS FOR VOMITING PHOBIA: HOW YOUR CHILD CAN TELL IF SHE'S REALLY SICK OR JUST WORRIED

Children often worry at the slightest grumble of the stomach or even just at the thought that they might get a stomachache that these are signs that throwing up is imminent. Help them tell the difference between sick and worried by using these questions:

1. "What happens next? Do you feel more scared or more sick? If more scared, then you know it's worry. If you feel more sick, like you have to lie in bed, no TV or anything, then you're probably sick."
2. "What makes it better? If distracting yourself helps by playing a game or doing something fun, then you know it's worry. Distraction won't help if you are really sick."

Boss back talk: My body knows what to do; eating is a normal part of life. My body would only throw up if it absolutely needed to; it won't do it just because I'm worried. Throwing up isn't the problem, my body has that under control, worry is the problem!

On-Purpose Exposure for Gagging and Vomiting Fears

- Have your child put a lollipop (or spoon or toothbrush) on the roof of her mouth or in the back of her throat—to show that she can manage that sensation. The gag happens, and then the throat relaxes again. If your child isn't ready to put the spoon all the way back, do a stairs of learning for practicing halfway back, three-quarters of the way back, and so forth.
- Practice making gagging sounds. Have your child put a spoon, or oatmeal, or mashed potatoes on the back of his tongue if he needs some assistance!
- Let your child watch a parent gag and pretend to throw up.
- Your child can rehearse the sights and sounds of vomiting (with fake vomit you can buy at any novelty store—or make your own with various creamy soups and frozen veggies) by staging a gagging contest with the whole family. Play catch with fake throwup.
- View hierarchy of vomit videos at www.emetophobiaresource.org.
- With supervision and parents previewing pictures and comments given some occasional inappropriate language, look at sample "throw up" on websites like ratemyvomit.com. Make the sounds that you think produced that vomit—and have fun (preferably not after a meal!). Replay the segment until there's no distress, only normal disgust.
- Pretend to throw up into the toilet. Put soda or soda with cereal in your mouth, or, if you dare, a few spoonfuls of a raw can of soup, and spit it into the toilet. This proves to a child that even practicing and trying to convince your body to throw up won't make it happen, so they don't need to worry about small things like coughing or even gagging—these natural reactions will not cause trouble.
- Eliminate safety measures: Don't carry around a plastic bag (just in case) or antacids. These tactics only keep the fear alive in your child's mind.

Choking Phobia

Children with this fear may have had an experience once with food getting stuck for a second, and even though they were totally fine, a new idea took root: What if I choked and died? As a result, they avoid eating certain foods (sharp, crunchy, sour) or in certain locations (not in the car, or when alone, nor when talking), and chew food until it is "mush"—all to prevent what they perceive as the very likely event of choking.

Rethink and shrink: Separate the feelings from the facts. Children need to know that chewing and swallowing are automatic. Your body is built to keep you safe. Ever since you were a baby your body has known how to handle food. Worry is making you overthink something that is really automatic.

On-Purpose Exposure for Choking Fears

- Have your child wear a turtleneck or a scarf around his neck, or have him hold his neck gently to tolerate the sensation.
- He can swallow small candies (jimmies, M&M's Minis, Mini Chiclets) to learn to relax while swallowing.
- Have your child chew dry foods (pretzels, potato chips) without water.
- Reduce the amount of time your child chews foods (some kids overchew food as an unnecessary safety maneuver).
- Your child can try to talk or read while eating, in order not to overfocus on chewing.
- Make a hierarchy of foods your child avoids—for example, tough food such as meat and dry food such as chips and nuts—and wants to eat again, and begin to try them.

For Kids Who Are Afraid of Choking on Pills or Vitamins

Use candy sprinkles, M&M's Minis, or Mini Chiclets to build up a child's GUTI confidence using something tasty first. Do the following exercise with your child: Take a bite of food out of your mouth and compare it with the size of the pill. Your child will see that his throat can handle a pill—he just has to learn that pills are okay. Though his throat is in overprotection mode because he thinks that the pill is a "foreign object," with enough practice he will be able to override that danger message and swallow his pills.

Fear of Fire Drills/Alarms

Rethink and shrink: Children with this fear don't like to feel surprised; the anticipation that something startling is going to happen is unbearable and keeps them on edge. Though your child's nervous system doesn't like "that startled feeling," it's normal—only a minute or less (help him to time it), then it's done. Help your child do the side-by-side comparison. What does worry say about alarms? What are the facts? Is an alarm unbearable, dangerous, and terrible or just uncomfortable? Can your body recover quickly? Is it better to have a minute or two of discomfort if an alarm happens, or to worry about it constantly?

Boss back talk: Fire drills are about safety, not danger! The loud sound can't hurt me. I can tell my amygdala to calm down—that it's just a drill. The worry is much worse than the drill. I don't have to like the alarm. I can learn to live with this kind of surprise.

On-Purpose Exposure for Fear of Alarms

- Practice with a kitchen timer, a dryer buzzer, a whistle, a smoke detector, or a car alarm. Take turns being in charge of the sound—sometimes you can start the alarm, and sometimes your child can. Have her time how long it takes to recover. She can imagine having earphones on so it won't be such a shock to her system.
- Give your child control: Have both of you make the alarm sounds yourselves. Record the sound of the fire alarm or house alarm from your own home, or download the sounds from the Internet. Let your child control the on-off switch and the volume.
- Do long-distance learning: Have a doll or stuffed animal in the car (if desensitizing to a car alarm) do the learning first so your child can be a secondhand observer of what happens.

Better yet, use something less precious than your child's stuffed animal—her brother's stuffed animal.

The Fear of Costumed Characters and Dolls

For some anxious children, clowns are frightening. They think: "He looks so real. Why isn't his face moving? What is it if it's humanlike but not human? Is it dead?" This is an "uncanny valley" experience—the mind is uncomfortable when there is uncertainty about whether something is alive or not, or real or not. Some children may react with panic attacks; others may feel nauseous and even gag.

When you encounter large costumed characters, hold your child up and away from the action. Narrate what you imagine your child may be observing in the scene, but model coping. "Barney does have big eyes—he's like a big doll. Barney is a nice big doll. Barney is waving hello! Hello, Big Barney. I know you are nice, but you are so big. I'm not used to you." Over time you can work on the idea of masks and costumes, trying them on stuffed animals and then on people, but in the meantime, short and sweet exposures may be preferable.

For children who are afraid of dolls, help them to examine the facts: Dolls are plastic; they are fake. Someone's job every day is to go into the workshop and make these figures. They are just stamped out of a machine—that's it. Then do systematic desensitization: Have your child draw a doll, look at pictures of dolls, look at an actual doll, hold the doll, play catch with it.

ON THE HOME FRONT: FEAR AND PHOBIA PREVENTION

If something traumatic happens—a dog knocks over your preschooler, or your eight-year-old falls off the waterslide and into the pool, or your fourteen-year-old gets stuck in an elevator, give it some time, and don't force your child right back on that horse, but revisit it—by talking about it and, whenever possible, by returning to the situation to ensure that your child masters the fear they had by seeing that everything ended okay. When worry gets stuck at the cliff-hanger moment in the story, ask your child to think through to the end (when the situation was resolved). Help them learn the right things about that moment: how to be safe and take charge, instead of that they need to be afraid.

RENEE'S STORY

Renee had always been fearful of dogs. Her mother remembers that they were trick-or-treating when Renee was five and she heard a dog barking and ran right in front of a moving car. Fortunately, she was not hurt. The family worked around the fear for many years, but Renee began missing out on many social activities because she couldn't go to friends' houses if they had dogs. Renee's parents suggested that the family get a puppy to help with her fear. Though Renee was able to go and help pick it out, rather than getting rid of her fear, having a new dog made her feel worse because she was afraid and she couldn't enjoy her puppy.

Renee came to treatment, and we set up a hierarchy of situations where she could work on thinking straight and breathing calmly as she looked at her dog, Spice, first from a distance (in another room), progressing eventually to "playing" with her from behind a screen door. She would also just look at the dog when it was sleeping. This gave her a chance to know what she thought about the dog without being so scared. She started being able to see that Spice was a sweet dog and was jumping up to play, not to hurt her. She also worked on her command voice so she could say "No" firmly to teach Spice not to jump up. Renee kept a journal each day of how she was getting closer to her dog, and how her fear level was decreasing. Seeing the results in black and white really helped her confidence. With a combination of exposures, great support from her parents, and Renee's support from her religious faith, she was able to interact with Spice more and more, and today she is Spice's best buddy. Renee believes that her experience has made her a stronger person. She says, "I am able to go to pet stores and actually admire the dogs. I go to people's houses with no problem, and I am enjoying it so much." Her advice to parents? "You always have to push, but some things need a little more time. Be patient; frustration doesn't help!"

WHAT IF YOU'RE AFRAID, TOO?

Many parents ask what they can do if they are squeamish themselves, or if they are afraid of dogs, heights, or bugs. You don't have to pretend that you don't have a problem—but you can't ask your child to do something that you're not willing to try yourself. This is your opportunity to be a good model. Model your self-talk: "I know this isn't really dangerous. I know what I need to do. My mind is making it harder for me; I am going to learn how to do this. Let's learn together." And remember, misery loves company: Your child may be more willing to listen to you if you are on the same page—and more willing to follow your lead, too. You don't have to be on the same step on the stairs of learning, and you don't even have to have the same fear. Stay honest, keep challenging your worries, and interact with the feared situation as much as possible.

HAZEL'S STORY

Fifteen-year-old Hazel was sitting in a biology lecture about the circulatory system. While the rest of the class's reactions to descriptions of blood, veins, and arteries ranged from rapt attention to dozing off, Hazel stopped hearing anything. Her ears were ringing, her hands were tingling, and she didn't know what was happening or what to do. She tried to hang in for as long as she could, and then she had to go to the nurse. As soon as she got to the nurse, she started to feel better, but she was very upset. What had just happened? Would it happen again? When Hazel was afraid to go to biology class the next day, her mother called me for help.

In talking with Hazel, I learned of the many difficult incidents she had had with needles—several people were required to hold her down when she needed to get an immunization at the doctor's office, then there was a visit to the ER for an IV after a fainting incident at camp. Essentially, Hazel's brain had been rewired. Blood, IVs, needles—those words and visuals set off an instant amygdala hijack. Undertanding that she wasn't crazy, that the associations to these objects had been *acquired,* and that they could be changed through desensitization gave Hazel some hope. Our practice began with desensitizing to the triggering words—one at a time. Hazel practiced saying: "shots," "blood," "heart," while doing deep breathing. She said to herself, "These things are okay. My brain is pushing the wrong message. I don't have to be on alert just because of a word." She knew she needed to "beat the system." My mind says danger! But I need to override that or it will hurt more. Eventually, she was able to say her hardest word—"IV" (intravenous). Practicing nightly, she was able to "wear out" the fear reaction and take the words in stride. She had neutralized them.

The next step, because Hazel did need to get immunizations, was to tackle the fear of shots. I keep on hand needles to inject (safely!) into pillows and pieces of fruit, but at first Hazel just looked at the needle, bringing it closer and closer. Knowing that she *wasn't* going to get the shot didn't make it any easier, but it made it possible to do the exposure. After that we practiced everything but the shot: wiping the surface with cotton balls, giving the shot to a pillow, and timing how long the whole process took (a mere three to four seconds). Seeing that she could control her reaction and not have that terrible wave of dread come over her was miraculous. Hazel decided to go to the doctor's the next day for the shot she'd been putting off. She reported proudly in an e-mail: "I did end up getting the shot! I was beyond excited that I had accomplished what I thought would be impossible."

DO IT TODAY: HELP YOUR CHILD BUILD COMPETENCY WHEN NATURAL EXPOSURES OCCUR

When naturalistic exposures happen—for example, encountering a dog when you are out for an errand—make the most out of them, but remember the sweet spot for amygdala-friendly learning. Because this is a surprise, and not planned, your child may not be able to do as much as he would in an "on-purpose" exposure. If you ask your child to do more than he's ready for, you will be "sensitizing" (reinforcing the danger cue) instead of "desensitizing" (neutralizing the danger cue). Help your child do a little more (or a lot more if he's game) than he would normally do. Observe the dog from a distance: Is it wagging its tail? Say hello to the dog or ask the dog's name. See if your child can stand back and watch the dog go by, rather than running away from the dog (which, as we know, and as you will no doubt teach your child, will only give the dog the signal that you want to play).

Chapter 13

FROM SHYNESS TO SOCIAL ANXIETY AND SELECTIVE MUTISM

My son has been shy his entire life. Now he's a teen and it's really starting to get in the way. He won't talk, he'll barely even text. I'm afraid that his friends will eventually give up on him because he gives so little back.

I don't mind helping my daughter break the ice with playdates and birthday parties, but we're not getting anywhere. She gives me such a look of terror and desperation when I mention that it's time for me to leave, how am I really helping her?

Social phobia is tragic and the tragedy is that it's relatively easily treated, but most people don't get treatment.

—DR. RON KESSLER, HARVARD UNIVERSITY

To see Rachel at home with her family, you might think she had political aspirations. Jumping into the middle of every argument, expressing herself with the righteous indignation of her teenage credo, she doesn't hesitate to let her feelings and thoughts be known. But as soon as she steps out her front door, that Rachel is nowhere to be found; a different person has emerged.

"I lose my confidence. I suddenly overthink everything. Well, I don't even know if I'd call it thinking. I'm racing; my face feels hot. I'm afraid my words will come out all jumbled. I just feel like I'm in the spotlight. I freeze. I can feel people's eyes on me—it's too intense. It gets so unbearable I run to the bathroom. As soon as I'm out of there I feel like I can breathe again. What is wrong with me?"

What makes Rachel suddenly not be herself outside the confines of her house and family? Her amygdala has spoken and it's saying: "You are being judged, scrutinized, and inspected . . . and you are failing miserably."

WHAT IT FEELS LIKE FOR YOUR CHILD

On one hand, it seems like there could be no simpler task—saying hello, saying your name, even just waving, but for children with social anxiety it is like asking for the impossible. Parents beg their kids to just look up, just give Grandpa a hug, just hand Susie the birthday present. Frozen with fear, they feel like they physically can't. They feel painfully self-conscious, just as you might feel when you are sure that all eyes are on a barely visible cold sore. While any of us may feel our anxiety ramp up a few notches when we are in the spotlight, kids with social anxiety are traveling around with their own spotlight. There is no backstage; everything is in public. Talking or singing in the car, being seen on your front lawn—in any ordinary moment your child feels that they are being constantly scrutinized.

When little kids hide in mommy's skirt, we understand. This is why children's birthday parties are for parents, too. But as a child turns five, six, seven, most kids start to acclimate to new situations with a bit of a nudge. Many will still not say much of a hello to the host, or may hesitate to give the gift directly to the birthday boy or girl, but when they see the trampoline or face painting, they jump right in. They might not know what to *say*, but they know what to do, and they want to do it. For children who are socially anxious, though, having time to warm up doesn't help. In fact, the temperature seems to shift the other way—they freeze. There seems to be no escape and no protection, and no way to express how they feel with words. Their body rigid, their throat dry, their cheeks burning, they are so taken over by fear that the world around them becomes a blur. Anticipating greater and greater failure as the seconds tick by, they see the possibility of turning things around as more and more impossible.

Children who are socially anxious are very avoidant of situations that require interaction of any kind—whether familiar or unfamiliar. Feeling defenseless and bound to embarrass themselves, they resist going. Unlike children with separation anxiety, whose reason to avoid a situation is for fear that something bad will happen to their parents, children with social anxiety cling to their parents or other loved ones because they've come to rely on them as their mouthpiece. Without a spokesperson, questions, even simple ones—How are you? What's your name?—feel impossible. The words get stuck in the throats of very capable, bright children. Out of utter frustration, tears and outbursts may result, usually when the child gets home. This is the rock and a hard place that becomes the uneasy life of children with social anxiety.

What is especially disabling for kids with social anxiety is the vicious cycle that develops. Anticipating or overestimating negative reactions from peers leads to more withdrawal; they want to disappear in the woodwork, but the more they recede, the more visible their discomfort may be—which could lead to *real* changes in how peers treat them. Anxious children, while not actively disliked, sometimes become significantly less popular for this reason. This leaves them fewer kids to connect with. It can also interfere with academic functioning. Afraid to raise her hand in class, speaking so quietly that no one can hear, becoming visibly flustered when called on—all of these situations are toxic not only to the child's learning, but also to her accrued social history with her peers.

THE DIAGNOSIS

As many as 5 percent of children suffer from social anxiety. Being around others, or even anticipating contact with others, can make them break out into the equivalent of mental hives. A rush of worries, rules, cautions, criticisms, and catastrophes blows through their mind, leaving little room for more composed brain activity. Left untreated, social anxiety in childhood limits opportunities and can lead to difficulties academically, socially, and professionally in adulthood. Fortunately, social anxiety is highly treatable, and kids can learn how to become socially competent and confident.

RED FLAGS

- Anxiety, worry, physical tension about unfamiliar people, places, situations
- Paralyzing concern that they will do something embarrassing or humiliating in a social or performance situation
- Avoiding eye contact even with familiar people (relatives, classmates)
- Speaking in a very quiet voice, or not speaking at all—for example, being unable to order in a restaurant, talk on the phone, raise their hand in class, use public bathrooms, or even getting sick on days when required to do an oral report
- Clinging, hiding at school, birthday parties
- Unable to change in the locker room for gym class
- Chills, shakiness, feeling hot, blushing in social situations
- Painful self-consciousness about appearance, hair, clothes, face
- Hesitant to respond to other children's social overtures, unable to initiate social contact
- May withdraw at unstructured times—lunch, recess, group activities—rather than risk rejection

THE TRICK AND THE GOAL: IT'S NOT A PERFORMANCE; NO ONE IS WATCHING (THAT CLOSELY); FIRE THE JUDGE, LOWER THE STAKES, AND PRACTICE SMALL STEPS!

The triple-play trick that social fears play on a child is that *everyone* is watching, they will *totally* mess up, and they're totally weird for feeling this way in the first place. These messages looping around in the mind would make it difficult for anyone to feel socially competent. But what are the real answers? Help your child fact-check and do the side-by-side comparison. First: No one is watching that closely (they are busy paying attention to themselves because everyone is at least a little self-conscious). Second: What does "messing up" mean? Little mistakes are what make all of us sound natural and not like robots. Third: We all have that little voice of the critic in our heads. There is nothing abnormal about it; we just need to learn to unplug the critic's microphone, rather than putting it on a loudspeaker.

The first goal (shrink the risk) is for children to develop better, more accurate self-talk in social situations, based on a more realistic assessment of themselves and of how much or how little others are paying attention. The next goal (approach the situation) is to create the stairs of learning—finding a child's starting point with social interaction and creating small, repeatable, on-purpose opportunities (texting a friend, asking the teacher a question, ordering at the ice cream store) to feel some fear and see that it goes away and that they can succeed in that situation.

In preparation for GUTI challenges, kids may need to brush up on some skills—understanding that communication is always a two-way street and learning some tricks and "lines" to keep conversation going. Once you determine the starting point—whether it's making eye contact, smiling at someone, saying "hi," or calling a friend on the phone—the child needs to practice these small steps until he can approach them with confidence rather than with dread. Another practical matter that must be addressed is the fact that many children become so avoidant of social situations that other kids may see them as aloof and disinterested and stop trying to include them.

HOW YOU CAN HELP: CREATE OPPORTUNITIES FOR YOUR CHILD TO BE SOCIALLY COMPETENT

Parents are torn: Do they push their child to go—knowing that their child will be stressed out—or do they let them stay home and become stressed out themselves knowing that their child is missing out on so much? Waiting and wondering compounds the anxiety for all and only seems to turn up the brightness on that roving spotlight.

As always, your goal as a parent is to support your child, not the anxiety. So your first job is to let your child know that you understand how bad this feels, that you know it's not their fault, and that worry is the one making it hard for them to make a move! Your second job is to use that empathy to create trust (that you won't corner your child in a situation that is too hard) and to create amygdala-friendly opportunities with the spotlight dimmed for your child to increase her interaction with others. Remember, think small. Any interaction—looking up, handing a waitress the menu (even if they can't yet say their order), smiling—will feel hard for your child, but will be a step in the right direction. Though you may want to hurry your child along and be surprised at how hard seemingly simple things may be for them, your goal is to help your child *feel* and look as socially competent as possible. The confidence these actions bring will give them momentum to climb the stairs of mastery.

How is this done, without inadvertently adding to the embarrassment by highlighting their difficulties? By sharing the job, in two important ways. First: Give your child a task. When many kids with social anxiety go out in public—say, to a store or a restaurant—they are passive bystanders, stiff, closed off from the action, waiting for the dreaded errand to be over, nagging you to finish. Without anything else to do, their only job is to listen to their worry. So give them something to do: Split up your shopping list, ask them to help you locate items at the store, eventually have them ask a clerk where an item is located. Interaction of any kind puts them on that runway of communication and eventually they will take off.

A second way to share the job is to include them in your conversations. Like those offhand comments on television, where the star talks to the audience instead of to her costars, imagine you are waiting at the bus stop and another parent comes up and starts talking. You are taking the primary role in the conversation, but then you turn to your child and say, "David, that sounds like something you were saying the other day," or, "Charlotte, I remember you had a similar experience." This gives your child an opportunity to be included. Create closed-ended (yes or no) questions that connect with the topic so that your child can nod in agreement, or say or gesture yes or no. Open-ended questions offer too wide open a horizon for choices of what's right or wrong or embarrassing to say. Essentially you are handing your child a line, giving them the opportunity to participate as much as they can given their current level of fear.

The problem with social anxiety is that often the level of challenge is so high even with simple things that the opportunity for failure or falling short is very high. So there is perhaps a bit more pressure on parents to be mindful of closing the challenge gap for their child by stepping in with their words or helping their child to graciously exit after they've given their smile, or hello with their eyes. Look for the small opportunities.

HOW TO EXPLAIN THIS TO YOUR CHILD

The Backstory: Fear of public speaking tops the list of fears—above fear of death or spiders, at least on surveys. Why is that? If anxiety is about overestimation of risk and threat, then social anxiety is the threat of being scrutinized, judged, or embarrassed. But where does the judgment come from?

Social anxiety may stem from ancient circuitry that allowed us to scan, not for poison berries or wild animals, but other human beings—and to read, by simply looking into someone's eyes, whether or not they were a threat to us: friend or foe. But that friend-or-foe filter is overkill in today's world. Is someone in class a threat to us, or might they just not love the answer we gave to the question? The good news is that we don't need to change; we just need to fire the judge we have in our own minds.

In fact, explaining social anxiety this way to kids, especially older children and teens, can be very reassuring, even humorous. "Your old brain—let's call it protector brain—can't stop looking for danger, and invaders to your tribe. The reason you feel so nervous and sweaty, why your heart races, is that your brain is sending the signal it would if someone were going to bite your head off. What you need to do is call on another part of the brain. We don't need protector brain when we are going to a birthday party.

What part would be better? Fun brain? Friend brain? Using a different part of the brain, you can reset the radar so that you bring the risk down to size—all you are doing is talking to classmates or approaching the playground, not approaching enemy territory. Keep your body quiet by doing your breathing; soon your brain, instead of readying you for an impending attack, will help you handle the situations you are in."

For young children: Everyone gets a little nervous going somewhere new or meeting someone they don't know well. It's like a worry mosquito is buzzing around saying the same thing over and over: "It's scary. You can't say hi. Don't look at anybody; you might feel silly. It's not going to be fun." A parent might say something like this to their child: "We need to teach the worry mosquito to quiet down and learn that birthday parties can be uncomfortable at first, but after a few minutes you get used to it and find fun things to do. So let's practice what happens at birthday parties—how to say hi, how to decide what you want to do first. That will show the worry mosquito that you're the boss!"

THE STRATEGIES: KEY INTERVENTIONS IN TREATMENT

STRATEGY: Help Change Your Child's Thinking: Do the Side-by-Side Comparison: Fears versus Facts

When it comes to social fears, help your child generate data for the side-by-side comparison. There are two primary assumptions that fuel the fire of social anxiety; the first is fear of humiliation, and the second is perfectionism—holding oneself to a higher standard than you would use for other people. While young children are primarily troubled by the prospect of being humiliated, teenagers get a double dose, tending to be afflicted with both concerns. Help your child turn their convictions into questions to be proven.

How? Ask her what worry is telling her, then help her fact-check using the strategies from Chapter 5. These include the thought sorter, the million-dollar question, the red pen edit, the Worry Shrinker machine, and more.

For young children: While some children will actually express fears about being laughed at or other kinds of social criticism, most simply experience general feelings of discomfort (freezing, disorganization, feeling scared and embarrassed) and uncertainty in social situations ("I don't know what to do"). You may need to focus less on correcting distortions, and more on encouraging self-talk that is calming and also strategic—scripting the normal steps and stages to follow at a birthday party, with relatives, on a playdate, or at the playground. Using role-playing and cartoon thought bubbles, children can first tell the worry story, then counter it with their smart thoughts or what they imagine another child might think in that situation, and finally, tell about the way they want the story to go. Write the smart thoughts on index cards and have the child rehearse them in front of the mirror or in the car before going to an event.

For older children and adolescents: Using the variety of metaphors in the master plan, kids can work on the idea of correcting the worry wrongs and creating a more realistic sound track for their life. Have your child run any situation down the brain train track, look at it with the worry glasses and the good glasses, write out the "what-ifs" and the "what elses." Ask your child, "What's the worst thing that could happen, and how would you deal with it?" Encourage him to challenge his fears. For example, if he worries that he might "say something weird," ask him, "Would a thinking person like you actually say something so random, or is your brain giving you false information?" Remember to turn statements ("Everyone will laugh!") into questions to be tested ("Will *everyone* laugh?").

Correcting Common Thinking Glitches

Everyone is watching me and judging me. Is everyone watching and judging? No, most people are watching out for themselves; teenagers especially are pretty self-absorbed.

People will think I'm weird, or that what I say or do is strange. What is so strange about saying hello? Asking for milk in the cafeteria? Asking someone for the homework? These are very ordinary things—yet under judgment brain's microscope normal things look strange.

Everything I do counts and it has to be perfect. Does everything have to be perfect? No one is perfect, and no one is paying that close attention to what you do.

Everybody remembers everything I do and it is set in stone. Like a Twitter feed, not everyone sees your news, and it becomes old news very quickly. Kids are focused on themselves and what's next; they don't hold on to what happened in the past.

No one else is struggling with these things. Teenagers especially assume that no one else has put on fifteen swipes of deodorant because they are afraid of someone seeing them sweat; or that they rehearse their lines before a party; or that they worry about who is watching them when they walk into the dance. Reassure your teen that teenagers have felt self-conscious since the olden days (like when we were kids). It's universal, not personal.

THE PARADOX OF SOCIAL ANXIETY: PUT OUT THE WELCOME MAT FOR MISTAKES

Kids with social anxiety dread making mistakes, but this raises their fear temperature many degrees before they even get into the situation. Instead, teach your child to expect mistakes, perhaps even to befriend them, but certainly to be prepared to finesse them. Allowing for failures and goofs, rather than expecting that you have to be perfect (or entertaining, hilarious, or brilliant) will paradoxically reduce your anxiety and make you less likely to make mistakes. Why? Instead of looking in the rearview mirror at what you just did, or racing ahead to where it will get you, all of your attention can focus on what's going on around you right now.

STRATEGY: Unplug the Tension and Get the Body on Board

Often children with social anxiety, especially adolescents, hold tension in their bodies. Diaphragmatic breathing (Chapter 6) gives them an instant solution for the racing heart and other discomfort they feel around others. With regular practice, breathing training (Chapter 6) allows them to support their breath, amplify their voice, and ameliorate tension in the upper body, face, and hands.

Socially anxious children think that people are watching their every move, so they will worry that other people can *see* them if they are doing breathing exercises to calm down. Practice doing this invisibly. Show them the difference between a deep breath at home, and an "incognito" deep breath in public. They'll see (or not see!) how this can be done inconspicuously (or certainly during bathroom breaks) during the school day.

STRATEGY: Take Action! Engage in Behavioral/ Doing Strategies

Remember, after your child shrinks the risk by correcting worry's mistakes and distortions, seeing is believing. GUTI is an essential part of overcoming social fears, and there are constant opportunities to do so. Remember the swimming pool: Your child is going to be very reluctant and nervous to try any exposure, so it is important that you empathize with where they are at, and help them remember that how they are feeling now is not how they'll be feeling later. It isn't a sign of trouble; it's just a sign of the beginning.

PRACTICE DOESN'T MAKE PERFECT; IT MAKES YOU CONFIDENT; REPEAT GUTI EXERCISES FREQUENTLY

Your child might not feel great the first time they make a phone call; they may be clenching the phone with white knuckles through the call, and as a result their anxiety may be more salient to them than their success. The second time will be a little easier. But it isn't until the third, fourth, or fifth time that your child will start to feel that confidence of overlearning. Like mastering a concept in math, there's a reason that teachers give twenty questions on one concept rather than just a few. You want your child to know how to do this like the back of their hand, and that will happen after lots of practice. Researchers have found what parents already know: Massed practice is far preferable to spaced practice. In other words, if you go to the mall to have your child practice asking questions in a store, don't do it just once so that your child feels like they barely squeaked by. Do it three or four times. What's the rule of thumb? GUTI. Your child will tell you if it's getting easier. Use the fear thermometer if you need to check in.

As with all exposures, take the time in advance to plan out the script, playing out possible scenarios of what could happen and generating with your child their choices for responding. Write down the phrases that your child likes and have them practice them in front of the mirror or on video- or audiotape. If your child is ready, rehearse those scripts with role-playing. If they are not ready, have your child imagine the various scenes from beginning to end, while doing relaxed breathing and inserting coping talk, such as, "I am okay. I can do this. Stay calm." These new associations of relaxation and competency in a given social situation will replace old feelings of anxiety and dread. To further decrease the anxiety, add some humor: Try role-playing with your child acting like a favorite cartoon character ("How would Superman say 'hi' here?") or Valley girl–style? Experimenting with different voices often warms up the child so they can find their own voice.

Early GUTI exercises are often best conducted with people your child doesn't ever have to see again, such as store clerks, deli counter staff, or waiters. Children can practice phone skills by calling businesses from the phone book. These should be legitimate calls, not prank calls—have your child ask the store for their hours or location. Encourage your child to make several of these calls in a row until she feels more at ease. Once she has gotten more comfortable with talking to people she won't see again, she is ready to move on to the next steps: increasing her interactions with people she knows. In order to prepare for that and get good conversational material, she can also casually listen in on other kids' "small talk" before class or in the cafeteria or the bus line and report back three or four things that kids were talking about. Then have her generate conversation topics—movies, homework, siblings, teachers—and come up with two ideas to share about each. Remind your child that if she is not ready to increase her verbal contact with others, she can work on decreasing her anxiety level in social settings, practicing her breathing, relaxed body posture, and nonverbal communication such as nodding or smiling.

Make sure that you reinforce all of your child's efforts at communicating with praise, stickers, and incentives. Broaden your definition of communication: eye contact and a smile from a child who previously always looked away qualify as a major step in the right direction. Always look for the ways your child has coped as compared to his baseline, not as compared to other children.

ON-PURPOSE EXPOSURE: SAMPLE EXERCISES FOR YOUNGER CHILDREN

- Smile at a friend at school.
- Say hello to your teacher.
- Tell your teacher one news item (weekend plans, lost a tooth, the dog threw up).
- Say hello to two children at school.
- Bring in something from home, such as a long jump rope or special toy to share; this can be an icebreaker.
- Ask a child to play a game with you.
- Join a group of kids on the jungle gym.
- Ask for a book at the library, answer the phone at home, or place an order in a restaurant.

ON-PURPOSE EXPOSURE: SAMPLE EXERCISES FOR OLDER CHILDREN

- Call a store and find out their hours.
- Call the library and ask if they have a particular book.
- Order a pizza by phone (with parent's permission!).
- Answer the phone at home.
- Ask a student in the cafeteria what time it is.
- Raise your hand and answer a question.
- Compliment a classmate on something.
- Order a sandwich at a convenience store (in person).

- Call a classmate and ask about an assignment.
- Call a classmate and invite her to the movies.

Note: If your child is having difficulty doing "active" exposures, ask them to be a good observer. If, for example, they don't think they can hold an "interesting enough" conversation, ask them to do research at lunch or recess and notice what others are talking about. They will likely learn to adjust their standards, as others' conversation is not necessarily fascinating; it's pretty ordinary, and that's fine.

POINTS TO CONSIDER FOR SOCIAL ANXIETY AT SCHOOL

Anxious children don't like surprises. The more that a child is prepared (getting information the night before at home) or has control over what will be asked of them at school, the more the child can keep the exposures in the amygdala-friendly zone. Here are examples of how to coordinate exposures with the teacher on your child's behalf:

- Have the teacher call on them only when they raise their hand.
- Get questions ahead of time, so your child can practice at home.
- Have the child put an orange card out on the desk when they're ready to be called on.
- Find out if they are more comfortable with an open-ended question or a closed-ended question.
- What is the subject in school they are most comfortable with? Do courage challenges with that subject first.
- Instead of doing a book report in front of the whole class, can they present material to a small group?
- Increase comfort and connection with the teacher by having letters or a notebook go back and forth daily with one or two lines, either about school or about news at home—for example, silly things their pet did, what they ate for dinner, what they are reading at bedtime.

ACTION STRATEGIES

Take a Look

Tape recorders, video cameras, or even mirrors can be powerful tools in helping children to take charge of the social messages they send through their body language and tone of voice. They can use these devices to see what they look like when they smile and experiment playfully with creating different impressions—confident, serious, worried—noticing what it feels like in their muscles.

Practice by Role-Playing

Start by either just asking what time it is, or even having a brief conversation about homework. Mix it up. Try doing this by imitating different people you know, different characters on television, or different people at school.

Do iPhone recordings of how you would answer questions at school, at lunch. Try to mess up on purpose first, then do it being yourself, then try to do it "perfectly"—see which one you like the best. Try to make it realistic—if you are rehearsing ordering in a restaurant, have a sibling make conversation and clanging noises in the background; have the "waitress" be patient in one exercise, grumpy in another, so that your child is prepared and not thrown by the variables that may commonly occur in the actual situation.

Practice the Mistakes on Purpose

If what children are afraid of is making mistakes, don't let mistakes be a mystery. Practice them on purpose so they can see that mistakes can be finessed, are survivable and part of the human condition. For class presentations, phone calls, or ordering in a restaurant, add a dash of "wrong word" or a slight stumble over words, or even forgetting their place. Like knowing how to find your way home if you get lost, by practicing these mistakes, children will be more confident that they can say things like: "Let me try that again," or, "Right, where were we?" or simply continue on. You can also be a "heckling" audience, or practice coughing, looking bored, falling asleep, or falling off your chair so your child can be prepared for those common responses and probably have a good laugh, too, at your antics.

Can You Hear Me Now?

Many children with social anxiety speak quietly. Establish with your child what is a good, audible voice level—but do the long-distance learning by starting with yourself as an example. Give your child an imaginary "remote control" and start talking with a low voice. Let your child pump up the volume until he decides that you're talking at a good level where he can hear you. Go beyond to "too loud," so he can dial back to "just right"; switch roles and have your child give you the remote control. Help your child find "audible."

BRUSHING UP SOCIAL SKILLS

Make eye contact. Young kids can be given the challenge of saying hello to someone and reporting back on their eye color; this way you know they are making eye contact. Older kids and adolescents should know that eye contact is another way of conveying interest in a person or in what they are saying. When you don't make eye contact, people might conclude that you are shy, but they also might wonder if you are being sort of rude or uninterested. If you don't want to send that message—look them in the eye!

Work on conversation skills. Encourage your child to listen and watch others to see how conversations work. Remind him that conversation is a fifty-fifty venture and he's not responsible for the whole thing. He can listen for typical conversation topics, hear how conversations start and end, and see the ways that others deal with awkward silences.

Making conversation can be like selling a product on TV. By your tone of voice you can suggest to your audience that what you are saying is interesting and important—"Did you see that great cartoon in the school newspaper?" Encourage your child to show enthusiasm for what he's saying. If he's interested, others are more likely to want to hear what he has to say.

Have your child practice conversation in comfortable settings—with other kids in a youth group; relatives; a same-sex peer; an opposite-sex peer.

Work on greetings. Often children with social fears will wait for someone else to say hello, not realizing that their peers may be looking for a positive sign that *their* greeting is welcomed. Encourage your child to greet people warmly, to say hello with their eyes or their smile first if they aren't ready to commit to a verbal hello. They may be surprised at how, just as they are happy to be acknowledged, others are too.

Keep the conversation going with a "hook." Tell something about yourself, then put out a hook in the form of a question for the other person: "I just saw the new Chris Rock movie. Did you see it? Did you like it?"

Have a short list of topics that you can bring up if conversation lags. This might be complaining about parents; or discussing school, recent movies, or CDs, upcoming projects for school, plans for vacation, what's happening in sports.

Don't think big conversation. Encourage your child to just practice taking "a few more bites"—like when you are encouraging your child to eat a little bit more of his peas. Just say a few more things than she would normally—a "yes," a "no," a "me, too!"

WHAT'S WRONG WITH SAFETY BEHAVIORS

Being safe seems like such a good thing when you're feeling anxious, right? Wrong. Here are some examples of safety behaviors:

- Talking quietly or mumbling (so people won't hear if you mess up)
- Talking quickly (so you can get it over with and get out of there)
- Not making eye contact (in case the person is disapproving)
- Standing in the back of the room (so no one will know you're there)
- Not expressing any opinions or showing any emotions (in case they are wrong or weird)

Safety behaviors don't really make you feel safer; in fact, paradoxically, thinking you need to do all these extra things just to be safe has the opposite effect: It tells your body that you're in danger and you need to do things "or else" you will really be in trouble. The amygdala will be pumping adrenaline into the system, which will only make you feel more jittery, less able to focus, more nervous, and . . . less able to see your successes. To keep the stress bucket low, don't hold on to unnecessary safety moves.

BRING IT ON! EXAGGERATE WORRY TO FIND THE ABSURDITY

Parents often object to their children being sarcastic, but sarcasm can have a great role in working on anxiety. Using exaggeration or sarcasm competes with anxiety and wins! Take worry's threatening words *("You're going to mess up! Don't try to say hello. You'll embarrass yourself!")* and turn them on their head by exaggerating them further. This helps kids take the power from worry and feel in charge. *"Listen to this: I'm going to mess up so badly; it will be the worst hello in the history. It will be all over the Six O'clock News!"* Amplifying the worry message reveals the absurdity and makes it easier to dismiss.

Listen to the difference between these two scripts, and ask your child to take their fear temperature with each one:

WORRY SCRIPT

"I'm going to fail."

"What if I sweat?"

"What if I blush?"

EXAGGERATED SCRIPT

"Yep, I'm going to mess up, big-time. I might say something really strange—because, you know, saying hello is so weird. Yes, everyone else does it all the time, but if I do it—that will be so strange. Like, 'What, you're saying hello—to me?'"

"I might sweat—like a pig! Like five pigs!"

"I might look nervous—I might blush from my ears to my toes! I will be known as 'The Blusher' from now on."

If your child feels more anxious with the sarcastic script, it just means that he hasn't gone far enough with it. Remember the wave figure from Chapter 7: anxiety may go up first (because you're saying things that sound scary), but then the more you say them, the more absurd they sound, the worry "fever" breaks, and the wave passes.

SCRIPTED ROLES: A REPRIEVE FROM DECISION-MAKING RESPONSIBILITY

A welcome inconsistency in some children with social anxiety is how wonderfully they can do in class plays or concerts. Parents are often confused about how it could be that the same child who refuses to talk at family gatherings or text a friend to get together is somehow able to leave their doubts at the door when they step up on stage. For these children, their anxiety is about the embarrassment that grows out of uncertainty and ambiguity: saying something stupid, or not knowing what to say, or being stuck with silence. A scripted role removes the responsibility for those "unknowns" and allows kids to relax, knowing that they have memorized "the right thing to say." In fact, acting classes can sometimes provide adolescents with the opportunity to get the practice "in groups" that they can't get by themselves. If your child has any inclination in the direction of the performing arts, pursue it.

ON THE HOME FRONT: ELIMINATING INADVERTENT REINFORCEMENT OF SOCIAL ANXIETY

Explaining that a child is "shy" is something that we all naturally do when we see him shrinking back from a welcoming overture, unable to reciprocate a friendly hello. The problem with "shy" is that it is a role, and once cast in it, a child begins to identify with it. It boxes him in. It's not that shy kids don't want to socialize.

Most kids who are uncomfortable with social contact want very much to connect, but they feel they have no choice but avoidance. "Shy" also suggests that the problem is not a big deal—either the child is stuck with it, or he'll outgrow it one day. As one mother put it, "When people say 'shy,' it minimizes the issue."

Begin to see your socially anxious child not as stuck in shyness, but as working slowly on a continuum toward connection. When your child seems frozen with fear at family gatherings or birthday parties, rather than saying, "He's shy," say, "Oh, Justin will be ready to play a little later. He just needs some time to warm up." Or, for your older child, find a way of welcoming him into the conversation, even if he is not ready to talk: "Michael is our thinker. You'd be surprised by the things he comes out with after he's taken it all in." To help start your child over the bridge to socializing, decide together before you go to an event whom he feels most comfortable saying hi to first, and role-play that hello.

SLOW AND STEADY WINS THE RACE

Though you may be tempted to rush your child into social situations, resist. Your child's history, and her imagination, are filled with social failures, embarrassments, and humiliating experiences. You want to choreograph her recovery to ensure that she is logging experiences in the "success" category. Think small. Push your child to keep working on some aspect of increasing participation and decreasing withdrawal in social situations. Be patient with the small steps, such as saying hi, and practicing with nonpeers. Better to bloom late than to have her social future nipped in the bud.

SUMMARY OF INTERVENTIONS FOR SOCIAL ANXIETY

Cognitive Glitch	Fix
Excessive self-focused attention; looking at your behavior under a microscope, micromanaging	Widen the view, back up; keeping such close track would mess up anyone.

Overthinking responses	Simplify: There is no one right answer to a question (other than in math!); everyone's entitled to their opinion.
Body preparing for an emergency, sudden onset of criticism, or attack by others	Reset the panic button to normal by doing breathing, muscle stretching, refocusing on the real situation in front of you.

DO IT TODAY: FIND SMALL OPPORTUNITIES TO SHARE THE MICROPHONE

Share the job, share the credit. Rather than ordering in a restaurant for your child, talking for your child, answering for your child, start seeing opportunities for them to do the work along with you. Find the small things that your child can do, and at the same time, decide that it's okay for them to do whatever they can. If you make a practice of giving them experience in the right doses, you will be giving them the opportunity to succeed!

JULIE'S STORY

Julie, age fifteen, has always been on the quiet side, but when she started junior high in a much larger school, Julie was getting lost in the crowd. She wanted to fit in and be part of what was going on, but her heart would race just thinking about talking. She spent most of her time in class trying to muster the courage to say something. What was wrong with her that she couldn't talk while everyone around her was gabbing away?

At school dances she was a nervous wreck. Following the lead of friends who seemed outgoing and popular, she tried liquor from her parents' cabinet a few times. An honest girl with good judgment, Julie didn't want to hold back from her mom, and she was also scared that this kind of drinking would lead to alcoholism. When Julie's mom did find out she was shocked and upset at the lying and the sneaking. But when Julie told her mother how hard it was to sit in school or look at people, let alone go to a dance, her mother knew that Julie's pain was real and needed to be addressed.

In treatment, Julie was relieved to learn that social anxiety is more than just shyness, that all of those nervous feelings and confusion result from the brain processing the situation as a very high risk and readying the body for a major attack. She worked hard to learn how to dismantle that thinking process herself. She decided to take some risks when she realized that nothing she would say could be that bizarre. Within weeks Julie saw great progress. Though her heart might race at first and she'd hear the old thoughts ("You're going to mess up," or, "You'll say something stupid"), her second thoughts ("You can do this. Smile. Just start; it will get easier") began to come to her without so much effort. Today Julie feels more confident in her own abilities, feels less tense going to school, and naturally smiles more because she no longer feels like she's auditioning on stage all the time—she has the part, this is her life.

SELECTIVE MUTISM: WHEN THE WORDS GET STUCK IN YOUR CHILD'S THROAT

If your child talks comfortably at home but is unable to speak as soon as she steps out the door, no matter how much you coax her, she may have selective mutism. Well-meaning adults often find the discrepancy in the child's speech baffling, but given the way the brain is wired in people with anxiety, it is not hard to imagine that the child is getting signals that home is safe and not being at home is not safe. The child is mortified by taking the risk of speaking (and after not talking for a while the idea of speaking gets scarier and scarier—what will his voice sound like?), so in self-defense he speaks only in selected situations—at home, at school only with peers or only with teachers, or neither. For some kids the behavior begins as purely physiological—they freeze up. For other children there are faulty but understandable assumptions about the risk of participation, and the task is to correct the assumptions and give the children multiple opportunities for practicing speech of some sort. Left untreated, selective mutism, like other types of social anxiety, only becomes more debilitating. However, with systematic cognitive behavior therapy, patiently delivered, kids will begin to participate verbally more and more.

RED FLAGS

- The child does not speak in certain situations, such as at school or social events.
- The child can speak normally in settings where they are comfortable, such as in their home.
- The child's inability to speak interferes with his ability to function in educational and/or social settings.
- The child appears to freeze up, becoming stiff and statuelike in target settings.
- Mutism has persisted for at least one month.

Treatment for Selective Mutism

As in children with other anxiety disorders, a child with selective mutism is not simply a little uncomfortable and will not just outgrow it. Children with selective mutism grow increasingly isolated, frustrated, and angry, and feelings of low self-esteem are inevitable as they experience daily negative attention from others who are waiting for them to talk. They are vulnerable to other psychological difficulties. Fortunately, according to a leading spokesperson on selective mutism, Dr. Elise Shipon-Blum, the prognosis is excellent with proper diagnosis and treatment. Effective treatment involves a combination of strategies to correct distortions in the child's processing of his speech and other's reactions to it, and an openness and flexibility in the situations in which the child struggles so he'll be willing to venture out of his comfort zone. Here are some ideas to get started:

STRATEGIES TO TAKE CHARGE OF ANXIETY

- Correct distortions in people's reaction to the child's lack of speech.

- Teach realistic, supportive self-talk.
- Begin systematic desensitization to the target setting—help the child gain comfort in school.
- Positively reinforce any approximation of communication in the target setting—begin with smiles, notes, playing a simple instrument, eye contact, reading a one-word script, eventually spontaneous speech.

Environmental Accommodations

Provide dry-erase boards or index cards with answers to commonly asked questions that the child can present when needed. Sometimes children will be able to speak with one or two peers but not with a teacher; if this is the case, the child can be linked with a buddy to deliver whispered messages. Allow oral presentations to be taped at home. Teachers should not call on the child unless this is something within the child's repertoire or comfort zone. Sometimes answering questions they are sure about, with some warning ahead of time, can help kids to feel that they are participating at their comfort level.

Flexibility in Selective Mutism and Finding the Moving Part

It can be perplexing to work with children with selective mutism—knowing that they can talk perfectly well (and often are the most talkative!) in certain settings; it can be frustrating for parents and even therapists to see the child "refusing" to talk in other situations. It is important to keep in mind the involuntary nature of this disorder. (Previously called "elective mutism," in 1994 the term was changed to "selective mutism" to reinforce the fact that children very much want to speak in these situations.) Some therapists and parents will insist on talking as the only acceptable outcome, but this quickly becomes a battle of wills. Instead find the moving part: The goal is not speech but communication. Give the child choices about how they are going to communicate: a white board, whispering, having a signal system for yes and no, and so forth. When it appears that a child is "refusing" to speak, reestablish the goal of communication: "I know you want this to be easier, and I want to help you. Let's figure out ways of doing this together. Here are some choices. You can say no to some, but we have to find something that you can say "yes" to. I can't do it without you!"

Some Examples of Exercises for Selective Mutism

Play the category game. Because one-word answers are a good place to start, go back and forth naming desserts, animals, vegetables, television shows until you run out of ideas. Play cooperatively; there doesn't need to be a winner. Another way to play is using the alphabet—see if you can take turns naming states, animals, desserts, and so forth, that begin with each letter of the alphabet.

The Mystery Motivator (an intervention developed by William Jensen). Choose a reinforcer such as extra computer time, a homework pass, or another small prize. Write it down on a piece of paper and put it in an envelope with a question mark written on it. When the child is able to ask for the envelope with an audible voice, they earn the prize inside. Over time, you can increase the challenge and keep a chart on which the child has to earn a certain number of stickers each week for communication to earn the mystery prize. The key is not to remind the child about it; when they are ready to earn the prize, they will do the work themselves.

The Parent's Dilemma: How Not to Be Rude or Indiscreet When You're Trying to Help Your Child Not to Be Rude

For many parents, there is a great push-pull with social anxiety exposures because they are concerned that their child is acting "rude." And then there's an added piece: When you are correcting your child or coaxing them to say something, well, it doesn't come across very kindly. Not only does your child feel he's doing something wrong, but, to add salt to the wound, now everyone is *noticing* his inability to participate.

So you have to ask yourself: What's your goal? In the short term you may feel pressure from your own needs: I need my child to be social. But remember, your goal is your child's growth. How your child behaves in this one moment is not a lasting assessment of his or her abilities, but how he *perceives* this moment, and how you handle it, could make him feel either that he's shut off—he's going to fail—or that there's an opening—he could "get better."

You want to try to help your child become a more social person, not to have their deficits highlighted. Many parents of socially anxious kids have social anxiety themselves. It's important to let go of the need for this moment to be perfect—or even good—and just see it as one moment. Focus not on the short-term and possibly insignificant needs of the adult whom your child is interacting with, but on the potential for your child to take a crucial step that will help them in the long run.

Chapter 14

FROM CLINGINESS TO SEPARATION ANXIETY AND PANIC DISORDER

An Inside Look at Separation Anxiety

Our seven-year-old can't be alone. She follows us to the bathroom, can't be out of our sight, begs us not to go out. She wrote a note saying that she can't be without us. We are the only ones who can help her. She says she would rather die than be without us. She is so distressed, I don't think she's trying to manipulate us, but what do we do?

Our middle child can't sleep alone. He's in our bed every night. He says he won't be able to fall asleep without us. I don't want him to be a wreck in the morning, but now our two other kids want to know why they can't sleep in our bed, too. Is tough love the answer? It seems like he'll fall apart and none of us will get any sleep.

An Inside Look at Panic Disorder

Maria came down the other night looking like she'd seen a ghost. She had these strange feelings like she was in a dream or a movie. She said it felt weird to look at her hands; they felt like they were someone else's. She was terrified that she was going crazy, and now she doesn't want to leave my side because she's afraid it will happen again.

The tough thing about panic is that it hits without warning and it is immediately at a ten on the anxiety scale. It's hard as a par-

ent to give up the illusion that you have the power to make it all go away.

SEPARATION ANXIETY AND PANIC DISORDER: BORN OF THE SAME (DIS)CONNECTION?

At somewhere between eighteen and twenty-four months, toddlers learn to climb the stairs and run around the yard, and just then, with the winds of freedom whistling at their backs, an interesting phenomenon occurs—they panic and want Mom! This acute separation anxiety is necessary for their survival; it ensures they won't break the ties to their source of protection, and it usually resolves itself within several months. The young child learns through practice back and forth from home base that even though she runs away to pursue an interesting bug, friend, or trip with Grandma, she can come running back into Mom's welcoming arms.

Over the next several years of the child's life, the lesson that separations are survivable, that freedom is good, and that reunions can be trusted is tested and reinforced. These experiences serve as the foundation for children's confidence in independent exploration of the world. Typically, by age five or six most children are able to separate confidently. Children and parents alike learn that those "missing Mom or Dad" feelings come and go, and it's much easier when there's a person or activity to transition to. Though the handoff may be teary, usually most children settle in within a few minutes of the parent leaving.

Children with separation anxiety disorder (SAD) have a glitch in making the connection between separations and reunions. Rather than building confidence over time, they continue to experience each separation as a crisis. They do not feel safe unless they are actually with a parent, and even then they may be troubled by future potential threats to their parents. A little boy may worry all the time about whether the parent is ill, happy enough, going to die, too tired, or upset. Separation anxiety disorder is a debilitating condition for both parent and child.

Panic disorder is less common in children than is SAD, and is characterized by sudden surges of anxiety accompanied by unexplained physical symptoms—dizziness, a racing heart, becoming hot, tired, or faint, or feeling detached or unreal—as if they are not there, or they're in a dream, or a movie. Though the physical symptoms themselves are harmless, the child doesn't understand what is happening to him and feels terrified that the symptoms signal impending doom. These sensations are experienced as signs of danger and lead instantaneously to thoughts of being out of control and fear of dying, suffocating, or going crazy. Children become fearful that this surprise attack of intense fear will occur again ("fear of the fear," or fear of the uncomfortable feelings of fear), and to play it safe they begin to avoid situations in which panic might occur. They may feel the need to stay close to home, so their problem may look like separation anxiety disorder, but they are not concerned with their parents' well-being; they are afraid for their own.

This experience of feeling safe only within a certain distance from parent or home is one that separation anxiety disorder shares with panic disorder, and one reason that current theory posits that separation anxiety (most common in seven- to nine-year-olds) is an early manifestation of panic disorder (most common in teenagers and adults). Further support for this hypothesis comes from the finding that nearly half of all adults with panic disorder and agoraphobia (not venturing out because of fear of a panic attack, literally "fear of the marketplace") report having had separation anxiety in childhood.

WHAT IT FEELS LIKE FOR YOUR CHILD

For children with both of these disorders, the simple need to feel safe in day-to-day life can be a full-time job. They despairingly ask, "Am I going to be okay?" But they are not able to wait for an answer, because the amygdala stays in the "on" position, readying the children to defend themselves as if they're not okay. This state of readiness comes at a cost. It results in the physical symptoms we have already mentioned. Children can become hysterical and out of control, beside themselves with fear about the meaning of those symptoms. Will they faint, have to go to the hospital, or die? They also fear that the bad feeling will come when they are away from their parents and no one will be able to help them. As one youngster told me, "My parents are the ones who've known me the longest. They are the only ones who can help." As a result, such children stay near home base.

Without a basic feeling of safety, it is difficult for children to focus on anything else. While other children are free to let their minds roam—playing with friends, learning in school, generally engaging in life—children with separation anxiety or panic disorder are on a tight leash. If they are able to lose themselves in an activity for a while, this may end abruptly when they realize they haven't been worrying. Rather than experiencing this reprieve as a relief, they are more unsettled because they've been off their watch. They are constantly making contact with home base (parents), whether by phone, text, or simply by calling upstairs, "MOM!" to make sure a parent is available; they feel the constant need to know the parents' whereabouts. Especially as children get older, the hold that anxiety has on their thinking and their mobility wears on them, often causing isolation, sadness, and even in some cases depression.

THE TRICK AND THE GOAL: FROM BEING IMMOBILIZED WITH FEAR TO CREATING A MOBILE SENSE OF SAFETY

Reinterpreting the Alarm

Children with separation anxiety need to learn to tolerate increasingly longer separations and replace the "away from Mom = danger" circuit with "I am safe even when I'm away from Mom." Rather than an alarm going off—"Mom? Mom??!!, MOM?!!?"—whenever they look up and see their mom isn't there, with your help they will employ the seven-second delay and learn to think, "Mom is not in the kitchen; she is in the bathroom or the basement, or at the mailbox outside," rather than panicking thinking that she has somehow vaporized.

Children with panic disorder need to relabel the sudden onset of physical symptoms as a benign fire drill in the mind, learn to tolerate the uncomfortable feelings and know they are completely *harmless* and aren't a sign of any physical danger, and reset their body's alarm. This is accomplished by breathing and relaxation exercises, and by venturing out into situations where there is a fear that panic may occur. As with all types of anxiety disorders, the goal is to see that the problem isn't the situation (they have no health risks, and there's nothing inherently dangerous about going to the mall, the movies, or to school), but that anxiety is mistakenly sounding the alarm when everything is actually completely fine.

Mastering the Skill of Being Alone

In the thick of things, the idea of being alone elicits feelings of fear, loss, and vulnerability. But on the other side of the challenge of separation anxiety and panic disorder, happy children are able to go to school without tears, play at friends' houses, sleep through the night, even go to a sleepover party. Once these accomplishments are earned, there's no turning back. Kids are confident that they can manage without Mom or home base, because they have learned to bring their comfort zone with them. So approach this challenge knowing that even though your child may fight you every step of the way, you are doing a good thing. Compassionately know that he is fighting because of the fear that being alone will be too hard. Your child won't naturally outgrow this without your help.

HOW YOU CAN HELP

Freeing your child from separation anxiety requires that you understand your child's no-fault faulty processing of separations, and reinforce the idea that he is safe, and that even though his alarm went off, nothing big is changing. The brain is playing the trick of having the child focus on how awful it would be to never see a parent again and manipulating his feelings terribly, all the while withholding the information on how unlikely that would be. Anyone presented with that worst-case version of the separation story would cling. The solution is not more reassurance or clinging, or avoiding all separations, but recasting the issue. The separation is temporary, and each of you will do what you need to do, and then there will be the happy reunion, when you can compare notes on your adventures. Your child with separation anxiety needs *more* practice with separations at his level in order to internalize your strength and confidence in him.

With panic disorder, the first and most important way that you can help is by not being afraid, yourself, of what your child is experiencing. Your child's own anxiety spiral is fueled by fear of not understanding what is happening. You can put a lid on that, but this may be difficult at first because you yourself are confused. What is my child afraid of? How can my child be anxious if I'm sitting right here with them? Remember, your child's symptoms are so frightening to them because they don't make sense to them, either. Rather than ask why, which will only make your child feel worse, use the thought stamper and relabel their experiences as anxiety, to separate the scary thoughts from your child.

Second, parents can help by being willing to take small steps. For many families dealing with a child with separation anxiety, parents going out to dinner and a movie is too big a leap for early exposures. Be willing to work in shorter shifts—a fifteen-minute walk around the block, a half-hour errand, a short trip to the mall. End the exposure on a good note, returning when your child has settled down. You don't want to reinforce that just because your child is protesting your being away, you immediately come home and cut the process short by jumping in to rescue your child: Remember from Chapter 2 that rescue is very reinforcing, but it's reinforcing the wrong things. You want your child to feel in charge and have a sense of mastery—I did this! That's the moment that you know it's okay to call it a day.

Third, it helps to have a pull, not just a push, to help your child's world expand. So although you want to be supportive of your child needing to stay close to home for a while, make sure that life at home isn't so interesting that they have no reason at all to make a change. Your child will be more motivated to venture out when there's a pull from out there—when it's not just about what (or whom) they are leaving, but what they are going toward. Help your child to see how interesting life outside of your home and family can be.

Finally, remember that helping your child separate is good parenting. It is hard to see your child distressed, but another part of you knows it is a very important thing that only you can do for your child, to broaden their base of confidence in themselves and the world. If you hesitate, your child may interpret your hesitation as a lack of faith in them—or as a sign that you are afraid. Choose to see your child's strength and potential rather than their (or your) fear and hesitation. Do your own "red pen edit." First thought: "I'm leaving my child to manage discomfort on his own! This is terrible. I'm a bad parent!" The rewrite: "I'm ~~leaving~~ giving my child *the opportunity* to *learn how to* manage discomfort on his own! This is ~~terrible~~ a really important skill—and I have to be brave enough to believe he can do it, because that's what I'm asking him to do. I'm a brave ~~bad~~ parent!"

The rest of this chapter will address these two disorders separately, providing solutions for creating a sense of safety both in the home and outside it by addressing both thinking errors and physical symptoms. If your child has symptoms of both disorders, as many do, familiarizing yourself with these strategies will help you cover all your bases.

SEPARATION ANXIETY DISORDER: THE DIAGNOSIS

Separation anxiety disorder is diagnosed when several of the following symptoms are present for at least four weeks and interfere with the child's and family's functioning (going to sleep, school, work).

RED FLAGS

- Extreme distress upon actual or imagined separations
- Crying, clinging, tantrums, vomiting upon separation
- Nightmares about harm to parents
- Reluctance or refusal to leave the house or be apart from parents
- Frequent checking, reassurance-seeking about safety of loved ones
- Discomfort or inability to be in a separate room or on a separate floor from parent
- Frequent calling out to parent (at home) to establish his or her whereabouts
- Frequent phone calls home or insistence that parent stay home when child is out
- Difficulty or inability to sleep in own bed
- Difficulty attending school, frequent calls home, trips to nurse's office
- Unable to go on playdates, field trips; unable to be in a car other than parent's
- Desire for parents to drive in separate cars as a safety precaution
- May report unusual experiences like "seeing" eyes staring at them or hearing whispers at night

HOW TO EXPLAIN THIS TO YOUR CHILD

Compassionately help your child know that his brain is playing the trick of having him focus on how awful it would be to never see you again or that bad things will happen. Meanwhile, that's not how the story ends. Brain bug doesn't know how things really work when kids go to school or parents go to the movies; we've got to teach it what good-byes really mean: They are temporary and everybody's fine.

THE STRATEGIES: KEY INTERVENTIONS IN TREATMENT: CONNECTING THE "GOOD-BYE" CIRCUIT TO "SEE YOU SOON"

STRATEGY: Change the Thoughts, and the Feelings (and Actions) Will Change as Well

Use the many thought-shifting strategies, such as doing the side-by-side comparison or asking the million-dollar question described in Chapters 4 and 5 and the master plan in Chapter 8, to increase realistic thinking.

STRATEGY: Get the Body on Board; Compassionately Turn Off the Alarms and Set Limits for the Nervous System

Kids with separation anxiety disorder can get out of control emotionally very quickly. The mere mention of a separation (a year from now) can send them spiraling. A child with SAD has difficulty reining in emotion because his nervous system delivers very intense distress. Sometimes crying can help a child move through a situation, but often symptoms for kids with SAD only escalate with crying.

Because being out of control isn't good for anybody, therapists, parents, and teachers need to compassionately direct these kids to slow the body down. You don't want to inadvertently reinforce the deterioration by talking with them through their tears. Say things like "In a minute when your breathing slows down, you'll feel a little better and we can talk about this." Or, "Hold my hands and breathe with me. Then we can talk." The directions that follow can be used with children with SAD and panic disorder if they are in the throes of an episode. Teaching children how to do balloon breathing (see Chapter 6) can proactively help them keep their anxiety from escalating. They can be instructed to use breathing techniques in challenging situations, such as when they're trying to fall asleep on their own or going to school.

Voice	"Try to tell me in a regular voice when you are ready. Let's slow down the crying. Wait till you've calmed down, then you can explain. Don't try to talk now."
Breathing	"Slow down your breathing. Breathe with me. Hold my hands. Look at me. Do balloon breathing. Breathe slowly into a paper bag."
Body position	Help the child to sit in a chair. Try to get them to hold your hands rather than clinging or lying on the floor.
Thinking	Orient the child to the present. Let them know that they are in no danger, that the feelings of fear will pass soon if they can stay calm. Tell them, "Your mind just gave you a bad signal that you aren't safe. You are fine. These feelings will pass when you turn off the alarm."

APPROACH THE SITUATIONS THAT ARE UNCOMFORTABLE AND PRACTICE GETTING USED TO THEM

Once you have established a more realistic picture of separation and reunion, your child is ready to begin acting on that new belief. Kids need lots of GUTI practice, at a manageable level, to get confident that they can handle separations. Though parents, especially frustrated parents who have been stuck at home for months or even years, may be tempted to book tickets for a weekend getaway at the first chance, it is important to remember that small steps are essential to lasting success. Small steps that begin in the proverbial "shallow end of the pool" will be best, and for children with separation anxiety and panic disorder, this means in your house (with you on a different floor or out at the mailbox), then in your neighborhood, gradually expanding your child's comfort zone to include more and more territory. You will get to that weekend getaway much faster if you work steadily with small steps.

GENERAL GUIDELINES FOR WORKING ON SEPARATION ANXIETY

- Establish a stairs of learning hierarchy for progressive exposure to separations, from the easiest to the toughest, using your child's fear thermometer as a guide. Remember, separation is in the eye of the beholder: Ask your child what step he is ready to take first. Though the goal is stretching the amount of time that parent and child are successfully apart, it may be preferable to accomplish this through stretching the amount of time that the parent is away, as opposed to increasing the time that the child is away. If the child can remain on the familiar territory of home (with a sitter), he only has to cope with the challenge of separating; if he ventures out, he is coping with the dual demands of a new situation and separation. Look at the Anxiety Equalizer figure in Chapter 7 to consider the impact of different factors, such as time of day or familiarity with the setting, in planning exposures for your child. Ask your child, "What would make it easier? What would make it harder?" See if there are other variables that they think you should add to the list that will impact the degree of difficulty of the courage challenge. And remember, every challenge can be broken down into smaller challenges (for example, going to the bathroom with a sibling or pet rather than a parent, and then building up to going alone).

- Remember that nighttime coping is generally the toughest; work in earnest on daytime separations first.
- Get your boss back talk ready. Your child should have "cue cards" to help him remember what to think (e.g., "This is fine. Don't think how awful it would be if something happened; think how awfully unlikely it is that something bad will happen. Mommy loves me. She'll be back soon. Worry bug, go away!").
- Role-play or rehearse what the child will say or do when the parent is away. Switch roles so that your child gets to be the parent. It is often enlightening for parents to hear how kids think you should be responding to them.
- Time flies when you're having fun. Make a schedule of activities that your child can do during a separation exposure. Even teenagers will benefit from this structure. What would you do with this time if you weren't nervous or worried?
- Use sticker charts to keep track of young children's courage challenges. For older kids, points can be logged to trade for extra computer time, a CD, or some other treat.

ON-PURPOSE EXPOSURES: SAMPLE EXERCISES FOR VERY YOUNG CHILDREN (AGES FOUR TO SEVEN)

- Make a "good-bye book" that your child can read when you go out or when the child goes to preschool. Have your child draw or dictate the story with a beginning, middle, and an end. In the beginning of the story, the child is saying good-bye to the parents; in the middle are pictures and directions for what the child can do while the parents are out (play games, color, read books) and what she can say to herself if she is worried ("Mom always comes back. Shoo, shoo, worry bug!"). The last page of the story is the happy reunion.
- Make a picture or list of things for your child to do while Mom and Dad are gone. Your child can illustrate and decorate the list.
- Make good-byes short and sweet (see discussion in "On the Home Front," later in this chapter).
- Role-play good-byes. Let your child play the parent role—you'll hear what he wants you to tell him. When you play the child, don't overdo the drama; it will frighten and overwhelm your child.
- Make a list of brave statements that your child can say if he's feeling scared.

ON-PURPOSE EXPOSURE: SAMPLE EXERCISES FOR YOUNG CHILDREN

Establish independence outside of the house:

- The parent goes to pick up mail; the child stays busy (supervised) in the house.
- The parent goes out for increasing periods of time (during the day).
- The parent goes out for increasing periods of time (at night).
- The child goes to a playdate and Mom remains there—in the same room, then in a separate room.
- Mom leaves the playdate (or birthday party) for increasing periods of time.
- The child goes to a playdate or birthday party alone.

Establish independence at bedtime:

- The parent tucks the child in, then increases physical distance from the child. If the starting point is the parent lying in bed, move to sitting on the bed, sitting on the floor, sitting by the door, then standing outside the door.
- Reduce the amount of time spent in the child's room at bedtime, checking on the child every few minutes instead.
- Reinforce the child for staying in bed.

ON-PURPOSE EXPOSURE: SAMPLE EXERCISES FOR OLDER CHILDREN AND TEENS

- Create a list of "courage errands" or "courage challenges"—going to a separate room, then a separate floor to pick up items, get a snack, and so forth. You can write these tasks down with your child's help on separate slips of paper and place them in a basket. Have your child choose one to two courage challenges from the basket each day.
- Increase the time spent at school. Decrease number of phone calls or texts to parents.
- Establish a bedtime routine in which the parent checks on the child; the child doesn't check on the parent. For seven- to ten-year-olds, have the child write in a journal or leave notes to Mom in a special mailbox rather than calling out.
- If you pick up your child from school, don't be the first in the pickup line. Tell your child that you will be among the first few cars, but make a plan for what the child can do while they are waiting.
- Use the Anxiety Equalizer in Chapter 7 to decide what steps your child is ready to take—going to a good friend's house in the daytime, in good weather, and so forth. Move up to stretching the amount of time spent at a friend's, including nighttime.

SAMPLE HIERARCHY OF COURAGE CHALLENGES FOR OLDER CHILDREN AND TEENS

- The child stays inside while the parents are outside in the yard.
- The child stays home while the parents go for a walk around the block.

- The child goes to a friend's house in the afternoon while the parents stay at home.
- The child goes to a friend's house till 7 p.m., and the parents stay home.
- The child goes to a friend's house during the day while the parents are not home but are at an agreed-upon location.
- The child goes to a friend's house without knowing the parents' specific plans.
- The child goes to a friend's house until 10 p.m.
- The child goes for a sleepover at a friend's house.

GENERAL RULE OF THUMB

Parents are on standby for exposures so your child can check in as needed, but your presence should not be built into the plan because children, generally, rely on the parent when he or she is there, but will tap into their own strengths and resources if they are not. This is the case provided that the courage challenge is amygdala-friendly or at the appropriate level for your child's current functioning. For example, rather than assume that you will walk your child to the bathroom at night, see if by using a flashlight or night-light or bringing along a stuffed animal your child will go to the bathroom by himself. It's better for your child to see how much he can do without you than for you to automatically be there.

CLEAR GOOD-BYES: NO SNEAKING OUT

When your child already feels unsafe, rushing them, sneaking out, or not preparing them for outings will only confirm for them that they need to stay glued to home base. Make sure that when you do exposures you say good-bye; though they may be tearful now, eventually they will learn to manage the temporary discomfort.

DON'T ALLOW SEPARATION ANXIETY TO LIMIT THE FAMILY

Other family members' needs matter, too, and they may feel limited because of the small radius of the anxious child's comfort zone. You can plan outings with your spouse or other children, leaving your child with a trusted relative or sitter. Though this may be stressful or challenging for your child, it is a stretch that they need to make for the good of the family, and you know that they are safe at home. This can be an important intervention not just for the family good, but for the anxious child too. She may see that she is able to calm down and manage without her parents—something her anxiety wasn't ever going to let her see!

HANDLING CALLS AND TEXTS

Parents will often come into a session showing me their cell phone's record of messages from their children—fifty calls in the course of one outing. It is important to put a limit on this contact, which will only keep the "missing you" circuit active in your absence. Rather than do this unilaterally, share the job. While being empathic that this separation is challenging, ask your child, "Who is going to be happy if you call me fifty times? Is it really good for your goal of becoming more confident, or is it really going to make worry happy? What would you be doing if anxiety weren't bugging you? Let's help you do some of that" Over time, work toward eliminating these check-ins by phone.

ON THE HOME FRONT: NEW STEPS IN THE PAS DE DEUX

Families aren't happy to find themselves in the separation anxiety dance, but one reassuring thing is that both you *and* your child can take the lead in changing this dance. Your child will be working on the courage challenges we have outlined above, and you can make sure that you are giving your child appropriate opportunities to practice separating. Many parents who have been dealing with separation anxiety disorder for a long time speak a language of defeat: "I couldn't go to the party; she wouldn't let me." Instead, proceed with your plan and work around it. Pose questions such as "How can we make this more comfortable for you? What part of this are you ready to do? What would you like to do while we are out?" You must take your child's distress seriously, but with a plan to help your child move past the distress.

Sometimes parents themselves have separation anxiety. If you are in this situation, use the strategies in this chapter on yourself first. Ask yourself, "What's your worry story about being alone? What's the smart story (the accurate one) you want to tell yourself instead?" Notice how your distress isn't coming from the situation itself—it's the story your mind is telling you about being apart—that it is "too much" or it is "damaging." When you are separating in a planned way and with love and compassion, it is not damaging for either of you; it is natural and it is freeing for both of you! Think of all the great healthy experiences your child will be able to have on the other side of this hurdle. You are bravely helping her get there. If you are finding it hard to address these issues in your child because of your own lingering separation anxiety, please seek help. It will make a world of difference for both of you.

TO SLEEP ALONE, OR NOT TO SLEEP ALONE: THAT IS THE QUESTION

Many kids with separation fears have difficulty sleeping in their own rooms. They may sleep in their parents' bed, with their siblings, on a sleeping bag in their parents' room, or sometimes even camped outside the door. Tackle this in steps. For one youngster, eight-year-old Kelly, we made a map of the distance from her parents' door to her room and divided the route into steps that she thought she could take each week, inch by inch. Just making the map helped Kelly see the challenge as more manageable, and the next week she was back in her room. Not all kids will be so eager, but put out the expectation that your child will be able to sleep alone someday soon. For specific strategies on dealing with nighttime fears, see the discussions in Chapter 18.

MAKING THE CLEAN BREAK: DEALING WITH CLINGINESS AND ENCOURAGING CONFIDENT, HEALTHY SEPARATIONS

- Find good ways to say good-bye early on. Don't sneak out without saying good-bye. Help your child build confidence and trust by having the courage to take a good look at your child so he remembers your smile, rather than the sight of you sneaking away.
- When you say good-bye, don't add fuel to the fire by saying something like this: "I wish I didn't have to work either. I'm going to miss you all day, too." Instead say, "It's always hard at the beginning, but the scared feelings won't last. We'll have a happy reunion when we get home."
- Help your child transition to another adult (teacher) or to an activity before you leave.
- Be positive and encouraging about new situations. Help your child look through the smart glasses and see what might be fun or interesting in the new situation.
- Give your child opportunities to practice small separations.
- Use transitional objects—pictures of family, stuffed animals, favorite snacks, favorite books—to bring a little bit of home to the new situation.
- Don't joke, ever, about not coming back, or tell your child that you'll call the police to pick them up if they behave badly. These words, however lightly delivered, can be devastating to a child with anxious wiring.

PARENT'S CHEAT SHEET FOR SEPARATION ANXIETY

- Remember, your separation-anxious child needs more practice with separations, not less.
- Practice frequent small separations, rather than occasional separations with a higher degree of difficulty.
- Help your child get his thinking straight; help him to separate the thoughts from the feelings.
- A watched door never opens. Schedule activities to keep your child busy while she is waiting for your return.

- Keep your part of the good-bye short and sweet. Be brave and confident; you'll show your child that this is safe.

LENA'S STORY

Lena, a teenager with extreme separation anxiety and panic disorder, was unable to attend field trips at school or even let her parents out of her sight at home. She couldn't go to friends' houses, had great difficulty when her parents left her with a sitter, and didn't want her parents to drive anywhere together because the idea of losing them both in an accident was overwhelming. In treatment she learned about panic disorder and separation anxiety and relabeled her worry thoughts as the work of "Fuzz Guy." She fought back with "Smart Girl." With treatment, Lena began taking small risks: walking to school, having her parents walk around the block while she stayed home, reducing the length and intensity of her good-byes. She was improving but still had challenges. Then one day Lena's mother announced that there was an out-of-town business conference she wanted to attend for a week. Having braced for a difficult reaction from her daughter, Lena's mother was completely taken aback when Lena said, "Mom, I want you to go. I know how important this is to you." This from a child who just a week earlier had been still clinging to her mom in tears when she was going to go out for the evening! Lena had turned a corner. What this confirmed for the entire family was that as much as Lena might have wished that her mom would not go—because that would be easier—the real Lena wanted her mom to go and do what she needed to do in her own life.

DO IT TODAY: DON'T WORRY; GO THROUGH YOUR CHECKLIST INSTEAD

Fear trumps logic, but logic can carry its own weight. Look for ways to be logical about separation anxiety disorder. For Christopher, we created a detective checklist of places to look first before calling out to Mom. This was a job-sharing intervention: Mom stopped having to run everywhere when Christopher called, and Christopher stopped going to look, because the burden of the work was on him. This work helped convince him that even though Mom was not exactly where he thought she should be, she was not on Mars, or in Europe, or even at the circus. She was just away for a minute—doing laundry, in the bathroom, getting the mail.

For Jane, we created a list to carry in her pocket to remind her of possible explanations for why Mom might be late: "There was traffic. She was held up in a meeting. She was walking the dog. She'll be here soon!" In the other pocket she kept a deck of cards so that she'd have something to do while waiting—other than worrying!

PANIC DISORDER

What It Feels Like for Your Child

Panic disorder can be one of the most crippling anxiety disorders to manage, because there is no specific triggering situation to be avoided. The possibility of a surprise attack is omnipresent; in fact, they often happen during an otherwise perfectly calm moment, even a positive moment—a family gathering, a party, a meal at a restaurant. All of a sudden out of the blue your child has a sensation—feels warm, dizzy, or light-headed. The feeling is frightening, unfamiliar, and inexplicable. It sets off within seconds a terrible feeling of dread that something very bad is about to happen at any moment—they may not be able to articulate what that bad thing is, or they may say, "What's happening? Am I okay? Am I going to have to go the hospital? Am I going crazy?" The more these questions are entertained, the more frightened they become; anxiety spirals, their fight-or-flight symptoms such as heart racing or sweating increase, which only perpetuates their fear and convinces them they are in danger. What is confusing and troubling to all is that there isn't an object of that fear—no snake, test, or bully to point to. It's the fear that the feelings will happen (and that they'll be away from parents or home), and they don't know when or where, so they feel trapped and vulnerable.

HOW CAN THIS *NOT* BE AN EMERGENCY WHEN IT FEELS LIKE IT IS?

How to Make Sense of Panic Attacks

A panic attack can best be described as a simulated drill of the nervous system to see if the first responder gear is fully functioning. Testing: one, two, three. The problem is there's no announcement that this is what the body is going to be doing. So trying to make sense of strange and uncomfortable symptoms, we assume we are in immediate peril. If only the brain could announce, "Fight-or-flight drill," then kids would be able to relabel those surges as false alarms or fire drills, and know that they are not in danger and that the "drill" will end.

In a panic episode, children are very distressed and often flatly refuse to go places because they are afraid. When you ask them what they are afraid of, what they answer is: "I don't want it to happen again," or, "I don't want to get that feeling again." When pressed for a reason beyond that, kids just feel embarrassed, angry, or simply unable to put their finger on anything other than a fear that they will feel mortally uncomfortable and need to come home.

Until your child understands how panic works, she can't protect herself from panicking. The treatment for panic disorder involves teaching your child about the quirks of the brain, much like a mechanic might alert you to the ins and outs of your car. When your child learns what all the signals mean, what happens when certain metaphorical buttons get pushed and how to deactivate them, she will be confident that the uncomfortable feelings are not signs of danger at all. Because parents become alarmed about seeing their child thrown into such a state, they too need to learn how panic disorder works so they can facilitate the deactivation process rather than getting pulled into the contagion of fear.

Children are diagnosed with panic disorder when they've had at least one panic attack followed by a month of persistent worry about the attack—Are they going to lose control, have a heart attack, or "go crazy"?—or by significant interference in their functioning: avoiding unfamiliar situations or where they fear that they are at risk of having another attack.

What a Panic Attack Is Like

For parents who haven't experienced a panic attack firsthand, it may be difficult to understand how misreading a signal could lead to such chaos. Imagine that you're driving in your car and an unfamiliar icon suddenly starts flashing in red on the dashboard. What does it mean? Should you pull over? What's next? In those seconds before you figure out that it's a harmless warning light letting you know that a bulb is out, your heart may be racing from the possibility that it's a signal that the engine is going to ignite in the middle of the highway. Before you can even think, your body is surging. Like the childhood story of Chicken Little, who believed the sky was falling when it was only a stick that fell on his head, we are wired to prepare for the worst—instantly.

By learning that panic feels frightening but is 100 percent harmless, your child can learn to stop the chain reaction. They may still have those first uncomfortable sensations, but they can relabel the signals rather than stoke the fires of panic: "It's just my heart beating fast. It's okay. A false alarm was set off for some reason. My body is testing its emergency response team. This can't hurt me. If I slow down my breathing and keep telling myself that it's panic and it will pass, then it will."

When a child is able to stop a panic attack from blossoming, we call this a "limited symptom attack." This kind of episode is a very important step in treatment progress. Better than the fluke of not having panic symptoms at all, when a child comes in having had a limited symptom attack, they begin to feel more confident that the uncomfortable sensations are manageable, so they are more willing to venture out knowing that even if the feelings start, they can determine what happens next. Essentially, the child is learning to say to his or her body: Follow my lead.

PANIC DISORDER: THE DIAGNOSIS

RED FLAGS

- Sudden, unexpected surges of intense fear that are unrelated to any specific worry or fear situation
- A surge of physical symptoms—overheating, dizziness, racing heart, feeling detached or unreal as if watching oneself on TV, feeling disconnected from parts of their body
- Attacks occur out of the blue and peak within ten minutes
- Subsequent to the first attack, the child fears venturing away from home for fear of having another attack, and avoids perceived triggers and locations of previous attacks
- The child appears to be seized by fear of dying, being unable to breathe, or losing control and may be inconsolable or hysterical

How to Explain This to Your Child

Once you help your child generate his own anti-panic script, he can write the messages on index cards and keep them with him to use at the onset of an attack.

For young children (under age seven): "Your body is fine. Worry is tricking you. Nothing happened, nothing changed. It's like if an acorn fell on a squirrel and the squirrel thought: 'Uh oh! This means trouble! The sky is falling!' Does it mean trouble? Does it mean the sky is falling? Right, no. So your protector brain felt a funny feeling—a little dizzy, a little hot, a little out of breath, and it started to jump around like the squirrel, saying, This is bad! But really those feelings are harmless; they can't hurt you at all. And they go away! Not right away, but pretty quickly if you keep using your smart strategies."

In the middle of an attack: You can say to your child, "Hold my hands. It's just that busy dizzy guy. We'll breathe those feelings right out. Slow down, look at my face, match my breathing. I'm going to count. You're just fine. Everything is okay. These scary feelings are going to pass. We'll blow them away by breathing together nice and slow. It's going to go away soon. It will go away sooner if we can breathe calmly together."

For older children: "A panic attack is when the brain suddenly, out of the blue, turns on the emergency response program as it would if you were suddenly in danger. Imagine what you would do if you suddenly saw a tiger. Your body would do everything to defend and protect you: Your heart rate would increase to pump blood to your arms and legs so you could run for your life, and you might feel light-headed as that happens. Your digestive system would come to a screeching halt so that you wouldn't be distracted by things like hunger when you're fighting the tiger—though this can feel like stomach cramps. You would sweat to ensure that your system doesn't overheat while you're fighting—and also so that you'll be slippery so that the 'enemy' can't grab hold of you. Isn't it great that your body does this? There's only one problem: There's no tiger. So you're going through all the motions of an emergency; meanwhile, there's no emergency. It's like a fire drill. At least with a fire drill you know there's no fire. This is what's missing in a panic attack. So you need to be the one to tell yourself that nothing's wrong and that the episode will be over soon—usually in about fifteen minutes if you do calm breathing and talk yourself through it. Just telling yourself that it will be over soon and that you're safe will help shorten the attack. And just as the body has the instinct to fight or flee, it also has the instinct to reset to normal if there is no emergency. It won't do that instantly, but if you use the strategies in this chapter, the feelings will usually fade within about fifteen minutes or so."

THE STRATEGIES: KEY INTERVENTIONS IN TREATMENT: WHAT TO DO WHEN YOUR BODY IS ALL STRESSED UP WITH NOWHERE TO GO

STRATEGY: Help Your Child See That Questions Fuel Panic and Statements Stomp It Out

Panic feeds on uncertainty. In response to the uncomfortable sensations of panic we instantly think: "What's happening? What will happen next? What am I going to do? What if it doesn't stop? What if something bad happens?" The questions come on in a spiral of anxiety, making the situation seem totally unknown. But it's not. It's completely predictable, and the panic can be stopped by making statements about the situation. Following the same pattern every time, panic starts suddenly, escalates within minutes, and ends uneventfully. Like watching a movie without the scary sound track, the more your child can recognize the panic pattern from the start, name it, and predict its course, the less he'll compound the panic.

To short-circuit panic thoughts, children need to make statements and stay in their time zone: the present.

Panic Script: Questions	Anti-Panic Script: Statements
What is wrong with me? This shouldn't be happening!	Nothing is wrong. I feel like something is wrong, but I'm in no danger; everything is the same as it was two seconds ago. Nothing has changed at all.
What is happening to me?	Nothing is happening. This is a panic attack. It is harmless.
What if this means something bad is happening or I'm going to die?	This is harmless; it can't hurt me. This is a false alarm: My brain sent the wrong signal.
What if this means I'm going crazy?	I feel like I'm going crazy, but I'm not. Everything I am experiencing is normal. These are signs of a panic attack, not signs of trouble. I am fine. Nothing is wrong with me.
What if I can't get out in time or people can't help me?	I need to slow my body down—there's no danger; nothing is happening; nothing has changed.
What if I faint or suffocate?	If I breathe slowly, I'll reset my system. My body will get a new signal and everything will go back to normal. No one ever dies or loses it from panic. It's not comfortable, but it can't hurt me. These feelings will pass if I don't add to them with my fear. Don't fuel the fire; put it out!

What if I have to go to the hospital?	Panic is harmless. Everything is fine. Nothing is actually wrong with you.
What if this time is different? What if it's real this time?	It's always the same. That's just more panic thinking. I'm fine, and if I keep thinking calmly, these feelings will pass.

STRATEGY: Help Your Child See That the Body Is Safe by Bringing On the Uncomfortable Sensations

What You Feel Can't Hurt You

The most effective way to demystify panic is to manufacture the symptoms on purpose. If you can make the same sensations happen—turn the switch on, then off—then children learn that they aren't dangerous and can be controlled. Once the child knows this secret, she can rein in her reactions and teach her brain to correctly interpret the signals as benign. Teenagers may see a parallel scenario in how computer-illiterate parents react when their computer freezes! The parent panics, fears that all is lost, that they've crashed the system, but the teenager may confidently be able to read that signal properly as a need for a simple reboot. Kids may even get a good chuckle at their parents' expense because they see their parents overreacting when the kids know clearly that all is well. Kids need to learn that panic is a similar system misfire. For them, rebooting their own system can be done with controlled breathing, self-talk, and focusing.

HOW TO INTERPRET THE FEELING OF "GOING CRAZY"

One aspect of panic that is especially frightening to preteens and adolescents is the feeling that they are going crazy. They feel so hyper in their bodies, yet at the same time so detached physically that this feels—to them—like going insane. Again, set the record straight: This is garden-variety panic. Kids may fear being psychotic or schizophrenic—this is what they imagine it may feel like. Those disorders, serious and painful in their own right, are not characterized by sudden surprise attacks like this but are chronic and progressive. They are, fortunately, treatable but are in no way related to panic attacks.

Learning to Manipulate Panic

While it may seem counterintuitive to want to bring on anxiety symptoms when you are trying to reduce them, think of the following exercise as an opportunity to trip off a circuit breaker on purpose so you can learn how to flip it back and not remain helplessly groping about in the dark. Below is a set of directions for "creating" different panic symptoms. These brief attacks show kids that even after they start to panic, they have the power to stop it. This is even more reassuring and liberating than a panic-free period during which they're wondering when the next attack will happen and how they will react. Before attempting any of these exercises, a child must know how to do diaphragmatic breathing so that he can calm back down after doing the exposure. See Chapter 6 for specific instructions.

Panic Symptom	Recipe for Simulation
Dizziness	Spin in a chair several times, then spin while standing for longer and longer stretches. See how quickly the dizzy feeling goes away.
Hyperventilation	Pant on purpose for thirty seconds.
Racing heart	Run up and down stairs several times till you are winded, or step up and down on a stool repeatedly.
Muscle tension and tingling	Tense up the muscles of your body—and hold the tension for thirty seconds.
Overheating	Bundle up in extra layers indoors and do jumping jacks, run in place, and spin.
Derealization	Use hyperfocus to create a feeling of detachment or unreality: Keep saying the same word over and over until it sounds so strange you start to doubt it's a word. Stare at yourself in the mirror for a minute until you feel a sense of unreality.
Disorientation	Lower your head, look down, and then lift your head up quickly.

After your child practices these symptoms, he can use his breathing and his accurate thinking to help the sensations dissolve and the fears dissipate. Your child can also be instructed to say, "Wait: I know this is just panic!" and begin focusing his attention on his environment: what colors he sees, what textures he feels, what smells he can notice. This routes him back to the present and derails the panic train.

How to decide which simulations to do? Children need to be ready to recognize the particular telltale signs of their panic reaction. Younger children may be given a "map" of the body and asked to circle the parts that get scared or feel funny when they have an episode. Older children can think about past attacks and track what symptoms they noticed.

STRATEGY: Practice Exposures and Help Your Child Learn to Carry the "All Clear" Signal in Their Pocket

Although panic is a surprise attack, there are certain situations or sensations that may bring on the fear of a panic attack: class trips, cars, elevators, auditoriums, open spaces, high ceilings (as in churches or auditoriums), getting overheated, open fields, stores, crowds, theaters, sporting events, or just being away from home. Once children are armed with the truth about panic and have their de-panicking self-talk and their breathing ready, they are then ready to make their stairs of learning and reapproach, step by step, the situations that they have avoided because of fear of panic.

Expect that your child will be nervous doing these on-purpose exposures. The anxiety will go away if the child stays in the exposure situation and sees that the bad thing doesn't happen, that panic was wrong again, and that they can actually even enjoy themselves because the feelings and fears do go away after about fifteen minutes if the child is doing their anti-panic maneuvers.

Remember, the more we run away from anxiety-inducing situations, the more this behavior reinforces the mistaken belief that we are in danger. If your child is having difficulty with an exposure, try not to leave the event entirely. Go outside or to the bathroom to regroup, and see if you can go back into the situation once you've reinforced and reestablished that the child is safe. Make sure you return to the "scene of the panic" rather than going home.

JUST IN CASE: HOW SAFETY MANEUVERS BACKFIRE

Eric started having panic attacks after he felt light-headed at a soccer tournament. He had been playing in the heat and wasn't optimally hydrated. After that he was very much on the lookout for that feeling and insisted on carrying extra water bottles just in case.

Ronnie began panicking when she saw someone else faint at camp. She herself had a moment after getting her blood drawn when she felt queasy and unsteady. The nurse gave her a hard candy to suck on. After that, she never went anywhere without the hard candies, just in case that feeling came back.

These children learned "the wrong things" from these experiences: They concluded they could feel light-headed or unsteady at any time (not just if they had actually not eaten, or had spent too much time out in the sun), and that unless they had their candy or water bottle, they wouldn't make it. In treatment, children who have their tricks—sitting by a window, by a door, bringing snacks, holding on to stair banisters with a death grip because they're afraid of falling—need to eventually shed these special extra measures, which may feel necessary at first to get them back in the situations, but ultimately will interfere with their mastering their fear, and will in fact maintain it.

ON THE HOME FRONT

Panic is very difficult for parents to manage, because even when they understand the mechanics and how to manage the attacks, there continue to be surprise attacks. The more you understand how panic works, the more you will be able to label what is going on, instruct your child on the steps she needs to take, and confidently let her know that she will be fine. This takes the attack out of the crisis category and turns it into a manageable situation that is not a matter of life or death but just a matter of time. Because of the physicality of panic, it is important to immediately guide your child toward slowing down her body. Though you may feel mean redirecting your panicking child, when you do it compassionately, you are really rescuing your child from much anguish.

PARENT COPING TALK FOR PANIC

- "I'm going to help you through this."
- "It feels like something is wrong, but these feelings are harmless—you are absolutely fine."
- "You are not going crazy; you are not in danger; your brain is sending the wrong signal—you'll be fine."
- "You got scared about what the feelings meant; the anxiety will pass in a couple of minutes."
- "Breathe with me. Let's slow it down."
- "You can move on even if the anxiety is there."

KAYLA'S STORY

Ten-year-old Kayla described her panic as "the weary feeling." While out for a walk with her brother on a hot summer's day, she began to feel tired and overheated and wanted to stop, but her brother wanted to keep moving. Kayla felt faint, dizzy, and "spaced out," and very afraid that something bad was happening. She wanted her brother to carry her home—afraid that if she tried to walk she might die. After that, Kayla was terrified that the weary feeling would happen again. She started to limit her walking. She couldn't go anywhere—even going to school was tough. Her family was getting frustrated. They didn't understand how normal activities could suddenly become so overwhelming to her. In therapy, Kayla learned about how her brain was sending her a faulty message that she was in danger of collapse when she really wasn't. She named her anxiety "Shadow" because it always followed her. Kayla soon learned how to devalue Shadow's false alarms, to do deep breathing, and to use good boss back talk: "Worry isn't going to make the choices—I do! Shadow, stop making me look so far ahead. If I'm tired I can stop; I'm not climbing Mount Everest; I'm just going to the bus stop!" By doing exposures in treatment, Kayla had the opportunity to face the fear and see that she could survive!

IDEA BOX

- *Separation anxiety:* Ask your child to draw an independence thermometer. Color in the thermometer in units of minutes or hours that your child is able to be apart from you, and plan a special celebration when your child reaches the top of the thermometer.
- *Panic disorder:* Ask your child to draw a map, marking the comfort zone. Hang the map on the wall and add pictures or pushpins for each destination or situation he conquers *outside* the comfort zone, thereby stretching his comfort (versus his discomfort) further and further.

MATT'S STORY

Eleven-year-old Matt suffered from panic attacks at sporting events and swim team practice and in school. Matt's parents were very concerned but also frustrated that they were held hostage by Matt's unpredictable attacks. After a couple of months of learning how to handle panic, they reached a turning point when Matt had a panic attack while his mother was driving him to camp. Feeling unable to bring him to camp in that condition, Matt's mother went on to her next stop, a doctor's appointment, with Matt in the car. As Matt's panic was amping up, his mother calmly directed him on what to do: "If you need to lie down you can, but I need to go to my doctor's appointment." While Matt's mom was on the phone letting the doctor know that she was going to be a little late, Matt, who had essentially been curled up in a ball and crying, suddenly began to calm down. It was as if Matt could take Mom's lead and life could come back to normal. This wasn't the terrible disaster scene that his brain had presented to him. When his mom got off the phone, Matt said, "You know, I think I can go to camp. I can handle this." By not getting swept up in the drama, not being afraid herself of what was happening, Matt's mom was able to show panic the door, and help the real Matt step forward.

Chapter 15

FROM SUPERSTITIONS AND RITUALS TO OBSESSIVE-COMPULSIVE DISORDER AND PANS

My brain is saying I have to do these things or I won't feel good. So I just have to do them to feel better.

Brittany is so afraid of germs, she can't get close to anyone—even us. She is sure that she is going to catch something. This goes way beyond good hygiene and health. She tracks every cough, sneeze, or stomachache at school. She yells at us if we even exhale too close to her.

I feel like I have to lock up my hands; that's the only way I can be free. If not I'm afraid I might do something to hurt someone. People tell me they're just thoughts, but I'm scared.

Martin woke up one morning and it was as if someone had taken away our son in the night and we were dealing with a child we didn't know at all. Nothing he did made any sense. He was confessing everything—strange, little things. He was worried about touching things. He was apologizing for everything. It's like all the circuits just went haywire in his mind. He's a wreck.

Like the children we met with generalized anxiety disorder (GAD) in Chapter 11, the more than one million kids with obsessive-compulsive disorder (OCD) worry too much, but with two important differences. First, unlike the everyday worries that get stuck in the nets of kids with GAD, in OCD the thoughts that get stuck are senseless and bizarre. Take eight-year-old Betsy, who was afraid of being in the school office because she was afraid she might suddenly swallow the thumbtacks on the cork board. Or Shawn, who was worried that if he read the word "death" in a book, it meant someone would die, unless he quickly "undid" it by saying the word "life." Second, kids with OCD get locked into rituals to relieve their worries—walking, talking, breathing, reading, praying, moving—rituals that consume hours of the day. *I breathed out when I saw the stop sign. It's red and that's the color of blood, and that means something bad will happen. I better breathe it back in, to "un-do" it. Oh no, I'll do it four times for good luck, because that's the number of people in my family. Maybe I should do it four times four just to be extra safe.*

Since we are all creatures of habit, this chapter will show you how to tell the difference between the rituals that accompany healthy growth and development, and the compulsions that can clog the arteries of your child's—and your family's—daily life. The primary litmus test is evaluating whether the pattern makes the child feel confident (checking his hair in the mirror before going to school) or anxious (spending hours combing and flattening until his hair is "just right").

Obsessive-compulsive disorder is a highly treatable condition, and early intervention can prevent years of suffering. Even if a child doesn't have full-blown OCD, she may have areas where she gets stuck, areas where she needs help—writing perfectly, being overly concerned with cleanliness, or being polite to a fault. The most effective treatment is exposure and ritual prevention (ERP), which entails resisting doing the rituals and instead on-purpose living the "old way" before OCD: breaking the rules that OCD has insisted are important to see that nothing bad happens. The strategies in this chapter will help you work on these behaviors at home.

CRACKING THE CODE: MAKING SENSE OF OCD

The bizarre nature of OCD symptoms can be frightening—kids and parents alike can fear that something is terribly wrong for these thoughts to be coming up in the first place. Don't try to make sense of OCD by looking into your child's personality or scrutinizing your parenting practices. People across history, of all cultures and ages, have experienced the same basic themes of OCD. Like other anxiety disorders, OCD is caused by a misfiring in the brain—but with OCD it is not the amygdala jumping to conclusions that starts the action. Instead, the caudate nucleus—the brain's filtering station for our thoughts—is malfunctioning. Unnecessary thoughts that a healthy caudate nucleus would filter instead find their way into the "Urgent Messages" box. There is no real urgency, but since the images are sitting there, kids feel frightened by the thoughts themselves and the fact that they are thinking them. Kids with OCD never act on their intrusive thoughts—such as the frightening violent thoughts of hurting others. These are gentle, sensitive children who wouldn't hurt a fly, but they are plagued by the possibility that they could.

WHAT IT FEELS LIKE FOR YOUR CHILD

"Step on a crack, break your mother's back." For some kids this is a game to enliven an otherwise tedious walk home from school; for others, a simple walk home becomes a matter of grave responsibility, warding off harm to a loved one. "What if I wasn't paying attention and something happened? It would be all my fault. Did I accidentally step on a crack? How can I undo it?" Having OCD is like having a tyrant whispering in your child's ears.

Children with OCD don't know that they are heading down the path to a disorder when it first begins. Little routines can give children a sense of control. But when these rituals take on a life of their own and become more important to follow than the advice of parents, these routines are no longer harmless good-luck charms. These superstitions often don't even make sense to the children themselves, but they're afraid to risk it—once the possibility is introduced that a connection *could* exist between such unrelated things as how they walk and the welfare of their family, they feel they need to obey OCD's "rules" just in case there is a connection and they are putting anyone at risk. If they try to resist, their mind keeps goading them: "You can't prove it's not true—so don't risk it." Children with OCD feel near-constant pressure and responsibility. Children naturally try not to think their OCD thoughts, but the more they try not to think of certain things—illness, sexual thoughts, death, counting—the imp OCD only makes them think those things more.

Rituals are the ways children think of, or that the mind introduces, to undo the bad feelings or ward off the danger. Following elaborate steps for ordinary operations, a child may have a ten- or twenty-step routine just for closing a drawer, turning on a light switch, or walking through a doorway. Simple tasks such as brushing teeth or tying shoes could take hours to get just right.

Like paying the OCD gods, this bargain makes the children feel like they have insurance against the bad thing. Until the rates go up. Children start to question the safe feeling that OCD rituals temporarily lend. It feels like they didn't do it well enough, or exactly enough, and a more elaborate ritual is needed.

Given the pressure of responsibility that these rituals place on children with OCD, they are often very irritable, angry, and even depressed, though to their credit they will show this side only to their family; to the outside world they look like extremely likable, successful children (and they are!). They walk around on eggshells, afraid that everything they do could bring harm or turn into another item on their ritual to-do list. As a result, their stress level is maxed out even before actual stressors enter the picture—like homework, friendships, or sports. The images in children's minds can be so disturbing to them that they may feel afraid to be alone (so their behavior can sometimes look like panic disorder or separation anxiety).

Somewhere underneath all of the rituals, kids with OCD have compelling, healthy thoughts: "Why do I have to do this? Other kids aren't doing this and their lives seem a lot better than mine. What do I do?"

THE DIAGNOSIS

What follows is a list of diagnostic criteria to help you determine if your child's habits are typical or not. If you recognize any of these, it is time to seek professional help.

RED FLAGS

- Presence of obsessions: persistent, disturbing, or inappropriate thoughts, images, or ideas that the child can't get out of his mind even though they may make no sense to him
- Repeatedly asking questions, and inability to be reassured by answers
- Engaging in compulsions: spending excessive amounts of time doing things over and over, or avoiding ordinary activities such as touching faucets, putting on shoes, answering questions, wearing certain clothes, or eating certain foods
- Needing a parent to answer often obvious questions in a precise way, often repeating the answer if the child hasn't heard it just right
- Obsessions and/or compulsions that create distress, interfere with child's functioning, and are time-consuming (take more than an hour a day)

OCD Rituals	Non-OCD Habits
Time-consuming	Not overly time-consuming
Child feels like he has to do them	Child wants to do them
Disrupt routine and take on a life of their own	Enhance efficiency or enjoyment
Create distress, dread, or frustration	Create a sense of mastery
Appear bizarre or unusual	Appear ordinary
Cause great distress if interrupted or skipped; child must start over	Can be skipped or changed without consequence
Become increasingly inflexible and elaborate over time	Become less important over time
Connected to a web of feared consequences, are performed to prevent harm or due to other superstitious belief	Performed for the sake of the activity itself; are comforting but have no elaborate connections to feared situations or superstitious beliefs

THE TRICK AND THE GOAL: BREAK THE RULES AND SET YOURSELF FREE

The cycle of OCD goes like this: First comes the intrusive thought "Maybe I left the closets open—my baby brother will get into the cleaning chemicals!" For most of us, we may get a passing bad thought from time to time, but when we identify a good enough answer ("I probably remembered to close the closet, and if not, there's no way my brother could open a bottle himself!"), we move on. But with OCD, the all-clear signal never comes. A solution that looks good at the time—recheck the doors—relieves the anxiety temporarily. The person thinks that the bad thing didn't happen *because* they did the ritual.

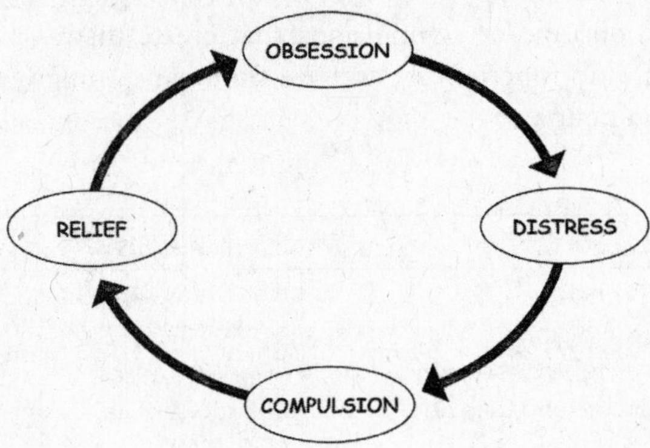

That connection "sticks," and the next time the child feels germy or scared, he feels like he *needs* to fix the feeling the same way he did before. Though they relieve anxiety in the short run, rituals actually maintain anxiety in the long run. Before you know it, one check turns into two or three—into checking without having any bad words or thoughts in mind, checking while standing on one foot, and so forth.

Compulsive behaviors deprive kids of the opportunity to see that nothing would happen anyway. If they never test that possibility, they never know that anxiety is a wave that comes and goes on its own! The feared consequence doesn't happen—not because of the compulsion, but because it was really unlikely in the first place.

The goal of OCD treatment is to teach children the tricks OCD plays to scare them, and then outsmart them by doing the opposite of what OCD is telling them to do. Here are some typical OCD tricks you'll want to point out to your child:

Trick One: "If I'm thinking something, this means it's true or I want it to happen."

A child runs to his mother saying, "What if you're really not my mom?" Or, "What if I'm dead and this is a dream?" Or, "What if I want to hurt myself?" These thoughts may sound bizarre and scary. Your job is to help your child do the side-by-side comparison to get distance from the thoughts. "Is it really that you *think* you are dead? Or is that thought really scary to think about?" "Are you really afraid that you're actually going to hurt yourself, or is it frightening to you that you are hearing that thought?" Having a thought is different from wanting or intending to do something. Seeing a knife doesn't mean you want to stab someone. Coincidence doesn't mean intention. When you separate your child from the thought, they are free to conclude that it's just a thought; it's not about them. Or, for short: It's not me; it's OCD. Even the most seemingly unusual OCD thoughts are typically garden-variety—thousands or millions of other people have experienced the same thoughts.

Trick Two: "If I have bad thoughts, this is about me: I'm a bad person."

A classic study by Rachman and DaSilva back in 1978 found that people with OCD and people without OCD have the same thoughts. Whatever OCD sufferers are thinking—contamination fears, or violent, religious, or sexual thoughts—are generic in content. Even OCD experts can't tell them apart! The difference is the meaning that people with OCD attach to the thoughts (they're personal!) and the reaction they have to them (rather than let them go, they feel they need to undo or neutralize them with a ritual).

Trick Three: "But if the thought is there, it's important, and I better listen or else!"

OCD makes you think about high-stakes matters—life, death, sickness, religious beliefs—but remember, the thoughts are there because your brain isn't filtering them out. Even if they are about important topics like health or death, this doesn't mean that they are important to *you*, or important for you to think about *right now*. They just jumped into your mind for no reason and got your attention because the filter isn't working. The thoughts aren't important; they are just stuck.

Trick Four: "If I don't do a ritual, bad things will happen."

There is no connection between ritual and results except what OCD makes you think. If you don't wash your hands just right, don't tie your shoes three times, or don't say "I love you" to each of the pictures of family members in your living room to protect them from getting into an accident—then not only does nothing *bad* happen; something very, very good happens: You are teaching your brain how to be free.

HOW TO EXPLAIN OCD TO YOUR CHILD

At first glance, explaining these symptoms to your child might seem to be just a matter of being extra logical and insisting how impossible OCD's claims are, but likely you've already tried and have seen that logic has no impact on OCD. Kids may know that what they are doing makes no sense, but they still feel they can't stop. The alternative is to use child-friendly phrases and stories to describe what is happening in an OCD moment and to build a language that you will use to communicate about these symptoms as you work together to outsmart the tricks OCD plays. Here are some ideas.

For young children: "No one wants bad things to happen, but your bossy brain is making up extra rules. Do you like extra rules? Are these rules that Mom and Dad are telling you to do? Right, no. And you know what, you don't have to follow them. When your bossy brain is telling you what to do, even if it's being a meany brain and saying, 'If you don't obey, something bad will happen,' you need to boss it back. Then you can train it to be quiet and leave you alone! It's like if you went to the ice cream store with a friend and the friend could get whatever he wanted, but you could get only what your meany brain said, and you had to pay triple what your friend did. Does that make sense? You shouldn't have to do anything extra! Don't let meany brain boss you around. Order what you want, do what you want, and meany brain will learn to leave you alone."

Have your child practice role-playing and switch off who is being the voice of meany brain and who is being the voice of reason. Have your child choose a name for OCD—descriptive names like Disaster Man or Guilty Gal can lighten the mood and inspire your child to fight the injustice. You can use hand puppets to convey the meany brain with a silly voice: "You can't have what you want. I'm the boss of you!" Then ask your child what the other hand—smart brain, or calm brain—would say: "You're not the boss of me. Sorry, meany brain—I'm putting you on mute!"

For older children: "Imagine you are sitting in class and all of a sudden your teacher stops talking and for no reason says, 'There's going to be a fire! But if you clap your hands you can make it stop.' At first you think, 'This is ridiculous; he's lost it.' You look around and there's no sign of fire. But he goes on repeating the same thing, and after a few minutes you start to get really nervous. Your heart's racing and you think, 'Maybe I should just clap. I don't want to be responsible for a fire!' So against your better judgment, you start clapping, and you feel relieved but also confused and embarrassed—this makes no sense. That's what happens with OCD; it keeps making connections between unrelated things, telling you to do this to prevent that. It's not real, but it becomes convincing because it keeps repeating. You can learn to disregard and underreact to the messages because they were never true in the first place. When you don't drop everything and give priority to the OCD thoughts when they intrude, you are retraining your brain to filter out those thoughts, and eventually they will stop coming to you.

HOW YOU CAN HELP

Your most important job is to separate your child from the rituals and worries. Rather than asking her why she is washing or checking or praying, point to the OCD as the culprit. Help your child be part of the solution, not the reason for the problem. Change the question and ask: "What is OCD wanting you to do here? What's it telling you will happen? What do you really think? Let's show it who's the boss!"

Break the Rules: Superstitions Are Fake

To prove to your child that there is no connection between what they do (stepping on cracks, washing their hands excessively, saying prayers a certain way) and what happens in the world, show your child that you are willing to do on-purpose exposures with yourself: If you normally hesitate to open an umbrella inside, walk under ladders, or do something thirteen times—this is your moment to break the rules. The connection exists only in your mind. Our worry brain may be saying, "Yikes, what have we done?!" but our voice of reason knows deep down that this is not how the world works. Notice how even though you fully understand that this is safe, you may hesitate to take these low-risk actions. This will give you a window into the (very doable but initially daunting!) challenges that your child now faces.

DRAW THE LINE: REASONABLE PRECAUTIONS VERSUS OCD

Is it healthy to wash your hands? Absolutely. Is it healthy to scrub up to your elbows for fifteen minutes till your hands are raw and bleeding? No. Rather than getting in a fight with your child about their rituals, talk to them about the line between reasonable precautions and excessive rules that are unfair to them because they are unnecessary and time-consuming. When your child is engaging in a ritual, point to the imaginary line and ask, "Which side is that action on? Is it reasonable, or overboard?" You can help define the line by asking what other trusted people generally do in these situations. For example, when does a doctor or chef wash his hands? For how long? With how much soap? OCD is making up excessive rules for your child, but he has a choice about whether or not to follow those rules.

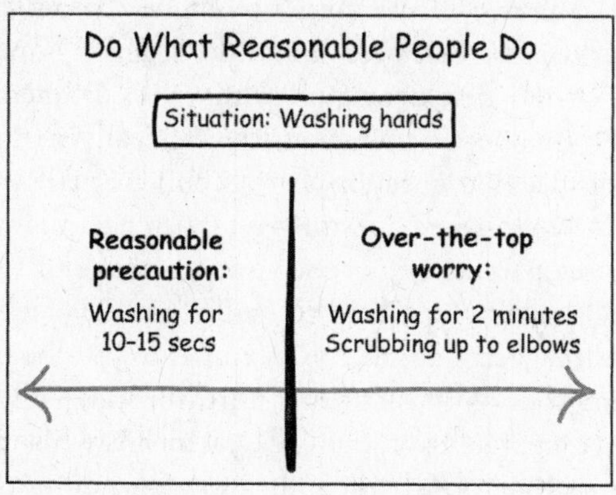

Do What Reasonable People Do
Situation: Washing hands
Reasonable precaution:
Washing for 10-15 secs
Over-the-top worry:
Washing for 2 minutes
Scrubbing up to elbows

Don't Reassure, Relabel: The Cantaloupe Question

Most parents of OCD kids who come to see me are exasperated and exhausted. Their child has questions about everything—"I touched the *this* that touched the *that*. Am I okay?"—and a reasonable response that would reassure most kids isn't working at all. If you answer the question seriously, you've become part of the ritual. You are reinforcing a cycle in which the only way to get relief from an obsessive thought or urge is to go to Mom or Dad, and sending the message that what your child is asking makes sense. Instead, the message you want to send is that there is *no risk*. While your child's distress is real, the risk is fake. As a worrywise parent, you're going to teach your child not to avoid or obey OCD, but to relabel it and resist it. The way to do this is not to fall into the OCD trap yourself—hearing bizarre things as reasonable.

Imagine if your very reasonable child said something else nonsensical, but said it sincerely and urgently—such as, "Mom, I'm afraid I am a cantaloupe; am I?!" What would you do? Would you engage seriously with the content of the question and say, "Well, let me see—you're not round, you don't have a tan, ribbed exterior. I think you're probably not a cantaloupe." No, you would call a spade a spade. You'd say, "Your mind is playing tricks on you. Let's not let it trick both of us." So while OCD questions ("Am I going to electrocute myself touching the outlets?" "Am I going to turn into a bad person and do drugs?" "Am I going to catch AIDS from that doorknob?") may feel different from the "Are you a cantaloupe?" question, they're really not. Ask yourself the million-dollar question: Is your child actually at risk from what he is fearing? These questions really aren't ambiguous at all, but sometimes parents get swept up in the haze of OCD along with their kids. When parents get pulled in, kids feel more convinced that their fears are real. Remember to pin the problem on the problem: Your child isn't being unreasonable—it's OCD. See your child as separate from the OCD, which is whispering in his ear. Tell your child, "OCD is coming up with a doozy," or, "Brain bug is making up stories again. Good try, brain bug, but we don't believe you!"

Don't Be Afraid of OCD: Parenting on the Edge

To the uninitiated, OCD therapy looks completely backward. Why would you encourage children to play catch with an empty pack of cigarettes, or touch their shoes and eat a snack, or say curse words? Aren't these signs of bad parenting, if not bad therapy? In short, no. OCD has warned your child that if they walk by a cigarette on the ground, they will smoke when they grow up (or that maybe they already did!); or that if they touch a table before they eat, they'll get sick and maybe die; or that because they thought a bad word while they were around a certain ethnic group, that they hate them and are a bad person. OCD goes overboard threatening kind, responsible, law-abiding kids with dire consequences, so you have to counter the exaggeration with something equally outrageous to downgrade the authority OCD has claimed over your child's thinking—and most importantly to prove it wrong! Get comfortable with "playing" with ideas about germs, sex, religion—you are showing your child that he knows right from wrong very well; in fact, he knows it so very well that simply saying or hearing a curse word doesn't change who he is. But most important: You are showing that it is safe to suspend decorum temporarily (within reason) in order to get better. Play catch with some used bubble gum, stomp on some cigarettes, eat off the floor, throw around some curse words. Your willingness to discredit OCD is much more powerful than the reassurance you give your child, a measure that has a very short shelf life and needs to be replenished over and over.

THE STRATEGIES: KEY INTERVENTIONS IN TREATMENT: COGNITIVE BEHAVIOR THERAPY USING EXPOSURE AND RITUAL PREVENTION—WHO'S THE BOSS?

What Doesn't Help

Distraction doesn't help. Many parents and even some therapists will advise kids to just think about something else, or do something else—listen to an iPod, think good thoughts. This doesn't work! Having to be distracted means that your child is hiding from her fears—like seeing a fire and going to the next room to distract yourself from it, rather than fighting it. Job one is to "put out the fire" by seeing that the thoughts are fake.

Reassurance doesn't help. "I promise that you won't get sick." "But how do you know? What if there were germs on the table my food might have touched? What if the spot on my bread was poison?" It doesn't take long to see that there is no such thing as an airtight explanation in life. Having OCD is like being allergic to doubt. Kids sense the smallest amount of it and have a big reaction. The goal is to help them see that living with *some* doubt and uncertainty is the only way anyone can live. While it seems like your reassurance should release them from their distress, they'll need to keep coming back to you for more, since doubt can jump in at any time. Point the finger at the real problem—not the door, the hands, the thought, but the fact that OCD is making them doubt that everything's okay.

Avoidance doesn't help. "I just won't use the bathrooms at school, or at the mall, or the one downstairs that guests use." What starts out seeming to your child to be a good solution to a given fear will eventually turn on him—the more he avoids something, the more everything will look suspect to him. And the world will get smaller and smaller, depriving your child access to things that are safe. The alternative: Face it head-on, doing exposures on purpose in manageable steps to see that OCD is wrong, the bad thing doesn't happen, the bad feelings pass, and you are free.

Relaxation doesn't help. Relaxation strategies can be extremely helpful for going to sleep at night, or dialing down stress before a test, but relaxation in and of itself will not treat OCD. As with avoidance or distraction, if you are telling a child to ignore OCD and just relax, the thoughts are still there. Imagine trying to relax while your phone is ringing or your alarm system is blaring and you believe the call is for you or the alarm is for real. How can you possibly relax? The second reason that relaxation doesn't work as a primary intervention is that your child needs to *feel* the anxiety in order to desensitize to it—to get to the point where he doesn't react to the warnings because he knows that they are meaningless. Just relaxing leaves him exactly in the same spot he was before the relaxation: unprepared for OCD's attacks

What *Does* Help: Exposure

Exposure and ritual prevention (ERP) is the most effective treatment for OCD. When children deliberately place themselves in a potentially OCD-triggering situation (touch something "dirty," lock a door, etc.) but refrain from doing rituals and do it *their* way, not OCD's way, they learn that resisting OCD feels uncomfortable at first—not because it's actually dangerous, but just because they are "breaking the rules." But the anxiety and discomfort caused by resisting the rituals will dissipate because they are learning that there's nothing wrong. The more they learn to "underreact" to OCD's warnings and demands, over time, they will rewire the brain, it will learn how to filter out the warning thoughts, the child will hear the warnings more as "blah, blah, blah" rather than as blaring alarms, and they will short-circuit and intercept the messages of OCD. So even if they hear the messages (which over time they won't) those messages will, with repeated exposures, be meaningless to them.

Diminishing the Power of Suggestion Helps

Kids with OCD have a bad thought, and then think, "I am possessed by the devil. I had sex with that person. I stole from a store." We need to teach kids that thoughts change feelings, but they can't change the facts. As we saw earlier in Chapter 5 during our discussion of the power of suggestion, thinking about yucky things like lice or pleasant things like ice cream sundaes changes how we feel but can't make things happen in the real world. They can't make things happen, and they don't change you. All people think good thoughts and bad thoughts. Thinking bad thoughts can't change a good person into a bad person. The world of thoughts and actions are totally separate.

Acceptance and Selective Attention Helps

Another route to extinguishing the anxiety associated with OCD thoughts is acceptance. Not accepting the *meaning* of the thoughts, but accepting their presence and not needing to do anything about them. Just as children may hear background noise (an air conditioner, traffic sounds, even a parent's voice reminding them it's time for bed), a child can hear the thoughts and think, "I hear you, and there's nothing more I need to do about you."

I'm going to outline the steps that children are taught in OCD treatment. While they bear some similarity to the master plan steps in Chapter 8, an important difference is the addition of exposure and ritual prevention (ERP), our most powerful tool in overcoming OCD. In ERP a child deliberately puts himself in the situations where OCD strikes, but refuses to follow OCD's rules. Though families may be tempted to rush to use ERP with every symptom, exposures should be conducted on the basis of establishing a stairs of learning hierarchy guided by the child's fear temperature (see Chapter 7).

Step One: Relabel the Thoughts

The only way you can solve the problem of an OCD thought is by identifying the brain glitch that put it there in the first place. The brain filter isn't working properly, so put the blame on the OCD, or the brain bug, pushy guy, Mr. Perfect. Parents and kids can join together in fighting a common enemy. Kids won't feel like they are in the hot seat, and will be inspired to focus their righteous anger and frustration at the brain bug instead of at you. How can a child tell which is an OCD thought and which is not? Even children as young as four or five can tell the difference between "strict or pushy thoughts" and regular thoughts. For all children: Draw two boxes on a piece of paper. Label one "What I want to think and do." Label the other "Things I feel like I have to think or do, or else." Have your child fill in each box. The "have to" box is the OCD—your child may enjoy drawing a trash can under it because that's where those ideas belong!

Step Two: Resist OCD with Show-and-Tell

With ERP your child is going to show and tell OCD who is the boss by bossing it back and refusing to engage in rituals. It is best to practice the ERP by doing role-playing first—whether with a five-year-old or a fifteen-year-old—about what tricky OCD is telling them about a situation and what they want to think instead. Role-playing helps the child hear what OCD really sounds like—which ignites their anger and frustration at the OCD, and motivates them to dismiss its validity and fight back. If your child is having trouble generating the right spirit for boss back talk, remind her that if her sibling or even a parent asked her to do what OCD is asking, she would flatly refuse. She has permission to refuse OCD, too. She shouldn't let it bully her.

CHANGING THE CONVERSATION: QUESTIONS TO ASK INSTEAD OF WHY?

- "What's OCD making you think there?"
- "What's OCD telling you will happen then?"
- "What is your head saying will happen if you don't?"
- "What trick is the brain bug trying to play this time?"
- "I hear that, brain bug—what's brain brat telling you to do here?"
- "What kind of brain bug bologna is being served today?"

STRATEGY: Use Ritual-Busting Techniques

We think of ERP as exposure and total prevention of any ritual, but in reality any break in the pattern is a step in the right direction: washing with the left hand first (if the rule is the right), or to say PMYBHITM instead of pleading, "Promise me you'll be here in the morning." Once a child has constructed an OCD hierarchy using the fear thermometer to identify the degree of difficulty of breaking each ritual, he can choose from any of the strategies below to change the OCD pattern. Though ultimately the goal is to resist the ritual altogether in a given situation, these techniques create the intermediate steps that will get him there.

- Delaying tactics: Delay the ritual for progressively longer intervals—two, four, and then ten minutes.
- Early dismissal: Shorten the ritual. Leave early. You will see that the "finished" feeling will catch up with you if you move on to something else.
- Ask your child, "What would your friends do?" Try to say good night the way your friends do, or lock your locker the way another kid without OCD would do.

- Change the emotional tone: Make the voice of OCD different in some way—make it silly, make it sound like Elvis, sing the words, say the words in pig latin, or picture the voice as a silly cartoon character. These techniques tone down the seriousness of OCD's messages.
- News reporter/sportscaster: Rather than doing the ritual, give a blow-by-blow description of what your brain is asking you to do. It will sound silly to you when you say it.
- Do the opposite: If OCD says start with your left foot, start with your right. If OCD says walk out the same door you came in, don't!
- Incentives: Give yourself a point for every time you walk out of a room without flicking the lights on and off or don't wash your hands after putting on your shoes.

STRATEGY: Say the Bad Thought: Flooding

It's scary for kids to think about bad thoughts. They get spooked and the thought becomes larger than life as they add ten more thoughts and questions. The antidote to being spooked by a thought is diving in and getting used to it by saying it out loud. This helps children get to the point of being able to tune out their bad thoughts without freaking out, by submerging themselves into the world of that thought and then coming out the other side. Children may start out saying one word of the thought—like "kill" or "steal" or "plagiarize" or "devil"—or by writing the words, whispering them, even just spelling them a few letters at a time. Remember that *any* contact or interaction with the idea your child is trying to avoid is better than none. Eventually, your child will be able to say the entire scary sentence enough times that the anxiety wears off and she is desensitized to the thought. You can write various trigger words in sets of two on index cards and play the concentration memory game, you can play catch and say the words whenever you throw the ball, create a song to "Row, Row, Row Your Boat," write a limerick about the word or idea, or even create a game show and have your child interview the word to find out what little power it really has.

Step Three: Refocus Your Child on What They Want to Do

Once your child has bossed back and broken a ritual, he is going to feel some anxiety. That's because he is changing a pattern. The OCD is in a tug-of-war with your child, trying to pull him back into a ritual—and when the child feels anxiety it is actually a sign that he is doing the treatment right. Remember that the anxiety will pass on its own within a few minutes. Remind your child that it's just like jumping into a swimming pool: It's cold at first, but then you get used to it. Have him take his fear temperature from one to ten, and then help him get involved in something that is more deserving of his time—a quick game of catch, a walk or a run, a dancing or singing groove. Notice how his fear temperature goes down a few points after engaging his brain and body—without doing any rituals. In a successful exposure the fear temperature should drop at least two points, but preferably 50 percent. This work will help forge a new circuit.

Step Four: Reinforce Your Child's Efforts

Fighting OCD is hard work, and winning doesn't happen overnight. It's like having an extra job, or taking extra classes at school—no one pays you and you don't get a grade, but your child should get credit along the way! Sometimes the relief from symptoms is enough reward, but if it's not, don't hold back. Use small, appropriate incentives to get the new circuits going. Rewards may be the reason your child starts working on reducing his symptoms; eventually, as he catches on and the work gets easier, you can fade out the rewards. You can keep track of your child's progress by using the two-jar system we saw in Chapter 8.

SPECIFIC SUBTYPES OF OCD

Next, we're going to take a closer look at the four themes of OCD: contamination, checking, symmetry/just right, and bad thought

OCD. A detailed description of treatment for each is available in *Freeing Your Child from Obsessive-Compulsive Disorder.*

Contamination OCD

RED FLAGS

- Fears about germs and illness; avoidance of places, people, or things that may contaminate (for example, towels, silverware, furniture, doorknobs, phones, banisters, pens, public bathrooms)
- Extra time spent in the bathroom washing, resulting in disappearing supplies, mounting laundry, and chapped, red hands
- Refusal to wear certain clothes or sit on certain furniture because of its possible contact history
- Dividing the world into two different time zones: Clean Time (post-shower—may not go downstairs, touch family members, allow family members to touch them) and Dirty Time (during the day until child is home again)
- Fears of contact with Magic Markers, cleaning chemicals, gasoline
- Superstitious or symbolic contamination—if I touch my work when I'm dirty, I'll do poorly on the test

Summary of Treatment

The bottom-line message to your child: "You are clean, but your brain hasn't gotten the message yet." ERP involves constructing a hierarchy of contamination situations—both those that are avoided entirely (e.g., they only use doors they can push open with their feet) as well as those that are followed by excessive washing (scrubbing after handling money in the lunch line). Starting with the easiest challenge, children practice touching the feared object and refraining from washing.

Checking and Redoing OCD

RED FLAGS

- Feeling overly responsible—for example, for security in the car (checking seat belts) or house (checking doors, windows, electrical outlets)
- Asking repeated reassurance questions: "What did you say? Are you sure?"
- Rewinding a video or rereading something multiple times to make sure he really understands; if he makes a mistake, he must start from the beginning
- Spending unnecessary hours redoing homework, rechecking the calculator results
- Reclosing drawers or car doors to make sure they are really shut

Summary of Treatment

If at first you don't get the feeling of completion, *don't* try, try again! When we finish an action—like closing a door or putting on our shoes—we get a signal from the brain that it's done. Treatment for checking OCD involves gradually reducing the number of checks. Using a hierarchy of symptoms, a child reduces the number of items he checks and the number of times they are checked, and learns to ride out the unfinished or uncertain feeling.

Symmetry, Evenness, Numbers, "Just Right" OCD

RED FLAGS

- Repeatedly straightening pillows, arranging dolls or books, redoing hair, smoothing clothing, retying shoes
- Feeling like an itch on the right side needs to be "evened out" on the left
- Erasing a letter or number until it looks exactly right

- Double touching: If child bumps into a locker with right shoulder, feels need to even it out by bumping locker with left shoulder
- Homework so neat it looks typewritten
- Needing to leave the room, a building, or a chair the exact same way it was when she went in
- Excessive slowness so that things are done in a precise manner
- Good-luck numbers, bad-luck numbers, chewing a certain number of times
- Needing to say or read syllables forward and backward
- Needing to count ceiling tiles, windowpanes, floorboards

Summary of Treatment

Precision and neatness are qualities that we hope for in our children, but with OCD these habits are taken so far that they become paralyzing rather than admirable or beneficial. The goal of treatment for "just right" OCD is for kids to turn off their minds and just go. Using the fear hierarchy, the child begins an adventure in unevenness—wearing two different socks or mismatched earrings, lining up objects in the "wrong" order, tilting pictures slightly askew—so she can see it doesn't matter.

Bad Thought OCD

RED FLAGS

- Fears of turning into a bad person or another person (loss of essence)
- Confessing or apologizing about insignificant or untrue things, things she "might have" done
- Confessing bad thoughts such as "I think I hate you," "I thought that person was ugly"
- Refusing to answer questions definitively and instead says "I don't know" or "maybe" because she's afraid she may be lying (she is not)
- Repeating prayers throughout the day; fears of offending God
- Intrusive, graphic sexual thoughts or images; confessing sexual

acts though innocent; intrusive fears that simple actions signify he or she is gay

- Thoughts of having pushed or kicked, run over, or stabbed someone
- Avoiding being near knives, driving a car, or riding a bike for fear of hurting someone
- Intrusive, disturbing images of violence, death, dismembered bodies

Summary of Treatment

"Bad thought OCD" plays a cruel trick. It calls into question your child's very sense of herself as a decent person, and tries to convince her that she doesn't know who she really is and what she's capable of. The child accepts and absorbs an uninvited thought as a key to her core identity. Many symptoms of bad thought are rooted in the following mistake or brain trick: coincidence = intention. For example, "If I happen to see a pair of scissors out of the corner of my eye, that means I want to use them to hurt someone," or "If I happen to swallow while looking at a girl when the teacher is talking about date rape, I must have assaulted her." Children become very afraid of thinking anything and may even try to "shut down" their thinking so that their mind won't keep tormenting them with the worst possible accusations. The more they fear the thoughts, the more they try to suppress, the greater priority these thoughts receive.

Treatment for all types of bad thought OCD involves identifying where these thoughts are coming from (impersonal, meaningless junk mail from the brain) and, by devaluing them as "brain hiccups," rather than true confessions or accusations, changing the emotional score that is accompanying these scary scenes. Your child can turn intrusive images of hurting people into cartoons, with little mice squeaking the scary thoughts, thus demoting them to the level of unimportance they deserve. Fighting "scary" with "silly" or "absurd" neutralizes the fear and puts your child in control. Give your child permission to diminish the authority of these thoughts: sing them to "Row, Row, Row Your Boat" or say them like Patrick from *SpongeBob*

SquarePants. As the credibility of those thoughts drops, so does your child's fear level.

ON THE HOME FRONT: CULTIVATING IRREVERENCE FOR THE PROBLEM AND RESPECT FOR YOUR CHILD

When parents take treating OCD seriously, they will make the treatment *less* serious. Use humor, sarcasm, and silliness to say, "I trust you, and you can trust you, too." When parents take their child's distress seriously but are crystal clear that the OCD message has no validity, they are leading the way in their child's recovery. So at first, parents should relabel those questions or concerns: "OCD, we see you—stop bullying my child!" After a while parents can get a little more "edgy" and play at being unreasonable—outdoing the OCD's weirdness—showing their child that nobody is afraid of OCD. One major caveat: Go at your child's pace. Never get ahead of your child's humor in dealing with the problem, and never use the humor against *him*. Use it against OCD to show your child you are confident and not afraid.

One parent I worked with, Martha, showed that she understood the idea of abandoning seriousness temporarily. Her son, Nick, was struggling with the bathroom—he felt he had to take off all his clothes and shower every time after he used it. Nick had been progressing steadily, but he really needed a push. When Martha gave him a ten-dollar challenge—use the bathroom without changing or showering—Nick immediately replied, "Germs can kill—anthrax, smallpox, yellow fever. You want me to die. Is that what you're telling me?" Jumping at the opportunity, Martha said, "You feel like you're going to die, but just because it *feels* that way doesn't make it true. Listen, I know this sounds terrible and morbid—not what a mom should say—but I'm paying you ten dollars a day to do this. If you die, it would cost me a lot more for your funeral! Doesn't that mean I think this is a risk you can take?" Nick was sort of shocked, but his mom's edgy, matter-of-fact stance sobered him, and it brought him back to reality. He was ready to make a deal.

OCD RITUALS: DO THE MATH: THEY DON'T ADD UP (OR ADD ANYTHING)

At the end of our first meeting, I was explaining to twelve-year-old André how with OCD the brain is hiccuping, making us feel like we need to fix something, but there's nothing to fix; nothing changes by doing a ritual. The outcome is the same. He was tired of doing his long list of nighttime rituals. With OCD, the more he did rituals, the only thing that happened was that he was up later at night, and more tired the next day. Suddenly it clicked. He said, "This reminds me of math class. Doing rituals doesn't add anything to your life. They don't give you good luck. They do nothing—just like adding a zero to a number, or multiplying a number by one. Everything is exactly the way it was before—nothing changes—you've just wasted your time doing that extra step. I'm not falling for it!" André was quickly on his way to being a worrywise kid, and in charge of his OCD.

PANS: WHEN OCD STRIKES OVERNIGHT

Most children with OCD experience a slow onset of symptoms over the course of months or (more typically) years. But in approximately a third of children with OCD, their disorder begins dramatically and definitively overnight. Parents can practically pinpoint the very day or moment when their child changed from being a normal kid to suddenly having what parents describe as "ferocious" preoccupations and rituals. Parents of such children feel that they've lost their child—the changes in their personality are so sudden and extreme and the child is inconsolable. The second identifying feature of this type of OCD is that it is episodic; it comes on dramatically and then it resolves. This "spike and resolution" pattern is referred to as sawtooth.

This sudden OCD is referred to as PANS (for pediatric acute-onset neuropsychiatric syndrome) and was initially referred to as PANDAS (pediatric autoimmune neuropsychiatric disorders associated with streptococcal infections). It was initially thought to be triggered by strep throat, though today there is mounting evidence that autoimmune reactions to a variety of diseases or illnesses can cause it.

Pediatric acute-onset neuropsychiatric syndrome is most common in children between the ages of five and nine, and generally occurs in children who have not yet entered puberty (it's unclear why). So how does an autoimmune reaction cause OCD symptoms? An infection, like strep, triggers the immune system to produce antibodies in the blood to fight the infection. In some children, the antibodies, rather than attacking the strep, attack healthy cells in the basal ganglia, the part of the brain where OCD occurs. This leads to the sudden attack of OCD symptoms (or exacerbation of existing symptoms). The good news? Within a few weeks of antibiotic treatment, most children will experience a gradual lessening of OCD and related symptoms. There are usually some residual OCD symptoms, often mild, which are generally well managed by cognitive behavior therapy. Some children with repeated PANS episodes are being treated with prophylactic (preventive) antibiotics, either ongoing or during strep season (winter and spring); the effectiveness of this intervention continues to be investigated.

For strep-triggered PANS, the guideline according to Dr. Michael Jenike of the International OCD Foundation is three to six weeks of antibiotics initially. If improvement is not seen within three to four weeks, a different antibiotic may be tried. Additional treatments such as Plasmapheresis and Intravenous Immunoglobulin (IVIG) may be indicated if symptoms persist. Steroids are often used for treating autoimmune conditions in order to reduce inflammation; in the case of PANS, the steroids would be treating inflammation in the basal ganglia. SSRIs (selective serotonin reuptake inhibitors) may be tried, although there is some evidence that children with PANS may be more likely to develop the unwanted side effects of behavioral activation (agitation, hyperactivity, disinhibition, mania, aggressiveness) that sometimes occurs with SSRIs.

Children with PANS may have none of the classic symptoms of strep—sore throat, fever, or headache—yet their strep cultures are still positive. Therefore, if your child has a mild cold but a marked increase in OCD and behavioral symptoms, take him for a throat culture.

RED FLAGS

- Sudden onset or exacerbation of OCD symptoms
- Sudden onset or exacerbation of tic symptoms—eye blinking, knuckle cracking, throat clearing, and so forth
- Motoric hyperactivity
- Emotional regression or lability, including rages, baby talk, screaming for hours
- Nighttime fears
- Oppositional, defiant, belligerent behavior
- Separation anxiety
- Increased sensory sensitivity—clothing tags, certain textures, socks and shoes may not be tolerated
- Unusual statuesque poses and movements, choreiform movements (piano-playing movements of the fingers, writhing arms, hands, or feet)
- Marked deterioration of handwriting, drawing skills, math skills
- Hyperactivity, fidgetiness, clumsiness
- Personality changes
- Refusal to eat or fear of eating
- Urinary frequency, urgency, bedwetting

There are some tests your doctor should run if you suspect that your child may have PANS:

- A throat swab. If results are not positive on the quick test, have the specimen cultured (takes two to three days). If the culture is negative, repeat within a few days or a week. Additional tests may be indicated, such as for Lyme or Mycoplasma.
- Blood tests for the presence of strep antibodies, called blood titer tests, can be done, though they may be difficult to interpret, as some children may have a normally elevated baseline. These tests are the antistreptolysin O (ASO) titer and Anti-DNase B.

- An additional test, called the Cunningham Panel, is a series of tests that indicate the likelihood that your child's symptoms are caused by an autoimmune signal in the brain. More information is available at http://pandasnetwork.org.

Children with PANS will require medical intervention, but when families understand the mechanisms of OCD, they can effectively avoid behaviors that will worsen symptoms, using cognitive behavior therapy, and begin to work on bossing back, changing rituals, and other aspects of exposure and ritual prevention therapy.

MARK'S STORY: GOT MILK?

Ten-year-old Mark was having a difficult summer. A straight-A student with a great sense of humor and an accomplished athlete in several sports, he suddenly became concerned that he was breaking the rules at baseball camp. He would replay his moves and try to make sure they were right. He was concerned that he was plagiarizing on some summer reading projects. Life was not making sense to Mark or to his parents. He remembered hearing on the news about how Osama bin Laden sent messages to his cohorts through hand signals or by the items arranged around him—a fruit basket with nine apples and eleven oranges let them know when to attack. Mark was terrified that when he held his arm out and blinked he was giving a sign to someone that would make them do something bad.

Mark and his parents were extremely relieved to learn in treatment how these symptoms, though bizarre, were garden variety, making sense within the illogical realm of OCD, and were very treatable. Within a few weeks of treatment Mark was looking brighter and unburdened. A turning point for Mark and his family occurred after about three months of treatment. Mark had an obsession at swimming practice that he might somehow leave practice and go out and kill someone. The resulting compulsion was to look at the clock after every few strokes to make sure that he could account for his time—that he hadn't, in fact, sneaked out of the pool to commit murder. Once he processed this behavior with his parents he knew that just having the intrusive thought about murdering someone didn't make it true—at all! Mark got it: He wasn't leaving the pool, but because of his OCD he was leaving his senses! His parents, having learned the drill of taking OCD to the edge, began some creative play with Mark. They'd say, "So when you leave swimming to go out and kill someone, can you stop by the store and pick up some milk for us?" This became a great code phrase for Mark in fighting the OCD; it brought the absurdity of his concerns into focus. Now when he leaves for swim practice he tells his mom, "Don't worry, I won't forget the milk!"

Chapter 16

FROM NERVOUS HABITS TO TOURETTE'S SYNDROME AND TRICHOTILLOMANIA

My son started doing this blinking thing with his eyes. He says it's nothing, but it's definitely not normal for him. Do we ignore it or try to make him stop?

Lizzie came down to breakfast one morning, and I knew right away that something was very wrong. I looked at her red eyes and saw that she barely had any eyelashes left. She told me she didn't know why she did it, but she didn't know how to stop.

Children are born to move. Peek into any elementary school classroom and you'll see a sea of constant motion: fidgeting, wriggling, tapping, picking, poking, and making faces. For most children these behaviors aren't a problem; they are how young children process the world. In fact, for children under the age of three or four, habits such as thumb-sucking or ear rubbing may represent an accomplishment in self-soothing; they are not considered disruptive behaviors, are best ignored, and will resolve over time. Not only would trying to interrupt the child be frustrating because young children have so little behavioral control, but it would run counter to a child's development and to the trust between parent and child.

For about 10 percent of children, eye blinking or twirling their hair isn't just a means of cooking up ways to entertain themselves. Instead, their bodies are sending them an intrusive automatic message that is hard to ignore: *Blink your eyes! Shrug your shoulders! Clear your throat!* These behaviors aren't their choice. They are tapping or clearing their throat or blinking their eyes because of a *tic*—an involuntary and "non-purposeful" instruction from the brain, like a mental itch, to do a certain action, typically repeatedly. The child doesn't want to engage in the behavior, and often may even be unaware of what he is doing until someone says: "Stop tapping!" A child may try to stop, but they only have so much control over the tics. Much of the time, like a suppressed sneeze, the behavior has to come out at some time. As one child described it: "It's like a champagne bottle. You can keep pressing the cork down, but eventually it will burst."

Similarly, many kids describe the beginnings of trichotillomania (compulsive hair pulling commonly referred to as "trich") as just a little tension reliever that they accidentally discovered one day when they were rubbing their eyes (or twirling their hair, or pulling their shirt), only to find that within weeks the innocent diversion had turned into a monster habit that they couldn't stop. Tics can be devastating for a child when others do not understand that they are involuntary and not misbehavior.

Many children's habits don't require treatment; they can be resolved with reminders, incentives, and techniques for reducing or controlling the behavior. When needed, a specific type of cognitive behavior therapy called Habit Reversal Training (HRT) can weaken the hair-pulling habit and train children to reroute a noticeable tic such as neck rolling or eye blinking to a less conspicuous form, and in some cases obviate the tic altogether.

This chapter summarizes the key elements of habit reversal training, and how to work out a habit reversal plan for any of these habits or repetitive behaviors. Also covered are guidelines for broaching these issues with your child in a sensitive, informed, and supportive manner.

WHAT IS A HABIT?

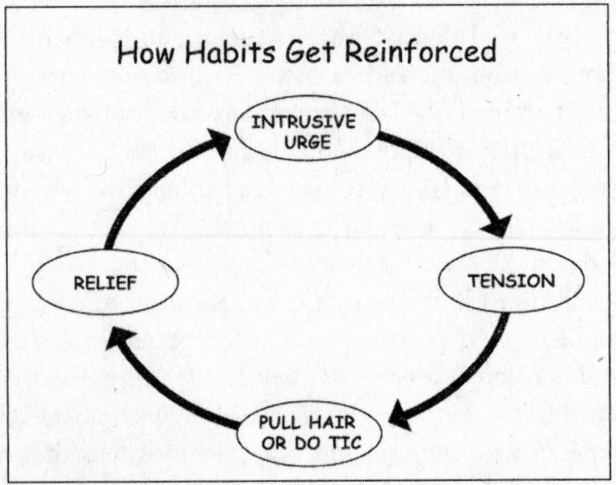

When a child responds to an urge by engaging in a particular behavior (doing a tic like blinking or pulling at a hair), this creates a powerful feedback loop in the brain and strengthens the vicious cycle. When the same urge comes the next time, the child is more likely to engage in the same behavior as it relieved the tension the first time.

It may seem hard to understand, but we experience some of the same things every day. The brain has a strong need to complete whatever it starts, so if you think "sneeze"! and then you don't sneeze, the idea seizes your attention, and you can't forget it until you sneeze. When we do "complete the action" by sneezing, the brain responds with a feeling of satisfaction. Urges get reinforced by a positive ending. So even if what might have started as a negative cue—pull that hair—ends with a positive result—feeling good—this feedback loop gets reinforced. The brain learns quickly what feels good and seeks to repeat it. We can interrupt that cycle with other choices of other ways to respond; this is how treatment works. More about that in a minute.

COULD IT BE NORMAL? RED FLAGS FOR PROBLEM BEHAVIOR

While it can be difficult to distinguish a passing habit from a problem behavior, the guidelines below provide a starting point. As always, don't wait for a collection of red flags; the techniques in this book can be used preventively, and some problems may be averted.

- The child is unable to stop when the behavior is brought to his attention
- The child feels frustrated by the behavior but unable to control it
- The behavior is something the child feels compelled to do, not something he chooses to do
- The child feels intense anxiety or frustration when he resists the behavior
- The child feels a sense of relief when he performs the behavior
- The behavior causes physical damage—a sore neck or sore knuckles from tics, or bald spots from hair pulling
- The behavior interferes with the child's functioning (in the middle of a sports event or math test, the child needs to interrupt the activity to perform the behavior)
- An ordinary habit—spitting, knuckle cracking, nail picking—is accompanied by multiple tics or habits, including vocalizations (humming or throat clearing)

WHAT YOU CAN DO TO HELP: UNDERSTAND THAT THE HABIT IS THE PROBLEM; YOUR CHILD IS NOT

One of the stresses that parents (and children) feel in contending with these conditions is that it is difficult for those around the child to understand why they have this habit, and why can't they *just stop*? The behaviors seem so stoppable to the outside observer—especially when the habits are bringing distress to the child, as they often do. But no child does this on purpose. One of the most important things you can do for your child with tics or trich—and you may be the only person in your child's life who truly does this—is to understand that habits are not something your child wants to be doing, can fully control, or, generally, wants to talk about. You can make your home a judgment-free haven for your child, a place where they will not be questioned, embarrassed, or insulted about their habits. If you can establish this trust with your child, when you do suggest strategies or getting help, they will see that you are doing this from a sense of caring for their well-being, not from a place of judgment.

Gaining Cooperation: What's on Their Habit Annoyance List?

The best way to elicit your child's cooperation in a behavioral plan is to help her draw up an "annoyance list"—what bothers her about doing the habit, does it hurt, does she feel embarrassed, and what are some reasons that she would like to gain more control?

Thinking Strategies That Help

We'll talk about physical tools for children to use to manage their urges in a minute, but thinking tools can help, too. Imagine if your child thought that Tic Guy was trying to boss him around every time he moved. He wouldn't be so likely to just follow directions; he'd stand up to Tic Guy and say, "I'm the boss!" One youngster drew a picture of a bug (we often call these urges "brain bug") the size of an actual tick. This helped him to think, "I'm not going to let a little tick boss me around!" An older child might think of The Picker as an unpleasant teacher or classmate and think—"Don't tell me what to do!" One teenager used her imagination to picture a SWAT team storming her room every time she went to pull a hair.

SUMMARY OF TARGET BEHAVIORS: TICS, TOURETTE'S SYNDROME, AND TRICH

Tic Disorders

There are two types of tics. Motor tics are gestures or movements that occur in any part of the body, such as the face, shoulders, abdomen, hands, or legs. The movement could include eye blinking, facial grimacing, licking lips, head jerking, shoulder jerking, chin on chest or shoulder, touching, tapping, rubbing objects, thrusting of arms, groin, or torso, hopping, jumping, clapping, dragging feet, kissing objects, touching genitals. There is some evidence that tics begin at the head or face and over time progress down to other parts of the body. Vocal tics include throat clearing, lip licking or smacking, grunting, squeaking, coughing, humming, yelling, echoing of sounds, clucking sound from the back of the throat, and the repeating of certain phrases.

Some children are unaware of their tics; others may experience a feeling of tension in a particular area as if something is going to happen—akin to the feeling we all get when a sneeze is coming on. When a child tries to resist a tic, as with a suppressed sneeze, there is a feeling of tension until the action is completed. Often before the tic occurs there is a "warning" or what is referred to as a premonitory urge. This is where your child has a window of opportunity to resist the physiological urge using habit reversal training and try to let it pass. Importantly, in children under age ten, simple tics (where one muscle group is involved) are more automatic, less controllable, and less likely to be preceded by a warning or premonitory urge, than are complex tics (in which multiple actions or muscle groups are involved).

Children who have motor or vocal tics, but not both, are diagnosed with either a provisional tic disorder (occurring regularly but lasting less than twelve consecutive months) or a chronic one (lasting longer than twelve months). Tourette's syndrome is diagnosed when children have both multiple motor and one or more vocal tics for more than a year. The tics need not be concurrent.

There is substantial evidence that tic disorders have a genetic component. They may be caused by an oversensitivity to the neurotransmitter dopamine, which controls movement, and they may originate in the basal ganglia, the part of the brain that controls behaviors.

A Note About PANS

If your child has a sudden onset of severe tics (overnight) or a sudden increase in the intensity and frequency of existing tics, it is possible that this episode may be caused by an autoimmune reaction to a common childhood disorder such as strep, or to another virus or infection, or even Lyme disease. Please refer to page 333 in Chapter 15 and check with your pediatrician. Medical treatment may be indicated to eliminate this acute trigger of your child's symptoms.

Prevalence and Course

Most children with tics begin by age six or seven with simple tics such as eye blinking. Usually vocal tics emerge by age eight or nine, followed by more tics and tic/OCD hybrids at age eleven or twelve. About 50 percent of children with tic disorders also display symptoms of OCD. Through the early years, the tics wax and wane, reaching greatest intensity in mid-adolescence and generally waning in late adolescence and into adulthood. About 60 percent of people will see a substantial reduction in their tics over time, even without treatment. Approximately 24 percent of children experience tics, but most are minor; estimates are that between 0.5 and 1 percent of the population suffers from a chronic tic disorder.

What Makes Tics Worse?	What Makes Tics Better?
Stress, being overscheduled, or feeling unnecessary pressure to perform	Having a balanced schedule with reasonable expectations for performance
Drawing attention to tics, feeling pressure to "not" tic, being blamed for being disruptive or inappropriate	Having a place to tic freely without comment or ridicule; having it understood that this is no-fault and not purposeful
Fatigue and poor nutrition; being overtired makes it more difficult to function in general and can exacerbate tics	Getting adequate sleep and good nutrition will help reduce stress and allow for better functioning and control

TRICHOTILLOMANIA

Trich is a no-fault neurological condition in which a child is responding to erroneous brain signals to pull her hair. It may be related to ancient grooming circuitry gone awry, and it may be similar to the urge to scratch an itch. Imagine that a hair calls to the child, often beginning with a tingling sensation on the scalp. Certain hairs may have a different look or feel—longer, shorter, thicker, or with a larger root—and these call out to the sufferer like the lone dandelion in a perfect lawn. If she resists the urge, the feeling hounds her. When she pulls a hair and gets it "just right" or has the "perfect pull," there is an instant feeling of relief. But that relief is quickly followed by a sense of shame and guilt over the damage that has been done. Sometimes areas of pulling will change as the nerve endings become desensitized to the feeling of pulling, and the person looks for other areas where she will experience that strong sensation of the perfect pull.

Course and Prevalence

Trich typically begins in childhood. Some children outgrow what begins as a self-soothing habit, but for others the behavior progresses into a disorder in later childhood. Trich occurs in 1 to 2 percent of college students; it is not clear how many young children have trich. Kids with trich are likely to have a family member with some sort of tic or habit, such as knuckle cracking or nail-biting.

THE GOAL: COUNTING STRATEGIES, NOT HAIRS OR TICS

Of course, we'd love for kids to just stop picking, pulling, and ticking. But as we've learned from studying intrusive worry thoughts, we have to address the thoughts themselves as well as the behavior. The keys to treatment are about (1) increasing the child's awareness of the habits; (2) increasing their choices of how to respond; (3) changing their relationship to the urge; (4) using fidget tools like Koosh balls to keep their hands busy and away from their hair; (5) keeping track of success by looking at how responsible the child has been been using their tools. Remember that the goal is for the child to have *their own* goals to tackle the problem.

THE STRATEGIES: KEY INTERVENTIONS IN TREATMENT

Habit Reversal Training

Habit reversal training is the specific type of cognitive behavior therapy first introduced by psychologists Nathan Azrin and Gregory Nunn in the late 1970s for treating common childhood habits such as nail-biting and thumb-sucking, as well as trichotillomania and chronic tic disorders. Habit reversal training has been studied for decades, and my plan in this chapter is based on the research findings about the critical components of habit reversal training. Medications may also be used in the treatment of tics, Tourette's syndrome, and trich—please see the online resource page on www.tamarchansky.com for more information.

Expectations: Catch What You Can

Children and parents need to be clear about the no-fault nature of these disorders. Make sure your child understands that he is not to blame in any way, but that if he would like to gain more control over these behaviors, there are effective techniques he can learn. Rather than focus on the tics the child performs, parents should commend him for the ones he catches. Likewise, with trich look for the times when your child interrupts pulling or fights the pulling urge. With tics there is often a premonitory feeling (like a foreshadowing, a preview, a hint, an itch), and with trich, children often describe feeling a strong itch or burning that precedes the pulling. Children can learn to use these feelings as a signal to buy some time and make a choice: Do I go with Plan A (pick, pull, tic) or Plan B (ride out the urge, surf the feeling, use my tools, leave the room to be with others)?

Step One: Increase Awareness

Many kids are unaware that they are engaging in their habit behavior at all. That's what gives the habit the advantage—it catches the child off guard. This is why one of the first steps in habit reversal is increasing awareness of situations where the target behavior occurs and the triggers that cause it. With trich, these triggers may be stress, boredom, anger, or fatigue. There aren't always identifiable triggers, but awareness can still be increased by asking the child to notice how the tic happens, how and where the first signs of the urge occur, and what happens next.

Awareness training techniques for your child to practice:

- Notice the earliest signal of the target behavior.
- For tics: Look in the mirror to see how the target behavior happens in slow motion; notice opportunities for blocking moves.
- For trich: From what part of the body is hair pulled? Are any tools used (tweezers, etc.)?
- Identify triggers and frequency through self-monitoring. Keep track on paper: the situation (bored in class, waiting for a test, in bed after having a fight with Mom), the feeling, the strength of the urge (0 to 10), any blocking moves performed.

If your child knows the likely triggers, he can go into those situations prepared with tools rather than getting caught off guard.

The trigger—for example, homework stress—can signal to the child that it's time to mobilize into Plan B action! The child can consult with a parent nightly to review the day and his progress by looking at his eyebrows or fingernails, or discussing tough tic moments. This time spent together should be supportive and strategic. For instance, the parent might say, "How would you want to handle that tomorrow?"

Step Two: Establish a Competing Response

When working with a habit or automatic behavior, a child will need to build up new blocking moves and muscles and find new skills outside the moment so that they are ready and easy to reach when he needs them. Below we discuss how to identify some of the many possible competing responses and how to set up practice. Find the pattern that works best for your child. Practices should be brief—a few minutes—and can even be fun—whether it's doing relaxation training together or doing boss back plays to fight "the picker." Change will not happen without this practice, but pushing too hard will only make conditions worse, and parents can't expect that their kids are going to be happy about having to practice each day. Work on the spirit of practice, not the letter. In the following paragraphs we look at approaches to blocking moves to use in response to an urge to pull or tic.

STRATEGY: Squeeze Your Lemons Rather Than Tic or Pull

Make a fist and hold it tight, as if squeezing a lemon in your hand for one minute. Releasing the fist can substitute for the release of tension that comes from pulling or engaging in a tic.

STRATEGY: Use Blocking Moves: Find the Best Incompatible Responses

The rationale behind habit reversal training is that with greater awareness of habits and options for alternate behaviors, children can train themselves to either block the behavior or disguise it by engaging in a more socially acceptable alternative. Ask your child to perform a tic in slow motion in the mirror so that you can both observe the opportunities for how to block it. The behavior is no longer an embarrassing moment; it's more of a physics project. If energy is going to move in this direction, how do we stop or redirect it? A neck roll or shoulder shrug may be interrupted by having a hand on the chin in a modified "Thinker" pose (like the famous sculpture by Rodin, the figure with a hand on his forehead). Throat clearing may be blocked by a slow, deep breath or a swallow, or by chewing gum. An abdomen thrust likewise may be blocked by a slow, deep breath (it's tough to breathe in and thrust out at the same time) or by the child crossing his arms in front of him. For lip licking he can picture his mouth as a baseball diamond, and instead of rounding all the bases, he can teach his tongue to go just to the corner of his mouth and back to "first base"—and eventually he may be able to resist lip licking altogether. For tongue thrusting, the child could picture a window shade, and rather than yanking the shade all the way out, just pull it out slowly and slightly. When the urge to touch someone is inappropriate, a child can instead learn to rub a piece of sandpaper in his pocket until the urge goes away.

After I explained competing responses to one young man, he said, "Can't I just take a deep breath instead? That way I'll feel more relaxed instead of more stressed." While most kids need a visual/tactile tool, if your child would prefer to have an incompatible response like breathing/relaxing to compete with the urge to engage in an unwanted behavior—go for it.

STRATEGY: Stay Out of the Danger Zone

When you are on a diet, it's not wise to hang out at the donut shop—why tempt yourself? When working on changing a habit, a child shouldn't keep her hands in the danger zone. If she has trich, or a hair-twirling or nose-picking tic, as soon as her hands are above her shoulders an alarm should go off in her mind—beep, beep, beep! Because once she's up there it's a slippery slope to the target behavior. Kids can give their parents permission to do the "beep, beep"s when they see a hand heading for trouble. Gloves help, as do long-sleeved shirts. Be creative. Any solution that works for your child is a good one.

TOOLS TO HAVE READY

Keep several stashes of fidget tools near problem locations—the car, the phone, the TV, the bedside table—and in your child's pocket for school. These tools may include Koosh balls, stretchy toys, textured balls, Silly Putty, Gak Splat, Theraputty—any undistracting but fidget-friendly toy will serve. The ground rule for fidget tools is that they can't be more interesting than or require more concentration than the task at hand. Sometimes schools are willing to make these fidget tools available to all children in the class, because they can be useful in increasing focus and to help the child who really needs them not stand out.

Additional Techniques for Trich: Making It Harder to Pull

The following items interfere with hair pulling or let your child know when their fingers are going for the danger zone:

- Band-Aids, tape on fingers, rubber finger covers (from office supply stores), or gloves create a more effective warning to your child that her fingers are in the danger zone (because they feel different than just skin, which she is used to, and in the case of Band-Aids, they have a scent) and make it harder for the child to pull her hair.
- Bracelets with bells or charms let the child know where his hands are going.
- Hand lotion that makes your fingers more slippery makes it tougher for the child to grip her hair.
- Keeping hair wet or not washing out conditioner completely keeps hair more slippery and makes it harder to pull.
- Long nails can make it harder for some kids to pull hair. A set of false nails can also be an incentive and reward for successful control over a given period of time.
- Wearing a hat, headband, or bandanna can slow down access to hair and give your child more of a chance to fight.

Practice Routines

There are various ways of practicing the competing responses outside the moment of the tic or other habit urge. In general, daily practice consists of your child imagining the urge and then rehearsing taking his hand away from his hair (for trich), using swallowing or calm breathing to counter the throat-clearing tic, or trying to squeeze a Koosh ball rather than pick his nails. Boss back talk can also be practiced. These rehearsals needn't take more than a few minutes but should be done regularly. In addition, you can begin to set up with your child "habit-free periods" when he will be working on blocking the problem behavior.

- Set up target habit-free times each day or night, beginning with a fifteen-minute block (it is best if the practice period is done at the same time every day, e.g., during your child's favorite TV show). Make sure he has his fidget tools ready. When your child is able to master the fifteen-minute block behavior-free, then build on that foundation in fifteen-minute increments.
- Ask your child to identify a class period during the school day that will be habit-free. Always start with the smallest challenge, so the best class to start with would be the one in which there is generally a lower frequency of the problem behavior. When your child has had at least partial success in that class, she can add another class to her challenge list.

Step Two and a Half: Manage Unpleasant Emotions or Sensations

Internal Experiences

Many tics are the result of kids acting on an uncomfortable feeling or tension—but it's not until after they tic that they realize they were feeling a certain way. Encouraging your child to be aware of what is going on in their body or mind and report on it ("I'm feeling upset right now, and I'm having the urge to pull to get rid of that feeling") helps them start a dialogue with themselves and make choices about how to handle the strong feelings. Once they have identified the feeling, they can work on getting perspective on the feeling by using visualizations. Feelings create a strong reaction in the body, but they are temporary. Pulling or ticcing doesn't "solve" the problem, it adds to it.

- Visualize that you are in a movie theater and the feelings are on the screen. Put yourself in the front row, then keep moving back. See how the intensity of the feelings changes as you move farther back from them.
- Visualize that you are lying in the grass looking up at the sky. Each cloud in the sky is a feeling or thought that you are having. Visualize that just like clouds, your feelings are moving across the sky and soon will disappear.
- Visualize that the feelings you are having are on a canvas in front of you. Put a frame around it. Stretch the frame to make the picture bigger or smaller.
- Visualize a stream flowing in front of you. Put your feelings on branches or leaves and let them flow down the stream.

Step Three: Be Prepared for Possible Relapses

After a period of responding to urges successfully, a child may go off their watch and a setback may occur. It's important that we teach our kids to expect that they are probably going to have urges throughout their lives and should have tools ready to manage them. They can prepare themselves to correctly interpret any slips, telling themselves: "This is about trich, not about me. I have choices about how to get back on track."

HOW TO MAKE PROGRESS: TRACK PROGRESS!

It's important to set goals, but keep things flexible. For teens with trich or nail-biting it may be wearing mascara or being able to paint their nails. For kids with tics, it may be not having a sore neck or being able to make their tics less noticeable during a particular activity. The important piece is that the child has a plan. Measuring the number of tics or amount of hair that is pulled is focusing your attention on the problem rather than the solution. It's also focusing on what your child *can't* control instead of what they can. Instead, track your child's efforts at using their strategies.

ACCOMMODATE WHEN YOU CAN'T CONTROL

Improvements take months of practice and won't happen overnight. In the meantime, help your child think creatively about how to make his life work around the habit. If your child has a spitting tic, he can carry a handkerchief and/or insist that he clean up after himself. If your child taps, she could tap on a piece of foam at school to muffle the sound. If your daughter's trich has left bald spots, hair extensions or wigs may be helpful for privacy (and as a pulling deterrent) until she progresses to a place where her hair has grown in.

REMEMBER: PARENTS HAVE CHOICES, TOO

Though you may feel the pressure of your child's distress and want to help him get better as soon as possible, pressure gets the amygdala beeping, and that means that no good work can get done. Remember that you have choices as to how you view your child's situation. The anxiety track will come first—you can't help that—but don't stop there. Think again.

Your anxiety track tells you: "This is terrible. I'm embarrassed. I'm worried"→It feels urgent to make your child stop no matter what→Child is upset, you're upset, low parenting moment.

Your competent track tells you: "This is a no-fault behavior. My child doesn't want this to be happening"→Encourage your child to use the available tools→Child feels supported, you feel of use as a parent.

ON THE HOME FRONT: WHOSE FINGERS, HAIR, OR NECK IS IT ANYWAY?

Habits, tics, and trich can become a battleground for families. Kids may feel that their parents are trying to control them, and parents may feel that their kids aren't trying to help themselves. You may also feel inadequate as a parent and blame yourself for not being able to stop your child's tics. But nothing could be further from the truth! Don't let your frustration with your inability to *stop* the behavior get confused with your ability to help. There is so much you can do as a parent to help your child separate himself from his urges. In fact, you are in a unique position to give your child a sense of safety and acceptance. Work toward this. No one is perfect.

Giving your child support and tools to fight back against the messages of the push-y, pull-y, or tic-y brain can reduce tensions and power struggles between you and your child, because your child can reclaim power over his hands, hair, and everything else. It still leaves open the question of whether the child wants to take advantage of these strategies, or be left alone to do it when he is ready. In general, you don't want to become as pushy as the Trickster, nor do you want your child to see therapy as a punishment. It is best if you present your child with the techniques or give him a peek at what behavior therapy can offer, and then let him decide when and how to take this on. Incentives certainly help, but ultimately the child needs to feel that the behavior is problematic enough to warrant the effort of making changes. Sometimes kids feel better when they know that it is normal to be mad that they have to work on this in the first place. If they meet with a therapist who understands why they wouldn't be gung-ho about the treatment, that may leave the door open for them to decide willingly to pursue it. The most important issue is that your child feels empowered. If you are forcing them to change by insisting they go to therapy, the only way for them to feel empowered is to resist you. If your child feels that you are on their side, then they are more free to assert their independence against the problem, not the solution.

THE PARENT'S CHALLENGE

Knowing that your child suffers with a condition that is visible to others—and more importantly, misunderstood by others—causes great heartache for parents. Parents add guilt to that pain when they find themselves reacting either directly or privately the way a stranger would. If you recognize yourself as this parent, spare yourself the anguish and know that this is a normal response. Make peace with yourself first by learning as much as you can about the condition and find the matter-of-fact phrases that you'll say first to yourself and then to others who don't understand—whether they are family members, soccer coaches, or folks at the checkout line. Your goal is to be supportive and not be more conspicuous or embarrassing than the behavior you're trying to stop.

You could say: "My child has a neurological disorder, a medical problem; it's called [trich, Tourette's syndrome]. He can't help it, but he's working really hard to control it, so it would be helpful if you didn't stare. If you have questions you can ask me." The Pennsylvania Tourette Syndrome Association has free double-sided cards available to parents for moments such as these, which explain that the child has a neurological disorder and is not misbehaving. You can help your child prepare a one-liner for questions as well. Some kids may feel best saying, "It's just something I do. I'm working on it." Or even to ask, "Do you bite your nails or have any nervous habits? Most people do."

JOHN'S STORY

John, a bright, creative youngster with Tourette's syndrome, was trying very hard to be an advocate for himself at the ripe age of nine. Fully understanding the erratic nature of neurobiological conditions, he knew that some days things were quiet on the tic front: "A good day," he explained, "is when I don't notice myself." Other days were, in John's words, "just pickish," which meant he needed to pick—at his shoes, sometimes the rug, sometimes his scalp.

John worked with his teachers to explain his needs. They came up with a plan where John could go to a quiet area of the classroom when he needed to get the tics out of the way, or just needed to move around. This small accommodation helped him immensely to be able to focus and participate in his educational program. John's teacher also explained to his classmates (with his permission) that John was working hard at controlling his behavior, but that his habits were often automatic and uncontrollable. This helped the other kids understand that John wasn't trying to annoy them or disrespect their wishes.

MELANIE'S STORY

Melanie, a confident, capable, and outspoken college student, reflects back on her experiences with trich, which began in junior high. She remembers that it snuck up on her as a solution for the stress she has always felt in her life. "Everything seemed to be more than I could handle, and I guess it was. I remember one night in seventh grade when my family was on vacation, I was lying in bed, thinking of all the things I was going to have to do for school when I got home. The anxiety took over my body, and I felt completely overwhelmed. I started feeling the upper outer corner eyelashes of my right eye. I pulled lightly, then a little harder, and out came an eyelash. Even though it hurt, it still provided me with a sense of comfort and relief. I felt again for another eyelash and continued this process. By the next morning I had no upper eyelashes. I was so embarrassed and knew people would notice.

"I used to sit in my bed at night and think I was the only person who did this. That was probably the worst feeling—the loneliness. I came to hate my fingers and hands and would try to prevent myself from pulling whenever I could. When I looked in the mirror I would cry. Why was I doing this to myself, why couldn't I stop? When we sought therapy and found out that this wasn't a phase or a weakness but a disorder, I felt so much better.

"Now I've learned how to quiet and control the trich urges. I have learned techniques that work for me. I try to address the reason why I am feeling upset rather than 'solving' it by pulling. I no longer feel bad about myself for having trich; it's not who I am; it's something I have to take care of. I know I will have to keep my eye on my trich and not let myself slip, but now I have learned to love and accept myself, to look in the mirror and be proud of the person smiling back at me."

DO IT TODAY: APPROACH YOUR CHILD WITH COMPASSION FIRST, STRATEGIES SECOND

Think about a time when you had a habit, or an aspect of your appearance, that you felt embarrassed about. A stutter, a weight issue, thinning hair, bitten nails, skin picking; imagine what it felt like when people noticed, or you were afraid that people were noticing—ten thousand spotlights, all focused on you. You could barely breathe! Imagine now what you would have liked in those times: people not to notice, not to judge, not to treat you differently. Take that idea and bottle it on the shelf; put it somewhere safe in your mind and go back to it regularly.

Stop asking about hair or tics. Instead focus on tools and make sure you have interactions with your child about other things in their life. This problem is not what they want the center of their life to be, and neither do you.

Chapter 17

FROM ACUTE STRESS TO POST-TRAUMATIC STRESS DISORDER

Charlie was only five when we had the car accident. He was so upset that he fainted. He is really afraid of going anywhere by car, and even sometimes when he is walking and a car drives by, he jumps as if it were going to hit him. It doesn't seem like the fear is fading.

I never meant for my son to be there when my mother died. But he saw the whole thing—her last gasps for air, the paramedics, the ambulance racing to the hospital. He doesn't want to talk about it. He is afraid that he's going to stop breathing. It's like this awful experience is frozen in his mind, but he won't let us help him move on.

We'd like to believe that time heals all wounds, but as parents we know it doesn't. When a child experiences a traumatic event, it can be very confusing for parents to figure out if their child's responses are normal, and when he needs help. The majority of children who face a traumatic event (see the next page for a definition of trauma) do not need treatment, but about one in four will develop post-traumatic stress disorder (PTSD). Either way, by understanding the mechanisms of trauma and how it is treated, you will be able to help your child resiliently summon all his resources and move forward from the trauma, rather than getting stuck in a place of vulnerability.

WHAT IS TRAUMA?

The DSM-V defines trauma as exposure to an event that causes or is capable of causing death, serious injury, or threat to the physical integrity of oneself or another person. It also specifies that the child's reaction must include intense fear, helplessness, or horror, or disorganized or agitated behavior. It has long been thought that children are resilient to trauma—that their youth acts like a protective shield, and because they don't fully understand the impact of the event, they have less to react to. But the very reasons we thought kids were immune—their not understanding—is the same reason we now believe they are particularly at risk.

All children exposed to trauma need to identify what they are thinking and feeling in order to begin to change those thoughts and feelings, but many kids are unable to articulate their distress. Think about how children indirectly show that they are hungry or tired by falling apart. When dealing with something as unfamiliar as shock or distress, they may show how they are feeling by changes in their behavior rather than saying it in words.

THE BRAIN MECHANISMS: UNDERLYING TRAUMA

Post-traumatic stress disorder researchers hypothesize that traumatic memories are imprinted in the senses and the emotions and remain static over time, unaltered by life experiences. This is a sharp contrast to how our brains process normal memories. Most experiences are coded through meaning—schematic, narrative, and available to be amended in response to new experiences—and are fluid in our minds, like stories. Traumatic memory, on the other hand, is fragmented, nonverbal, and characterized by vivid feelings in the body—colors, sounds, and smells.

This is one reason that nonverbal treatment methods, including Eye Movement Desensitization and Reprocessing, and play, dance, and art therapies are often used for trauma survivors: These methods can be very effective in accessing memories that are more sensory in nature.

WHAT IT FEELS LIKE FOR YOUR CHILD

For children who are suffering from a traumatic reaction to an event, it may seem that they are operating in an altered state. Their system is on high alert, and their physical and emotional resources are all taken up by scanning the environment for signs of danger, and not available for processing the present. This reaction can manifest itself by the child shutting down or ramping up. Physically, the amygdala and related symptoms are locked into defense mode so children will seem preoccupied, on edge, hypervigilant, jumpy, irritable, tearful, and they can't be calmed or talked out of this state of arousal. They may have trouble sitting still or paying attention and may look like they have ADHD. Emotionally, children who are contending with trauma reactions have their stress bucket filled up. Any additional stressor can put them on overload. They may feel separate from others, and because of this (temporary) inability to connect, they may not want to socialize with others—either because they realize that their friends won't understand what they are going through, or simply because socializing won't be fun for them.

WHAT IS THE DIFFERENCE BETWEEN A NORMAL HEALING PROCESS AND PTSD?

Many children experience potentially traumatic events, and it's normal for a child to exhibit a wide array of emotional and behavioral responses. This might include acting confused, disorganized, or emotional; showing sadness, anger, or even denial; crying, distress, irritability, belligerence, avoidance, and withdrawal. For most children, these reactions are brief and contained, and diminish over time. Normal activities, such as school or social events, begin to exert a positive pull and the child becomes more and more eager to return to his or her normal activities. In contrast, with PTSD the symptoms move in the opposite direction: Children become more symptomatic, their behavior more extreme, and their world shrinks, as managing day-to-day can be overwhelming.

IF YOUR CHILD HAS EXPERIENCED A TRAUMATIC EVENT

If not properly treated, a child can carry the invisible wounds of trauma throughout life. Our darkest moments as parents come when we cannot shield our children from trauma—whether abuse, terrorism, or witnessing the death or injury of others. The good news? There is nothing—no therapy, no medication—more powerful for promoting the healing of an injured child than a parent's unconditional love. And there are so many things that parents can do to help limit the warp effect that traumatic experiences can have on children, and help their child develop his or her own resources for integrating the difficult experiences and moving forward out of the past, with a strengthened view of their own resilience.

Research shows that what makes an event traumatic is how a crisis is processed and consolidated in memory. Our job is to help kids process the trauma itself, and to teach them how to make sense out of the very frightening symptoms of trauma, such as flashbacks, nightmares, and sudden surges in adrenaline. A comprehensive discussion of all the specific types of trauma is beyond the scope of this book, but many excellent references are available (please see the online resource page on www.tamarchansky.com for more information). This chapter is a starting point. I'll present a general framework for coping with trauma—how to explain it to your child, what you can do at home, and when your child will need to get professional help.

WHAT YOU CAN DO TO HELP

Of course, parents wish that they could have shielded their child from the traumatic event, but this can't be done. The good news is that parents are the most vital piece of what can happen next. Your job is to translate the frightening experiences that the child is having into normal, expected reactions to these events. This saves your child from worrying that, on top of the trauma, there is something "wrong" with him and that he'll always be this way. By separating your child from the PTSD, you can reinforce the idea that you know that your child wants to move on; his brain isn't letting go yet, but he will be able to teach it to do so.

Creating a sense of emotional safety is another important way that parents can help their children recover. This means accepting your child's symptoms, not challenging why they are happening, or why sometimes she may seem fine, and other times not fine at all; limiting unnecessary conflict in the household; and returning to maintaining routines, family meals, bedtimes, and so forth. Within this return to structure, your flexibility will be invaluable, too. If your child is having a particularly difficult time, you may need to spend extra time with her at bedtime, or scale back on some activities if they are overwhelming to her. Remember, make these accommodations with an eye toward growth and recovery and your child ultimately not needing them—but your short-term flexibility can help keep your child moving forward, rather than seeing the challenges of day-to-day life as insurmountable and feeling no option but to shut down and retreat.

It is also important that you attend to *your* own emotional needs. It is not unusual for parents of children who are suffering with any kind of emotional or health problem to have their own secondary reactions. They may feel sad, guilty, hopeless, and anxious because of what their child went through, compounded by a second layer of similar reactions to the fact that their child is still suffering now. Your child has gone through a trauma, but even if you were not present for it, by extension it is a trauma for you as well. As a result, treatment for parents can be an equally important part of the recovery process for your child. Be mindful of your relationship with your spouse or partner, too; experiences like this can strain a relationship because both parties are feeling so much, perhaps even blaming each other. But this can also be an opportunity to come together for your child.

THE DIAGNOSES

The DSM-V recognizes two primary trauma-related diagnoses. Both diagnoses specify that the child's initial reaction to a traumatic event include intense fear, helplessness, horror, or disorganized or agitated behavior. Acute stress disorder is immediate, beginning and resolving within a month of the traumatic event; it is characterized by a shutting down or numbing to emotional experience. PTSD, on the other hand, can begin anywhere from a month to many months after the traumatic event and is manifested by hypervigilance, emotional reactivity, and re-experiencing of traumatic events through flashbacks. What is critical in the development of trauma symptoms in children is the perception of a life threat, even when no one has actually been injured or hurt in a given situation.

Red Flags for Trauma Reactions

Each child reacts differently to a traumatic incident, but most children exhibit some significant changes in their behavior and mood. Very young children will not display classic PTSD symptoms, as the majority of these symptoms require verbalization of their internal state.

For young children:

- Regression in language (baby talking)
- Toileting accidents
- Clinginess or freezing up in situations—unable to respond
- Irritability or fussiness
- Lack of emotional responsiveness, or more sudden and extreme emotional reactions
- Increased generalized fear and anxiety
- Separation anxiety
- Sleep disturbances
- Trauma-related play—enacting aspects of the traumatic event

For older children:

- Increased anxiety and separation fears
- Fears about a recurrence of the trauma
- Hyperarousal—on edge, startles easily
- Intrusive images about the event

- Concerns about personal responsibility for the event
- Physical complaints
- Sleep disturbances, nightmares
- Changes in eating habits
- Loss of interest in activities
- Withdrawal
- Regressive behavior

Red Flags for PTSD

- Frequent memories of the event; or, in young children, re-enacting some or all of the trauma repeatedly
- Upsetting and frightening dreams, whether general or about the trauma
- Acting or feeling like the experience is happening again
- Worry about dying at an early age
- Losing interest in activities that were previously enjoyed
- Physical symptoms such as headaches and stomachaches
- Sudden and extreme emotional reactions, irritability, angry outbursts
- Problems falling asleep or staying asleep
- Problems concentrating
- Acting younger than their age
- Hypervigilance or increased alertness to the environment

THE TRICK AND THE GOAL: WHAT HAPPENED THEN IS NOT HAPPENING NOW

PTSD can be considered the body's way of freezing in alert mode to make sure that if the traumatic event happens again, we won't be caught off guard again. With the incident over, however, being in constant preparation and protection mode actually becomes the problem. This is the trick of PTSD—the constant demands of being on alert, reviewing what occurred through flashbacks, or expending a great deal of energy trying *not* to: The "protection" interferes greatly in your child's life. They aren't able to be present in activities in their life, which makes it harder to engage and enjoy interaction with others and may make them want to generally pull back in their lives. You will need to help your child understand why his body thinks it needs to be on high alert, explain and normalize this reaction so he isn't afraid of what is happening to him, and help him teach his body that the coast is clear.

There are three main goals of treating trauma. First, because the symptoms themselves can be frightening and confusing, children are guided to understand—at their level—that the symptoms are not dangerous, and that there is nothing wrong with them; and stating clearly that they can recover and that it won't always be this way. The second goal is to teach breathing and relaxation skills to give children tools for relief from the distressing symptoms that can occur suddenly and dramatically in situations that trigger replaying of traumatic memories. The third element of treatment is to help children create a more accurate explanation for events that were not under their control, transforming the often disconnected and frightening memories of the trauma into a narrative that has a beginning, middle, and end. Usually the beginning and middle are vivid in their minds; the end point—that they survived, that the trauma ended, that there is some resolution—is what is elusive for people experiencing trauma. Reaching a point of closure in treatment can be critical to a child's perception that his world makes sense again, is whole again in some way, even if it is tragically changed.

Other elements of cognitive behavior therapy for children with PTSD can include making a plan for managing unpleasant symptoms such as racing heart, anger, or flashbacks; identifying triggers and reminders and making a plan for each; and ultimately creating a stimulus hierarchy for traumatic reminders that the child will gradually approach to neutralize his associations to these events. For example, a child who was in a car accident will eventually ride in a car and then visit the location where the accident occurred. That place is currently in the "dangerous" file, so whenever he thinks of it or drives by, it immediately sets off the threat/protect program, which is accompanied by uncomfortable surges of adrenaline. By revisiting this stimuli, now that the trauma is not happening, and staying for longer periods of time, the child can move the place out of the file of "current threat," to the safe file of "in the past," which doesn't require any physical or emotional readying at all.

A child will require professional intervention if the symptoms are interfering with his functioning and/or causing him significant distress. At the child's pace, therapy focuses on reconstructing a narrative of what occurred in the trauma, beginning with the child's recollections and listing and processing difficult flashbacks or intrusive thoughts.

HOW TO EXPLAIN TRAUMA TO CHILDREN

Children need clear explanations of the alarming symptoms of trauma as well as reassurance that their reactions are normal. Similar to the relabeling of symptoms that we've seen with other anxiety disorders, children with trauma need to befriend the "protector brain" and provide the important information that it is missing: that the trauma is over, that they are safe, and that it wasn't their fault. They need to understand that these pictures and flashes of information are the brain's way of trying to bring everything together because it was too overwhelmed at the time of the trauma to organize all the input that was occurring then. The traumatized child needs to stay with those pictures and allow the brain to piece together a story that makes sense, rather than having the narrative stop in the middle or having fragments or flashbacks rush in and out.

The following scripts can be used to help children understand their experiences:

For young children: "It was really scary what happened. It's not happening now, right? But it was so [scary, sad, etc.] that your brain keeps thinking that it has to be on high alert to protect you as if it were still happening. Your protector brain will always be there for you, but now we need to tell it that this is over, and that you are safe. Otherwise it just keeps making you feel like the bad thing is still happening. You can tell your protector brain: 'Thank you, but you're scaring me.' There are other things that we're going to learn from a special doctor who works with children who have had scary things happen to them. The doctor will help you do exercises with your mind to help you be in charge again."

For older children: "Our brain has a way of helping us understand and digest experiences that are difficult for us. We might feel upset about some things at first—if, for instance, a friend teases you, or your hamster dies—but then maybe the next day we feel a bit better, or we have forgotten about it. That system works very well for most ordinary disappointments or upsets. But when there is something very scary or very sad that happens, the feelings are so big and the memories so many that our bodies can't digest it all in a day. It is such a big job that sometimes feelings sort of shut down and we may feel numb, like nothing matters, or we may feel so upset that it seems like we are crying all the time. Sometimes sad feelings change into angry and frustrated feelings. When you think about what happened, you may get very nervous, upset, or frightened—it's like having a video of a scary movie where the tape is stuck at the scariest part. All of those feelings are normal.

"The normal equipment in the brain that we have to process events is overwhelmed and shut down because of how frightening this was. Instead of helping you process the story of what happened, your brain made a choice to just help you get through. Now there are a lot of isolated, static pictures that you have that your brain hasn't integrated into one story with a beginning, a middle, and an end. So they may keep popping up randomly in what are called flashbacks. It might almost feel like you are reliving it all over again because the brain can make it so vivid. So what you'll do in treatment is help reprocess those pictures and let your brain know that what happened then is not happening now. Being on high alert, keeping you on edge, is making things harder for you. That's actually the problem now. You lived through those difficult times; now you need your protector brain to catch up with that news."

It is important for you (and your child's therapist) to explain to the child that she is in charge of the pace of the therapy. She will decide what she's ready to work on or talk about. Using the fear thermometer, your child will let you know what her temperature is, choose the items to discuss that are the lowest temperature, and build from there. A signal such as red light/green light should be established between the child and therapist, so the child has full confidence that the therapist is listening and will respect her needs.

THE STRATEGIES: KEY INTERVENTIONS IN TREATMENT: FINISHING WHAT FEELS UNFINISHED

STRATEGY: Rethinking the Problem, Making It Safe to Revisit
Children who have experienced traumatic events often have misperceptions about why the events occurred, what exactly occurred, and, importantly, fears about even exploring any of those questions, because the mere thought of going back to that event—even in their minds—feels terrifying and dangerous. It is essential to help children to see that it is safe to go back and understand what happened, that it happened in the past and it's not happening now, and that it wasn't their fault. The following are suggestions for how to discuss these common concerns with your child.

Thinking Glitch/Error: "It's my fault." Children often have a distorted perception of their responsibility for a traumatic event: "If only I hadn't wanted that doll so much, my mom would never have gone out to the store."

It is important to normalize this process. Explain that good kids wish they could control things, and that taking the blame for something can make us feel there was a reason it happened. But we don't cause bad things to happen; we all try to be safe, and sometimes things just happen and it's nobody's fault.

Thinking Glitch/Error: "Thinking about what happened is dangerous. If I do, it will be too much and I'm going to lose control or go crazy."

Our brain sends us strong protective urges to avoid anything related to the trauma: It feels as if it's going to be the same as going through it again. What children need to know is that they will never go through the traumatic event again. Remembering the trauma is not the same as reexperiencing it. They are doing *planned* exposure: On purpose, when they do have control, they can decide to expose themselves to the thoughts and images, so that they can teach the body that it doesn't have to mobilize and protect it from those things. Eventually they'll see that it's not happening now and that the anxiety is lessening each time they remember. With the therapist's help, they will only remember and think about one part at a time. And remembering will help the child put together the pieces that now are separate and feel overwhelming.

Thinking Glitch/Error: "If I feel upset and remember those feelings, I'll never feel better."

Children (and adults) often fear that the high level of anxiety they feel when exposing themselves to images and thoughts related to the trauma will always stay high. But, in fact, the opposite is true. Exposure is the way to get used to those images and help the body and mind lower or lessen its reaction to those triggers with repeated exposures. Remember GUTI: With repeated practice we get used to things.

Use Physical Strategies to Obtain Relief from Symptoms

STRATEGY: Use Body-Calming Techniques

It is essential for children to have strategies to counteract and take charge of the sudden attacks of physiological symptoms that may occur (heart racing, feeling on edge, feeling unreal). Parents can consult the breathing and muscle-calming strategies described in Chapter 6. The child should become competent at breathing and relaxation before embarking on exploration of trauma material. To maximize the relaxation, the child should have self-talk that redirects him to the present—"I am safe now. Nothing bad is happening now. That is in the past." Children may have difficulty, especially at night. Parents can use the doors exercise in Chapter 8 to give them choices for fun, positive places to direct their thinking as they are falling asleep at night.

STRATEGY: Explore the Use of Medication

Though PTSD is the result of an external event, medication may be helpful in relieving some of the anxious arousal (reactivity, startle response), panic, sleep difficulties, and depression that are often associated with it. These medications include the SSRIs, as well as the short-acting anxiolytic medications (see Chapter 3 for discussion). Though the benefits of these medications are considered to be modest, they may enable some kids to go to school or sleep at night.

Practice Exposure Exercises and Desensitization

In PTSD therapy, exposure focuses on both the thoughts and the actual stimuli related to the trauma. For example, a child who was in a car accident will first undergo systematic desensitization in the office for aspects of that event, using relaxation and realistic thinking to manage the anxiety that arises. Once the child has successfully been desensitized, treatment then focuses on reapproaching triggering situations, such as driving in a similar car, or on a rainy day, or at the location where the accident occurred.

While a child's natural and understandable inclination is to avoid thinking about the trauma and avoid any reminders of it—including people, places, and things that may be associated with the event—we know that avoidance keeps the body in a state of alert and reinforces the belief that these experiences are too difficult to manage. Avoidance keeps the child in a heightened state of vulnerability. The protection again becomes the problem. Everything must be processed through the lens of whether or not it is related to the trauma, or is going to remind the person of the trauma. Exposure therapy, what is called prolonged exposure, gives the child the opportunity, in small steps, to habituate or desensitize to experiences related to the trauma. Using the concepts that have been woven throughout this book, a child will decide which "brain" to take to the exposure—telling protector brain or memory brain that they need to hang back, and smart brain that it needs to be the one in charge.

STRATEGY: Use Integrating Activities Such as Writing Letters

For some children, telling the story of what occurred, or having the therapist tell it from the information they've provided, helps them create a cohesive narrative for the traumatic event. Because it is often the feelings associated with the trauma (vulnerability, anger, fear, rage) that children are afraid to experience because they are so intense, exposing themselves to the feelings through writing can help them see that they can have the feelings and nothing bad happens. Writing letters (often never sent) to people who may have been involved in the traumatic event in which the child spells out what it was like for them can be another way of integrating elements—triggering event, feelings, and the people involved—so that they can feel less afraid of those feelings surging out unexpectedly. With treatment a child is able to construct a narrative of the disparate memories of the traumatic event (the fragments) and, importantly, see that they can turn the pages rather than get stuck, and they can come to the end where the traumatic event is not happening and they have survived.

Length of Treatment

The length of treatment varies according to the severity of the trauma and the child's readiness to work at treatment, though many children can experience significant improvement after a few months of treatment with a qualified professional.

Even after treatment is successfully completed, children can be affected by PTSD again at any time; for example, a child who was in a car accident may have difficulties when she begins taking a school bus, or begins to drive on her own. A child who sustained sexual abuse may have difficulties at puberty when boys show interest in her. Children who suffer severe PTSD will likely need ongoing treatment. In a 2000 review of state-of-the-art treatment for PTSD, Drs. Cohen, Berliner, and March indicate that for children who may need ongoing treatment, a "pulsed intervention" may be indicated, rather than a finite number of weekly sessions.[9] Pulsed treatment refers to the suspension of short-term treatment until the child needs further work—for example, when there are increased symptoms, or at a developmental transition. The benefit of this schedule is that the child has an ongoing connection with a provider but is able to feel confident in his abilities and return to therapy only when needed.

Eye Movement Desensitization and Reprocessing

We have focused on cognitive behavior therapy for anxiety disorders, but there are other treatments that show promise in treating trauma in children. Eye movement desensitization and reprocessing (EMDR) is an intervention that was developed by psychologist Francine Shapiro to treat PTSD. Like cognitive behavior therapy, it involves exposure through recalling aspects of the traumatic event, but the recall occurs while the child is visually following specific back-and-forth hand movements by the therapist, or alternate rhythmic tapping by the therapist on the child's hands. The rationale is that the eye movement or tapping simulates the deep information-processing activities that occur during rapid eye movement (REM) sleep, where we work through the difficulties of our day. There is not sufficient empirical evidence of the utility of EMDR with children, but anecdotal evidence indicates that it may be beneficial.

ON THE HOME FRONT

With so much of the work of trauma requiring professional intervention, what is the parent's role? There is a balance between modeling useful, effective efforts to manage the situation, and reassuring your child that whatever reaction he is having, he is accepted and safe. If a child is crying, or even laughing, remember that all reactions to trauma are normal. Clearly, if your child is hurting himself or others, limits must be set on him, but in a caring fashion. Help your child work out the feelings in a different way.

One of the strongest predictors of how a child responds to the stress of war is the reaction of his parents and other significant adults. By extension, in any traumatic situation, a parent's ability to model coping behavior is crucial. Important aspects of this process include the following:

- Reestablish a sense of safety and authority. Let your child know that you are back in charge, and that you will take care of him.
- Correct misperceptions of blame.
- Attribute the trauma to its true cause accurately, but with only as much detail as necessary and in a developmentally appropriate manner.
- Provide a return to structure and routine as soon as possible, including regular bedtimes and regular meals. Though families may feel it is best to give the child lots of room, the child may see this change in routine as a sign that life will never return to normal. This makes it hard for her to predict what will happen next on a given day. Though on the surface that latitude may seem appealing, it is ultimately stressful, for there is no pattern, and no semblance of order, which is necessary for a child to thrive.

DELIA'S STORY: MOMENTS OF MOVING ON

At age nine Delia witnessed an unusual traumatic event. In the middle of a play performance at a community theater, a man sitting right in front of Delia lost control and began shouting, punching and beating up the person sitting next to him. Terrified, Delia leapt over her seat and ran out of the theater. When her parents found her outside, Delia was in shock—irrational, crying, inconsolable. After this, Delia was terrified to go anyplace where there was a crowd—church, assemblies at school, sports events—for fear that someone would lose control again. She was unable to attend many family events, or managed them with a very high level of anxiety, constantly scanning crowds for people who looked unstable. She would jump when someone made a small movement near her.

When Delia came to treatment three years later, she still remembered vividly the entire sequence of events: the glasses flying off, the man being pushed to the ground, the color of his jacket, the feeling and sounds of hysteria in the crowd as if it were yesterday. In therapy Delia learned how trauma works and how the memories were following her because the event was sort of caught in her mind and hadn't been finished and filed away.

After establishing strong breathing and relaxation skills and creating a "safe place" to go to in her mind, we next used EMDR to return to the exact original scene and facilitate Delia's desensitization to those characteristics associated with the event. Through this exposure in her imagination, she was able to see that many capable people had taken charge, and that though she had been terrified that she was going to get attacked, she was in fact safe and hadn't been hurt. We used cognitive behavior therapy strategies to change her thinking patterns, and she began to reapproach situations using a hierarchy of fear challenges we defined together. Delia was able to climb up the stairs of learning so that she could relearn safety in her world. The top of the stairs, and a real triumph for Delia, was being able to attend a play—for the first time in over three years—because her best friend was performing in it. Nervous but determined to overcome her fears, she walked in and took her seat in the theater, vowing not to scan the crowd for danger. Her friend's mother, who understood what an enormous step this was for Delia, leaned over and said to her, "Even though you are not in the play—you are truly the star!" Delia glowed and began to feel like a normal life was possible again.

Part IV
ANXIETY: BEYOND THE DIAGNOSES

We have just explored how the different anxiety subtypes require different types of interventions. In this next section, we go beyond the diagnoses and look at factors that affect children across the spectrum of anxiety disorder diagnoses, including sleep, school, friends and family, real-world fears, and our success-oriented, stress-causing culture. In our closing chapter, we witness how learning about anxiety management can effect a positive sea change for the entire family and beyond.

Chapter 18

THINGS THAT GO BUMP IN THE NIGHT

From Nighttime Fears to Sleep Anxieties

Heidi wants to sleep with the lights on—a night-light isn't enough. When we tuck her in, she follows us out of her room saying that she can't sleep. She is so upset, and we don't want her to be tired the next day, so we sleep with her, or else she crawls into our bed. How do we get out of this cycle?

Alex is seventeen and is going away to college next year, but suddenly he has this fear that he can't fall asleep. He gets so worked up thinking he'll be the last one up in the house that it turns out to be true. Now he's saying he can't go to college because he'll be up all night.

Sleep—a magical restorative that bolsters memory and focus, or a battleground between kids and parents? For most families at some time, it's been both. I know it's not fun. Your child, having worked himself up to a second or third wind, is insisting he's not tired, or that he can't sleep in his room, or can't sleep without you. You know what's right: Everybody needs sleep, everybody needs to be in their own bed. Yet in the haze of sleep deprivation and anticipatory stress of tomorrow's busy schedule, your survival instinct kicks in, saying, "If I don't get some shut-eye, nothing will get done in my household." And so . . . you cave. You do all the things you know you shouldn't: You bring your child into your bed, you fall asleep in his, or you resort to electronics to put your child to sleep. But take heart. You have a second survival instinct—to think long-term, and to help your child build good sleep habits over time. This chapter will help you do just that.

SLEEP AND ANXIETY: WHAT'S THE CONNECTION?

Anyone who has spent a sleepless night watching their clock hour after hour knows that sleep and anxiety are diametrically opposed and, for that reason, inextricably linked. Sleep is about letting go, and anxiety is about holding on. Working out a peaceful resolution between the two is an essential life-management skill.

Much emphasis is placed on the sleep habits of infants and toddlers who are working on separation as well as fears, but older children and adolescents can be equally plagued with difficulties getting a good night's sleep. Anxious kids struggle at bedtime for the simple reason that it is the first time all day when they can't distract themselves from their fears and worries: They are their own captive audience. When all is quiet the mind gets up and wanders, looking for trouble; that is when the questions start to pop up. "What's that shadow on the wall? What was that noise? Do my friends like me? When am I going to study for my math test?" Some kids have specific fears of robbers, aliens, or monsters, but others may fear sleep itself—will they die in their sleep?—or will they be up for hours in the middle of the night? Whatever the worry, one thing is clear: Everyone in the family is losing sleep over it. The recipe for successful sleep has three main ingredients: (1) worry-management skills for kids to quiet their minds and slow down their bodies; (2) consistent expectations and routines maintained by parents; and (3) a sleep-friendly environment in your home (TV off, lights dim, to distinguish night as different from day). You can't *make* sleep happen, but you can make conditions optimal to invite sleep. Because sleep is something the body wants, needs, and knows how to do, it will take over from there.

SLEEP TAKES WORK: SEE THIS AS A PROJECT

After nutrition, sleep is the key ingredient to healthy development, both physical and emotional. A lack of sufficient sleep has been associated with a risk of obesity, poorer academic performance, bad decision making, and even depression. The good news is that once kids begin to get more sleep, these bad outcomes can quickly reverse. On average, children need ten to twelve hours of sleep a night, and nine hours a night for teens.

When you set good patterns, you will be rewarded with easier bedtimes, and hours and hours of sleep—for you and your child. It is never too early or too late to start. Even after years of sleepless nights, you can still expect excellent results if you and your child work faithfully on creating good sleep patterns.

Many parents struggle with leaving a protesting child awake to fall asleep on his own, particularly when such factors as separation anxiety or phobias are present. But research suggests this is exactly the right thing to do. Infants whose parents are present when they fall asleep wake up more often than those who are put to bed awake and left alone; given the opportunity, babies learn to soothe themselves. Without that opportunity, if they wake up in the night, they will need you there in order to fall asleep again. The same is true for older children. Though you may feel like your child is too insecure to be left alone to fall asleep, he, like an infant, can acquire that competency to sleep through the night, but first he needs to learn the skills. Once the skills of breathing, relaxation, and calming self-talk have been mastered, you can begin to fade yourself out of the picture, switching from lying in bed with your child to tucking him in followed by check-ins.

Keep in mind that just because sleep is a natural state doesn't mean it will come automatically. Sleep will come if the signals from the environment and the mind are all set on sleep mode (are conducive). If a child is worrying about something—especially about whether or not they will sleep—this will signal the "stay awake mode" in his or her mind. The body detects the message that there is a problem, and thinks it needs to stay up to solve it. When your child is worrying about sleep, she's blocking the very all-clear signal that lets her know it's okay (safe) to sleep. Kids need to switch off their protector brain and turn on their sleep brain.

YOUR ROLE: SEE YOUR CHILD AS A SLEEPER IN TRAINING

Many parents worry that they are asking too much of their child by expecting that he learn how to fall asleep on his own. The child's distress only heightens that fear and the whole thing becomes a tale of two amydgalas. The child is saying: "How can you leave me?! I'm in danger." This immediately triggers a parallel response in the parent: "I'm a bad parent. I need to help my child." That reaction lasts until frustration gets the better of everyone. But it doesn't have to be this way.

Stay grounded in the knowledge that helping your child learn how to sleep is essential good parenting—whether your child learns these lessons quickly or more work is required. Your child may not like the lessons, and will probably pull right on your heart strings, or your last nerve. But keep centered in the project. Your goal is for your child to be as independent as possible with settling in on his own, while you are stretching the amount of time between check-ins or other comforts. Yes, your job is to "be there" for your child, but this doesn't mean literally being scrunched up in her tiny bed with her. Being there for her means teaching her strategies for shrinking her worries, expanding her competency, and accomplishing this most essential staple of life: sleep.

PRESCRIPTION FOR A GOOD NIGHT'S SLEEP

The following is a list of factors that are known to facilitate good sleep. In addition to addressing anxiety issues directly, the strategies provided here will increase the likelihood that your child will sleep well.

- Allow sufficient wind-down time; plan a good wind-down activity. Extending exciting activities up to the last minute only prolongs the falling-asleep process. Stop exciting activity—rough play, television, computer games, especially those with scary content—well before bedtime. Teenagers shouldn't study up to the last minute. Establish a wind-down activity—reading, bath, quiet music.

- Keep it safe. Avoid scary material before bed—for young children, no scary books or videos, no frightening games with chases; for older kids, no scary books or movies before bed—or maybe at all: They are not necessary!
- Have a plan for nighttime fears. Make up realistic self-talk on cue cards for the child at bedtime, teach diaphragmatic breathing, and keep a flashlight on hand.
- Make sure your child gets sufficient exercise during the day—but not close to bedtime.
- Keep it positive. Avoid all negative associations with sleep or the child's bedroom. Don't use sleep as a punishment (going to bed early for bad behavior). Use another area if "time-outs" are needed so that they are not associated with the child's room. Keep the associations with being alone and being in bed positive.
- Watch the child's diet. Eliminate caffeine—chocolate, teas, sodas (even some root beers and clear or orange sodas contain caffeine). The effects of caffeine, which can exacerbate anxiety, may last up to ten hours after intake.
- Plan for the "ploys." Don't reward nighttime "ploy" behavior. Though nighttime conversations can be golden, if you stay an extra twenty minutes to get the scoop on school, it will likely become a new nighttime ritual. If you want time to catch up with your child, push back bedtime to accommodate or encourage your child to share news with you after supper. If your child always needs a glass of water, have him get one himself and put it beside his bed before he gets in.
- Focus on readiness for sleep, not a deadline. Don't focus on expectations about when your child should fall asleep; she can't control that. The harder she tries to sleep, the more awake she will be.
- Avoid the problem of getting kids out of your bed: Don't invite them in. Don't make more work for yourself or your child by having him just "visit" in your bed before bedtime; make your

room off-limits before bedtime and thus avoid the problem altogether.

- "Don't call us, we'll call you." The rule is that your child stays in bed: You will be the one checking on him; he is not to come find you. You can use incentives: happy-face charts, stickers, or small prizes for young children, and more tangible rewards for older children. Without getting angry, be firm and be clear: Your child needs to stay in bed.
- "Location, location, location." Settle your child down to fall asleep in the same setting (her room) where she will wake up. For young kids, falling asleep in your room and waking up in the middle of the night in their own room will be disorienting. Teenagers who fall asleep in front of the TV won't be comfortable falling asleep without the TV.
- Make parting less sorrowful—be brief. Be consistent in how long you stay in the room. You'll be supervising the wind-down more with young children (under eight); with older children you will facilitate their independent "settling routine." Stay for shorter and shorter times.
- End with a pleasant interaction. In whatever way fits for your family, send your child to sleep with a message of love—singing, hugs, kisses, a funny saying, or "sweet dreams."
- Reinforce good cooperation with extra hugs, an extra story, and so forth.
- Don't watch the clock! Turn clocks around or take them out of the room. The only thing they do is keep your child up calculating exactly how long he's been up, how much less sleep he's getting, and how tired he'll be tomorrow.
- Keep the room dark or dim (light will block the production of melatonin and will interfere with the body's natural rhythms of sleep). Fade light gradually over time using lower-wattage bulbs and shifting the source of light from overheads, to night-lights, to night-lights in adjoining rooms or hallways.

WHAT TIME SHOULD BEDTIME BE?

Children get a second wind, telling you they are not tired, willing themselves through those early signs of bedtime readiness, but bedtime needs to be bedtime. While every child is different, these general guidelines will help.

One- to three-year-olds: twelve to fourteen hours, bedtime between 6:30 and 8:30 p.m.

Four- to six-year-olds: ten to twelve hours, bedtime between 7 and 9 p.m.

Seven- to twelve-year-olds: ten to eleven hours, bedtime between 7:30 and 9:30 p.m.

Teens: eight and a half to nine hours; if they're in bed by 10 p.m. they are significantly less likely to suffer from depression

SOLUTIONS FOR COMMON NIGHTTIME ANXIETY CHALLENGES

Like their daytime counterparts, nighttime fears are addressed by enlisting a child's thinking skills to turn a distorted, frightening, or worrisome situation into something that is more manageable. The fact is that just because a child feels scared, this doesn't mean he is in danger. His internal alarm system has gone off, but it was not triggered by anything real. Find out what your child is worrying about, or what is frightening him: Is he not tired enough? Is he afraid of monsters? Is he worrying about school tomorrow? This way you can find strategies to address the particular challenge your child is facing.

GETTING TO THE ROOT OF THE PROBLEM

Some children have been good sleepers and have suddenly hit a jag—a worry or a scary movie that's keeping them up at night. Others have never slept well and the situation is becoming impossible. Some kids have one bad night's sleep at a friend's house and then believe they can no longer fall asleep; many teens are up late with homework, or on social media, and find they can't fall asleep like they used to. Use the questions below to find the root of the problem.

- "What's hard about bedtime?"
- "What's worry telling you?"
- "What do you think will happen when Mom goes into her room?"
- "What do you think will help?"

By asking your child what is on her worry list at bedtime (or simply noticing the kinds of questions she is asking you), you will learn what targets to use realistic thinking on. Your child can look at the shadows through the worry glasses and then the smart glasses, and get her imagination to work for her rather than working for the anxiety. It is best to start this work during the daytime when your child is not tired and therefore in better shape to think calmly.

Monsters in Closets or Under the Bed

It is very common for young children, who are still trying to master what is real and what is pretend, to be frightened of monsters, cartoon characters, or the proverbial boogeyman under the bed. Use your creativity to deliver the message that there are no monsters. Remember that gentle humor is a way to fight "fear" with "funny." You could make a silly announcement into an imaginary megaphone: "This is David's mother, and I am saying that this house is officially safe. There are no monsters here!" Open the closet, look under the bed, and again make your pronouncement: "See, it's dark under there—but there are no monsters, just a shoe and some dust, and . . . oh, and my bologna sandwich from yesterday. Hey, how did that get under there?" Then have your child repeat after you: "There are no monsters in my house. My house is safe." Slightly older children can say, "I'm the boss. That's just a story. My imagination is set on 'scary,' but just because I can imagine scary doesn't mean I'm in danger. I'm not." You can lead the way at first, but over time invite your child to take more responsibility for the project. He can be the one to open the closet door, or pull back the blankets. After your child feels comfortable (this may take days or weeks), then you can transition him away from checking for monsters in the closet or under the bed to just using his brave talk. Also keep on hand a flashlight and a list of ideas (this can be a pictorial collage by the bed that your child helps to make) that your child would rather think about instead.

DO THE MONSTER MAKEOVER!

If your child is afraid of monsters that his imagination has created, put that imagination to good use and fight scary with silly. (Check out the Monster Makeover drawing in Chapter 5.) Have your child draw a picture of the monster in his mind. Next have him do a silly makeover, adding accessories like funny hairstyles, bows, polka dots, tutus, trumpets, roller skates, banana peels, or silly positions like balancing on one foot, doing a handstand, riding a unicycle—let your child decide.

Movies or Pictures Stuck in Your Child's Mind

Use your own special effects. If your child has seen an upsetting movie and has a particular scene stuck in his mind, help him take charge by doing a variation on the monster makeover. Like a photo effects program, they can take the scene and make it silly; they can add food; they can turn everyone into a cartoon; they can imagine the characters speaking in gibberish; they can have all the characters doing some embarrassing bodily functions (your child will have no problem finding ideas there). A younger child can create a remote control on paper for all the choices they have generated, and then when the scary picture comes to mind, they can select a button to change the scene. For older children, they can simply picture the actors doing the scene in a silly manner.

"Bloody Mary" and Other Scary/Ghost Stories

One of the rites of childhood, it seems, is to hand down frightening stories, especially around campfires or at sleepover parties. Some children think nothing of these tales of blood, horror, death—to them it is a great time, and they go peacefully right off to sleep. Other children feel true terror. Contemplating the possibility that the legends could come true, they begin to avoid bedtime, and even the anticipation of evening frightens them. They may become more clingy and avoid being alone—in the bathroom, or at all. The story of Bloody Mary—an urban legend that if you look in the bathroom mirror at midnight, Bloody Mary will jump out at you—is one such scary story that continues to be passed down. In order for your child to know that this is made up, be willing to do the "ritual" in the bathroom (some variations include turning a certain number of times—saying the name a certain number of times) to prove to your child that nothing happens. The story is frightening because of the imagination responding to the power of all of those scary suggestions, not because it's real. It is unlikely that you'll need to stay up till midnight to do the ritual unless your child insists that he won't know for sure that it isn't true unless all conditions are met.

Have your child make up a story like Bloody Mary, but do a silly makeover. Instead of saying "Bloody Mary," maybe you have to quack like a duck or moo like a cow twenty times. And there could be cotton candy coming out of the mirror, or rubber duckies. Or just make up your own story. One child made up a story called "Muddy Larry." Whenever his mind was bugging him about Bloody Mary, he would come back with that and then he knew that it was all made up.

Fear of the Dark

Fear of the dark is most common among young children and preadolescents, but some teenagers and even adults struggle with this fear. It may be at the core of a child's difficulty sleeping alone. The fear of the dark is typically tied to the frightening ways the imagination fills in for what we can't see.

Children need to first work cognitively on looking at the dark through worry glasses and then through smart glasses. Then they might come to the conclusion, "It's just as safe. I just can't see as well, but I don't need to see. There's nothing to see." Then they can generate boss back talk to fight the fear: "I can do this. I am brave. Other kids manage this, so can I. I just have to get used to it." Once the thinking is straight, have your child work on the fear of the dark in stages, first during the day, taking fear challenges in the basement or attic with a flashlight, then in the early evening, going upstairs to his room in the semidarkness and doing something fun—reading a book, listening to music. What about playing flashlight tag in the dark? Or staging a scavenger hunt for hidden glow-in-the-dark items (dollar stores are great for these). Finally, begin to reduce the amount of light in your child's room at night. If your child sleeps with the overhead light on, switch to a low-wattage lamp; if a child has three lamps on, reduce the number to two, and then move to a night-light or hallway light. Once you put out the idea of the stairs of learning, your child can tell you what step he's ready to take first.

Because younger children are just starting to understand the dark, be a good tour guide—showing them that it can be fun, safe, and familiar. At night, start the bedtime routine with low lighting so that the transition to the dark won't be such a sharp contrast. Let your child know that at first he can't see in the dark, but within a few seconds—faster than he can sing "Happy Birthday"—his eyes will adjust and then he will be able to see. Using a familiar object of your child's choosing, such as a teddy bear, do an experiment: Turn down the lights, start singing, and see how long it takes before he can make out the shape of his teddy bear. Also let him know that sometimes it feels like your eyes play tricks on you in the dark and things don't look the same, but they really are. Do another experiment by asking your child to tell you what things look like in the dark, and then shining a flashlight on them so your child can see what they really are.

Fear of Sleeping Alone

Managing sleeping alone requires a combination of cognitive tools to calm the worry, balloon breathing, progressive muscle relaxation to help the body unwind, and quiet activities your child can do until sleep arrives. Simply insisting that the child stay alone will not work. Once you've identified the source of the fear and have taught your child the thinking and relaxing skills he needs, you should begin to fade yourself out of the bedroom gradually. Or, if your child is sleeping in your bed, he can begin to head back to his room step-by-step. Though fatigue and sympathy can weaken the strongest parent, it is best not to lie down with your child. It makes the departure tougher for her (and parents often fall asleep). Instead, sit on the edge of the bed or rub her back. Then tell your child that you'll see her in the morning. Ask her how many times she wants you to check on her—two times or four times (a bargaining strategy). Make your check-ins very brief, definitely under a minute. Tuck her in and wish her sweet dreams. Make it clear that she should not call out, that you'll come back to check on her. If your starting point is that your child is sleeping in your bed, or you in hers, make a hierarchy to gradually match up the right people with the right beds.

Nighttime Worries, Last-Minute Questions

When kids have worries on their mind it is difficult to fall asleep, and it is difficult to be alone. If your child is a nightly worrier, or has ten urgent questions that must be answered at bedtime, schedule a worry time well before bedtime—taking five minutes to write down or say his worries, then challenging the worries with more realistic thoughts, using one of the strategies listed in the master plan. This could also be a "last call for questions time." Then at bedtime remind your child that he is the boss of his mind. Keep coping thought reminders on cards by the bed, and keep a list of other thoughts or ideas that your child would like to think about. Your child can also write down his questions on a card for you, or in a journal, and at breakfast, after you are well rested, you can focus on his questions at length.

Keyed Up, Unable to Relax

Tedium is the stuff of good sleep. If your child is too alert and awake at bedtime, check out "Prescription for a Good Night's Sleep" on page 380 and use relaxation strategies from Chapter 6, or some gently "boring" mind games, to settle him down.

The Paradox of Being Afraid of Not Being Able to Fall Asleep

When children fear being unable to fall asleep, the fears quickly build up, and the thoughts sound like this: "No one else will be awake. I will have a terrible day tomorrow. I'll fail my test," and so forth. Explain to your child that worrying is an "awake activity" and will actually interfere with their going to sleep, that their goal is to "shut down the brain" and only do things that keep them in the sleep zone by not "overthinking" sleep. Do the side-by-side comparison: Ask your child whether their worry thoughts or their calm thoughts would be better for falling asleep. Let them make the choice. Write the calm thoughts on a card and keep the card by their bed for easy reference when they are feeling worried. Following are some ideas.

THINGS TO THINK

"I may be getting more sleep than I think."

"I may need less sleep than I think."

"I am sleeping well enough."

"Other nights I have slept well."

"Letting go of sleep worries is how I'll sleep better."

"My body wants to sleep."

"I'm going to keep my mind in the sleep zone."

"This isn't worry time; this is sleep time."

"I can fall asleep because my body knows how."

"I will fall asleep when I'm ready, or eventually."

"I can't control when I fall asleep, but I can control which thoughts I pay attention to."

USE THE DOORS EXERCISE

Help your child do breathing and relaxation exercises from Chapter 6. It is also helpful to have a new place to direct the mind once you've dismissed the worries. Look back at the illustration for the doors exercise at the end of Chapter 8: Ask your child to think of four things they'd *like* to think about: cupcakes, animals, celebrities, Legos, whatever it may be. Have them draw four doors and label them with these topics. Each night as you say good night, have your child tell you which two doors they are going to choose to explore. They can report back about their adventures at breakfast.

Nightmares

The majority of children have occasional nightmares. The period from toddler years through early grade school is a particularly busy time for contending with fears such as separation and fear of the dark, and bad dreams may be more frequent during this time. In fact, nightmares occur in as many as 50 percent of all children between the ages of three and six years. The occurrence of nightmares tends to decrease over time, but some children continue to have nightmares into adolescence and even adulthood. Reassurance and gentle coaxing back to sleep is the best approach. Though you may be bleary-eyed, it is best to walk your child back and settle him in his room. After a few moments of gentle reassurance that the dream won't come back, change the channel to a new dream, flip the pillow over for a fresh start, and help your child resettle.

Refusing to Go to Bed

Bedtime resistance is defined as a child's difficulty in getting to bed three or more nights each week for at least four weeks, with the child struggling for forty-five minutes or more each night. You may think that this describes most kids, because it is the rare child who wants to go to bed. But more often than not, even feisty nighttime fighters will surrender to the inevitable when parents hold their ground with the bedtime routine. If you are keeping to your part of the bargain but your child continues to have difficulty settling, make sure you are not overlooking any fears. Your child's compliance in getting to bed and staying there can then be reinforced with incentives—extra playtime, an extra story the next night, extra computer time. Although in general incentives work best, some parents find that withdrawing privileges temporarily gets the job done.

The Challenge for Parents of Teenagers: Don't Give Up on Setting a Bedtime!

Rather than a power struggle, think of this as a collaboration. Your child doesn't want to be exhausted, and likely is juggling a lot of conflicting demands between school, friends, sports, and sleep. Join with them in an open conversation about how they might best meet all of those needs. Many teens work (or text!)

right up until bedtime; talk to them about the importance of a wind-down routine. A quiet play list on his iPod while he reads or gets ready for bed will become a cue that his body will remember. Teens need to know that their body wants to sleep, and they will help it do so by sending the right signals. You can empathize when your teen says, "I'm not tired [at 10:00 at night]," or, "I'm not nearly done with my homework." Schools' and sports' early-morning starting times are not conducive to teens' internal circadian rhythms, but any effort they can make to get to bed earlier will be positive. See if they can back up bedtime by a half an hour or even 15 minutes; over time this extra sleep will really add up. A large-scale study found that teens who went to bed by 10 p.m. were 15 percent less likely to experience depressive and suicidal thoughts,[10] not to mention how much brain functioning in general is improved by sleep.

Parents Who Work Late or Travel

Late hours and frequent overnight travel have become a reality in many households. Families struggle to stay connected long-distance, or to arrive home without riling up the kids before bedtime. Skype conversations after dinner, or leaving notes to be read at bedtime, can help make the connection without getting the routine off track.

ANNE'S STORY

Insomnia runs in Anne's family: It is not unusual to find at least one member of the family up in the middle of the night. According to Anne's mom, Ellen, Anne has had trouble with sleep since she was an infant. As she got older, one of the factors perpetuating her sleep difficulties was her worry that she wouldn't be able to sleep. Like many children with sleep anxiety, Anne is haunted by the memory of one awful night when she was up for hours, unable to fall asleep. Ever since that night, Anne would stay up late worrying that she wasn't going to be able to sleep. She would get so frantic and worked up that her worst fear would come true.

Through self-talk and breathing exercises, Anne was able to see how she could work with her anxiety level at night by what she was saying to herself and what she was doing with her time while waiting to fall asleep. As she writes, "I would feel so scared at night thinking that I would never fall asleep and that I was the only one who felt this way. I worked my way through it. Even though that night I was scared, I started to realize even if the worst thing came true and I stayed up all night again that I could deal with that. I realized too that when I didn't make that into a big deal it actually helped me stay calmer—and even if it took a while, I could fall asleep. When I saw that I could survive not sleeping well—that I could still be fine the next day at school—I knew I would be okay, and I actually worried less at night. Now that I've learned not to let anxiety about sleep control my sleep, I think to myself: 'Wow, I can't believe I did it! It's a great feeling.'"

DO IT TODAY: ARE YOU SLEEPING?

According to the Centers for Disease Control, insomnia in adults is a public health epidemic. With many of us falling asleep in front of our televisions or laptops, our own sleep hygiene could use a makeover. Look at the Prescription for a Good Night's Sleep (see page 380) and take this opportunity to be a good role model for your child, by watching your caffeine intake, turning off electronics at a reasonable hour, and finding a wind-down activity. Your child will learn from your example and you'll get a better night's sleep!

Chapter 19

EXPANDING THE FOCUS: ANXIOUS CHILDREN AT SCHOOL AND WITH FRIENDS AND FAMILY

It is so difficult to get Vicki to school that I begin to wonder, Is this really necessary? Maybe she should just stay home.

Sometimes I think I'm the one who is losing it. My mother-in-law says that all these problems would go away if I was just more strict. What do I tell her?

SCHOOL: MAKING IT WORK FOR ANXIOUS CHILDREN

Children spend over eleven hundred hours a year in school. Anxious kids' difficulties can range from an occasional sticky situation when they don't want to attend, to a serious stalemate where nothing can get them to go. When schools tune in to the needs of anxious kids, it can make the difference between a child attending and thriving in school or not attending school at all. In this section we'll take a look at why anxious kids often refuse to go to school, and educational options and accommodations that can help them.

Reasons for School Refusal

When your child's struggles over attending school are not occasional but part of daily life, it is urgent that you identify the source of the problem. It is best to take a wide view when investigating the reasons for your child's refusal: Take in information from your child, from the school, from looking at peers, home life, and health. Is your child escaping from some unpleasant or difficult situation, such as panicking about tests or about being unable to handle a social problem? Or is she being positively rewarded in some way for staying home, such as being given unlimited access to computer, television, or Mom? Or has she missed so much school that she is afraid that she'll never catch up on the work she's missed, and won't know how to explain her absence to her friends?

Think in Parts: What's the Source of the Problem?

STRATEGY: Use a Pie Chart

To identify what is making school hard for them now, ask your child to create a pie chart—most kids understand the concept of big chunks and little chunks. If they are unable to give an answer, and can only say, "I don't know," tell them it's time to go "fishing." Mention a few things other kids sometimes say that make it hard to go to school, and if something you mention matches what they feel, they will tell you you've "caught a fish." Mention things such as the teacher yells, isn't nice, is strict; the work is hard (narrow it down to which work); the work is boring (sometimes code for hard); I have no one to eat lunch with; kids are teasing me. Then ask follow-up questions: Is the work boring because you get it done too quickly and it's too easy? Or is it boring because it's really hard to understand and you can't get it done? Is it hard to find friends to play with at recess or eat lunch with? Are you worrying about other things and that makes it hard to be at school? Often if you "go fishing" long enough, a child may see that you are earnestly trying to help and may either tell you you've caught some fish, or, in realizing what the problem *isn't*, may discover what the problem *is*. Once your child has generated a list of problems, then return to the pie chart and ask him to fill it in.

What makes school hard?

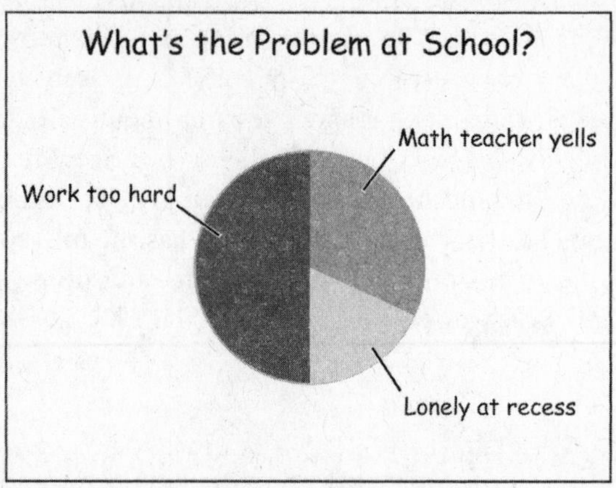

STRATEGY: Get Specific

Another strategy is to use the Worry Shrinker from Chapter 5. Start with the biggest box: "I can't go to school." Ask your child questions to get specific: "Is it the kids? The teachers? The work?" Keep narrowing it down to identify exactly what feels hardest to your child. Once the child has identified the problem, you can begin to solve the problem. For example, if a child is fine with everything about school except for taking tests—and, more specific than that, taking tests in social studies—you are going to get even more specific to find out exactly *why* the tests are hard. Because it's hard to memorize or even understand the material? Because he doesn't have a friend in that class? The teacher is strict? He's nervous because he has gym next period and the boys aren't nice to him in gym? If your child isn't forthcoming or clear himself, play a game of twenty questions. Watch the problem shrink.

STRATEGY: Fast-Forward to the Solution

To instill a sense of momentum and hope, and to get your child working on solving the problem, ask the questions a different way:

- "If things were worked out with this problem, what would be different from how it is now?"
- "What would a typical day be like?"

- "What would you change at school and at home to make things better?"

This series of questions helps get more detail about external situations that may be bothering your child, as well as puts your child in the equation—"I wouldn't be so scared to tell that kid to stop kicking my chair" or "I wouldn't fight with my mom in the morning about going to school." Once you've established what would make things better, then you can ask: "Okay, let's figure out the things we need to practice or teach you so that you can do those things that will make it better."

Through this assessment process, you've gone from dug in to working it out, and all the while, the child knows that you are on his side—the side of wanting things to get better and not have these problems.

Once you have identified the possible source of the problem, consult the earlier chapters for strategies to address the issue. When a child is not going to school in order to avoid a perceived fearful situation, remember that escaping only reinforces the power of the fear. Take steps to reduce or resolve the source of the discomfort, and then work with the child to reapproach school in manageable chunks. This may involve having a shortened schedule or spending part of the day in the guidance office.

The Parent's Stance: Believe That School Is the Right (and Best) Thing for Your Child

When a child refuses or struggles to go to school, our own worry often super-sizes the moment. With your child's words "I'm not going!" quickly the arc of the future of their disability unrolls before us. Immediately, our blood pressure rises. We feel like the foundation of our family's routine—the child going to school—is being upended, and we panic. We yell, we accommodate, we lose our footing. Take a deep breath and do the side-by-side comparison of fears to facts. This will help you eliminate the pressure that if you don't fix the problem this minute, things will always be like this. You need to calmly pace yourself for the work ahead.

Once the stage has been set and a constructive plan put in place, your job is to be positive and supportive about your child's attendance. Your conviction that your child can manage the challenge of school will help him put his best foot forward. If a parent has mixed feelings about the child attending school, the child will sense this and use it to dig in. Likewise, children will pick up on any conflict between the parents and the school and will side with the parents, thus devaluing the school and feeling less compelled to attend.

School Avoidance: Prevention and Intervention

Partnering with the School

After you have identified the issues and tried to work them out with your child, you may still need the school's help. Ask for a meeting with your child's teacher or, for middle or high school students, the guidance counselor or the student assistance program. Enlist their help by discussing your concerns with the team in a positive way. "We are working on Daniel's anxiety, but he is struggling and really needs your support during the day. We are all concerned that this be kept private and discreet. Daniel doesn't want to be treated any differently, but he knows that his anxiety is getting in the way of his concentration at school."

Getting Out the Door

Children who avoid school are plagued by intrusive anticipatory anxiety. A running commentary of negative thoughts and images of the worst-case scenario—which often starts the night before—is calling the shots. Using the strategies in the master plan, help them to challenge the anxiety and come up with a story about what they really think will happen at school and how they can cope with it. In addition, consider the following approaches:

- Try to keep stress low for your morning routine.
- Even though your child may be upset, keep her moving in the morning—getting dressed, brushing his teeth, having breakfast.

- If you have the flexibility, bring your child to school yourself, at first, rather than having her take the bus.
- Have a teacher or guidance counselor meet younger kids at the bus or in the parking lot upon arrival. Sometimes a call from a teacher the night before or in the morning can break through the "what-ifs" and remind the child that someone is on her side.
- Use tangible reinforcers (prizes, tickets to sports events, computer games) for succeeding at the hard work of attending school.

Children Must Be in School (Even If That's at Home)

Whether your child misses school for a day or a week or a month, it is crucial that you maintain the concept that daytime is school time. This means that children don't sleep in but wake up for school, even if they don't go. Get work from teachers at school, or find worksheets or teaching modules on the Internet. During this time there is no television, iPod, phone, and so forth. This isn't a punishment, and it shouldn't be presented this way—otherwise you will spark a conflict spiral. Just be matter-of-fact. Tell them, "The law is that children need to be in school, and this is where school is today." Truly, you are doing your child a favor. If she's already having trouble going to school, and there is no structure at home—it's like a Disneyland vacation of television and snacks—there will be no push to return to school. Structure creates the first steps in the stairs of learning. To fill up the day, you can create a structure that includes three to six hours of school time, an hour of physical exercise, and an hour of "common good" tasks—helping out around the house. Socializing can occur only after the school day and other tasks have been completed. Socializing may help create the pull for children to want to return to school, so provided that your child has met her other daily requirements, it should be encouraged.

Having a Plan at School for Tough Moments

In order to help your child feel more supported at school, identify a teacher's or guidance counselor's office as a safe place for moments when they need to leave the classroom temporarily. What makes a safe place safe? Make sure the teacher or counselor understands enough about anxiety to know that however illogical the fears sound, they feel very real, and that his or her job is to help the child separate themselves from the worry, correct the distortions, and take a second look at the situation through a more accurate lens. For example, staff wouldn't ask a child who has an anxiety disorder about throwing up or fainting if they need a bucket or want to lie down; that would support the worry, but not the child. Instead, staff would ask the child, "What is worry saying to you? What do you think is really true, and why? What do you want to tell yourself instead?"

It's hard for a child to predict when they'll be feeling anxious, but when the worry hits, it's best to nip it in the bud. So it is preferable to give children a free pass for brief check-ins with a counselor. The goal for these five- to fifteen-minute conversations is for a child to get their thinking rerouted back to reality, with an eye toward heading back to class. The counselor may even walk the child back to class if they need that extra help.

Although a child may immediately ask to go home or to talk with a parent, contact with parents should be the last rung of the plan. Often when children talk to their parents during school, it makes it harder for them to stay.

For the Child Who Has Been Out of School for Weeks or Months

When kids have been out of school for an extended period of time, they have a great deal of anticipatory anxiety built up, and therefore transitioning back to school may need to be even more gradual, or in any case well thought out so that potential wrinkles are addressed proactively, saving every one from glitches (a teacher expecting a child to take a test that day for which she is unprepared because of missing school) that may result in setbacks.

When something at school is the problem: If there is an academic, social, or teacher–student issue, the school should get involved on the child's behalf to work out the problem. Always work closely with the child; they know best how things feel and what is likely to help.

When leaving home is the problem: Typically, this is due to either separation anxiety (fear of harm befalling a parent) or panic disorder (fear of being out of a safe zone if panic occurs). Generate a hierarchy of steps, like the one that follows, using the child's fear temperature as a guide. Stay at each level until that step has been mastered and is no longer challenging.

Challenge	Fear Level
The child makes a visit after school to talk with teachers about the plan.	6
Mom drives; the child goes to class for one hour while Mom waits in the parking lot.	6
Mom drives; the child goes to class for two hours, checks in with guidance counselor, while Mom stays home.	8
Mom drives; the child goes to class until lunch while Mom stays home.	8
Mom drives; the child goes to classes through lunch, has lunch with the guidance counselor and two friends; Mom is not at home.	8
Mom drives; the child goes to class for five hours.	10
Mom drives; the child goes to school for the day; Mom drives the child home.	10
The child takes the bus to school and stays at school all day; Mom drives the child home.	10
The child takes the bus in the morning, stays at school all day, and takes the bus home.	10
The child goes to school and stays after class for a music lesson.	10

The hierarchy above shows how Matt, the child with panic whom we met in Chapter 14, was able to return to a full school day within two weeks. If there had not been the flexibility on the part of the school to welcome Matt and support his anxiety management, Matt might have simply been unable to attend because the bar was too high. Unfortunately, in the sink-or-swim method of approaching school refusal, the tragedy is that most children bail.

Forcing a Child Is Not the Way to Go

Simply forcing a child to attend school is not a treatment plan. You need to know the "whys" of the situation. Find out what has become unbearable to the child. Once the specific issue, or roadblock, is addressed, your child will be more willing to return to school, and forcing will not be necessary. Until your child can return full-time, keep the connection to school going, either through partial-day attendance or, when that is not possible, tutoring at home.

Academic Accommodations: Your Child's Rights

Some anxious children need additional supports or accommodations in school, such as adjustments to their schedule or assignments. For some children, these accommodations can make the difference between attending school and not attending school. Like children with physical disabilities, children with anxiety disorders are entitled by law to adaptations in their academic programming so that they may be successful in school. The Individuals with Disabilities Education Act provides specific procedures and funding for children who require such services. Contact your school's student assistance team to initiate the process of procuring an Individualized Education Plan (IEP) for your child. IEPs can include modified schedules, one-on-one aides, and modified assignments. (Keep in mind that in order to qualify for this process, your child must be identified as having special needs as established by a comprehensive assessment.)

For children with milder impairment, a document called a 504 plan can be drawn up by the school with parent input. A 504 plan is less formal than an IEP and could be used to grant prorated credit for partially completed assignments, or allow a later arrival time at school, a phone call to parents, or similar concessions. Refer to the online resource page at www.tamarchansky.com for more details and advice on securing these types of accommodations for your child.

SAMPLE SCHOOL ACCOMMODATIONS

Accommodations	Benefits child with	Implementation
Excused lateness, delayed start in the morning	Multiple OCD morning rituals, medications that make child sleepy in the morning, separation anxiety or panic: requiring a shorter day	Arrange for the child to receive class and homework for the missed class the day before. When possible, arrange study hall or free period first so the child isn't missing instruction time when late.
Tests or assignments given orally rather than written	OCD: The child is slowed down by perfectionism in writing.	Use a scribe (a person who takes dictation), tape recorder, or voice recognition computer program; keyboarding may be substituted where appropriate.
Reduced homework	OCD perfectionism, PANS, children recovering from trauma, GAD taking excessive time on assignments	The teacher sets a time estimate for the assignment, and the student attempts to stay within that time frame; the grade is prorated based on completed work; the number of writing assignments is reduced; the child may do every other problem in math.
Reduced public speaking; oral reports taped or conducted one-on-one with the teacher	Social anxiety, generalized anxiety, panic disorder	The child gives a presentation to the teacher alone; works toward small public speaking challenges; can be given prearranged questions so they can prepare; works up to spontaneous public speaking.

Reduce in-class note-taking	OCD: perfectionism in writing, other interfering anxiety, overfocus on notes and missing important anxiety	Provide the child with prepared notes that she can highlight in class; arrange a note-taking buddy who will provide a photocopy of his notes.
Safe place at school, free pass for brief breaks	OCD, panic disorder, separation anxiety, phobias	Have a prearranged signal system so the child doesn't have to ask to leave (place a bright orange card on the desk, wink at teacher); child makes a brief trip into the hallway for water; child takes a brief five- to ten-minute break with identified target staff.
Untimed tests	Any anxiety condition, especially test anxiety	Extended time and an alternate test location (quiet office) where the child doesn't see others finishing their test quickly. The child may not choose to make use of the extra time, but knowing it's there reduces stress and enhances concentration and performance.
Preferential seating for assemblies and large group activities	Panic disorder: child may need to sit by the door initially in order to leave briefly if overheated or overwhelmed; OCD: contamination fears and bad thoughts make it difficult to be around many people; may wish to sit up front where they can't see others, or in back where they can leave easily.	Children may need to build up their tolerance for large group events. See if child can keep increasing the amount of time they are able to stay for assembly; if the child needs to leave, try to have them return later to end the exposure on a good note of success.
Social skills groups	GAD, separation anxiety, social anxiety	Provides a shared experience for children who need help making social connections or help with assertiveness, expressing a differing opinion, or handling teasing.

An accommodation for all: Every child struggles with getting work done from time to time; anxious children battling perfectionism and feeling overwhelmed by too much work can benefit from the following strategy.

THE THREE-SPEED METHOD FOR PACING (AND FINISHING) WORK

"A cheetah, a turtle, and a horse show up for homework time. . . ." Every time I suggest this intervention for an individual child with anxiety, teachers latch onto it and teach it to the whole class! The three-speed strategy works for children who are perfectionists or otherwise anxiously slow, deliberate workers, and for kids who race through their work either because anxiously they want it to be over, or they have focusing difficulties and they're not paying attention. Have your child choose three animals: a super-fast one, a slow one, and one in between. Popular choices are a cheetah, a turtle, and a horse, respectively. When a teacher gives an assignment, she should specify the speed required; for example, "This one takes slow, careful work, so turtle speed," or, "This one we just need to get through quickly, so cheetah speed," or, "Do good work, but keep moving, so horse speed, please." Your child can use this technique when doing homework, if she's stuck moving too slowly on an assignment—she can shift her program into higher speed.

BURNING DOWN THE HOUSE: PREVENTING ANXIETY-GENERATING TEACHING IN OUR SCHOOLS

Schools have been undergoing a great challenge in recent years to meet the diverse learning needs of all their students. But unfortunately many schools are still sorely behind in terms of recognizing differences in emotional sensitivity. When it comes to considering the needs of anxious children in dealing with potentially frightening topics, we are still operating with a one-wiring-fits-all curriculum. There are a few very small, easy steps that can reduce the amount of unnecessary anxiety exposure in classrooms. Parents may want to share this information with teachers.

Important and well-meaning drug- and alcohol-prevention programs or health classes can be triggers for many anxious children. Science teaching can often be problematic because of the subject matter, but offhand comments in other subjects can do inadvertent damage as well. Teachers need to be aware of the fact that anxious children, through no fault of their own, may be more affected than their peers by what they hear at school, in ways that teachers don't intend.

No teacher knowingly traumatizes a child or would ever wish to, but teachers should consider the following: By conservative statistical estimates, more than 20 percent of the kids in their class are anxious and have difficulty processing risk accurately. They need perspective, and the use of phrases like "rarely," "small chance," or "slim to none" will mean a great deal to them. So when teaching about how a small cut can lead to gangrene and eventual amputation, teachers shouldn't forget to emphasize that this circumstance is extremely rare and explain why (because people notice infections and take care of them). Otherwise, kids will be coding this information as "infection . . . blah, blah, blah . . . CUT OFF YOUR HAND!" Or when talking about oxygen and using an example like "Imagine your house is on fire. How quickly would you have to get out before the oxygen would be used up?" a teacher should consider how this example would affect an anxious child, and if there's another way to illustrate the point that isn't so provocative.

Teachers may find the following guidelines useful:

- Emphasize safety precautions as much as, if not more than, risks.
- Make sure to put the risks in perspective and emphasize how rare or unlikely the situation is.
- Assume that there are anxious ears listening and correct any generic misperceptions or misunderstandings that are likely.
- Emphasize above all the appropriate and accurate take-home message.

FRIENDS AND FAMILY: MANAGING RELATIONSHIPS

Friendships

Anxiety interferes with friendships on many levels. Whether your child is second-guessing what her friends think, worrying about approaching other kids, or simply spending so much time on anxiety issues that there's no time left for anything else, anxiety gets in the way. Children often feel different because of their anxiety—like they are the only one suffering—and feel not only lonely but also unacceptable. Children with anxiety may be relieved to visit websites online, or even to read the kids' stories in this book, to see that they are by no means alone. Here I will introduce tools to help your child navigate her friendships as she tackles her worries.

Talking to Friends

Many anxious kids don't want to tell friends about their anxiety until they are feeling better. This makes sense in some ways; they are feeling too vulnerable to deal with the risk of potentially insensitive reactions, and with the possibility of being seen differently. But if your child does decide to talk to her friends about anxiety, she can tell them that she doesn't need any special treatment, but that it just helps if someone else knows. Some children do appreciate when their friends know that they don't like to hear really gross jokes about throw-up, or don't want to see horror movies, or that being around dogs makes them feel uncomfortable. If your child is searching for words to describe what's going on for her, here are some ideas of what to say that kids have taught me over the years:

- "I worry a lot—I don't want to and I'm working on it, but my brain just comes up with tons of stuff that scares me or makes me feel like I'm not safe."
- "My brain gives me the wrong messages—it's like it's stuck on the worry channel. I always think of what could go wrong. It's a pain, but I'm learning how to change the channel."

- "I get nervous about a lot of stuff. It doesn't just come and go, it sticks around and makes me feel really bad."
- "Sometimes I feel like something really bad is going to happen; it's scary. My brain just goes into hyper–worry mode, but I'm learning how to shut that off."

If your child seeks your help in making the decision about whether or not to tell a certain friend, suggest that she consider how that friend has handled confidential information in the past. If a friend has shared a secret with your child, that suggests a certain level of trust.

Returning to Socializing After a Break

When your child is ready to return to his social life after having been in the thick of working on anxiety management, he may worry about what awaits him. If he's been refusing invitations for a while, he may find that the phone calls have slowed down or stopped, and he may take that as a sign that people have moved on. It is often helpful to explain that friendship is a two-way street, and that the friends may have felt rejected when your child kept saying no. Help your child find the small steps he's ready to take to put the word out that he's interested again. Maybe that's sitting with an old group of friends in the cafeteria, texting a friend, saying hi in the hall again, or even making a weekend plan. Also, let your child know that it is likely that if these are true friends, they have missed him and will be thrilled to have him back. Finally, while it's true that your child may have missed out on gatherings, often they've missed a lot less than they think. Check in with other parents and you may be able to reassure your child that his peers haven't been socializing much and have been exhausted or busy, and he's not as "behind" as he believes.

All in the Family: Managing Relatives and Siblings

Extended Family

Identify family members who have the potential to help you with your situation, and cultivate their support. For those who seem critical or unwilling to learn, identify other ways that this relative could help: taking the siblings out to the movies or other entertainment if your anxious child is not yet able to go, or helping you with errands so that you have some downtime for yourself. Certainly, if a relative is making unsupportive comments to your child, you need to intervene more directly. Let them know that your child is stressed and these comments will only reinforce negative feelings he is already having about himself. Suggest alternatives that would be helpful for your child to hear.

Siblings: Reconcilable Differences?

Parents of anxious kids often feel pressure from all sides. They have the struggles of their anxious child, and their other children's needs and frustration with how their sibling seems to be getting away with murder (and ruining their plans) just by saying, "But I'm too scared." Parents may put additional stress on the other siblings to just "be nice" or "leave their sibling alone," but this shouldn't be a special favor or special treatment that the anxious child needs—this should be a family-wide policy: "We are good to each other and we try to give everyone what they need. That's how our family works."

Because anxiety isn't a physical disability that kids can see, and the limitations it imposes aren't so easy to grasp, you can do the long-distance learn and try to make a connection with something with which your child is already familiar so that they can relate to their sibling. For example, if your child had a sport's injury, like a broken toe, or when he was having trouble seeing and needed glasses, you can say: "Did you want those things to happen? Were they your fault? Of course not. Did they slow you down? Make it harder to do things? Right, they did. Did we get mad about that, or did we do what you needed?" Use your child's answers not to induce guilt that he wasn't thinking about his sibling in this way, but rather to create a connection: This is what families are for; this is what we do for any of us in the family, even if it is hard sometimes.

I recently saw a family that operated like a well-oiled machine: The anxious child could have a sense of humor about his anxiety, because no one teased him; the other siblings had his back and were on the lookout for what might be hard for him and what could help. If this is not your family—and I don't think that this is any family *all* the time—this is a great time and reason to start to head in this direction: everybody counts, everybody pitches in, everything works better for all. So if there is name-calling, mean-spirited teasing, or other sibling strife, this is a great time to clean up across the board. Not just for your anxious child. Everyone benefits from a safe environment, rules, respect, compassion, collaboration—this is what makes children feel safe.

All Family Members Pitching in for the Common Good

Families are a unit. They work best when all parts are getting some of what they need.

Even though managing anxiety may feel like a full-time job, it is important for all that even your anxious child is contributing to the family in some ways. Whether this is clearing his plate from the dinner table, putting his laundry in the hamper, or engaging in tasks that are more communal—watering plants, emptying the dishwasher or trash—have a family meeting to encourage your children (of whatever age) to think about things that they can do to help the family. This isn't a punishment. It's about improving and strengthening the family system, creating trust and feelings of competency. Keeping them accountable for their part in the family (even if tasks have to be accommodated by degree or type of task) is important for the anxious child—and for the others in the family to see.

STRATEGIES FOR WORKING WITH SIBLINGS

- Be clear that no personal attacks will be tolerated. Hold your children accountable for their actions.
- Teach your children that fair doesn't mean equal—otherwise, everyone would have to eat the same food regardless of preference, have the same bedtime regardless of age, and wear glasses whether they needed them or not.

- Don't blame your children: Always validate your child's feelings, even those very sharp-edged ones ("I hate him. He's ruining our lives. Nothing is fun anymore"). Help her express those feelings in a non-hurtful way. Teach your children to identify the problem in any situation, because that may lead to a solution. "You're frustrated because we can't go to the movies. I know; I am too. Your brother really wanted to go, but he got overwhelmed. You're right, this does stink. Let's make a rain check for you and me tomorrow. Meanwhile, how about Ping-Pong and ice cream sundaes at home?"
- If your child does do or say something hurtful, remember, sincere apologies are a million times better than forced apologies—and worth the wait. Think reparation—how to contribute or help out in a positive way to the family—rather than punishment or time out.
- Arrange special one-on-one time with your other children when possible. Friends and relatives can either free you up for this time, or if necessary can take the sibling out themselves.

Approaching these challenges from the angle of rounding up what you think of your child, engendering a sense of responsibility, accountability, and agency (making good choices)—these are concepts that build self-esteem. Blame, shame, and embarrassment only breed resentment.

WORDS TO BUILD FAMILY STRENGTH DURING CONFLICT

"We are a unit; let's work together on this."

"We all want things to work out."

"None of us wants to fight."

"Can you help me out with this? I can't figure this out without you. It will be better if we think this through together."

"We don't make threats or make fun of people in our family. That doesn't work well for anybody."

"We all need to feel safe in the family, and we need each one of us participating to make that happen."

"What you are saying is important, and other people's feelings are important, too."

"There are going to be some times when it just doesn't seem fair, but it won't always feel like that."

"The more we can each be flexible, the more options we have."

"Sometimes we need to do things for each other, even when we don't want to. Another time it may be your needs that come first."

"It won't always feel like we are lucky to have each other, but if we work on things as a family, more and more we'll know how lucky we are."

Chapter 20

WORRY PREVENTION IN THE REAL WORLD

When Luke overheard that his dad has to watch his cholesterol, he came running to me in a panic: "Does that mean he's getting old? Does that mean he's going to die?"

I'm afraid to take Cheryl to the movies; it's not worth it. If anything bad happens it stays with her for weeks. She can't sleep and she makes me promise it will never happen to her.

I know I need to talk to Sean about the terrorism alerts; otherwise he'll hear about it from kids at school and that's not right. I just don't know how much is too much to tell him.

PROMISE ME THAT WILL NEVER HAPPEN: TALKING TO YOUR CHILD ABOUT REAL FEARS

We would do anything to protect our children, but there are some truths that we can't shield them from. Illnesses, deaths, tragedies—these are part of our reality. When tragedy strikes, we grieve for those who have suffered, and we grieve again for our children, safe as they are, that these are the realities of their world. When thinking about sharing news of a relative who is dying, or a tragic school shooting, we may be saying to ourselves, "This is too sad. I can't bear it; and I can't bear to bring my child into this." This is true, and there is another truth, too. Deep down we know, and once we've absorbed the initial shock and have regained our footing, we remember that the world is both too sad and still the same collection of myriad wonderful things it was before the sadness. This is the perspective that even as adults we have to remind ourselves to reach for, and when we do, we share this profound and bearable view with our children.

We are role models for how to live through difficult things. Our job is to show our children how resiliency is possible, that we can take charge of our lives even though we don't hold all the cards. We have choices about what we highlight for our children—fear and danger, or safety and healing. Though we do not want this job, it is often in these most difficult places that we connect most deeply with each other; we strengthen our communities, we find gratitude for and appreciation of all those who work to protect us, and we deepen our compassion for others. Parents are the best ones to impart these lessons.

Children live, like we do, in a media-saturated world that brings us a daily regimen of illness, crime, war, and terrorism. All children have questions, but anxious children have many more, and they are listening closely to the answers. Although we, too, in our reactions to difficult or even shocking news, get flooded with emotion, this chapter will provide the clear guidelines for what is helpful for our children to hear. Most of all, a child needs to know that we are there for them, that they can talk to us about anything, and that we will do everything to keep them safe.

When the fears are big, we can feel immobilized and unprepared. You may also think that because our children are facing real situations, not ones that worry is inventing, the techniques that we've discussed thus far don't apply. But worry is worry, and all fears—great or small, real or imagined—require a return to the basics and the facts. This means narrowing our focus to the present, focusing on our strengths and possibilities, and fostering our competency rather than our vulnerabilities.

THE WORRIED LEADING THE WORRIED

When coping with events like terrorism or a school shooting, you may think that you can't guide your worried child because you're just as scared as he is. This is normal. But in this world of changing circumstances, we must ground ourselves and revisit the same lessons we are teaching our children.

First Things First: Put Limits on Your Own Worry and Imagination

When we are contending with something of great gravity, we may find ourselves thinking about it all the time, or feeling guilty when our thoughts have strayed. No matter how serious the matter, we need to take worry breaks or we will find ourselves depleted by the worry, with little energy left to act on the reality. We can visit the chaos—imagining various catastrophic scenarios—but we must also know how to quiet it down. When worry tries to sneak back in, we can push it back as we would a child pestering us for dinner. Tell worry: "No, it's not your turn yet." Just as we coach our children to choose what tape to listen to, the worry tape or the neutral one, we need to make those choices, too.

Adopting the Right Mind-set: It's Not About Risk; It's About Staying Safe

We live with the reality of kidnappings from children's beds and yards, school shootings, violent crime, terror threats and attacks, and life-threatening illnesses. While we need to prepare our kids for these possibilities, we need to do it in a worry-smart way, rather than inadvertently borrowing our tactics from a burglar alarm or exterminator salesman, or more commonly, the twenty-four-hour news broadcasts with up-to-the-minute details. We don't want to play up the scary side of things. Although these incidents are horrific, they are extremely rare, isolated events.

Instead of focusing on the risks, we need to focus on safety and on what kids can do to increase their safety. Share the job to help your child feel more in control. What are the safety rules for being outside? at school? at the mall? Stating "the family rules for safety are . . ." feels very different from telling a child that there are strangers out there who want to hurt him, for example. Make sure that your explanations do not make the dangers seem bigger and scarier than they are. Get clear on the message first for yourself, and then communicate it to your children.

Right from the start, consider your purpose in sharing any news. If in your mind you're thinking: "I could never forgive myself if something were to happen and I hadn't warned him," your distress and urgency will be the loudest and clearest message, and your words, rather than being constructive, may be confusing or even frightening to your child. As much as possible, be calm and explain what your child needs to do to be safe.

Rather than simply rattling off rules, share the job, ask your children: "Who knows the safety rules for the mall?" Or, "Who can tell me why it's important to stay with Mom and Dad?" Your child may be able to provide good answers. This is an opportunity to reinforce their competency, not their fear, and you can feel reassured that your child knows what he needs to do to be safe.

It's Not What You Say; It's How You Say It

In moments of uncertainty or crisis, children are looking to us for direction. No matter what words they actually use, they want to know three things: Is it okay that this is happening? Am I okay? Are you there for me? We will be supplying information with our answers, but children will be watching our faces, our emotions to see if we are telling them between the lines: "This is okay, even though it's not good. You are okay. And I am here for you." Even if we are in the midst of our own reaction to what is going on, we can convey the information our children need from us. Remember that parents are models for their children. Grief and sadness are normal, healthy emotions in times of crisis. It is from our more raw, unprocessed emotions—our rage or despair, which we experience when we have not yet gotten control over ourselves—that we want to shield our children whenever possible. Children may feel confused and disorganized by your raw emotion, and responsible to make you feel better. If this were to happen, and sometimes it is unavoidable, we can and should come back to it when we have gathered ourselves and say: "Mom [or Dad] was really upset. That's normal. This took me by surprise. I'm still sad, but this is a sad time. These feelings sometimes are very strong, and then, like a wave at the beach, they pass. Sometimes the waves come again, but Mom [Dad] can take care of herself [himself]."

If your child was very upset about seeing you that way, you can ask further: "What did you think when Mommy was crying like that?" Your child may not be able to articulate their feelings, but it gives you an opportunity to reinforce that even when parents are sad like that, they can take care of themselves, and they can take care of their children. Children are reassured by sincerity and groundedness. When we try to ignore the issues or minimize them—when we aren't available to our children because we aren't being truthful—they read it only as confusion. Also, their curiosity or need to know won't end just because you have said, "We aren't talking about this." They will seek out other answers from their peers or other sources, and you will have lost the opportunity to join with them in a difficult time.

MANAGING THE FLOW OF INFORMATION

TELEVISION NEWS SHOULD BE RATED "R"

News programs are not made with children in mind. So it is fine for parents to watch television news, but children under the age of thirteen should not watch it with you. They may get nightmares from the images on the screen, and in some cases they may believe that the event is recurring each time they see it replayed. Share news yourself, or with materials created with children's needs in mind. These include news magazines that have websites and print editions of the news specifically geared for children.

Whether you are talking about war, illness, terrorism, or crime, you won't have all the answers, and much of what you can tell your child will not be good. Still, don't let your feeling that you have to have it all solved and fixed stop you from broaching difficult subjects. Even if you did have all the answers, it would not be in your child's best interest for you to share them all at once. Use the following guidelines to prepare to talk with your child about fear-generating topics:

- Always start with the questions that come from your child. Ask her what she thinks or knows about a situation, or what she has heard. This will allow you to build on her knowledge base. Listen for her emotional needs, and correct any misperceptions. If your child is feeling distressed about what she knows already, it's not the time to add a lot of information; instead, you are going to help her to stabilize, and then come back to it another time.
- Be as *concrete* as you can, not as *complete* as you can. Create a simple narrative—a couple of lines—in which you say what happened, who helped, and, importantly, that it's over.
- Identify the people who are working on the problems that your child is asking about. There is power in numbers, and overly responsible, anxious kids (as well as we ourselves) need to know that others are on the job. Share the layers of protection and remind both of you of the millions and millions of people who want things to be safe in the world.
- Be truthful, but only in degrees. Build on your explanations slowly. Don't feel rushed or pressured to force-feed your child. Give your child a chance to digest the facts, keeping in mind what is appropriate for him. It is preferable to come back later with more information, rather than to overload him now.
- Don't be afraid to state the obvious, and don't be afraid to repeat it or restate it often. Often very basic information can be very comforting. You might say, "Your grandmother loves you very much, and the doctors are taking good care of her," or, "We have the strongest army in the world," or, "You are safe. I will always protect you."

- Focus on what your child can do. Give your child something to do with the information: a small job, a favor, a project. The goal is to focus on competency, or what your child can do to cope or protect himself given his age and abilities.
- Anxious children often feel responsible for situations that are not their fault. Make sure your child has an accurate understanding of the causes.
- Show confidence that we can live with uncertainty. Put a ceiling on how high the anxiety goes by simply saying, "This is one of those situations that is not easy, where we don't have all the answers." Empathize with her over the fact that this is a situation where there aren't good enough answers but that's okay.
- Reinforce realistic thinking—focus on the unlikelihood of a risk rather than how devastating it would be.
- Limit exposure to television. Turn it off yourself. Try to watch the news when your kids are not around. If you want your child to be aware of certain appropriate topics, make use of other media—newspapers and magazines. The written word is easier for most kids to process than a constant stream of violent images, which tend to stick in their minds.
- Return to routines as soon as possible. While crises throw off the equilibrium of a family, household, or community, we all need structure to feel safe. Going back to regular mealtimes, with the television off, reading books at bedtime, or other bedtime routines will settle children and let them know that recovery and getting back to normal is possible. Be flexible within your routines to make it work. For example, family meals should be maintained whenever possible, even if that means takeout or soup from a can rather than a home-cooked meal. Or the family could have quiet reading time together if you feel you can't read aloud to your child. In so doing, you are reestablishing that the crisis or situation isn't controlling your lives and the rhythms of your day. This will be reassuring to you, too.

A Sample Narrative for an Act of Violence

"Sometimes people do bad things. We don't always know why. We do know that these occurrences are very rare, which means that they almost never happen. Today a very sad thing happened. A man who was very disturbed and had a lot of problems went into a school and shot twenty people. It was very wrong. The shooting is over now. Immediately, the police and ambulances came to help take care of the people who were hurt. The families are very sad. Many, many people who care and love them are helping to take care of them. Schools are very safe places. Your teachers and principals work very hard to keep you safe at school. That is their job. And there are many other people—thousands—who are helping to make sure that those things don't happen and to keep you safe. Everybody is sad about what happened today. When something like this happens, we feel sad for those who got hurt, and we can think how we can help them—like making cards for their families or collecting food or money for them. Their families are taking care of them, too, but we can help. The more help, the better."

Sample Narrative and Important Points for Talking About the Loss of a Loved One

"I need to tell you some very sad news. Uncle Vince died today. You know he was very sick with cancer, and even though he got a lot of help from doctors, his body couldn't fight the cancer anymore. We are very sad and we will miss him very much, but we are glad that he isn't suffering anymore."

A child asks: "What happens when you die?"

First, ask your child what he's heard or what he thinks. Then do longdistance learning: "Do you remember when your hamster died? It means that his body stopped working because he was very sick and old. Our bodies work great until these things happen. When people die, they don't feel anything anymore; they aren't in pain."

You can connect this with the life cycle—everything has its time to live and to die. "You know how in the spring the trees have new leaves and even flowers? Remember the cherry blossoms we saw? And then what happens to those leaves in the fall—remember we had to rake them up? They die and fall. With people it's more like when the batteries stop working on a toy. Without the batteries, the toys don't work. People's batteries only die when they are very old or when they get a disease. It's different from when you or I get sick. Our bodies can handle those sicknesses just fine."

If your child asks about heaven . . .

Families will choose to discuss religious or spiritual issues as they feel comfortable. If a family isn't sure, the parents may say, "Some people think that people go to heaven after they die. I'm not sure what I think about that. What do you think?"

Whatever your belief, it is important not to create more fear inadvertently by saying things like "She's sleeping now," or, "She died in her sleep." This can make kids start to worry that they will die in their sleep. Saying that we "lost" someone will have the same impact. Children are literal and may take this as meaning that the person is lost—and can be found again.

HOW MUCH SHOULD WE CHANGE OUR LIVES?

Immediately after a tragedy occurs, we all must reorient to a new reality—what changed, what didn't? Parents struggle with whether to stop going to movies, to shopping malls, to schools. The fact is that these events, though devastating, are still rare, isolated events, and our children are best when order, structure, predictability are restored in their lives as quickly as possible.

CHANGING OUR LIVES IN POSITIVE WAYS: STRENGTHENING TIES TO COMMUNITY

We want our children to understand and trust in the layers of protection available through adults whose job it is to keep us safe, whether that's doctors who take care of our loved ones or police officers who work hard to prevent as well as respond to tragedies. At the same time, when families or communities work together to support those who need help, with food drives, letter writing, clothing drives, children not only feel reassured that help is there; they feel empowered to be part of the solution. Finding ways for kids to help out strengthens the fabric of our communities' and our children's resilience.

Chapter 21

TAKING THE PRESSURE OFF OF PRESSURE COOKER KIDS

Shifting the Mind-set from Proving to Improving in Sports, Tests, Grades, and the Race to College

Anxiety makes you put more time into your work, but you don't get to feel good about it anyway. It never feels like you've done enough. It never feels good.

—A FIFTH-GRADER, STRAIGHT-A STUDENT

The college application experience is one that is going to prove to me what a failure I am. And how I've wasted the last four years.

—A STRAIGHT-A NATIONAL HONOR SOCIETY STUDENT

We beg our son to get a B, to stop studying and pushing himself so hard. Other parents may think that it's a good thing that our son is so studious—but they don't know; he never feels good about anything.

— PARENTS OF A TWELVE-YEAR-OLD PERFECTIONIST

HOW NOT TO FALL FOR THE TRAPDOOR TRICK OF LOSING INTELLIGENCE AND TALENT

How is it that these children, with all their advantages and promise, perceive their path to the future as a tightrope walk? One false move, they think, one miss and they're done for. Is that the reality? Is it just their imagination? Is it something that we are doing wrong? It's not exactly any of those things, but fortunately there's something that we can do about it. It starts with rethinking the concepts of mistakes and "failure."

Children put tremendous pressure on themselves by believing that they have to be perfect and that every moment of their lives is a performance—a spotlight reflecting on their absolute self-worth. If they falter in that moment—get the B+, lose the game, get the answer wrong in class—it's not just about that moment for them. In the child's mind, that one disappointment or "failure" erases all of their previously established abilities and accomplishments. They believe they are stupid, they've outed themselves; people will now think they are dumb. This is what I call the "trapdoor trick of losing intelligence or talent." The child believes that all their intelligence or talent has fallen out, never to be recovered again. They are starting from zero.

This kind of misunderstanding is rampant in the athletic arena as well: If kids miss a shot, they immediately start to believe they stink, they're a terrible player, and they're going to be cut from the team. Never mind that professional athletes who are paid millions of dollars each year miss the goal or the ball every day! We still respect them, cheer them on, and, importantly, expect them to show up to work the next day.

Though we as parents know that mistakes are inevitable—that they are even great opportunities for taking risks that lead to growth—for many children, mistakes are unacceptable spotlight moments that expose their inadequacy. What we need to emphasize is that "smart," "successful" people make mistakes all the time; it's what those people do with the mistake that makes the difference. Same for our children. They can hide in embarrassment or learn the secret power of mistakes: They are gateways to even better information, and more knowledge and success.

THE RULE OF SOME: THE ANTIDOTE TO ALL-OR-NONE THINKING

Anxious children feel that they are always just one step away from disaster—because if they aren't succeeding, they are failing. There is no middle ground. So how do we counter this balancing-on-the-head-of-a-pin thinking? Help children think in parts, partial successes, wins within the losses, and learning within the mistakes. The antidote to all-or-none thinking is learning—and the rule of some. "Some things went well; some things didn't. Some things worked; some didn't. Some things I expected; some I didn't."

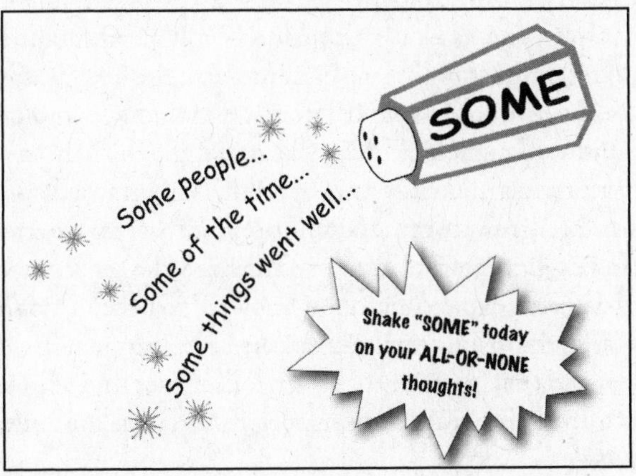

SUSTAINABLE LIVING AND LEARNING STARTS WITH YOU

It would be unreasonable to talk about pressure cooker kids without acknowledging that some of them are interpreting accurately the world we live in today. They receive more than their fair share of unhelpful messages about success: You can do anything you want; you better keep your advantage; just get into an Ivy League school and you'll be set; it's impossible to get into an Ivy League school. The fact is that anxious kids are more likely to be on this track because they're afraid of failure, and they have a broader definition of failure and a very narrow definition of success. By shifting our mind-set and broadening the definition of success, we can prevent our children from becoming "crispies" (a term used by admission board members to refer to students who they can tell—from the three varsity sports, ten extracurricular activities, and straight As—are likely to be overcooked and burned out by the time they arrive at their college doorstep).

GETTING OUT FROM UNDER THE PRESSURE: SWITCH MIND-SET FROM PROVING YOUR ENTIRE SELF-WORTH TO IMPROVING YOUR ABILITIES

To challenge the fixed or "all-or-none" model of intelligence or talent that many children have (either you're born with abilities or you don't have them, aka you're "dumb"), it's important to teach them a new understanding of how our abilities really work. Psychologist Dr. Carol Dweck, of Stanford University and author of the groundbreaking book *Mindset,* counters this all-or-nothing model with what she calls the "growth" (as opposed to "fixed") mind-set. For growth-minded children, effort, failure, and mistakes are not signs of limitations. They are the grist for the mill of *increasing* and expanding one's knowledge base. This mind-set includes the view that intelligence can be developed. The brain is like a muscle that gets stronger with exercise, and children can choose to feed the brain experiences to broaden and strengthen those muscles.

As children switch their goal from feeling the need to constantly "prove" to others their worth (an external locus of control) to "improving," increasing what they know or can do (an internal locus of control), they become more motivated to seek out challenges that previously they would have avoided. They are also more resilient when faced with disappointment or failure, because there's less at stake and they understand the gain in learning that comes on the other side of things that don't go exactly as planned.

HOW DO YOU TALK TO YOUR CHILD ABOUT THIS FROM AN EARLY AGE?

- Think about your own theory of intelligence and mind-set. Are you reinforcing the idea that getting good grades (or, for young kids, being able to name their planets) means someone is smart, and that less than perfect means they are not smart?
- Focus on and encourage learning and curiosity. Create the sense that it's a process. We only learn when we work. It's hard at first. Not getting things now just means that you haven't gotten them *yet.*

- Help your child understand how they learned concepts in the past. Did they always get them right away? Or were they confused at first? Was that confusion a sign that they weren't smart, or that they were *never* going to get the concept? Or was it a sign that they were just at the beginning of the learning curve and needed more time before achieving success?
- Pay attention to effort and process, not just outcome. Broaden your conversation beyond grades or results. Whether it's building a block tower with a preschooler, or writing a term paper with a high school student, focus on "how" they got to the result, what they brought to the project, rather than "what" the result was. This will keep your child chipping away at challenges rather than just looking for opportunities for easy wins in order to gain praise.
- Emphasize, as Dr. Heidi Grant Halvorson suggests, the importance of "getting better" at things rather than "doing good."

NEW INTERPRETATIONS OF DISAPPOINTING MOMENTS

Anxiety is all about the moment. We get the alarm of not knowing something, and then we begin to attach meaning to that not knowing. Instead, help your child do the "amygdala bypass" and be accurate: "I just don't know it *yet*. I'm about to learn this. I'm on my way to understanding. It's hard *at first*. I'm working on improving. I will probably learn this soon; I usually do. And then I get to know more! This moment of not knowing doesn't mean I'm not smart. Just like making a mistake, it doesn't change my value as a person."

THE MIND-SET OF A PARENT OF A CHAMPION: HOW TO MAKE YOUR CHILD WORRYWISE IN THE FACE OF DISAPPOINTMENT

While the idea of "taking the pressure off" of important things like grades and college may get your amygdala beeping, don't fall for your first reaction. By taking the pressure off, we are shifting the focus to the things that will *actually* help your child succeed:

learning, improving, being flexible and resilient. When we think about the adults who are most successful, they are those who work hard, are flexible, can adapt to new circumstances, take chances and risks to innovate, and recover quickly from mistakes.

How to Interpret/Handle Mistakes and Failures

When you fall, don't get up empty-handed.

—ANONYMOUS

What if Sir Isaac Newton had been a negative thinker? After getting bonked on the head with the apple, what if he hadn't suddenly thought of the Law of Universal Gravitation ($F = G \times m1m2/r^2$) but instead thought, "Why do bad things always happen to me?" Or what if Michael Jordan had given up after being cut from his high school basketball team, or if Steve Jobs had thrown in the towel after being fired from Apple? These are great examples of "famous failure" moments you can use with your child. These moments led to greater clarity and conviction, and with some perseverance they became important stepping-stones to greater success.

The following strategies will help your child accurately interpret the events that make them feel like a total failure, and help them see what happened as temporary, survivable, normal, and likely improvable:

Narrow it down. Use the Worry Shrinker boxes from Chapter 5 to put the mistake or failure into the smallest box. "I am terrible at piano" may end up being narrowed down to "I just need to practice this new piece."

Consult your possibility panel. Have your child "ask" for second opinions: What would an athlete he respects tell him about a (difficult) day like today? Do you think that this person ever experienced something like this? What do you think he or she said to himself to get through?

Divide up the pie. Have your child do an instant (or a few hours later) replay. Looking at what occurred, ask him to identify what part of this did he control, and what part did he not. What would he do differently with the part he controls?

Taking the Pressure Off About Grades: When Things Don't Go Well, Don't Crumple Up the Test

Not getting what you want is sometimes a wonderful stroke of luck.

—THE DALAI LAMA

Some perfectionistic, pressured children become so upset when they get a few problems wrong on a test that they throw out the test! They can't see that the crumpled-up test holds the key to how they can do better next time. Help your child learn to switch mind-sets and to befriend those mistakes, seeing them as a way to organize their "to-do" list of what they need to learn next. Disappointment may still hit like a wave, but it will pass, and then they can get to work on getting better. Taking advantage of every nook and cranny of a mistake (as well as taking credit for what went well) will help them get there.

How to Talk About Disappointing Performance

Find the partial success. Name the parts that went well and the parts that your child wants to improve on. Turn that second part into a to-do list and an action plan. Ask, don't tell: "What do you think is the best way to use that information? What do you want to do with that?"

Get optimistic expectations going. Ask your child, "What do you think you need to do next time to master this? How long do you think it will take?"

Teach your child about trends and outliers. High-pressure kids think that if there is one thing that goes wrong (like they get one B), it changes everything. Teach them about flukes, exceptions, and outliers. They don't count, because they are rare and aren't what is typical of a person's performance in general. A favorite teacher who forgets his notes one day doesn't become a "bad teacher" because of that one instance. A figure skater who falls one time (or even many!) doesn't become a "terrible skater." We characterize people and predict future performance by what is most commonly seen, not the exceptions.

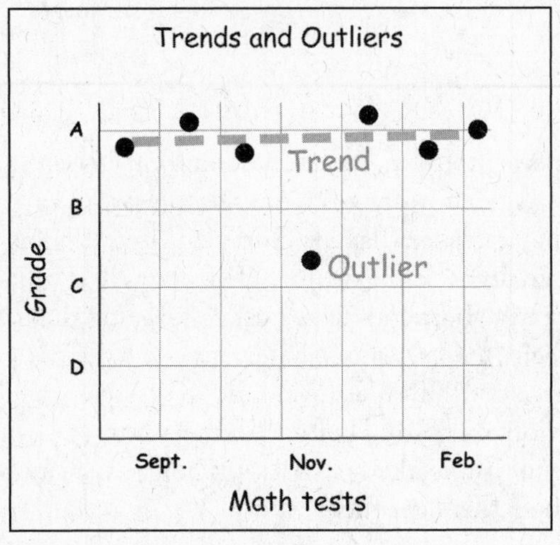

Introduce the idea of a learning curve. If your child is having trouble learning something, help them see that this means nothing about them; difficulty is just in the nature of learning. You have to work hard at first till you understand it; then it gets easier. Talk about other skills they've learned in the past: "What was it like in the beginning—and in the end?"

HOW DO YOU TALK WHEN THINGS DO GO WELL?

Research has shown that the way we praise our children can either reinforce their effort (which they control) or the outcome (which they only partially control). If we focus on outcome, kids don't learn how things really work, and they may discontinue putting effort in because it seems like the outcome is the only thing that matters. Praise effort, and engage your child in what the process was like, not just the result.

- "I know you worked really hard on that project. I see how you really planned your time."
- "What part did you like the most?"
- "What did you learn the most from?"
- "What was your favorite part of the project?"
- "Was there anything you would have done differently if you were the coach?"

HOW DO YOU TALK ABOUT THE FUTURE?

How is your child going to be successful in the future? If they are being encouraged to do well in the present: being hardworking, balancing work and play, being caring and connected, keeping physically active, finding satisfaction and meaning in their day-to-day life. Just like we wouldn't want someone measuring us by where we will be five or ten years from now (notice how just the thought of that makes you anxious), make sure that in your discussions with your child you are noticing and reinforcing the habits, behaviors, activities, and efforts that they are currently engaging in. The future is a natural consequence of the present, and the present is something we can directly do something about. Keep your focus there.

TAKING THE PRESSURE OFF ABOUT STUDYING

Let's Get Scientific: From It's Never Enough to Enough Is Enough

Many anxious children over-study and are afraid of not filling every moment with work. Worry says: "How do you know you are going to do well? Don't take a chance. Keep studying. Don't stop till you drop." But what does reason say? Help your child's brain be more truthful with them.

Do a needs assessment: Rather than just push, push, push, have your child evaluate whether they need to keep studying, or if they've already mastered the material and are ready for the test.

SEPARATE THE FACTS FROM THE FEELINGS

Feelings	Facts
I'm afraid I'm going to fail.	I have never failed a test; it's not likely that this will happen now.
I have no idea how I'm going to do on the test.	I have a pretty good idea of how I'm going to do, because I pretty much always do well, even when I feel scared like this.
I have to keep studying—what if I'm not prepared?	I am good at studying. I tested myself and I do know the material. There may be a curveball or surprise, but I am as prepared as I can be.

Ask the million-dollar question: "Even though part of you says, 'I have no idea how I'm going to do on the test,' or, 'I'm going to fail!' if you could win a million dollars by guessing right how this is going to turn out, would you be the big winner?"

TAKING THE PRESSURE OFF ABOUT SPORTS

Many children feel so much pressure to do well in sports that they stress for hours before they hit the field. The pressure and concern about their performance interfere with the performance itself. Remember the sweet spot for the amygdala: Worrying too much goes far past that middle ground and puts our children into the danger zone. Professionals know that you can't be on the field performing and out in the stands judging yourself at the same time. Like the pros, your child needs to put their game face on—forget about what people are thinking, and put 100 percent of their focus on what they need to do to play well. Shift their focus to improving their game overall, rather than letting the snapshot of their performance in one instance prove whether or not they are a good player. Since what is distracting your child from this focus on "getting better" is the overwhelming fear of "messing up," they are going to need to make friends with, or at least not be mortal enemies with, losing.

How to Talk to Your Child About Outcomes

Lower the stakes, not the standards, while separating your child's value from the outcome of the game. Your child's value as a human being isn't at stake every time they step on the field. Don't dispense with the importance of playing well, but dispense with the inaccurate interpretation of what it means to lose or have an off day: Ask your child what it means to him if he loses, and then ask him to think about what it really means in life. What is the interpretation that the coach has? The other players? Even MVPs lose games and strikeout—lots of games, lots of strikeouts. The outcome of the game is temporary and changeable; your value is permanent and will only improve with effort.

Find the wins within the losses and learn from the mistakes. While every game or event has winners and losers, the real loss is when your child doesn't give credit where credit is due. Ask your child what went well. Help make the crisis an opportunity for learning how to improve: Have your child analyze like a detective what went wrong and see if there are things they can do to make it happen differently next time (practicing a particular skill, staying focused on the game).

Separate the feelings from the facts and ditch the absolutes. When we're upset, our feelings are extreme. Fortunately, the facts are not. Point this out by reflecting back what your child says, and reminding him that feelings are strong at first but they don't last forever. So, if your child says, "Everyone is better!" you say, "It feels like everyone is better than you, but is that what you really think is true?" Help your child correct the absolutes: "Everyone is better" becomes "Some people play better, and some don't"; "I never do anything right" becomes "I usually play well, but this was a tough game."

Identify the outlier. When perfectionistic kids make a mistake, they assume that error redefines their life and starts a new trend for them as a loser. Help them see that exceptions here and there do not make a new rule.

Identify where your child is on the learning curve. Ask your child when she started to learn how to _______. Think through with your child about how long it will take to learn a new skill and how she will know when she has mastered it. Ask your child to draw a curve and make an X to denote her current position.

Control what you can and set your own personal goal. Help your child go into a game with one or two ideas about what he wants to do differently in this game. That way, regardless of the outcome of the game, your child can circle back to the goals and see how he did with the part he could control.

Bring in the pros, asking how their favorite player would narrate the story. Identify with your child one or several athletes whom they look up to and "ask" (imagine) what those stars would say about a tough game. Imagine or research how they have dealt with their own challenging games. Every sport has examples of winners who also lose—this is the norm.

TAKING THE PRESSURE OFF ABOUT THE PERFECT COLLEGE

As our dark honors student clearly stated in the beginning of the chapter, college feels to most students (and their parents) like the ultimate stamp of approval of success, and, by the same token, potentially, of failure. But does it make sense to be searching for the perfect college? What does that even mean? There is no perfect college; it's really about the best match between the child and the school. So, when it comes to a teen's future, many roads lead to Rome, and the more they can "travel" with the facts and the big picture, the more they will see that this important crossroads moment doesn't lead to a dead end if things don't work out exactly how they pictured.

College is one place where parents and students alike are thinking in terms of "best," and career choice is another. But, again, there isn't a best. It's all about the match. Of course, parents want their children to have financial security in the future—but what will truly be the most secure work is something that brings your child satisfaction and purpose. Rather than forcing a direction, ask, don't tell. Robert Hellmann, a career consultant who teaches at New York University, suggests an exercise called the Seven Stories.[11] Ask your child to brainstorm the top twenty great experiences in their life that they really enjoyed. Then have them pick the top seven and analyze the patterns: What felt best and why? What did you do best? This can provide some direction on paths to pursue that are right for your child.

Remember, too, to keep expectations realistic. Very few seventeen-year-olds know exactly what they want to do in life! We know that many adults reinvent themselves and may switch careers in their life. But by investigating their likes and dislikes, strengths and weaknesses, they begin to build up their store of information about themselves and what they may want to do. Here are some ideas to keep the anxiety down about the college and career process.

Success isn't about a place . . . it's about you. Research shows that there's little connection between where you go to college and success in the workplace. Success in college and job satisfaction overall are not about numbers and prestige; they're about finding meaningful work and doing it well. Success comes from within—not from your address or salary.

Separate the facts from the feelings. Your child may insist that there is one school and one school only for them. Empathize with their feelings, but help them also explore the facts. Given the numbers games of college applications (some schools having as low as a 6 percent acceptance rate in 2013—think of all the very qualified students who were "rejected"), they would do best to find several choices that they would be happy with in order to buffer themselves from possible disappointment. If your child gets rejected from a college, remember, it's one data point and one moment in time. They are still all the things they were before the rejection happened, and they hold on to those after.

Successful people are flexible people. The most successful people, whether they are entrepreneurs, world leaders, or athletes, have goals, but they are resilient and willing to find the good when things don't go as planned. This is an important life skill, and the current challenge offers your child an opportunity to be "successful" in many ways. That means being flexible in your search for the right school for you, not just going with what others think is right. And it also means being flexible at managing rejection. Don't over-interpret or misinterpret rejection.

This step doesn't lock you in. Students are not locked in to the first college they go to. Even people who go to their "first-choice school" often decide to transfer as they realize that their needs and interests have changed.

HOW DO YOU TALK ABOUT YOUR OWN LIFE?: SHOWING THE SEAMS

For better or worse, even though we may not feel this way most of the time, children idealize adults' lives—certainly celebrities', but even their own parents', teachers', and coaches'. Kids tend to think that whatever success these adults have now came to them effortlessly, that there were no unfortunate chapters, dead ends, or rejections along the way. Take the opportunity to correct and demystify the process of how people really get from point A to point B and beyond! I call this showing the seams. It helps kids to hear the backstory, the failed attempts, the starting over, the collaboration, the learning from others, the trying again, that led to the "finished" product they see. Don't be afraid to show a little of the backstory to your child—not when you are in the throes of disappointment or failure, but shortly after you've done what you've needed to recontextualize the moment, can see it in the larger perspective, and are ready to move on.

TURNING DOWN THE HEAT IN EVERYDAY LIFE: SUSTAINABLE SCHEDULING, SLEEP, NUTRITION

It has long been known that stress can trigger or exacerbate anxiety in children and adults. A process-oriented mind-set will lower stress when it comes to thinking about the future, but how does this attitude translate into everyday decisions about sports, extracurricular activities, and lifestyle? It's important to engage in the conversation, with even our young children, about choosing how many activities are too many, how to get to sleep at a decent hour when they are busy with sports or school. If we surrender to the schedule, it will simply steamroll over our lives.

Our fears about the future and what will look good on their resume one day can make us prioritize activities over a healthy, balanced life. What this choice says to our children is that the "project" of where they are *going* is more important than who they are *right now*. The irony is that we may be signing our kids up for all these activities so that they can "succeed in life"; meanwhile, their overscheduling is creating the very conditions that may impede children's health, growth, and success.

An anxious child may be even less able than other children to accommodate the demands of our stressful culture. Help your child learn to make reasonable choices about extracurricular activities—that is, not letting your child play three sports and play two instruments while still expecting straight As from her. While such decisions may create some additional stress for you if they differ from those of other parents in your circle, decisions that favor your child's good health are only difficult until you make them. Once they are made, seeing your child happier, more productive, and less stressed will be all the evidence you need that you've done the right thing. Perhaps others will follow your lead. Here are some easy-to-implement ideas for de-stressing your anxious child's life.

We know that caffeine makes anxious kids feel more jittery and tense, and that diets high in carbohydrates or sugar do not supply kids with energy that lasts. Kids need to know that one way they can take charge of their anxiety is by reducing sugars and eliminating caffeine. Take a look at your child's diet and talk with them about some convenient ways to improve it. Let your child help you make the decision.

Many kids—like adults—don't get enough sleep. See Chapter 18 for strategies to improve sleep. Have your child (especially your teen) note what happens with his stress level when they increase sleep even by thirty minutes a night. You can throw in an incentive, although feeling calmer and having more energy is its own reward.

CONNECT WITH YOUR CHILD

A predictable and supportive relationship with you provides the safest context for your child to develop the skills to reduce anxiety. Whether texting, talking at dinner, or making a "date" that you can both look forward to next month—stay connected. Even if you travel or work late, or work a night shift, be creative—have your nightly e-mail exchange, leave notes in a communication journal, ask your child to tell you what's the coolest thing she thought about or saw today.

LIMIT SCREEN TIME (AND UNPLUG YOURSELF)

If your dinnertime is nonexistent or a din of ringing phones and blaring TVs, it's time to unplug. One predictor of school success is whether the family eats dinner together.

- Decide what works for your family and stick to it.
- Screen devices such as handheld electronic devices or video games should be used as diversions, not full-time distractions.

A MIND-SET OF PRESSURE VERSUS A MIND-SET OF SUCCESS

Pressure: Do Good Mind-Set

Everything has to be right from the get-go.
You have to prove that you know what you're doing—already, without learning about it.
You compare yourself to others ("Am I as good as they are?").
When things don't go well you immediately doubt your abilities.
Worry interferes with performance.

Success: Get a Better Mind-Set

Think about growth and development of new skills.
Compare yourself to yourself—are you making progress?
Rather than focus on proving how smart you are, focus on learning things that will make you smarter.
Break big challenges down into smaller goals to increase motivation.
If you focus on learning, mistakes become an opportunity rather than a disaster.

FLASH OF HOPE

You'd think that Ryan's parents—both high-level executives and CEOs—would have been thrilled with their son's straight As. But realizing his need for those As was all-consuming and making him break down in tears on a daily basis, and this was only fifth grade, they did something radical—and worrywise. They stopped asking about grades, and they stopped getting excited about the As. It took some convincing that life could be easier for Ryan and that he didn't have to believe his worry, but it started to click for him. Ryan said, "When I started to think about it differently, I realized, even though I thought things like 'I have no idea how I did on the test,' or, 'I am going to fail and not get into a good college,' I realized I did know, and I wasn't going to fail. When I tested worry—collected the real data—that for me it's kind of hard to get a D or an F, or even a C, I learned about trends and outliers and realized that even the Bs I got were 'outliers' or unusual for me." Ryan was really into buying and building model cars. I asked him, "If you could buy a model for twenty-five dollars, would you pay fifty? Time is like money. You are paying double or triple for your test grade when you could get it for half the price." The light-bulb went off. After that Ryan agreed that rather than do the default studying no matter what, he would do the side-by-side comparison and only study when he actually needed to. Suddenly he had much more free time and was doing great in school. And simply not being in emergency mode with studying made him feel less anxious overall. For the first time in two years, Ryan feels relaxed. That is a result that sells itself.

TURNING DOWN THE HEAT ON ANXIETY

- Focus on learning, achievement, interest, and curiosity.
- Ask about the content of a test (was it interesting, fair, challenging) before asking about grades.
- Focus on your child's strengths and how they can use them to build a stronger base.
- Focus on your child's weaknesses as areas they could work to improve.
- Focus on your child's competencies in managing his life. Discuss the future in positive terms.
- Discuss role models for your child. Emphasize resilience and perseverance.

DO IT TODAY: MIND-SET CHECK

A Stanford professor instructs her business school students to create a Failure Resume starring their biggest mess-ups, flops, and bloopers. For sheer humiliation? No, to prove what they can learn from a thorough review of what went wrong. Though none of us would be comfortable with this *at first*, it demonstrates just how far we could go to get more comfortable with the downs that often precede the ups in life. Maybe you aren't ready for that today, but as you are trying to help your child's brain be more honest with him, this is also a chance for you to be more honest with yourself and your child . . . and be ready to change your relationship with grades, achievement, college, and so forth. Do some data sampling. Tonight notice how you talk to your child about school, grades, sports. Focus on the "how" rather than the "what" and look for opportunities to praise your child's effort. And, while you're at it, share the job. Why not open these questions up at the dinner table? Everyone can benefit from a mind-set tune-up.

- "What makes a person successful?"
- "What do you think mistakes signify?"
- "What do you think success means?"
- "Do you think that successful people make mistakes?"
- "What do you think the role of failure is in success?"

Chapter 22

FREEING YOURSELF FROM ANXIETY

Your Child Will Lead the Way

It took a long time before I could just listen to Connie's fears. Before that, I would feel this incredible sense of panic and urgency to make her stop. I was worried that she couldn't handle it. Now we both know what to do. Connie's job is to work through her "what-ifs" and "what elses" so she can get to the heart of the worry, and my job is to stay calm and just listen. She benefited from this approach right away; I'm a slow learner, but now I'm catching on.

The other night I had the best dilemma. My daughter Carol wanted to stay up later because she wanted to finish watching some "vomit videos" online. There were two more YouTube videos in her hierarchy and she didn't want to stop till she'd met her goal to get over her phobia. After years of not even being able to whisper the word "vomit" without her covering her ears, how could I say no? I didn't think it was even possible.

After just a month of working on her social anxiety, I can see the progress. Jill's not out there leading, but she's not hiding behind me anymore or missing out. I was so sad and worried myself that anxiety was just going to be a part of her life always. The smartest thing I did was not to wait to get her help.

All parents wish they could steer their kids around the inevitable bumps in the road of life. But in every life—no matter what your child's wiring—bumps happen. Picturing our children in the grip of fear and worry is painful and debilitating, but it's also only one side of the story—the worry story. What's missing from that picture is your child's will to be free to take charge of their anxiety, to live a good life. Every single child wants this. Believe in the strength of the protagonist in the story, and you will soon come to a page where the hero, your child, performs amazing feats and, leading the way, comes through just fine by the end. Your belief in your child's abilities is like a great big green light—go!

Doing the side-by-side comparison for themselves of fears versus facts, parents switch the goal from reassuring and shielding their child from that which frightens them, to realizing that courage challenges are the path to greatest strength and resilience for their child. Then, instead of scooping up your child at the least sign of fear, you begin to notice, create and prioritize opportunities for your child to face and overcome their fear. So like Carol's mom, you've laid out a path for them to master their fears and worries.

I recently had the opportunity to work with a child who exemplified the idea that kids will find their way out of anxiety. Seven-year-old Julia was a spirited girl but had always been more fearful than other kids. She was especially squeamish about spiders, and uncomfortable with the mention of death. One fall, Julia developed a sudden onset of OCD triggered by a strep infection. Suddenly, she stopped answering questions because she was afraid she was telling lies and that people wouldn't be able to understand her. Piles of black clothes couldn't be touched because black meant death; furniture was off-limits because she had a memory of an ant or spider having been there. Julia and her family came in for treatment—alarmed and despondent, their world turned upside down. After our first session, in which I explained about Julia's "brain bug" (which she decided to call Jello because it always wiggled around the truth—you couldn't pin it down), Julia returned confidently to my office with a convincing action plan in hand. She unrolled a beautiful poster that she had made on her own initiative, which listed about fifty different slogans and ideas for how she was going to win the battle over her anxiety: "I'm going to do it. I'm the boss of me. Changing your mind is not lying! These questions aren't important. This isn't a chess game—it's not that complicated! I'm going to win this tug-of-war game. I can do it! These are little risks, not big risks. Let the answers be free!"

Given a new understanding of what was going on in her life, Julia felt free to interact with the problem undaunted, with clarity of purpose, hope, and even a smile on her face. Although there was a lot of work to be done, she could draw on her creative resources to find her way out of anxiety. On the challenging path that followed, Julia would have to endure two more strep infections and one case of scarlet fever, exacerbating her symptoms over the course of seven months. The peaks and valleys of her family's roller-coaster ride during that time were very dramatic—but through every one, Julia emerged triumphant. With each fall, Julia was determined to get right back up again, and she did, kept on track by her understanding of her condition.

It was, of course, more difficult for Julia's parents, who had barely had time to recover from one episode when the next one started. They found it hard to trust Julia's smile. But it was hard to ignore Julia's progress as she jubilantly juggled her black clothes that had been off-limits, decorated her hair with black ribbons, wrote in black ink, said the words "death" and "croak," when only months before she couldn't hear those words without covering her ears and screaming.

At my last meeting with Julia, she reported that she had one issue left, but she told her mom that she didn't want to talk about it. Of course, my ears perked up: Was she avoiding something? We'd have to track it. No, it turned out the reason that Julia didn't want to talk about her last challenge—sitting on a couch that had been off-limits—was that she had already figured out a plan for how to approach it. I told her that as a colleague, I would just consult with her. Julia laid out all of the steps: "I know when something is hard I need to do it more, not less. Then it gets easier. I'm going to do it a fun way, not a serious way. I'm going to start small, work up, and practice over and over till it gets easy." Julia's mom is working on her own anxiety, but she takes her cue from her daughter. She said, "I need to stop projecting into the future and realize that our daughter's future is bright, even if she has an anxiety disorder."

Not all kids make the connections as quickly as Julia did, or jump into treatment with both feet. But all kids want to get better—they just need to be taught how. When parents know the lesson plan, things go much better. We know that you can't leave kids to their own devices, or wait for them to simply "outgrow" fear or "get over it." We need to introduce a new vocabulary that gives kids options in their thinking, and in so doing prevents a worried way of life and ensures a better way of living.

Parents love it when kids surprise them with things they've learned at school. Don't be surprised when your children start to use their worry strategies on you. Listen to what seven-year-old Isabel recently said when trying to teach her mom to rollerblade: "It's easier than you think, Mom. Just do a little at a time, you don't have to learn it all today." And when her mom was planning a summer trip in January, Isabel said: "Mom, how many months away is that? Don't you think we should start working on it now so we can be ready?" This coming from a child who months earlier would completely break down and fall to the ground at the thought of a school trip, a change in schedule, or a trip to the doctor. As children change themselves, free themselves from worry, there is a contagion of health, and they change their families and the world for the better.

Or take nine-year-old Henry, whose separation anxiety disorder had been reinforced by serious medical problems he suffered as a young child. Previously his mom's shadow around the house, Henry learned in treatment how to be alone and even enjoyed doing so. Now it was Mom who was getting up to check in on Henry when she hadn't seen him for a while. Henry protested, "I don't need you to check on me. I need space!" Now Henry's mom is very happy to have a new parenting skill to practice—not worrying so much about her son! Parents can model the lessons, but our kids may master them before we do.

Or finally, how about five-year-old William, who came to see me because of a terrifying fear of needles, sensitized by some serious medical procedures he had undergone as a younger child. After just a few sessions, he learned to boss back his worry brain and became the master of shots and beyond. According to his mother, months later William was at a local park and another child was crying because he was very afraid to go down the slide. William took it upon himself to go over to the child and explain, "It's just your worry brain. It's okay. You can do it! You're going to like it. Worry is just making it seem really scary, but don't believe it! It's fun!" What William grasped quickly is the key idea that what traps us isn't the situations we're in but the thoughts we have about them.

Once we, as parents, stop doing all the reassuring and give permission and skills for our children to do the learning for themselves, there is no stopping them. They like to succeed. They know that this is a result of being brave on purpose, teaching your protector brain it is wrong, and replacing their worry thoughts with new ones. Like André, whom we met in the OCD chapter, who came to realize that doing rituals was equivalent to adding a zero to a number in math—it made no difference! Or Charles, whom we met in Chapter 11, who took the ideas we discussed in a session for dismissing anxious thoughts and created his own version, which he called "Control-Alt-Delete," like the function on his computer keyboard to *control* worry by creating *alternative* perspectives and *deleting* the fears. Or Miriam, who said: "The thoughts try to challenge me now—they can't defeat me! They can try, but they kind of know they can't beat me anymore." These are children who aren't just "coping" with anxiety. They are taking charge, putting worry in its place. These are children who want to be free and are making the process their own.

They've learned what they end up with after going through worry's list of dire predictions: Did something jump out from under the stairs? Did we fail the test? Did we forget the words to our chorus solo? Did we get sick because we just washed our hands the normal way and not for ten minutes? Nope. Disaster is a no-show. It's the big *So what.* It was just our amygdala acting up again.

We have so much influence over how our children think. And the biggest influence we have by far is in reminding them that there is a choice. That they don't have to go with their first thought—the amygdala in overdrive—but they can learn how to wisely underreact and bypass the hijack, outsmart it, and move on. We have changed the conversation about worry. It's not about reassuring them. It's about helping our children see that they are in a relationship with their worry thoughts, and they call the shots. We can't call dibs on the conclusions they reach—that is their prerogative—but by our own examples and reactions we can bring out the choosers in them and encourage them to consider their options, think soundly, realistically, and freely.

We know that our children are smarter than their worry. Our job is to make sure they know that, too. The endeavor can be as serious or lighthearted as you want it to be—make it your own. Whether you talk to the worry bug with your imaginary microphone, say "Circuits misfiring," or text the scientist in your child for the facts, you are letting your child know that there are choices. The way that he feels is not a given, and there are many things he can do to feel more confident and competent!

This is the essence of being a worrywise kid. It's never too late to make a turn for the better and get back on a healthier, happier, more realistic track. By putting worry in its place, your child will find that the world opens for her. There is no limit to the possibilities of where our children will go next. And fortunately, they're going to take all of us with them! Here's to less worry all around.

NOTES

INTRODUCTION

1. Jean M. Twenge, "The Age of Anxiety? Birth Cohort Change in Anxiety and Neuroticism, 1952–1993," *Journal of Personality and Social Psychology* 79, no. 6 (2000): 1007–1021.
2. J.T. Walkup and G.S. Ginsburg, "Anxiety Disorders in Children and Adolescents," *International Review of Psychiatry* 14 (2002): 85–86.

CHAPTER 1

3. J.A. Claus and J.U. Blackford, "Behavioral Inhibition and Risk for Developing Social Anxiety Disorder: A Meta-Analytic Study," *Journal of the American Academy of Child and Adolescent Psychiatry* 51(10) (2012): 1066–1075.
4. G.S. Ginsburg and M.C. Schlossberg, "Family-Based Treatment of Childhood Anxiety Disorders," *International Review of Psychiatry* 14 (2002): 143–154.

CHAPTER 3

5. P.C. Kendall, "Treating Anxiety Disorders in Children: Results of a Randomized Clinical Trial," *Journal of Consulting and Clinical Psychology* 62 (1994): 200–210.
6. National Institute of Mental Health, *Antidepressant Medications for Children and Adolescents: Information for Caregivers.* Retrieved September 20, 2013. National Institute of Mental Health. www.nimh.nih.gov/health/topics/child-and-adolescent-mental

-health/antidepressant-medications-for-children-and-adolescents-information-for-parents-and-caregivers.shtml.

CHAPTER 10

7. J.J. Wood, C. Kiff, J. Jacobs, M. Ikefwunigwe, and J.C. Piacentini (2007), "Dependency on Elementary School Caregivers: The Role of Parental Intrusiveness and Child Anxiety Disorders," *Psychology in Schools* 44(8), Wiley Periodicals.
8. B.D. McLeod, J.J. Wood, and S.B. Avny (2011), "Parenting and Child Anxiety Disorders," Chapter 15 In D. McKay and E.A. Storch (eds.), *Handbook of Child and Adolescent Anxiety Disorders* (213–228), Springer Science + Business Media.

CHAPTER 17

9. J.A. Cohen, L. Berliner, and J.S. March, "Treatment of Children Adolescents," in E.B. Foa, T.M. Keane, and M.J. Friedman, eds., *Effective Treatments for PTSD* (New York: Guilford Press, 2000): 106–138.

CHAPTER 18

10. Kathleen McCann, "Poor Sleep Can Affect a Student's Grades, Increase Emotional, Behavioral Disturbance." Retrieved January 30, 2014. http://www.medicalnewstoday.com/releases/110640.php

CHAPTER 21

11. Eilene Zimmerman, "Career Couch: Helping Teenagers Find Their Dreams." *New York Times.* Oct. 25, 2009.

ACKNOWLEDGMENTS

It is a great privilege to be able to reflect back on the last ten years and all I have learned from my patients and colleagues and to undertake the challenge of writing a second edition of *Freeing Your Child from Anxiety*. I am very grateful to my editor at Random House, Anna Thompson, for giving me that opportunity, and for her vision, editorial expertise, and wonderful collaborative spirit in making this project happen. Big thank-you to Leah Miller at Random House for joining the team and bringing the book to fruition. Much appreciation goes to Maggie Carr for her careful copyedit of the final manuscript. Thank you to my agents, Gareth Esersky and Carol Mann, for their encouragement and making all the connections. I appreciate immensely the input and collaboration from my community of colleagues: fellow therapists, pediatricians, teachers, counselors, and psychiatrists, all of whom enrich this work and make it possible. Deepest gratitude to my courageous patients, who teach me so much, every day, about the strength and determination of the human spirit to overcome obstacles—however big or small—and lead a good life unencumbered by the distortions worry creates. A very special thank-you to the patients who generously agreed to share their stories and wisdom here so that others could learn from their experiences.

I would never consider attempting this work without the incredible love and support of my family. My daughters, Meredith and Raia, have grown up now expecting their mother to usually be in front of a laptop working on a book, and have been amazingly patient and supportive of me. My husband, Phil Stern, has gone far beyond the call of duty again and again, clearing space for this work and creating it right alongside me. Your drawings have made my work come alive and speak beyond what I could do in a thousand (or more!) words. I am eternally grateful for your incredible support, collaboration, and the way you've shown me how to live a creative life every day.

INDEX